Solomon asked in Proverbs 31:10, "Who can find a virtuous woman? For her price is far above rubies." Throughout the Proverbs Solomon defines the virtuous woman. Debbi Bryson has carefully searched through the Proverbs to ferret out those definitions. I believe that this research by Debbi, which has been put into an easy-to-read daily format, will be a spiritually enriching addition to any lady's devotional reading. I highly recommend it to any lady who is seeking to become the woman that God would have her to be. I believe that it will provide valuable understanding as to a Biblical definition of a virtuous woman.

PASTOR CHUCK SMITH
Founding Pastor of Calvary Chapel Costa Mesa

We all have questions, and many times we look in all the wrong places for answers. Debbi beautifully and clearly shows that the Bible is sufficient to give us answers and that we need not look anywhere else. We get wisdom only when we get it from God!

GEORGIA PURDOM, PhD
Research scientist and speaker

This devotional, *Wisdom for Women*, will become a tool to guide you in listening to the voice of God as He speaks to you through His word.

FERN NICHOLS
Founder and President of Moms in Prayer International

The One Year®
Wisdom for Women Devotional

The One Year®

Wisdom for Women Devotional

365 devotions through the Proverbs

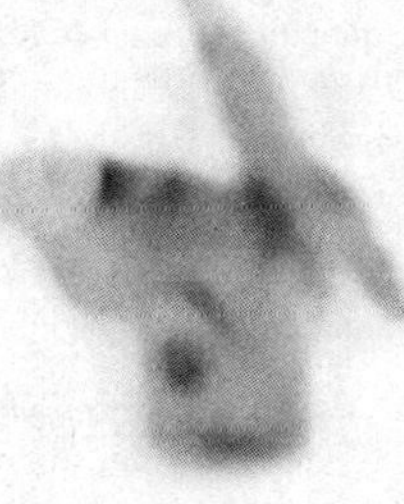

DEBBI BRYSON

Tyndale House Publishers, Inc.
Carol Stream, Illinois

Visit Tyndale online at www.tyndale.com.

Visit Debbi Bryson's website at www.biblebusstop.com.

The One Year® Wisdom for Women Devotional: 365 Devotions through the Proverbs

Designed by Jacqueline L. Nuñez

ISBN 978-1-4143-7529-8

Printed in the United States of America

19 18 17 16 15
7 6 5 4

Introduction

Life is a journey. Along the road, do you ever ponder the big questions: *What is the meaning of life? Where did I come from? What happens when I die?* Where do you find the answers? Do you wonder: *Are there no maps, no GPS systems, no road signs at the crossroads? Are there no yellow warning lights or guardrails on sharp curves and narrow bridges?* If there is a God, would he be so cruel as to leave us to flounder and wander and lose our way? When we are overwhelmed, when troubles surround us, when we're sinking in the quicksand of life, is there no one who hears our desperate cries for help? Is there no one to send out a search-and-rescue party? These are questions that, if left unanswered, can and will leave us lonely and hopeless, fearful and confused.

The good news is, there is a God, and he has a message for you. His message is so big, clear, safe, and strong that it can radically and permanently change your entire life. God is not a distant God. He is near and kind and wise and good. Of course he cares about your personal journey, because he cares about you. No one has or ever will love you more.

We see reality from our narrow, limited position on planet Earth. We have tunnel vision. We can't see the forest for the trees. But God sits above the fray. He understands your past more than you do. He knew you before you were born (Psalm 139). He is so aware of every detail of your present, that the very hairs on your head are all numbered. And the mysterious, uncharted waters in your future are crystal clear and eternally important to the one who wants you to know him as "our Father who art in heaven."

What does all this have to do with wisdom? Absolutely everything. Wisdom is not a stale, rigid, boring set of rules engraved in stone long ago. Wisdom is alive and fresh. It's as dependable and unshakable as the sun that rises every day. The sun is far removed from the control and whims of man. You can't put it or the wind or a lightning bolt in a box. They are dynamic—meaning they are not static. They are full of power, energy, and activity. So is wisdom. What then is wisdom like? How can you recognize the real deal? James, the brother of Jesus, gives us this insight: "But the wisdom from above is first of all pure. It is also peace loving, gentle at all times, and willing to yield to others. It is full of mercy and good deeds. It shows no favoritism and is always sincere" (James 3:17). Wow! This beautiful description piques our interest and stirs our hearts. How then can we acquire this amazing commodity? Surprisingly, wisdom is there for the asking; even a child can attain it.

> If you need wisdom, ask our generous God, and he will give it to you. He will not rebuke you for asking.
> JAMES 1:5

> [God's] word is a lamp to guide my feet and a light for my path.
> PSALM 119:105

The Bible—banned, burned, beloved. More widely read, more frequently attacked than any other book in history. Generations of intellectuals have attempted to discredit it; dictators of every age have outlawed it and executed those who read it. Yet soldiers carry it into battle believing it more powerful than their weapons. Fragments of it smuggled into solitary prison cells have transformed ruthless killers into gentle saints.
CHARLES COLSON

I believe the Bible is the best gift God has ever given to man. All the good from the Savior of the world is communicated to us through this book. But for it, we could not know right from wrong.
ABRAHAM LINCOLN

The One Year Bible

I, like many, have always had a respect for the Bible. But even after becoming a Christian, I found it difficult to be consistent in reading it through, cover to cover. Then one day (over twenty years ago) I discovered *The One Year Bible* (by Tyndale House Publishers). As I thumbed through the pages, I knew God had given me a simple, doable way to read every day. Each morning I open it to the page with that day's date. There I find a reading from the Old Testament, New Testament, Psalms, and Proverbs. What a joy! For the first time in my life I experienced deep growth and a sense that I was daily hearing God's voice and guidance for myself. Honestly, the first few years I missed reading some days. But I learned not to try to catch up. I skipped what I missed and began again with the current day's reading. Through the years, thousands have joined what we now call "The Bible Bus." Friends, families, couples, and ministry teams find reading the same portion of Scripture cultivates fellowship and like-mindedness. Instead of dull duty, reading daily is fresh and personal as you "journey to the heart of God." If you would like to join us, in the back of the book I've included a page of helpful instructions on how to develop a quiet time.

Wisdom for Women

Wisdom for Women was birthed on an ordinary day in Juneau, Alaska. That morning I went for a walk to the glacier with my friend Lisa. As we walked, she shared her sorrow that women are often confused, discouraged, and sidetracked. Hard situations or bad choices cause painful life consequences. Then she stopped and said, "Debbi, write something for us. We'll put it on the radio up here." Quite to my surprise, by the time we got back to the house, *Wisdom for Women* had a name and a plan. Before long it began airing on the radio. God truly does work in surprising ways. It then took several years to write and record 365 audio devotionals now heard on stations across the nation and as far away as Belize and Israel. "Let's sit down and talk" is the heart and tone. QR codes on the back cover and throughout this book allow you to scan and listen to the audio devotionals as you read each day.

Are you ready to travel through the profound and practical book of Proverbs? Will you look for God's sunbeam of wisdom to guide your path? Do you long to grow and become a Woman of Wisdom? A journey of a thousand miles begins with just one step.

Now as we begin, I wholeheartedly pray this prayer over your life: "This is Debbi Bryson, praying that the practical wisdom of God's Word will make you wise."

January

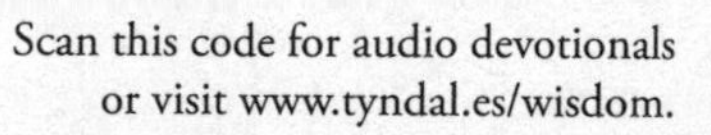

Scan this code for audio devotionals
or visit www.tyndal.es/wisdom.

Fresh Start

For attaining wisdom and discipline;
for understanding words of insight
for acquiring a disciplined and prudent life,
doing what is right and just and fair;
for giving prudence to the simple,
knowledge and discretion to the young—
let the wise listen and add to their learning,
and let the discerning get guidance.

PROVERBS 1:2-5 (NIV)

January 1: the very first day of a brand-new year. Picture with me this year laying out before you like a blanket of clean white snow. As yet, there are no mistakes, no new regrets, no fresh wounds to mar your path. This is the perfect time to let the past go and start afresh. As we begin in Proverbs 1, above, Solomon explains the purpose and life-changing effect the Proverbs can have.

But if you look around you, the pressures and influences to go in the wrong direction are strong—very strong. People are making foolish choices. Morality and integrity are ridiculed. God is mocked, the Bible neglected. Hosea said, "They sow the wind and reap the whirlwind" (Hosea 8:7, NIV).

Therefore, we must choose. W. C. Fields once said, "Remember, a dead fish can float downstream, but it takes a live fish to go against the flow." So choose wisdom! God has not left us to chart our course alone. He's given us his Word. Let me invite you to pick up a One Year Bible. It lays out a very doable reading schedule. It is simple and yet life changing. So today will you open your Bible to the first chapter of the book of Proverbs and begin this year as a journey to becoming a Woman of Wisdom?

Make It Personal . . . Live It Out!

Will you take a moment right now to personally picture this new year as a field of fresh snow? Now picture a ray of light marking the path. God has a promise to help you start your year right. He says, "Ask me and I will tell you remarkable secrets you do not know about things to come" (Jeremiah 33:3). Will you pray right now? As you pray, be aware and excited that God hears and is waiting to help.

One Year Bible Reading

Genesis 1:1–2:25; Matthew 1:1–2:12; Psalm 1:1-6; Proverbs 1:1-6

Godly Reverence

The fear of the LORD is the beginning of knowledge,
but fools despise wisdom and discipline.

PROVERBS 1:7 (NIV)

"The fear of the Lord." On our journey to becoming women of wisdom, it is vital that we truly understand what it is to fear the Lord. First of all we must know what it isn't. To fear the Lord is not the same as being afraid of him like he is mean or selfish or harsh or cruel. Nothing could be further from the truth.

To fear God is to know that he is righteous and he hates wickedness. God is holy. God hates sin because it enslaves us and destroys our lives. Sin separates us from his love. Jesus said, "God did not send His Son into the world to condemn the world, but that the world through Him might be saved" (John 3:17, NKJV).

So what is it to have a proper fear of God? It is to have a deep reverence for him. It is to be in awe of him because he is awe-some. It is to understand that he is the God of the universe, and we are not. He is the Creator, the King Eternal, the Only Wise God. When we respect him for who he is and live under both his authority and his love, there is no sweeter, safer, more peaceful way to live. This is truly wisdom.

A holy fear of a holy God—it does our souls good to have such an awe-inspiring reverence. Tonight, look up at the stars and know they all can fit in the palm of his hand. As the song proclaims, "Our God is an awesome God; he reigns from heaven above with wisdom, power, and love. Our God is an awesome God" (song lyrics by Rich Mullins).

Make It Personal . . . Live It Out!

There are two kinds of people in this world. There are Big God-ers and there are Little God-ers. David, Daniel, Moses, and Mary believed that God can move giants and mountains and men. Do you? Or do you live with a greater fear of men than you do of God almighty? Now the important question is, Will you choose to embrace him not just as *an* awesome God but as *your* awesome God?

One Year Bible Reading

Genesis 3:1–4:26; Matthew 2:13–3:6; Psalm 2:1-12; Proverbs 1:7-9

Peer Pressure

My [child], if sinners entice you,
Do not consent.
If they say, "Come with us," . . .
Keep your foot from their path.

PROVERBS 1:10-11, 15 (NKJV)

This is a warning. Be on guard. Don't be influenced or pressured into doing something you know is wrong. Sin has a powerful lure all by itself, but when others try to pull us in, it can become even more powerful. Does this happen? All the time. Sometimes sin comes in the back door through friends—the wrong kind of friends.

I'm going to list some of the ways that we sometimes yield when we have friends who influence us to do things that aren't the best. Do you have a friend who shops till she drops? When you're together you, too, shop too much. You spend too much money, and you buy things you don't need.

Complaining. Do you have a friend you complain with every time you are together? Both of you feel free to complain about your husbands, relatives, friends, people at church.

Do you have friends who compromise? Do they entice you to compromise by recommending R movies or trashy books? Do they invite you to join them for a drink at the bar? Or—warning!—do you have anyone in your life who is flirting with you, stirring you up to unhealthy desires?

Dear sisters, two things: (1) Pay attention to the red flags of danger. Do not have a friend who entices you to sin. And (2) be careful about the type of friend you are. A godly friend is a good friend

Make It Personal . . . Live It Out!

What's wrong with ungodly friends? Didn't Jesus intentionally spend time with sinners? Yes, he did. But his intentions were entirely different than just letting his hair down and fitting in. He brought light and truth into every atmosphere. He loved sinners and they knew it. He was grieved by the emptiness and pain he saw on their faces. Darkness did not drag him down; instead, he used light to lift them up.

Let's Pray

Lord, seal my heart against compromise so I can be a vessel of your light in a lost and dying world.

One Year Bible Reading

Genesis 5:1–7:24; Matthew 3:7–4:11; Psalm 3:1-8; Proverbs 1:10-19

Wisdom Calls!

As we read the proverb for today, picture wisdom as a woman—a woman like a mother standing on firm, solid, safe ground. She is calling out to those she cares deeply about. She knows, as every loving, wise, godly mother knows, that if they do not choose the higher ground of wisdom, they will be swept away by foolish, dangerous choices. So listen and picture the voice of God's wisdom calling out to you in today's Wisdom for Women.

Wisdom calls aloud outside;
She raises her voice in the open squares. . . .
She speaks her words:
"How long, you simple ones, will you love simplicity?
For scorners delight in their scorning,
And fools hate knowledge.
Turn at my rebuke;
Surely I will pour out my spirit on you;
I will make my words known to you."

PROVERBS 1:20-23 (NKJV)

Did you hear both the warning and the promise? Right now I feel an urgency. This year may be indeed the most complicated and challenging year we have ever faced. There are dangerous changes brewing in our world. Do not let circumstances, or others, or the ungodly world around you pressure you into making wrong choices. Do not let the lines between right and wrong become fuzzy to you just because they are blurry to others. Choose wisdom!

If you do, God himself promises that he will pour out his Spirit upon you and make his words known to you. Choose wisdom!

Make It Personal . . . Live It Out!

What is the antidote for the toxic and demeaning role models that are broadcast to us as women everywhere we look? God's Word! God's Word teaches us that women have a place of honor. We can be amazing influences for good. When God's Word is in you, you realize that the false images and values shown in the media are just cheap substitutes.

Look at the One Year Bible Reading list on this page. It gives you a simple, easy-to-follow guide. Try it. God's Word is God's love letter, God's truth, and God's light for your life. God's wisdom is calling, Will you listen? Will you follow?

One Year Bible Reading

Genesis 8:1–10:32; Matthew 4:12-25; Psalm 4:1-8; Proverbs 1:20-23

January 5

A Sober Warning

Since you rejected me [wisdom] when I called
and no one gave heed when I stretched out my hand,
since you ignored all my advice
and would not accept my rebuke,
I in turn will laugh at your disaster;
I will mock when calamity overtakes you—
when calamity overtakes you like a storm,
when disaster sweeps over you like a whirlwind,
when distress and trouble overwhelm you.
Then they will call to me but I will not answer;
they will look for me but will not find me.

PROVERBS 1:24-28 (NIV)

Today's proverb is very serious and, I hope, a sobering warning.

God's mercy, his love, his kindness to call us out of darkness is amazing. He will send conviction to our souls over and over with great compassion and patience, but if we repeatedly disobey, if we harden our hearts, he will refuse his grace. There will come a time when it is too late.

A few years ago I needed to catch a plane, but I was careless. I got a late start to the airport and hit traffic. It was my own fault. When I got to the gate, the door had closed. Too late. The plane took off without me. But I guarantee you the next time I was to fly, I got up early, and the plane arrived late. So if you are listening, if you have turned your back on wisdom in the past, it's time to learn from your mistakes. Don't repeat them. Don't be careless with your life and don't be careless with your soul.

Make It Personal . . . Live It Out!

Some people don't like to hear or heed warnings. The captain of the Titanic was one of them. The morning before the disaster, the sky was blue and the sea calm. So he canceled the scheduled lifeboat drill. No need; the Titanic was unsinkable. He received—and ignored—seven iceberg warnings, until it was too late.

If God has sent a flashing light of warning or conviction in your heart, listen. Life has icebergs ahead. Slow down, change course, and allow him to navigate you back to safety.

One Year Bible Reading

Genesis 11:1–13:4; Matthew 5:1-26; Psalm 5:1-12; Proverbs 1:24-28

Truth or Consequences

Because they hated knowledge
And did not choose the fear of the LORD,
They would have none of my [wisdom's] counsel
And despised my every rebuke.
Therefore they shall eat the fruit of their own way,
And be filled to the full with their own fancies.
For the turning away of the simple will slay them,
And the complacency of fools will destroy them.

PROVERBS 1:29-32 (NKJV)

Today's Wisdom for Women talks about consequences. It's been said that sometimes the best way to convince someone he's wrong is to let him have his way. Or, as James MacDonald puts it, "Choose to sin, choose to suffer."

Galatians 6:7-8 explains it very clearly. Listen to what it says: "Do not be deceived, God is not mocked; for whatever a man sows, that he will also reap. For he who sows to his flesh will of the flesh reap corruption, but he who sows to the Spirit will of the Spirit reap everlasting life" (NKJV).

Okay then, let's look at your life like a garden. Every farmer knows that at every stage he makes choices. In the spring he can choose to plant tomatoes. He knows that if he plants tomatoes he won't get potatoes. He can choose to pull the weeds when they are small. He can choose to water, and fertilize, and kill every pest that threatens his crop. But he also knows that his choices add up, and one day he will have tomatoes to eat and plenty to share with others.

All this to say: don't reject the Lord's wisdom in your life. That's foolish. Call out to the Lord for the wisdom you need today in all of your choices. They will bear fruit as a blessing today and a blessing tomorrow.

Make It Personal . . . Live It Out!

Although this proverb applies to all of us, this is an important message that moms especially need to hear. Those little toddlers to teenagers under your care today will be the decision makers and parents of the next generation. Like a good gardener, will you be diligent to plant the good seeds of integrity, purity, humility, kindness, thankfulness, and godliness in your children's hearts and minds? Plant the seeds and pull the weeds!

One Year Bible Reading

Genesis 13:5–15:21; Matthew 5:27-48; Psalm 6:1-10; Proverbs 1:29-33

January 7

Insight and Understanding

My [child], if you accept my words
and store up my commands within you,
turning your ear to wisdom
and applying your heart to understanding—
indeed, if you call out for insight
and cry aloud for understanding,
and if you look for it as for silver
and search for it as for hidden treasure,
then you will understand the fear of the LORD
and find the knowledge of God.

PROVERBS 2:1-5 (NIV)

As we begin, let me ask you a personal question. Please be honest in your answer. How important is the Bible to you—really? If you say it is important and yet you live day to day like it is less important than your hobbies or your favorite TV show, you're kidding yourself. Worse yet, you are missing out on the most wonderful, interesting, and life-changing experience there is: digging into the treasure chest of the living Word of God. So listen very carefully to today's Wisdom for Women.

If you would like to go deeper in learning and growing in God's Word, good. I love it when someone wants to know how. Let me invite you to my website. It's called BibleBusStop.com. There are lots of helps there to get you started.

And then when you do read, read prayerfully. As you read, read like you are searching to know God himself. Stop and pray often. Interact with God, using your reading time to discover more than just information. Truly, this is your Father God–child time. Picture it as a journey, a journey to the very heart of God.

Make It Personal . . . Live It Out!

The gaining of insight is a key topic of our proverb today. So, what exactly is insight? Why do we need it? And how do we get it?

Insight is the ability to see and understand clearly the inner nature of things.

We need insight because things are not always as they appear. As moms, we need insight to read what is troubling our children. We need insight when something is amiss in our marriages. We need insight when a friendship is broken.

How do we get insight? Call out! We need to take God at his Word: "Ask and you will receive" (John 16:24, NIV).

One Year Bible Reading

Genesis 16:1–18:15; Matthew 6:1-24; Psalm 7:1-17; Proverbs 2:1-5

Shielded

The LORD gives wisdom;
From His mouth come knowledge and understanding;
He stores up sound wisdom for the upright;
He is a shield to those who walk uprightly;
He guards the paths of justice,
And preserves the way of His saints.

PROVERBS 2:6-8 (NKJV)

The Lord does have a special relationship with those who love him and seek him, who walk in his ways and desire what he desires. God never promises that we'll have trouble-free lives, but he does promise that we'll never face anything that comes our way alone. Sometimes we forget that all we have to do is ask God for wisdom when life gets complicated, when we're confused, or when we're making a hard decision. Jesus said, "Ask and you will receive" (John 16:24, NIV).

The Twenty-third Psalm is a great psalm of comfort and hope. "The LORD is my shepherd; I shall not want" (Psalm 23:1, NKJV). As you read the entire psalm, it's more than just sweet sentiments. It's a list, a strong list of promises that cover every need and every phase of life from being hungry to dying.

Think of the phrase "thy rod and thy staff they comfort me" (Psalm 23:4, KJV). Both the rod and staff are tools to protect us, not just from predators but also from ourselves. We, like sheep, are prone to wander. A good shepherd needs to firmly strike a stubborn sheep, but for those sheep who love to stay near him, a little tap is all that's needed.

Make It Personal . . . Live It Out!

Let's personally grab hold of the promise in today's proverb: "He is a shield to those who walk uprightly." The fiery darts of fear, discouragement, criticism, and temptations are aimed at us. But God is telling us that when we choose to stay close to him, he personally shields us. No, he does not put us in a "holy bubble." But he does stand with us and for us. We are not alone.

Let's Pray

Lord, sometimes I do feel overwhelmed and outnumbered. Sometimes evil does seem stronger than good and right. Help me to trust that you are near, holding your shield over my heart.

One Year Bible Reading

Genesis 18:16–19:38; Matthew 6:25–7:14; Psalm 8:1-9; Proverbs 2:6-15

Fireproof!

Wisdom will save you from the immoral [man],
from the flattery of the adulterous [man].
[He] has abandoned [his wife]
and ignores the covenant [he] made before God.
Entering [his] house leads to death;
it is the road to hell.
The [woman] who visits [him] is doomed.
[She] will never reach the paths of life.

PROVERBS 2:16-19

Today's Wisdom for Women is a sober and vivid heart-to-heart talk. It was written as from a father talking to a son, telling him that getting tangled up with an immoral woman will ruin his life. But I have taken the liberty of switching it as a warning to women about the dangers of yielding to an immoral man. The principles are exactly the same.

Ladies, right now I have a burdened heart regarding this. I could tell you hundreds of stories of broken families, wounded children, scars, and shame that women feel for the rest of their lives because they left the guard off their heart and played with the fire of sinful sex outside of marriage. Don't do that. If someone at the office, an old boyfriend, a stranger on the Internet, or someone else's husband starts flirting with you, that's a red flag. Some men think flattery will get them everywhere. Slam the door on that. It is far easier to stop something that never got started than to reel in lust turned loose.

So be wise, and you'll never regret being foolish. Amen? Amen!

Make It Personal . . . Live It Out!

How can you fireproof your heart from the pitfalls of sexual temptation?

Avoid trashy movies, magazines, and atmospheres. They ignite sparks of trashy thoughts, emotions, and images.

Loneliness and isolation make you emotionally vulnerable. Get connected and involved in serving. Serving will fill your emotional cup and brings you joy.

Pray! Ask the Lord to stir your heart to fall freshly in love with him. "Take delight in the LORD, and he will give you your heart's desires" (Psalm 37:4).

One Year Bible Reading

Genesis 20:1–22:24; Matthew 7:15-29; Psalm 9:1-12; Proverbs 2:16-22

Trust

Trust in the L*ORD* *with all your heart,*
And lean not on your own understanding;
In all your ways acknowledge Him,
And He shall direct your paths.

PROVERBS 3:5-6 (NKJV)

There is a great hymn with the words "Trust and obey, for there's no other way to be happy in Jesus but to trust and obey."

A few years ago I was in New York City and decided to take a bus tour. As we passed the Brooklyn Bridge, the guide told us a fascinating story. When the bridge first opened, thousands came to cross over, but a few weeks later, a woman who was walking up the steps tripped and screamed. The scream triggered a panic that the bridge was ready to collapse. In the panic and crush, twelve people were killed. The fear of a collapse remained in people's minds, and few trusted the bridge. It sat virtually unused. Then P. T. Barnum was asked to take twenty-one of his elephants across the bridge. Under that massive weight, the bridge held up, and confidence was restored.

So let me ask you, have you ever fully put your *full* trust, your *full* weight—heart, soul, and mind—into the promises of God? Let me tell you, there is no greater thrill, joy, and reward. This verse will never be truly yours until you do that. "Trust in the LORD with all your heart, and lean not on your own understanding." He will direct your paths . . . because he promised.

Make It Personal . . . Live It Out!

"Trust in the LORD with all your heart." Among the roadblocks to faith and trust are our emotions. Can we trust them? No! Emotions can spin us down into anxiety, fear, and depression.

Trust is a choice, an act of intentional obedience to God himself. Will you consciously and intentionally surrender a specific area of concern into his safekeeping right now?

Let's Pray

Lord, I lift this burden up to you. Please forgive me for the many times I have worried and tried to work it out with my own understanding. Today I want to trust you completely and see you unfold your perfect plan.

One Year Bible Reading

Genesis 23:1–24:51; Matthew 8:1-17; Psalm 9:13-20; Proverbs 3:1-6

Be Teachable

Do not be wise in your own eyes;
fear the LORD and shun evil.
This will bring health to your body
and nourishment to your bones.

PROVERBS 3:7-8 (NIV)

"Do not be wise in your own eyes." Let me repeat this for us, ladies. "Do not be wise in your own eyes." Pivotal phrase: "your own." Okay, repeat that phrase with me. Shun evil like you would shun a bad snake. The results are given in verse 8.

Backing this up to the first part, don't . . . Don't be a wise guy. Don't be so full of yourself that you get stuck in thinking that you are always right. This implies that everyone else is always wrong. That's annoying to others, and it's short-sighted and foolish on our part.

So don't think you can't learn and grow. Don't think you don't need to. Be teachable. Be receptive. Be hungry to learn—first of all, from God himself, but then also from others. Make all of life and every day your classroom.

Some of the most godly, mature people I know read God's Word like an eager child, hanging on to every word. Their hearts are open. And they love to glean from others. They are always asking others, "What have you been learning from the Lord recently? Tell me. Let me learn too."

My friends, don't you love people like that? But most of all, don't you want to be someone like that? You do? Me too!

Make It Personal . . . Live It Out!

What if someone asked you, "What good thing have you learned lately?" I hope your answer would go deeper than a new health tip or a new recipe for cupcakes.

Have you relied upon a promise of God lately? If not, do! You will learn he is faithful. And you will end up with an amazing "God story."

Have you taken notes as you read a story in the Bible lately? Matthew 8:23-27 describes the day a storm hit while the disciples were out at sea. Their boat was sinking and they thought they would die. Why don't you read it for yourself and see what you learn and how it applies to your storms?

One Year Bible Reading

Genesis 24:52–26:12; Matthew 8:18-34; Psalm 10:1-15; Proverbs 3:7-8

Honor the Lord

Honor the L*ORD with your wealth,*
with the firstfruits of all your crops;
then your barns will be filled to overflowing.

PROVERBS 3:9-10 (NIV)

This is both a challenge and a wonderful invitation. The first part of this formula for blessing is "honor the Lord." Let me tell you: every single thing that we do for the Lord needs to start there, or else it's just meaningless performance of duty.

To honor the Lord is to always remember God is more than worthy of honor. He is the King of majesty. He is God almighty. He is the God of comfort and love. The Lord is honorable. It is our great privilege that he would allow us to bring him anything. After all, he is the giver of all things that we have to give. Never forget that.

And so when you write out a check to give, be joyful, because the Lord loves a cheerful giver. But more than your money or your things, may I ask you to give the Lord of glory the firstfruits of yourself. Give him your first hour in the morning, meeting with him, letting him lay out your priorities for the day. Honor him with the way you keep your commitments, with the way you treat people, with the way you serve, with the way you work at your job. If you're a Sunday school teacher, pour your heart into those kids. If you're a greeter at church, welcome people as if they truly are entering the house of God and you're the doorkeeper.

So if you want a rich, overflowing life, live your entire life with this principle: "Whatever you do, do it heartily, as to the Lord and not to men" (Colossians 3:23, NKJV).

Make It Personal . . . Live It Out!

Is there an area of your life where you have failed to honor the Lord? Have you wondered why your life seems barren and fruitless? Will you take God at his word? Will you ask him today to show you a need you can fill? Give it a try! You will see that it is more blessed to give than to receive.

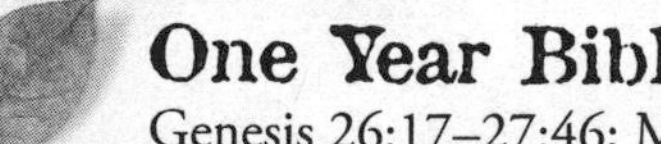

One Year Bible Reading

Genesis 26:17–27:46; Matthew 9:1-17; Psalm 10:16-18; Proverbs 3:9-10

January 13

The Lord Disciplines

My child, don't ignore it when the LORD disciplines you,
and don't be discouraged when he corrects you.
For the LORD corrects those he loves,
just as a father corrects a child in whom he delights.

PROVERBS 3:11-12

J. Vernon McGee said, "God is going to chasten you as you go along through life if you are his child. . . . That is a good evidence that you belong to him. . . . Chastening is not punishing. . . . The criminal is to be punished; the child is to be corrected."

So let's consider the Lord's discipline in our lives. Here it is directly connected with God's love and even his sweet delight. Think about this. For a parent it is easy to be delighted in a child who is delightful, but have you ever seen a little girl who is a brat? She is spoiled. She is selfish. She throws tantrums when she does not get her way. Have you ever seen a big girl like that? It's not pretty, really.

That behavior is a direct result of a stubborn bent that did not have or did not yield to correction. Ladies, dear sisters, this is not our destiny. You do have a Father who loves you very much. He loves you enough to discipline you when you need it.

So if conviction comes, if the Holy Spirit has been speaking to your heart about a bad habit or bad attitude, yield. Because whom the Lord loves, he disciplines.

Make It Personal . . . Live It Out!

Can you look back on your life and remember times that you have stubbornly chosen your own way, to your own harm? I can. My mother told me that one time I stood in the corner for hours just because I wouldn't say I was sorry. One time I sat at the table until bedtime because I wouldn't eat my peas. Childish stubbornness is childish. God wants us to grow up and out of these childish ways.

Let's Pray

Lord, show me when I have allowed my selfishness or pride to box me in. Soften my stubborn heart and help me to yield and listen to you.

One Year Bible Reading

Genesis 28:1–29:35; Matthew 9:18-38; Psalm 11:1-7; Proverbs 3:11-12

Better Than Gold

Blessed are those who find wisdom,
those who gain understanding,
for [wisdom] is more profitable than silver
and yields better returns than gold.
She is more precious than rubies;
nothing you desire can compare with her.

PROVERBS 3:13-15 (NIV)

Take a minute and stand back with me. Let's take a really good, long, hard look at the world. Let's look at the diminishing value of material things. This is a great time for a reality check. The stock market has fallen; housing values, fallen. If you buy a new car, it is worth less the minute you drive it off the lot. Last year's top fashions look hokey today. Reality check: even things like our health and the way we look deteriorate as we get older. Diminishing returns.

First John says this world is passing away, and so if you're a child of God, you—we all—need to stop living like this is all there is and like this is all that is important. Don't pretend that you don't do that. They say you can look at someone's checkbook and Day-Timer, and you will be able to tell what is really important to her. What do yours say?

Jesus has some really important things to say about this. If you are listening, let him give you his reality check: Matthew 6:19-21. "Do not lay up for yourselves treasures on earth, where moth and rust destroy and where thieves break in and steal; but lay up for yourselves treasures in heaven. . . . For where your treasure is, there your heart will be also" (NKJV).

Make It Personal . . . Live It Out!

God's wisdom, his love, and his peace are all things that the world isn't selling and money can't buy. God calls us back to the things that matter. He calls us back to him: "Why spend your money on food that does not give you strength? Why pay for food that does you no good? Listen to me, and you will eat what is good. You will enjoy the finest food. Come to me with your ears wide open. Listen, and you will find life. I will make an everlasting covenant with you" (Isaiah 55:2-3).

One Year Bible Reading

Genesis 30:1–31:16; Matthew 10:1-23; Psalm 12:1-8; Proverbs 3:13-15

Pleasant Ways

Long life is in [wisdom's] right hand;
in her left hand are riches and honor.
Her ways are pleasant ways,
and all her paths are peace.
She is a tree of life to those who embrace her;
those who lay hold of her will be blessed.

PROVERBS 3:16-18 (NIV)

The central phrase that grabs my attention is this: "Her ways are pleasant ways, and all her paths are peace."

This is a good way to live. It is pleasant—pleasant for yourself and pleasant for others who are around you. This reminds me that it is not wise to be impatient; it is not wise to be rude or harsh or critical of others. It is wise to be a peacemaker; it is wise to be kind.

Being wise is more than just being smart or skillful at life.

James gives us an excellent and clear description of godly wisdom that shows that it is both practical and wonderful. "The wisdom that is from above is first pure, then peaceable, gentle, willing to yield, full of mercy and good fruits, without partiality and without hypocrisy" (James 3:17, NKJV).

And so, in conclusion, dear ladies, choose wisdom—because all her ways are pleasant ways and all her paths are peace.

Make It Personal . . . Live It Out!

Some people view wisdom as a dusty old thing, antiquated, good only for old people with nothing much to do. No! Wisdom opens wonderful doors and takes you on journeys where few travel. Wisdom fills your heart with the pure, simple, exhilarating joy that comes when you just do the right thing. Wisdom from above is "full of mercy," for instance. So, just for the joy of it, try this out: Is there someone in your world who does not deserve mercy? Someone who has been cranky or rude? Will you choose to show mercy?

Let's Pray

Lord, please give me a tender heart to forgive. Help me say one pleasant word or do one kind deed. I know you love the difficult people in my life; help me to love them too.

One Year Bible Reading

Genesis 31:17–32:12; Matthew 10:24–11:6; Psalm 13:1-6; Proverbs 3:16-18

Look Up!

By wisdom the L*ORD founded the earth;*
by understanding he created the heavens.
By his knowledge the deep fountains of the earth burst forth,
and the dew settles beneath the night sky.

PROVERBS 3:19-20

I grew up in a nominal Christian home. We believed in God, but we lived like he was far away and unconcerned. When I was eighteen, one of the first college classes I took was Philosophy of World Religions. I was drawn to spiritual things but had a lot of questions. Some of the questions were *What is the meaning of life?* and *Where did we come from?* The first day of class, the professor held up a Bible and asked if anyone believed in that book. I weakly raised my hand, not because I had ever read it, but because somehow I felt it must be important. With a tone of authority he said, "It is my stated goal that at the end of this class no one will believe in the Bible, because life is all about you; you are the center of the universe." Well, as an eighteen-year-old, I already lived like life was all about me. He was singing my song. So at the end of the semester I dropped out of college, left home, and traveled to the tropics of Mexico to "find myself."

Two years and many travels later, I had found myself, but didn't like what I found. I was disillusioned, confused, and empty. Walking along the beach one evening, I was overwhelmed with the power and beauty of a tropical sunset. Falling to my knees I cried out to God, "God I know that you are real, and I do not know you." I didn't know that the Bible says, "The heavens proclaim the glory of God. The skies display his craftsmanship" (Psalm 19:1). But that night, surrounded by such majesty, I experienced both an awe and a hunger to know the one who created it all.

Make It Personal . . . Live It Out!

Has it been a while since you cried out to God, not asking him to do something for you, but to know him? Has it been a while since you went outside and looked up at the beauty of a starry night? God heard my voice that glorious night, and he will indeed hear you.

One Year Bible Reading

Genesis 32:13–34:31; Matthew 11:7-30; Psalm 14:1-7; Proverbs 3:19-20

Have No Fear

Have no fear of sudden disaster
or of the ruin that overtakes the wicked,
for the LORD will be your confidence
and will keep your foot from being snared.

PROVERBS 3:25-26 (NIV)

Have no fear. Many right now are living in constant fear. We are—no doubt about it—living in unstable times. I wish I could say, "Don't worry—be happy! There is nothing to worry about," but that would be naive.

What I can tell you is this: don't worry—trust God. In times like this, we do have a safe harbor for our souls. "The LORD [himself] will be your confidence."

Let me suggest something. In the One Year Bible tomorrow we start reading the incredible story of Joseph (in Genesis 37). It is the perfect illustration of our proverb today. Why don't you take the time to read it too?

Disaster—it did come into Joseph's life through a series of unfair circumstances, but he was not ruined, for the Lord was his confidence.

Joseph's foot was not snared by the jealousy of his brothers, not snared when he lost his home and was sent to slavery. His foot was not snared when he was tempted by Potiphar's wife and thrown into prison. And the final wonderful test upon tests: by the grace of God, Joseph's foot was not snared when his brothers became needy for food and he was in a position to send them away hungry. Truly, what man meant for evil, God used for great good. Good job, Joseph!

Make It Personal . . . Live It Out!

Do you feel you are barely hanging on? Sometimes I feel like a half-drowned cat washed up on the shore. You too? But then I remember: the tender mercies of the Lord, they fail not. "Great is his faithfulness; his mercies begin afresh each morning" (Lamentations 3:23). Will you take a moment right now to still your heart? Picture the burdens that are weighting you down. Will you lift them up to our merciful and kind Father in heaven? Will you rest your heart with confidence in him? Peace is not the absence of trouble, but the presence of God.

One Year Bible Reading

Genesis 35:1–36:43; Matthew 12:1-21; Psalm 15:1-5; Proverbs 3:21-26

I Can Do Something

Do not withhold good from those who deserve it,
when it is in your power to act.
Do not say to your neighbor,
"Come back later; I'll give it tomorrow"—
when you now have it with you.

PROVERBS 3:27-28 (NIV)

The New Testament companion to this proverb is found in James 2:15-16, which says, "Suppose a brother or sister is without clothes and daily food. If one of you says to him, 'Go, I wish you well; keep warm and well fed,' but does nothing about his physical needs, what good is it?" (NIV).

Good question: What good? I love that God cares about all of this. I think of some of the missed opportunities in the Bible. I think of the innkeeper who turned away Mary when she was about to give birth to the Son of God. I think about the people in Noah's day who saw him build that huge boat with just his sons. They could have helped.

And so we are encouraged to not miss the many opportunities around us. Okay, let me just throw out some things to pray about. Do you have elderly neighbors? Why don't you ask, next time you go to the store, if they need anything? Do you know a single mom? Why don't you ask if her son or her daughter needs new tennis shoes? Do you know someone who is sick? What if you made some extra soup or an extra casserole this week and took it over to them? Do you know of a family whose dad has lost his job? What if you filled a grocery bag with cereal and milk and eggs and peanut butter? Jesus said, "Inasmuch as you did to one of the least of these My brethren, you did to Me" (Matthew 25:40, NKJV).

Make It Personal . . . Live It Out!

I am only one, but I am one. I cannot do everything, but I can do something.
And I will not let what I cannot do interfere with what I can do.
—EDWARD EVERETT HALE

Let's Pray

Lord, please show me one thing I can do today to meet a need or lift a burden.

One Year Bible Reading

Genesis 37:1–38:30; Matthew 12:22-45; Psalm 16:1-11; Proverbs 3:27-32

Grace to the Humble

The LORD's curse is on the house of the wicked,
but he blesses the home of the righteous.
He mocks proud mockers
but gives grace to the humble.
The wise inherit honor,
but fools he holds up to shame.

PROVERBS 3:33-35 (NIV)

"Grace to the humble." That's our topic today. Many of us theoretically would like to be humble, but then we realize that to be humble might take the process of being humbled.

But let's listen to what 1 Peter 5:5 tells us: "All of you, clothe yourselves with humility toward one another, because, 'God opposes the proud but gives grace to the humble'" (NIV).

Here we see humility is a choice, and the context is in relationships. Pride and stubbornness build walls, but humility can melt them.

Let's apply this first to marriage. Has your husband disappointed you? Have you then in your frustration struck back with words or actions? Now you have a standoff. No one wants to budge. Ladies, when families fight, nobody wins. You be the first to say the kind word. You be the first to say, "I'm sorry." Mark my words. No matter how your husband responds, God will bless you because he promised that he would give grace to the humble. It's been said, "Humility isn't thinking meanly of yourself. It's merely not thinking of yourself at all."

So let's humble ourselves under the mighty hand of God because he guarantees that he, God himself, will lift us up.

Make It Personal . . . Live It Out!

I'll be perfectly honest: it's hard for me to humble myself when I think I am right or the other person is wrong. But God has taught me little steps that help me every time. (1) Try to step in the other person's shoes to see his side. How does he feel? (2) Ask yourself, *Have I been thoughtless or unkind?* It is humbling, because I always see how I could have or should have done things better. (3) Take it to God; then (4) God himself will give you the next step.

One Year Bible Reading

Genesis 39:1–41:16; Matthew 12:46–13:23; Psalm 17:1-15; Proverbs 3:33-35

Fatherly Advice

My children, listen to me. Listen to your father's instruction.
Pay attention and grow wise,
for I am giving you good guidance.
Don't turn away from my teaching. . . .
My father told me,
"Take my words to heart.
Follow my instructions and you will live.
Learn to be wise, and develop good judgment.
Don't forget or turn away from my words.
Don't turn your back on wisdom, for she will protect you.
Love her, and she will guard you."

PROVERBS 4:1-2, 4-6

Maybe as you listened, this actually made you a little sad because you never had a father who talked with you and taught you wise things. Maybe you're a single mom and you wish your children had a father who did that. Having a father is a very important thing. Listen to some tragic statistics: 90 percent of all homeless and runaway children and 71 percent of high school dropouts are from fatherless homes.

But although you may have lacked this kind of strong, wise input on a human level, God himself is able to make it up to you. He is willing and able to step into that role to father you and father your kids, giving them wise advice. He can stand beside you when you're weak. He can comfort you when you're lonely or afraid. He will be the Father you never had but always wanted.

Make It Personal . . . Live It Out!

"Learn to be wise and develop good judgment" is your Father God's advice for you today. *Learn* and *develop* are the key verbs. Wisdom does not just come overnight. We learn what is right as we read the book of Proverbs. Then we have a responsibility to apply what we learn. Each time we do what we know is right, we forge paths of obedience in our characters. Does that make sense? Wise choices and good judgment become your "new groove." And that's a good thing!

Let's Pray

Lord, please teach me what is right and help me to apply what I learn.

One Year Bible Reading

Genesis 41:17–42:17; Matthew 13:24-46; Psalm 18:1-15; Proverbs 4:1-6

January 21

Crown of Beauty

Whoever thinks that the godly life of wisdom is a life of sparseness or drabness or poorness is absolutely dead wrong. God is the King of the entire universe. He alone made the diamonds from coal. He alone created gold and snowflakes, waterfalls and sunsets. God loves to make things that have beauty and nobility. And we, as daughters of God, are actually princesses. Romans tells us that we are heirs of God and joint heirs with Christ; so keep this in mind as we read this lovely description in today's Wisdom for Women.

> *"Getting wisdom is the most important thing you can do!*
> *And whatever else you do, get good judgment.*
> *If you prize wisdom, she will exalt you.*
> *Embrace her and she will honor you.*
> *She will place a lovely wreath on your head;*
> *she will present you with a beautiful crown."*
> *My child, listen to me and do as I say,*
> *and you will have a long, good life.*
>
> PROVERBS 4:7-10

Crowns. Wisdom will present you with a beautiful crown. Crowns are both valuable and weighty. In the Kremlin in Moscow the actual crowns worn by past rulers are displayed. Some are large, heavily encrusted with jewels. The person wearing it would always be aware that they had it on and aware of all that it meant. With a crown came great responsibility. When Queen Esther put on her royal robes and crown it was not just to rule, it was to serve.

And so, dear sisters, may we wear God's wisdom as a crown, a crown of nobility and honor and beauty.

Make It Personal . . . Live It Out!

We women wear many hats: daughter, friend, cook, shopper, organizer, sister, counselor, homemaker, teacher, wife, mother. The question is, do you do what you do with honor? Embrace wisdom! I know—you might be thinking, *I can't! I fail.* Okay, I agree; none of us can, in our own strength.

Let's Pray

Lord, here I am again, like an empty cup held up to you. Please fill me with your wisdom that I may live with honor and beauty.

One Year Bible Reading

Genesis 42:18–43:34; Matthew 13:47–14:12; Psalm 18:16-36; Proverbs 4:7-10

Guided

I guide you in the way of wisdom
and lead you along straight paths.
When you walk, your steps will not be hampered;
when you run, you will not stumble.
Hold on to instruction, do not let it go;
guard it well, for it is your life.

PROVERBS 4:11-13 (NIV)

This is the ever-recurring picture of life being like a journey.

Alice, in *Alice in Wonderland*, came to a fork in the road.

"Which road do I take?" she asked.

"Where do you want to go?" responded the Cheshire cat.

"I don't know," Alice answered.

"Then," said the cat, "it doesn't matter."

But, dear sisters, your life does matter; therefore, it is important that you head in the right direction. Each step that you take, each decision that you make takes you further along the path for better or worse.

If you have a GPS in your car, you program in the address of where you need to go, your destination. The GPS then plots the best and shortest path. It guides you along the way with arrows letting you know when and where to turn. One of the greatest things is the voice. If you make a wrong turn, it will say things like, "Make a U-turn," or, "Recalculating your course." The GPS never loses sight of the goal, even if you do. This is especially helpful when I have gotten turned around, lost my way, or accidently driven into a rough area at night.

Good news! God has given us his personal, persistent, internal GPS system, the Holy Spirit himself. Follow his arrows and obey his voice.

Make It Personal . . . Live It Out!

I really love the words "recalculating your course." These are words of hope and help. Maybe you feel you have lost your way. Does it seem you've hit a dead end? Take heart. The very fact that you are reading this right now is evidence that you desire to get back on track. Grab hold of God's promise for you today: "I guide you in the way of wisdom and lead you along straight paths."

One Year Bible Reading

Genesis 44:1–45:28; Matthew 14:13-36; Psalm 18:37-50; Proverbs 4:11-13

January 23

We Must Shine!

Before you read today's Wisdom for Women, close your eyes and imagine the word picture of the phrase "Like the first gleam of dawn."

> *The way of the righteous is like the first gleam of dawn,*
> *which shines ever brighter until the full light of day.*
> *But the way of the wicked is like complete darkness.*
> *Those who follow it have no idea what they are stumbling over.*
>
> PROVERBS 4:18-19

"The first gleam of dawn." Maybe it's been a long time since you've gotten up early enough to see a sunrise. It is totally worth it. There is something about it that makes you feel like you're witnessing a secret, almost holy moment. The darker the night, the more exciting and dramatic the first ray is. Once the light comes, nothing can stop it. It gets stronger and stronger until there is no darkness left.

Child of God, we are living in perilous times. Darkness is dark, really dark. We see people—people we love—falling, falling into darkness. We see young people making foolish, sinful choices, and then falling in a series of life-changing, life-damaging choices. They had no idea where those first steps would lead.

And so we must shine. We must shine like the lighthouse set high on the rock of God's Word, the rock of truth, the rock of safety. We must shine. Jesus said, "You are the light of the world. A city that is set on a hill cannot be hidden" (Matthew 5:14, NKJV).

Make It Personal . . . Live It Out!

Okay, I am fired up about this. God is calling us! It is time for the people of God to stoke the fires of their love for God and their passion to make a difference in this world. There are people who have never heard the gospel that God loves them. There are people who have heard it but never seen it lived out. He can use our lives like "the first gleam of dawn." Come on! Let's fall on our knees and ask him to ignite us. If not us, who? If not now, when?

One Year Bible Reading

Genesis 46:1–47:31; Matthew 15:1-28; Psalm 19:1-14; Proverbs 4:14-19

Guard Your Heart

My son, give attention to my words;
Incline your ear to my sayings.
Do not let them depart from your eyes;
Keep them in the midst of your heart;
For they are life to those who find them,
And health to all their flesh.
Keep your heart with all diligence;
For out of it spring the issues of life.

PROVERBS 4:20-23 (NKJV)

The importance of the heart is the topic of today.

The New Living Translation Bible says, "Above all else, guard your heart, for it affects everything you do." Ladies, this may be some of the most important advice we'll ever receive. For us as women, our hearts are places of great vulnerability; on the other hand, they're also places of tenderness, compassion, and love.

And so may I ask you, what is the state of your heart? Do you have a broken heart, or a wounded heart? Do you have a troubled heart, a weary heart, an empty heart? Worse yet, do you have a cold, hard, or bitter heart?

In our proverb today God himself, our Father God, our Great Physician, gives us his prescription, his healing balm, the Word of God.

God's Word cleanses. It frees our hearts. It softens and restores. It's surgically sharp and can actually completely and permanently heal our hearts. We must also know that God's Word guards our hearts with truth. It's the antidote for the lie. God's Word is the Sword of the Spirit that defends and protects. It's light that gives our hearts hope; therefore, keep your heart with all diligence, "for out of it spring the issues of life."

Make It Personal . . . Live It Out!

There is lots of advice out there for emotional and spiritual brokenness. Take a pill, take a trip, read a book, or talk to a professional. Some women just give up and drown their sorrow. But let me give you the best prescription ever given to man (or woman). Read Psalm 23 three times a day for one week. "Keep them [the promises] in the midst of your heart" and you will see; he will restore your soul.

One Year Bible Reading

Genesis 48:1–49:33; Matthew 15:29–16:12; Psalm 20:1-9; Proverbs 4:20-27

Pandora's Box

My son, pay attention to my wisdom,
listen well to my words of insight. . . .
For the lips of an adulteress drip honey,
and her speech is smoother than oil;
but in the end she is bitter as gall,
sharp as a double-edged sword.
Her feet go down to death;
her steps lead straight to the grave.
She gives no thought to the way of life;
her paths are crooked, but she knows it not.

PROVERBS 5:1, 3-6 (NIV)

Today's proverb is a blunt, sober warning to men about the dangers of adultery, but if you were to watch almost any popular TV show today, the message is quite the opposite. They make casual sex look like a harmless game where the more you play, the more fun it is. Nothing could be further from the truth. It's a dangerous game, and no one wins. If you use emotions or people as toys, they break, leaving everyone broken.

Ladies, I don't care if you are fourteen or forty-four or seventy-four. Women have an ability to bring men down. The situation portrayed in this proverb is of a woman who flirts and flatters and causes a man to fall.

So if this has hit a chord, if you know that you have been flirting with danger, if you know you've opened a Pandora's box, first of all, may I beg you, repent. Call a godly friend and ask for prayer, ask for accountability, and draw near to the Lord himself, who is able to reel you back from this dangerous path of death.

Make It Personal . . . Live It Out!

Let me talk to mothers for a moment. You are either planting good seeds or bad seeds in your sons' or daughters' minds regarding their attitude toward "casual sex." Do you enjoy the latest sitcom that winks at sex on the first date or at couples living together? Do you buy the magazines that update you on the sex life of the stars? If you do, you are endorsing that behavior, no matter what you say. All I can say is, it's time to clean your own house.

One Year Bible Reading

Genesis 50:1—Exodus 2:10; Matthew 16:13–17:9; Psalm 21:1-13; Proverbs 5:1-6

Utter Ruin

Now then, my sons, listen to me;
do not turn aside from what I say.
Keep to a path far from [an adulteress],
do not go near the door of her house. . . .
[Otherwise,] at the end of your life you will groan,
when your flesh and body are spent.
You will say, "How I hated discipline!
How my heart spurned correction!
I would not obey my teachers
or listen to my instructors.
I have come to the brink of utter ruin."

PROVERBS 5:7-8, 11-14 (NIV)

Today's proverb is a warning to stay away from immoral sex. Although written for sons, it applies to our daughters as well. Even though this was written many years ago, it mentions the very same type of damage that occurs with immorality today.

It's been wisely said that "tomorrow is the best reason for doing the right thing today." Yes, there is pleasure in sin for a season, but beware: it takes a serious toll.

And so I feel it's important for us as women to be aware of the devastating consequences of sexual sin. STDs (sexually transmitted diseases) have become epidemic. We are learning more and more of the long-range damage this does to your body.

But more than that, immoral sex does not just mess with your body. It messes with your emotions, your thought life, and with your soul. Each time you have sex with someone, you bond in a deep place. When that relationship is torn, it tears a piece out of you. Sin is such a liar. Sin promises simple pleasure, but it delivers a powerful and complicated punch of pain and problems.

Make It Personal . . . Live It Out!

Maybe you are thinking, *If only I had known then what I know now.* Because everyone was doing it, you caved in to pressure to sleep around. Now you can look back and see a long trail of disappointment and pain. So, what now? I am so happy to say that God is the God of the fresh start. Purity is first spiritual, then it becomes emotional and physical. Jesus came to redeem and restore. Will you ask him and will you let him restore you, "white as snow"?

One Year Bible Reading

Exodus 2:11–3:22; Matthew 17:10-27; Psalm 22:1-18; Proverbs 5:7-14

Faithful Husbands

Drink water from your own cistern,
running water from your own well. . . .
Let them be yours alone,
never to be shared with strangers.
May your fountain be blessed,
and may you rejoice in the wife of your youth.
A loving doe, a graceful deer—
may her breasts satisfy you always,
may you ever be captivated by her love.
Why be captivated, my son, by an adulteress?
Why embrace the bosom of another man's wife?
For a man's ways are in full view of the LORD,
and he examines all his paths.

PROVERBS 5:15, 17-21 (NIV)

Ladies, our proverb today is written to our husbands, telling them to be faithful to us. This is a wonderful thing.

I was with some of my friends recently who were telling me about their daughters who have taken oaths of purity. Not only are they committed to wait until marriage to have sex but they are committed to not even kiss. One of the young girls told her friends, "I don't want to kiss a man who might later be someone else's husband." Good job, girls!

But is this possible in this generation? Is it worth it to even try? It helps to break some of the fallacies about sex outside of marriage. Studies show that couples who live together are not more satisfied, because there is no commitment. Cohabiting men are four times more likely to cheat than married men, and cohabiting women eight times more likely than married women—showing again that the grass truly is greener on your side of the marriage fence.

Make It Personal . . . Live It Out!

Although this proverb is addressed to husbands, let's now talk about our part. Make no mistake, there are many wives who make it hard for their husbands to be satisfied at home. When your husband comes home, are you still in your oldest, ugliest sweats? Is there no sign of dinner, and do the bills show you have been shopping too much? Your husband deserves more, and trust me, someone out there would like to give him more. Tonight, cook his favorite dinner and give him a reason to be captivated by your love.

One Year Bible Reading

Exodus 4:1–5:21; Matthew 18:1-20; Psalm 22:19-31; Proverbs 5:15-21

Slave of Sin

An evil man is held captive by his own sins;
they are ropes that catch and hold him.
He will die for lack of self-control;
he will be lost because of his incredible folly.

PROVERBS 5:22-23

The clear moral of this proverb is never to underestimate the power of sin to make you a slave. It can hold you hostage. Listen to this powerful description: "Sin will take you farther than you ever wanted to go. It will leave you longer than you ever wanted to stay, and it will cost you more than you ever wanted to pay."

But lest we get a mental picture of someone else we know whose sin is obvious and we shake our heads and say, "Yep, that poor person is ruining her life," we need to be conscious of our own sin. Sin is subtle. You may not be wasting your life at the bar, but maybe you are harboring pride and resentment. Don't kid yourself. That kind of sin can tie us in knots too.

When evangelist Billy Sunday was preparing for a crusade in a large city, he wrote a letter asking the mayor of that city for the names of individuals who had spiritual problems and needed help and prayer. How surprised Billy was when the mayor sent him the entire city telephone directory.

"All have sinned and fall short of the glory of God" (Romans 3:23, NKJV), but "if we confess our sin, he is faithful to forgive and to cleanse" (1 John 1:9, paraphrase). Now, that's freedom.

Make It Personal . . . Live It Out!

Can you visualize the grip sins can have? They are "ropes that catch and hold." Let's take a moment and be honest and specific. The sin of bitterness and resentment, for instance, can captivate your thought life. You find yourself reliving a hurt over and over and over. Do you see how driven and enslaved it has made you? Cut those ropes! By the power of God's grace, cut those ropes! Today, every time those thoughts come to your mind, will you ask God to help you forgive and forget—and set you free? Ask, and *you shall receive.*

One Year Bible Reading

Exodus 5:22–7:25; Matthew 18:21–19:12; Psalm 23:1-6; Proverbs 5:22-23

Financial Foolishness

My child, if you co-sign a loan for a friend
or guarantee the debt of someone you hardly know—
if you have trapped yourself by your agreement
and are caught by what you said—
quick, get out of it if you possibly can!
You have placed yourself at your friend's mercy.
Now swallow your pride;
go and beg to have your name erased.
Don't put it off. Do it now!
Don't rest until you do.

PROVERBS 6:1-4

The topic of today's Wisdom for Women is the danger of getting entangled in other people's financial dealings. If we can learn any lessons from the financial crisis we are currently in, both publicly and personally, we can see that we have not been wise. It's risky business to back up someone else when they are involved in risky business and can't stand on their own. Oh, if Capitol Hill and Wall Street and those who live on our street would listen and heed God's wisdom as stated in today's proverb!

So, ladies, what can we learn? We need to be less dependent on credit for ourselves, our kids, and others. If we can't save up for something we want, we need to truly assess if we really need it.

When my husband and I bought our first home, we had no one who could give us a down payment or cosign for us. The first house we tried to buy fell through because we didn't qualify. In retrospect, it was a blessing. It was a house in an area that wasn't good for us, and it was a payment we really couldn't afford. So even though at the time it felt like a bad thing, it was a good thing. It taught us to be realistic. We spent the next year and a half saving. Then when we did buy, it was a victory and a blessing.

Make It Personal . . . Live It Out!

Does God really care about our finances? Yes, actually he does. Foolishness and carelessness with money has been the ruin of many marriages. Loaning money to someone who isn't wise with money and doesn't pay you back has soured many friendships. Let's be wise savers and frugal spenders.

One Year Bible Reading

Exodus 8:1–9:35; Matthew 19:13-30; Psalm 24:1-10; Proverbs 6:1-5

Ants Aren't Lazy

Take a lesson from the ants, you lazybones.
Learn from their ways and be wise!
Even though they have no prince,
governor, or ruler to make them work,
they labor hard all summer,
gathering food for the winter.
But you, lazybones, how long will you sleep?
When will you wake up?
I want you to learn this lesson:
A little extra sleep, a little more slumber,
a little folding of the hands to rest—
and poverty will pounce on you like a bandit;
scarcity will attack you like an armed robber.

PROVERBS 6:6-11

You might not realize that the proverb that we look at every day is taken from the daily proverb in the *One Year Bible*. I love this reading schedule. It takes us sequentially through the whole counsel of God. I love that the Proverbs address practical and important life issues.

Today's Wisdom for Women deals with the topic of personal diligence and uses the amazing little ant as an example. These tiny creatures put some of us to shame. What's the secret of their success? They just keep at it, even though no one is standing over them telling them to.

Child of God, consider the ant. One of the fruits of the Spirit is self-control because it's a by-product of the Spirit's presence in our life. We need to start there. Diligence needs to start, first of all, in spiritual things, seeking first the Kingdom of God and his righteousness. Then asking him to fire you up. Ask God to give you the work ethic of our wise little friend, the ant.

Make It Personal . . . Live It Out!

I love the ant! She is the perfect illustration of the principle "Inch by inch, anything's a cinch!" Let's apply her example. For instance, why don't we clean out our closets? Because, once they start getting messy, messy takes over—right? Well, let's reverse the process. March into your closet and put five items in place. I'm going to. Now, savor the small victory and it will inch you on to others. Yay ants!

One Year Bible Reading

Exodus 10:1–12:13; Matthew 20:1-28; Psalm 25:1-15; Proverbs 6:6-11

January 31

Troublemakers

Here is a description of worthless and wicked people:
They are constant liars,
signaling their true intentions to their friends
by making signs with their eyes and feet and fingers.
Their perverted hearts plot evil.
They stir up trouble constantly.
But they will be destroyed suddenly,
broken beyond all hope of healing.

PROVERBS 6:12-15

A naughty person. Most of us remember some boy in elementary school who was always messing around—causing trouble and getting others in trouble. Well, some little boys and some little girls never grow up and out of that behavior.

What's the value of talking about them? Moms, talk to your children. Teach them not to make trouble or to look at bad behavior as cool or fun. "Do not be misled: 'Bad company corrupts good character'" (1 Corinthians 15:33, NIV). But don't —please don't—hate those kids, either. Sometimes they are just acting out. Maybe they're craving attention. Maybe they have no one at home to reel them in. Did you ever think about who is assigned to pray for those children? Sit down and write down the names of those kids who are troublemakers and pray for them by name.

And while you are at it, do you have any troublemakers at work or among your relatives or in your church? Maybe they are acting out, craving attention, too. Don't hate them, either. Did you ever think about who is assigned to pray for them by name? Maybe, just maybe, you are!

Make It Personal . . . Live It Out!

I have a friend who has a jail ministry. She has truly found her niche. Every day when she goes in, she knows she will talk to someone who is considered a "lost cause." But she has also seen that for some, jail is a wake-up call. She is a light to show them the way out of the darkness. You don't have to go into the jail to find someone who needs that. Will you ask God to assign you just one person who needs a ray of hope? And then, will you shine it?

One Year Bible Reading

Exodus 12:14–13:16; Matthew 20:29–21:22; Psalm 25:16-22; Proverbs 6:12-15

February

Scan this code for audio devotionals
or visit www.tyndal.es/wisdom.

Things God Hates

There are six things the LORD hates,
seven that are detestable to him;
haughty eyes,
a lying tongue,
hands that shed innocent blood,
a heart that devises wicked schemes,
feet that are quick to rush into evil,
a false witness who pours out lies
and a man who stirs up dissension among brothers.

PROVERBS 6:16-19 (NIV)

No doubt about it, not only are we to be students of what pleases the Lord, but we must be vividly aware of what displeases him. Here are seven things. Maybe as you read the list you thought, *Wow yes, those are so bad. Bad people do those bad things. I would never do any of them.* Really?

Let me pick out two that we as women are sometimes especially prone to—faults we see in others and yet sometimes don't see in ourselves.

- Haughty eyes. This is "that look"—that annoyed look, that rude look. It is the look at someone you think is below you, that you look down on. Have you ever heard the expression "if looks could kill"? Well, looks kind of do kill. Have you ever known someone who just made you cringe when you were around them because they looked at you like dirt? Enough said. Don't do that.
- Another thing that the Lord hates is causing rifts—causing division. Planting little seeds between people that make them distrust each other. Pointing out flaws and failures. Never forget: God hates it, so don't do it—ever.

The antidote for both is love. Jesus said, "By this all people will know that you are my disciples, if you have love for one another" (John 13:35, ESV). Love covers a multitude of sins.

Make It Personal . . . Live It Out!

God hates it when we use the expressions on our face to put others down with frowns and scowls. I have a friend who was doing that without realizing it. Then she stood at the mirror and could see that her frowns were becoming permanent.

The Lord spoke to her heart: "You can fix your face." It seemed silly and even impossible at first. But she knew it was the Lord's prompting. God had softened her heart, and she decided to practice on the outside what he was doing on the inside. Good idea! Let's try it.

One Year Bible Reading

Exodus 13:17–15:18; Matthew 21:23-46; Psalm 26:1-12; and Proverbs 6:16-19

Guard Your Heart

Our proverb today warns us that when sexual temptation comes, it is strong. Therefore the Word of God must hold us stronger. Godly parents who teach their children to love God's Word are giving the greatest gift and protection a child could ever have.

My son, keep your father's commands
and do not forsake your mother's teaching.
Bind them upon your heart forever;
fasten them around your neck.
When you walk, they will guide you;
when you sleep, they will watch over you;
when you awake, they will speak to you.
For these commands are a lamp,
this teaching is a light,
and the corrections of discipline
are the way to life,
keeping you from the immoral woman,
from the smooth tongue of the wayward wife.
Do not lust in your heart after her beauty
or let her captivate you with her eyes,
for the prostitute reduces you to a loaf of bread,
and the adulteress preys upon your very life.

PROVERBS 6:20-26 (NIV)

In Homer' story *The Odyssey*, Odysseus was warned that he and his crew would sail near the land of the Sirens, whose song would enchant them and lure them to their death, where they would join others who had fallen and whose bones had rotted. Circe warned, "You must sail straight on past. Lash yourself with ropes on the mast, and if you are tempted, have someone tie you even tighter."

Temptations will come; none of us should kid ourselves. The Word of God, hidden, treasured, and obeyed deep in our hearts, will hold us fast and keep us safe.

Make It Personal . . . Live It Out!

The moral of the story of the Sirens is this: don't trust your emotions. Don't leave your heart unguarded. It's a dangerous world out there. There are lots of women who did not receive instruction about morality and wise living as they grew up. Maybe you didn't. It's never too late. Get involved in a women's Bible study! The combination of fellowship, accountability, and growing together in God's Word is powerful and wonderful.

Let's Pray

Lord, help me to bind your words close to my heart; tie me tighter to you. Please guard my heart and hold me safe.

One Year Bible Reading

Exodus 15:19–17:7; Matthew 22:1-33; Psalm 27:1-6; Proverbs 6:20-26

Shame and Disgrace

Can a man [or woman] scoop fire into his lap
and not be burned?
Can he walk on hot coals
and not blister his feet?
So it is with the man who sleeps with another man's wife.
He who embraces her will not go unpunished. . . .
But the man who commits adultery is an utter fool,
for he destroys his own soul.
Wounds and constant disgrace are his lot.
His shame will never be erased.
For the woman's husband will be furious in his jealousy,
and he will have no mercy in his day of vengeance.
There is no compensation
or bribe that will satisfy him.

PROVERBS 6:27-29, 32-35

Today's proverb starts with a rhetorical question: "Can a man [or a woman] scoop fire into his lap and not be burned? The answer is "No, of course not." You would be crazy to think you could. So why do some people think they can play around with the fire of adultery and not end up with scars and ashes? Why?

Adultery—how easy it is to fall into, but how deep are the wounds. I remember a friend telling me her story. As a child her family's world revolved around the church. All of her best memories are of her time there with the family of God. But one day when she was just six, her parents had a meeting with someone in the church office. They sent her outside. She heard screaming and cursing. She knew something terrible had happened and her mom was to blame. When they left, her dad never returned home and they never went back to church. It was adultery. Adultery changed her entire childhood.

Make It Personal . . . Live It Out!

Has your heart been broken by the damage of adultery in your own family or those you love? Maybe you are the one who fell. John 8 relates Jesus' encounter with a woman "caught in the act." If you haven't read it lately, will you turn to it and relive the scene? As painful as it is to read, it ends with an amazing moment of grace. Just simply Jesus says, "Neither do I [condemn you]. Go and sin no more" (John 8:11). Nothing less, nothing more.

One Year Bible Reading

Exodus 17:8–19:15; Matthew 22:34–23:12; Psalm 27:7-14; Proverbs 6:27-35

Preventive Medicine

Follow my advice, my son;
always treasure my commands.
Obey them and live!
Guard my teachings as your most precious possession.
Tie them on your fingers as a reminder.
Write them deep within your heart.
Love wisdom like a sister;
make insight a beloved member of your family.
Let them hold you back from an affair with an immoral woman,
from listening to the flattery of an adulterous woman.

PROVERBS 7:1-5

There you have it: a love affair with God's Word will make you immune to love affairs with the world, the flesh, or the devil. How great is that?

So exactly how do you do that? How do you fall in love with the Word of God? Let me give you three practical things.

1. Ask the Lord himself to stir up your heart and to give you a joyful hunger for his Word. This is a supernatural work. Please know that this is the kind of prayer the Lord is so happy to answer.
2. Since it's helped me so much, I will recommend that you go out and buy a *One Year Bible*. This helps you with that beloved habit of daily personal reading.
3. Scripture memorization. I know you might think this is impossible for you to do, but just try it. Write out a verse that you would really love to know on a 3 x 5 card. Carry it everywhere. Read it and practice it. In days it will be written on your memory, in your thought life, and also in the deep places of your heart.

Make It Personal . . . Live It Out!

Our proverb today tells us not only to treasure God's Words, but to "obey them and live." This is where the rubber meets the road. Let me challenge you to a seven-day test. For seven days straight, read your Bible first thing in the morning and write down two lessons you learn.

Then, don't just put your Bible away and move on. Still your heart and ask God to show you one specific thing you can apply to your life right away. Something amazing and personal happens when you sense the unction of his Spirit moving on your heart.

And then, of course, do it! The results in the days to come will indeed reveal God's teachings as your precious possessions.

One Year Bible Reading

Exodus 19:16–21:21; Matthew 23:13-39; Psalm 28:1-9; Proverbs 7:1-5

Steps of Temptation

I was looking out the window
of my house one day
and saw a simpleminded young man
who lacked common sense.
He was crossing the street near the house of an immoral woman.
He was strolling down the path by her house at twilight,
as the day was fading,
as the dark of night set in.
The woman approached him,
dressed seductively and sly of heart. . . .
He followed her at once,
like an ox going to the slaughter
or like a trapped stag,
awaiting the arrow that would pierce its heart.
He was like a bird flying into a snare,
little knowing it would cost him his life.

PROVERBS 7:6-10, 22-23

Oh, the fatal mistake of crossing the street! We are sadly mistaken if we think that we fall into temptation all at once. No, most the time it begins small and subtle. It's not the first look that trips us up; it's the lingering look that becomes the longing look. Then there is an action that takes us dangerously near. Before we know it, just like the foolish man described in the proverb, we are become trapped and snared. Whether it's the chocolate cake on the counter or the R-rated movies on your TV, or the bottle of alcohol in a cupboard, it only takes one moment of weakness for us to "cross the street." It's like a magnet; the closer we get, the harder it is to resist.

What's God's advice? "Flee . . . youthful lusts" (2 Timothy 2:22, NKJV). Shake the magnetic pull by turning around and walking away.

Make It Personal . . . Live It Out!

One final word to us as mothers and friends: sometimes we allow something questionable in our homes or lives because we feel it will never tempt or trap us. But we must remember that a weak friend or a vulnerable teenager might use our liberty as an excuse to cross a dangerous line they can't easily resist. I urge you to adopt Paul's advice in Romans 14:21: "It is better not to eat meat or drink wine or to do anything else if it might cause another believer to stumble." That is truly love and wisdom in action.

One Year Bible Reading

Exodus 21:22–23:13; Matthew 24:1-28; Psalm 29:1-11; Proverbs 7:6-23

Seduction

The topic of today's proverb is seduction. It is a warning call not to be swayed and lured by temptation. Look down that path before you step one foot in that direction. Oh, the grief that would be spared if we thought through where that path of temporary pleasure would end up. Stop and ask yourself what kind of damage it would do to your marriage, to your kids, to your Christian witness, to others who have looked to you as an example.

Listen to me, my children;
Pay attention to the words of my mouth:
Do not let your heart turn aside to her ways,
Do not stray into her paths;
For she has cast down many wounded,
And all who were slain by her were strong men.
Her house is the way to hell,
Descending to the chambers of death.

PROVERBS 7:24-27 (NKJV)

So now let's look honestly at two emotional paths that can lead us as women to a crash landing of sexual sin.

1. At your office, emotional affairs start with sharing personal information and negative feelings about your husband with a man in the office. Then you meet for coffee, then for dinner—and then danger!
2. You bump into an old boyfriend and exchange e-mails. Stirring up old emotions can open a can of worms and lead to a secret life and fantasies. It starts as an escape and becomes a trap.

Let the red flag of wisdom stop you before you even get started.

Make It Personal . . . Live It Out!

Men are visual. Whether it's our intent or not, they notice when a woman's clothes give hints of sensuality. It's not fair to them to be careless. Just between you and me, there are a lot of women who need to lean over in front of the mirror before they go out wearing certain tops. A skimpy blouse, a short skirt, tight pants—they send the wrong message.

You don't have to look frumpy to be discreet. Let's have some honest discussions with the young girls in our life. And let's do a little wardrobe reality check ourselves.

One Year Bible Reading

Exodus 23:14–25:40; Matthew 24:29-51; Psalm 30:1-12; Proverbs 7:24-27

There's No Excuse

Does not wisdom cry out,
And understanding lift up her voice?
She takes her stand on the top of the high hill,
Beside the way, where the paths meet.
She cries out by the gates, at the entry of the city,
At the entrance of the doors:
"To you, O men, I call,
And my voice is to the sons of men.
O you simple ones, understand prudence,
And you fools, be of an understanding heart.
Listen, for I will speak of excellent things,
And from the opening of my lips will come right things;
For my mouth will speak truth;
Wickedness is an abomination to my lips."

PROVERBS 8:1-7 (NKJV)

No excuse. That is what I'll call the message of today's proverb. There is absolutely no excuse for any of us to make foolish choices or foolish decisions, because God is so eager to make wisdom available. All we have to do is pause and pray, and God will, as he promised, give us wisdom at every crossroads and for every need.

George Müller is one of the great heroes of the faith. He housed and cared for over twenty-three thousand orphans in the 1800s without asking anyone but God for support. When seeking God's wisdom in a matter, he said, "I seek at the beginning to get my heart into such a state that it has no will of its own in regard to a given matter. Nine-tenths of the difficulties are overcome when our hearts are ready to do the Lord's will, whatever it may be." Müller's life is living proof that God is a God who hears our cries for help and he is a God who answers.

Make It Personal . . . Live It Out!

Do you ever look back and ask yourself why you made some of the big decisions in your life? Do you wonder, *What was I thinking?* I do. Regretfully, I sometimes wonder, *Why wasn't I praying?* I can attribute every wrong turn and every careless decision to the fact that I did not wholeheartedly, patiently seek the Lord's direction and his perfect will before I moved ahead. Are you at a crossroads? Will you stop and ask and wait for God to give you the wisdom and insight you need? Take him at his promise; he will direct your paths.

One Year Bible Reading

Exodus 26:1–27:21; Matthew 25:1-30; Psalm 31:1-8; Proverbs 8:1-11

Humility

I, wisdom, dwell together with prudence;
I possess knowledge and discretion.
To fear the LORD is to hate evil;
I hate pride and arrogance,
evil behavior and perverse speech.

PROVERBS 8:12-13 (NIV)

In this proverb, wisdom says it hates pride. That's good. Pride always causes trouble and is a sign of foolishness. So then if pride is out of sync with wisdom, humility is in sync. Let me tell you a story.

A small Christian college was having financial difficulties. One day a very wealthy man came on the campus, found a white-haired man in overalls painting a wall, and asked if he could see the college president. The painter pointed out a house on campus and said he was sure the president could be seen there at noon.

At the designated time, the visitor knocked at the president's door and was admitted by the same man he had met in overalls, but now he was in a suit. As the visitor accepted an invitation to come in, he realized this man was the college president. He asked a number of questions about the needs of the college and told the president he would be sending a small donation. Two days later a check arrived for fifty thousand dollars. The donor had been touched by the humility of a man who was fitted for his position as college president but not too proud to put on the clothes of a workman and do a job that needed to be done. This is a picture of humility.

Make It Personal . . . Live It Out!

Why is it that humility is so endearing when we see it in others, but it is hard to accomplish in ourselves? Maybe it's because we are not bowing and humbling ourselves before our God. When we do that, somehow it eases our need to hold so tightly to our rights and to have the last word in a dispute. Are you in a stalemate with your husband; has a friend offended you; has someone broken a promise? It's been said, "It's better to bow than to break." Take God's advice on this, "Humble yourselves in the sight of the Lord, and He will lift you up" (James 4:10, NKJV).

One Year Bible Reading

Exodus 28:1-43; Matthew 25:31–26:13; Psalm 31:9-18; Proverbs 8:12-13

Created by God

Our proverb today tells us that God first created wisdom before he created the world.

The LORD brought me [wisdom] forth as the first of his works,
before his deeds of old;
I was appointed from eternity,
from the beginning, before the world began. . . .
I was given birth,
before he made the earth or its fields
or any of the dust of the world.

PROVERBS 8:22-23, 25-26 (NIV)

The natural world around us is a masterpiece of engineering design, wisdom, and perfection. But many scientists have looked at our world and universe from an evolutionist perspective. From that perspective, chaos, randomness, and accidents are said to explain everything from the snowflake to the sacrificial mothering instinct of the penguin. However, God himself definitely has a more logical, reasonable, and credible explanation: intelligent design. When we look at a well-designed building or bridge, it gives evidence that somewhere there would be an intelligent designer.

Just studying the human body alone argues for an Intelligent Designer. Did you know that every human spent about a half an hour as a single cell, but within that one cell there was the entire DNA written code to determine everything from eye color to height? One human brain generates more electrical impulses in a single day than all of the world's telephones put together. Scientists have counted over five hundred liver functions, and not only does your finger have a unique print, but so does your tongue. You truly are a living display of God's wisdom.

Make It Personal . . . Live It Out!

We can marvel that God designed rainbows and zebras. But clearly he applied his most personal touch when he designed you. Have you forgotten that? Maybe you grew up in a home where you never truly felt wanted, or maybe the hard things in life have left you feeling insignificant. From God's perspective, there is no one like you. Psalm 139 tells you that he has always known you, even when you were in your mother's womb; you are "fearfully and wonderfully made."

Let's Pray

Lord, help me see that you know me better and love me more than anyone. My significance comes from you, the brilliant and wise Creator of all.

One Year Bible Reading

Exodus 29:1–30:10; Matthew 26:14-46; Psalm 31:19-24; Proverbs 8:14-26

Wisdom—the Brilliant Architect

The proverb today had a profound impact on me. Wisdom is telling us that she was present observing the formation of the big elements of our world. She observed and understood and actually participated in determining complicated things like the distance of the sun from the earth and the placement of the reservoirs of water, oil, and gas deep within the earth. This same wisdom is available to you and me. Wisdom will oversee the complicated, multifaceted, and challenging processes and dilemmas that we face in our own personal lives. Think about that; really think about that. Yes, this can challenge us, but more, this should excite us, bless us, and give us great assurance. Why would we ever lean on our own understanding when we can rely upon God's?

> *I [wisdom] was there when [God] established the heavens, when he drew the horizon on the oceans. I was there when he set the clouds above, when he established the deep fountains of the earth. I was there when he set the limits of the seas, so they would not spread beyond their boundaries. And when he marked off the earth's foundations, I was the architect at his side. I was his constant delight, rejoicing always in his presence. And how happy I was at what he created—his wide world and all the human family! And so, my children, listen to me, for happy are all who follow my ways.*
>
> PROVERBS 8:27-32

Make It Personal . . . Live It Out!

What a masterpiece the universe is! Stars don't collide, the sun rises every morning, there's a rainbow after a storm. If your personal world seems in chaos, spinning out of control, this is the perfect time to fall on your knees and ask God to take control. Maybe you have told him what you want him to do, but have you asked him to show you what his ways are regarding this?

Will you stop and pray right now?

Let's Pray

God, I am looking to you. Help me to visualize all the things in the universe your wisdom has accomplished. With the same wisdom you use to guide the stars and the oceans, please direct me. And help me to rest with confidence.

One Year Bible Reading

Exodus 30:11–31:18; Matthew 26:47-68; Psalm 32:1-11; Proverbs 8:27-32

February 11

Your Choice!

Hear instruction and be wise,
And do not disdain it.
Blessed is the man who listens to me,
Watching daily at my gates,
Waiting at the posts of my doors.
For whoever finds me [wisdom] finds life,
And obtains favor from the LORD;
But he who sins against me wrongs his own soul;
All those who hate me love death.

PROVERBS 8:33-36 (NKJV)

Did you ever watch the TV show *The Price Is Right*? On the show, the contestant stood before a selection of doors. He knew there was a big grand prize behind one door and a booby prize behind the other. But it was a mystery which one was which. He had to take a wild guess and then take what he got. Not so with God. Our proverb today tells us that God is not making you guess. Door number one offers blessings, wisdom, and life. Door number two rejects wisdom and chooses soul-damaging death. This seems like a no-brainer. Let's choose door number one.

But you might be thinking, *That is easier said than done. When I come to a difficult decision, sometimes the wrong choice is disguised as the good choice.* Women have made bad choices in men because they were wolves in sheep's clothing. Money schemes, cults, jobs choices can all look good on the outside too. How are we to know? James 1:5-6 gives us the perfect answer. "If any of you lacks wisdom, he should ask God, who gives generously to all without finding fault, and it will be given to him. But when he asks, he must believe and not doubt" (NIV).

Make It Personal . . . Live It Out!

An important element of wisdom is personal responsibility. Many people blame others for their wrong choices and unhappiness. It is time to realize that we are each accountable for our own emotional and spiritual well-being. Did you know that you are exactly as joyful and wise and peaceful and full of God's love as you choose to be? No one can make that choice for you. Today, will you choose to put on some praise music if you feel down, will you sit and read Psalm 33 if you are discouraged, will you cast your care on the Lord if you are weary and heavy laden? Your choice!

One Year Bible Reading

Exodus 32:1–33:23; Matthew 26:69–27:14; Psalm 33:1-11; Proverbs 8:33-36

Wisdom Calls Us Home

Wisdom has built her spacious house
with seven pillars.
She has prepared a great banquet,
mixed the wines, and set the table.
She has sent her servants to invite everyone to come.
She calls out from the heights overlooking the city.
"Come home with me," she urges the simple.
To those without good judgment, she says,
"Come, eat my food,
and drink the wine I have mixed.
Leave your foolish ways behind,
and begin to live; learn how to be wise."

PROVERBS 9:1-6

This proverb paints a picture of wisdom as a woman calling us home. Dinner is on the table. It's a beautiful and inviting picture. Truly there will never be a more important place to learn and be nourished by good wise living than at home. Mary Farrar, in her book *Choices*, writes, "For most of known history, the home has been central to woman. It has been her primary place of work and influence and thus the natural place to express her womanhood. Therefore, throughout history . . . as the home has gone, so has gone woman." But because the structure of the home has been shattered over the last few decades, women have struggled with their sense of identity and worth. People are adrift.

We are longing for a place where we belong. Therefore, we need to redeem the concept of home as more than just a crash pad. Dear ladies, no matter what your age, marital status, how you grew up, or if you work outside the home, we are called to be homemakers. Wisdom is calling us to create within our homes a place of order and welcome, warmth and wise living.

Make It Personal . . . Live It Out!

Above all things, our homes should be godly homes. Will you look around your home and see if there is anything that you would be ashamed of if the Lord himself knocked on your door unexpectedly? Will you prayerfully walk around and ask him if there is anything you need to eliminate? That said, will you also pray about how to add some things to your home that reflect his presence? I love to have Scripture in every room of my house, in keeping with Deuteronomy 6:9. You can go to my website (BibleBusStop .com) and download Scriptures that are beautifully designed and perfect for framing.

One Year Bible Reading

Exodus 34:1–35:9; Matthew 27:15-31; Psalm 33:12-22; Proverbs 9:1-6

Rebuked in Love

Whoever corrects a mocker invites insult;
whoever rebukes a wicked man incurs abuse.
Do not rebuke a mocker or he will hate you;
rebuke a wise man and he will love you.

PROVERBS 9:7-8 (NIV)

It's been said that some people would rather be destroyed by compliments than saved by criticism.

Well, that's true. In the real world you can win some of the people some of the time, but some people, absolutely none of the time. So, first of all, never venture into the realm of correcting others without praying for discernment to know which is which. With some—maybe with many—don't waste your breath. Even the kindest, most gracious, honest comment will be twisted and overthought and misconstrued. Yep, we've learned that the hard way, haven't we? To correct a fool is barking up the wrong tree.

But don't give up on everyone. Recently I needed to have a little heart-to-heart talk with a dear friend. I was not annoyed or mad, just concerned. I hoped she would hear me out. I hoped she would know that what I said was not to hurt her but sincerely to strengthen and stretch her. Miracle upon miracle, she did receive my word, and in the end, this manifested not that I was wise, but that she is.

Make It Personal . . . Live It Out!

A wise man (or woman) loves rebuke. Therefore, if you are serious about becoming a woman of wisdom, you need to let your own defensive guard down. It is not good if your family or friends or coworkers are afraid to address issues honestly with you for fear of your response. And even an unfair, unkind criticism can be a blessing, for it can send you to the foot of the Cross. There, the Lord himself will help you sort it out to see if there is an element of truth that you need to take to heart. He can then help you live it out in godly sorrow and true repentance. That is why they call him Savior.

One Year Bible Reading

Exodus 35:10–36:38; Matthew 27:32-66; Psalm 34:1-10; Proverbs 9:7-8

Fear of the Lord

Give instruction to a wise man, and he will be still wiser;
Teach a just man, and he will increase in learning.
The fear of the LORD *is the beginning of wisdom,*
And the knowledge of the Holy One is understanding.

PROVERBS 9:9-10 (NKJV)

The fear of the Lord. I think for many this is a very misunderstood concept. But since over and over both the Psalms and the Proverbs tell us that "the fear of the LORD" is key to the attainment of wisdom, we need to get a grip on what it really is—and then let it get a grip on us.

The fear of the Lord. A. W. Tozer, one of my favorite authors, said this: "The current trick of frightening people into accepting Christ by threatening them with atom bombs and guided missiles is not scriptural, neither is it effective. By shooting off firecrackers in the face of a flock of goats, you could conceivably succeed in herding them into a sheep-fold; but all the natural fear in the world cannot make a sheep out of a goat. And neither can fear of [an enemy] invasion turn impenitent men into lovers of God and righteousness. It just does not work that way."

On the other hand, one of my all-time favorite moments to capture this is in Isaiah 6:1-5. Isaiah had just experienced the death of a king he respected. He was desperate. He looked up and he saw the Lord on his throne in heaven, glorious, high, and lifted up. Isaiah was totally in awe, filled with reverence, and it shook him up. Now, that is the fear of the Lord.

Make It Personal . . . Live It Out!

Are you afraid of God? Do you fear his punishment? Do you fear you could never please him? This kind of fear only brings torment and causes you to keep him at arm's distance. Did this false fear come from a harsh and cold relationship with your father or someone in authority? Please give your heavenly Father a chance to break that mold.

Let's Pray

Lord, I know it is unfair for me to blame you for the mistakes of others. Please help me lower my defenses and let you show me both your tender mercies and your awesome wonder.

One Year Bible Reading

Exodus 37:1–38:31; Matthew 28:1-20; Psalm 34:11-22; Proverbs 9:9-10

Wise Living

By me [wisdom] your days will be multiplied,
And years of life will be added to you.
If you are wise, you are wise for yourself,
And if you scoff, you will bear it alone.

PROVERBS 9:11-12 (NKJV)

It's been said, "People cannot decide their future. But they can decide their habits, and their habits decide their future." So true. Although it's right to live right and that alone is a reward, there are also many, many benefits to making wise, right choices.

So let's take a moment to look at some of the just plain practical, personal benefits of wise living for us as women.

- *Health.* Wise living teaches us to be good stewards of our health. It is not wise to smoke or eat lots of junky food. It is wise to exercise and eat well. It is unhealthy to internalize anger and worry. It's healthy to live simply and forgive easily.
- *Beauty.* A wise life is a beautiful life. I know several godly, gracious, wise women over eighty, and I have to say, I think they're beautiful. Pastor Chuck Smith's wife, Kay, is one of them. She is peaceful and contented and joyful. Actually, she glows.
- *Blessing.* Lastly, Jesus said, "It is more blessed to give than to receive" (Acts 20:35, NKJV). Being selfish, living just to please ourselves, is a lonely and empty life—bottom line: foolish. Living to be a blessing doesn't always add more days to your life, but it sure does add more life to your days.

Make It Personal . . . Live It Out!

As you read this, do you regret that you did not learn to be wise sooner? Do you feel that you have made too many bad, foolish choices and now you don't qualify for the "abundant life" that Jesus promised? That is soooooo wrong! One of the great wonders of God is that he loves to pour out grace. Have you been foolish with your health, a relationship, your tongue? Ask God to help you sort out one old foolish habit and replace it with a wise habit. It might sound trite, but today truly is the first day of the rest of your life. Be intentional about change. Get started today.

One Year Bible Reading

Exodus 39:1–40:38; Mark 1:1-28; Psalm 35:1-16; Proverbs 9:11-12

A Foolish Woman

A foolish woman is clamorous;
She is simple, and knows nothing.
For she sits at the door of her house . . .
To call to those who pass by. . . .
"Whoever is simple, let him turn in here";
And as for him who lacks understanding,
She says to him, "Stolen water is sweet,
And bread eaten in secret is pleasant."
But he does not know that the dead are there,
That her guests are in the depths of hell.

PROVERBS 9:13-18 (NKJV)

A foolish woman is clamorous. To be clamorous is to murmur, growl, roar, rage, to be troubled, in an uproar, in a stir, a commotion, boisterous, turbulent, raging.

Here is a big clue for us. Every one of these definitions describes anything but a meek and quiet spirit. Usually if we women make an uproar on the outside, it's because there's an uproar on the inside.

A clamorous woman lures other people into her whirlpool or maybe a better word is cesspool. I know that the first level of application of this proverb is the lure of sexual sin, but actually in the broader application, it can be the cesspool of just plain junk.

A woman who is all stirred up inside is usually just dying to pull others into whatever commotion is going on in her. Since misery loves company, she riles up others at church, at work, in friendships, and in families. She indeed is a foolish, clamorous woman.

Make It Personal . . . Live It Out!

One thing you could never say about the Proverbs is that they are subtle. Remembering that God used King Solomon to write them gives a clue to the tone of this proverb. Solomon had way too many wives, and a few too many of them must have been clamorous. But any husband or family or workplace that has a clamorous woman has one too many. When you are tempted to murmur or growl or rage or roar, will you take a moment before you vent? Ask the Lord to calm the storm inside you before you stir up a storm around you.

One Year Bible Reading

Leviticus 1:1–3:17; Mark 1:29–2:12; Psalm 35:17-28; Proverbs 9:13-18

A Penny Saved Is a Penny Earned

Ill-gotten gain has no lasting value,
but right living can save your life.

PROVERBS 10:2

The economic crises of recent years left our entire nation reeling. What happened? How could such a rich and prosperous nation as ours be bankrupt? Then we looked at the rich and long-standing companies. How could they be bankrupt? Then we looked at people, really, really rich and powerful people. How could they go bankrupt? Something went wrong. Why? Because something wasn't right.

In Luke 12:15 Jesus warned, "Watch out! Be on your guard against all kinds of greed; a man's life does not consist in the abundance of his possessions" (NIV).

So, ladies, children of God, we need to go back to the basics. Our proverb today says, "Right living can save your life." Financially we don't need a bailout. We need to straighten out.

Here are some suggestions:

- Did you know that if you packed your lunch every day, in one year you could save $2500?
- My friend told me that ladies at her church brought together their good, used clothes and they had a swap day; lots of fun and lots of money saved.
- Look at the flyers at the grocery store and shop specials only. Plan your menus for the week according to only what is on sale.
- Instead of going out to lunch with friends, I often make a good soup or salad, and we have lunch at my house.

As Ben Franklin once said, "A penny saved is a penny earned."

Make It Personal . . . Live It Out!

God is very interested in our being good stewards of our resources, and the Bible has more sound financial advice than any book ever written. Debt is a bondage and burden. It is time to break the grip by getting serious and proactive. You can make it a game. Enlist your kids. Keep a notebook to keep record of your savings. Instead of stopping at the coffee shop, make your own coffee and put it in a to-go cup. Then calculate the amount saved over a month and apply it directly to a specific bill. One taste of victory will motivate you to look for other places to save.

One Year Bible Reading

Leviticus 4:1–5:19; Mark 2:13–3:6; Psalm 36:1-12; Proverbs 10:1-2

God Provides

The LORD will not allow the righteous soul to famish,
But He casts away the desire of the wicked.

PROVERBS 10:3 (NKJV)

Here's a wonderful promise from God himself: "The LORD will not allow the righteous soul to famish." Maybe you're struggling right now and wondering if you are going to make it. Will your children be deprived? Will you lose everything and live in misery? These can be unspoken fears for us as women.

Listen to what Harry Ironside had to say: "Let the outward circumstances be as they may, the soul of the righteous is lifted above them all and finds cause to rejoice in the midst of tribulation."

In times like this, we need to read the stories of people who have faced physical famine and hardship in the past. Sit down and read the story of Elijah. God used ravens to bring him food (see 1 Kings 17:1-6). Then (in 1 Kings 17:9-16) God fed both Elijah and the widow of Zarephath. Remember? She was the one whose bin of flour never ran out. And how about the story of Joseph? He lost everything, really everything. But even though his situation was harsh and unfair, there is one line that stands out in his story: "The LORD was with him" (Genesis 39:23). This is the key. As we read Genesis 37, 39, and 40, another thing stands out too. Joseph took a stand for righteousness, for integrity. His pockets may have been empty, but his soul wasn't. God has promised he will not allow the righteous soul to famish.

Make It Personal . . . Live It Out!

Your greatest need is God's opportunity to show you his greatest supply. Jesus said, "Look at the birds of the air . . . your heavenly Father feeds them. Are you not of more value than they?" (Matthew 6:26, NKJV). The answer to that question is, yes, of course you are more valuable! There is something very sweet about seeing God meet a need in your life. It allows him to show you that he hears you and that he cares.

Let's Pray

Lord, I am coming to you alone with my need. May your supply meet my need and bring me to a fresh knowledge of your love.

One Year Bible Reading

Leviticus 6:1–7:27; Mark 3:7-30; Psalm 37:1-11; Proverbs 10:3-4

Soul Harvest

He who gathers crops in summer is a wise son,
but he who sleeps during harvest is a disgraceful son.

PROVERBS 10:5 (NIV)

Regarding the harvest, each of us is either diligent or lazy. Jesus said, "Lift up your eyes and look at the fields, for they are already white for harvest!" (John 4:35, NKJV). He was not talking about a wheat harvest. He was talking about souls: people who are lost but ready. The question is, are we? Are we ready and willing to share the good news of the gospel with a lost and dying world?

So, my dear sisters, let me encourage you with some practical helps.

- The best place to start is to ask the Lord to give you a burden for souls. Ask him to help you see people and love people as he does.
- Be prepared. I always carry copies of the Gospel of John everywhere I go. I have to admit I am much bolder if I have something to offer someone.
- Pray for a divine appointment. God will give a "holy tug" to notice someone. It may be a cashier or cab driver or just a teenager hanging outside the mall.

Recently a lady came up to me in the Costco parking lot. She was selling something. We talked, and then I got out a Gospel of John. I handed it to her and merely said, "I really feel I'm supposed to give this to you. It tells about God's love and that you can know him." I looked up and tears were running down her face. She said, "Thank you. You have no idea. Thank you." Simple, so simple. Look up; the field of lost, hungry souls is ripe.

Make It Personal . . . Live It Out!

Statistically, only 5 percent of all Christians ever share their faith. I know why that is: fear of rejection, fear we won't know what to say. But let me tell you, if you will just follow the three simple steps I shared, you'll be surprised. You will notice someone that you just "have to" speak to. There are some people who have never heard the words, "God loves you and has a wonderful plan for your life." Will you give it a try?

One Year Bible Reading

Leviticus 7:28–9:6; Mark 3:31–4:25; Psalm 37:12-29; Proverbs 10:5

Memory of the Righteous

Often the Proverbs use contrasts. On one side of the line there will be the blessings and benefits of godliness. On the other side of the line are the end results of selfishness, foolishness, and ungodliness. What is the point? The point is for us to take a look and choose. If we choose badly, we have no one to blame but ourselves. We could have chosen the other side, the blessedness of godliness. It's more than just information. It's an invitation.

Blessings crown the head of the righteous,
but violence overwhelms the mouth of the wicked.
The memory of the righteous will be a blessing,
but the name of the wicked will rot.

PROVERBS 10:6-7 (NIV)

"The memory of the righteous will be a blessing." This is their legacy. Wherever they go, they leave behind a fragrance of sweetness, of kindness, of grace and encouragement.

We need to rub shoulders with people who have lived like that, and one of the best ways we can do that is to read biographies of great godly people. If you haven't done that in a while, pick one up. It will do you good.

So let me suggest a few.

- *A Passion for Souls* by Lyle Dorsett is the story of D. L. Moody, one of my personal heroes in the faith.
- Another must-read is *George Müller: Delighted in God.* His story will stretch your faith and stir your heart.
- Anything about Billy Graham. Just saying his name is a blessing. One of my favorite books about him is *The Leadership Secrets of Billy Graham.*

Make It Personal . . . Live It Out!

"The memory of the righteous will be a blessing." Sometimes we think that only famous people make a real impact on others around them. You need to know that's not true in God's economy. Today you can give someone a word of hope, today you can lift someone up in prayer, today you can simply and sincerely tell someone you that love them and that they are important. Be assured: sometimes it is the little things that truly are the big things.

One Year Bible Reading

Leviticus 9:7–10:20; Mark 4:26–5:20; Psalm 37:30-40; Proverbs 10:6-7

Integrity

The man [or woman] of integrity walks securely,
but he who takes crooked paths will be found out.

PROVERBS 10:9 (NIV)

When was the last time you heard a discussion about integrity? Here's a good definition: integrity is doing the right thing even if nobody is watching.

W. Clement Stone said, "Have the courage to say no. Have the courage to face the truth. Do the right thing because it is right. These are the magic keys to living your life with integrity." Well said, Clement.

Abraham Lincoln is well known for many things, but there is one word that is always linked to his name: *Honest* Abe. As a young man, he worked in a store and found he had overcharged someone a few cents, so he walked miles to return it. As a lawyer, he defended the weak against swindlers, taking little for fees. It's no wonder that as he saw the wrongness of slavery, he paid a great price to make it right.

In Matthew 6 Jesus talked about integrity—not just before man, but before God. He said that when you do a good deed, you should do it before God alone. About prayer, don't pray so that people will see you do it but pray to your Father who is in the secret place; then your Father will reward you openly.

Integrity. As I look at this amazing, almost extinct character trait, I know I fall short, but I also know I want it! Don't you?

Make It Personal . . . Live It Out!

Again, "[a woman] of integrity walks securely." This means that if we purpose in our hearts to do the right thing, we will never have to cover our tracks. There will be moments when being a woman of integrity is tough. It is easier to tell a little lie or take a little shortcut—or so it seems. But when we are tempted, that is when we can shoot up a short arrow prayer: "Lord, give me grace to do right." Maybe you have never thought of that. You have thought you could only pray in formal "prayer times." Trust me, arrow prayers have been my saving grace many times. And if you get in the habit, they will be yours, too.

One Year Bible Reading

Leviticus 11:1-12:8; Mark 5:21-43; Psalm 38:1-22; Proverbs 10:8-9

Face-to-Face

The evasive eye is a sign of trouble ahead,
but an open, face-to-face meeting results in peace.

PROVERBS 10:10 (*THE MESSAGE*)

I'm a firm believer in eye-to-eye contact. Moms, this is an important part of your mothering. Give your children complete eye contact sometimes. Let them know you are connecting with them. But also require it from them. If they are lying or avoiding the truth, watch carefully; you can read it by the way they won't look at you. Call them on it—lovingly, but call them on it. If you don't hold them accountable, that's not good. Help them know they have to be honest above almost all other things.

And in friendships, in any important relationship, it is so good to get together and talk about things face-to-face. Is there a friend you feel somehow is struggling? Don't call another mutual friend and talk it out; we have to stop doing that. Call her yourself. Take her out for a latte in a cozy coffee shop. Take the time to let her know she is important. We are all neglecting our friendships way too much. If you sense something is troubling her, ask her if she will trust you enough to be honest. Make sure the goal on your side is to build bridges, and make sure your friend feels safe even if you hit some rough waters in the discussion. Right now, many people are going through tough times. We may lose houses and savings, but let's make sure we work hard to save our friendships. Amen?

Make It Personal . . . Live It Out!

Most of us are not very good at navigating conflict and disagreement. Sometimes we let small issues fester. Then we impute wrong motives and end up with a wall. If you are in a conflict situation with someone, here are some important principles to remember. Many disagreements come from misunderstanding. Will you ask the Lord to give you insight into the other's feelings and perspective? Will you choose not to overthink it? And then will you choose, if possible, to overlook it? "If anyone has a complaint against another; even as Christ forgave you, so you also must do" (Colossian 3:13, NKJV).

One Year Bible Reading

Leviticus 13:1-59; Mark 6:1-29; Psalm 39:1-13; Proverbs 10:10

Love Covers

Hatred stirs up dissension,
but love covers over all wrongs.

PROVERBS 10:12 (NIV)

Listen to the way *The Message* puts this verse: "Hatred starts fights, but love pulls a quilt over the bickering." I really like that.

Les Miserables, by Victor Hugo, is an amazing and beautiful story of the redemption of an ex-convict, Jean Valjean. When he was released on parole, he couldn't find work. A priest found him, took him in, and gave him food and shelter. In the night, Valjean stole the priest's silverware. He was caught by the police, but the priest saved him by claiming that the silver was a gift. Then the priest gave Valjean two silver candlesticks, the last of his valuable possessions. In this scene in the musical, the priest sings these amazing words—first to the officers and then to Valjean:

So Messieurs you may release him, for this man has spoken true.
I commend you for your duty; may God's blessing go with you.
But remember this, my brother. See in this some higher plan.
You must use this precious silver to become an honest man.
By the witness of the martyrs, by the Passion and the Blood
God has raised you out of darkness. I have bought your soul for God!

And so the moral: nothing *but* love can cover a multitude of sins.

Make It Personal . . . Live It Out!

"Love covers" has become one of my favorite phrases. As I say it, it becomes more than just a fact; it becomes a decision. When your friend is late even though you broke your neck to arrive on time, "love covers." When your toddler spills the milk, the waitress forgets your order, your mother-in-law criticizes your housecleaning, will you make the decision to "let love cover"? It is a very good policy, because as Jesus said, "Blessed are the merciful, for they shall obtain mercy" (Matthew 5:7, NKJV).

One Year Bible Reading

Leviticus 14:1-57; Mark 6:30-56; Psalm 40:1-10; Proverbs 10:11-12

Wise or Foolish Words?

Wise words come from the lips of people with understanding,
but fools will be punished with a rod.
Wise people treasure knowledge,
but the babbling of a fool invites trouble.

PROVERBS 10:13-14

Wise words or foolish babbling. It's been said that even a fool can appear wise, until he opens his mouth.

So, ladies, let's really think about it. What are you known for, by the people who are around you and those who know you best? When the heat gets turned up in any situation, are you likely to add fuel to the fire, or are you the voice of reason and peace, of kindness and grace?

When you're criticized, do you use your words to cut back? If you have the perfect chance to pass along that ugly story about someone, do you? Truthfully, what are you known for?

James 3:9-10 has something to say about this: "With the tongue we praise our Lord and Father, and with it we curse men, who have been made in God's likeness. Out of the same mouth come praise and cursing. My brothers [and sisters], this should not be" (NIV).

So—here's a little poem by William Norris:

If your lips would keep from slips,
Five things observe with care:
To whom you speak; of whom you speak,
And how, and when, and where.

As my grandma Gladys used to say, "If you can't say nothing nice—don't say nothing at all."

Make It Personal . . . Live It Out!

On the flip side of the coin, Proverbs 25:11 says, "A word fitly spoken is like apples of gold in settings of silver" (NKJV). You can purpose in your heart to find one opportunity every day to use your words to encourage or inspire. When your husband comes home tonight, tell him one thing you appreciate about him. Catch your kids being good and praise them. Write a note to your pastor or Bible study leader to tell them how their teaching has blessed you. Tell the clerks at the bank you appreciate their help. Your words of kindness might be the only ones they will hear all day.

One Year Bible Reading

Leviticus 15:1–16:28; Mark 7:1-23; Psalm 40:11-17; Proverbs 10:13-14

About Our Father's Business

The labor of the righteous leads to life,
The wages of the wicked to sin.

PROVERBS 10:16 (NKJV)

"The labor of the righteous leads to life"—not more money, not more things, but life. Psalm 37:16 says, "Better the little that the righteous have than the wealth of many wicked" (NIV).

So this is a great moment to pause and ask ourselves, what is life? Do you have a passion to fulfill the purpose that God put you on this planet for? Do you know what it is? Do you ever ask the Lord to show you what it is? Because, as Walker Percy said, "You can get all A's and still flunk life."

Jesus gave us a clear, solid place to start that will shake us loose from just falling into the world's version of success. He said, "Lay up for yourselves treasures in heaven, where neither moth nor rust destroys and where thieves do not break in and steal. For where your treasure is, there your heart will be also" (Matthew 6:20-21, NKJV).

When I think about these important words, I realize that material things get broken, go out of style, and get lost. It's really people who are important. Jesus invested in people. So the greatest purpose that he could give us here on earth is to love people. That's true living.

As Winston Churchill said, "We make a living by what we get, but we make a life by what we give." That's right, Winston.

Make It Personal . . . Live It Out!

All right, ladies, let's do something about this. As Jesus said, "[We] must be about [our] Father's business" (Luke 2:49, NKJV). And our Father's favorite business is people. He has a special tenderness for broken and lonely people like widows and orphans. The ache of losing someone you love lingers for many years. Often we feel inept around grieving people because we don't know what to do or say. We cannot fix their pain. But God can use you to give a moment of comfort, a hand on the shoulder, a kind card slipped into a pocket at church. I'll tell you the truth, when you do any of those things, not only will you be a blessing, but you will indeed be blessed.

One Year Bible Reading

Leviticus 16:29–18:30; Mark 7:24–8:10; Psalm 41:1-13; Proverbs 10:15-16

Don't Refuse Instruction

He who keeps instruction is in the way of life,
But he who refuses correction goes astray.

PROVERBS 10:17 (NKJV)

I love what commentator H. A. Ironside had to say about this proverb: "It is only when man learns to mistrust himself and to rely alone upon the unerring Word of God, unfolded by the Holy Spirit, that his feet walk in the way of life. . . . Let me gladly, then, receive correction."

The journey of the children of Israel from Egypt to the Promised Land is full of important lessons for us. As they were crossing the Jordon, that river that separated them from the land of rich blessings, they were told to follow the Ark of the Covenant, which held the Word of God. And then God used this compelling phrase: "For you have not passed this way before" (Joshua 3:4, NKJV). This captures me. And here's the lesson for us, we are just two months into this new year, and each day holds events and obstacles and dilemmas. There will be moments like crossroads, when your choice in a moment of time can affect your life for years. You need to come to God's Word each morning, eager and expectant. Let him speak to you. Write down at least one truth that stands out. Look for a lesson and instruction to ponder, and then ask the Lord himself to help you apply it. This is truly where the rubber meets the road. Our proverb says, "He who keeps instruction is in the way of life."

Make It Personal . . . Live It Out!

Reflecting on the lessons we can learn from the wilderness journey, Hebrews 3:10 gives us bottom-line insight into why some never entered the Promised Land: God said, "Their hearts always turn away from me. They refuse to do what I tell them." Basically, they weren't good listeners or quick learners. Every time we know the right thing to do and shrug it off or put it off, we are slipping back into the dry barren wilderness. Let's not do that.

Let's Pray

Lord, teach me to hear your voice. And then give me the desire and courage to obey.

One Year Bible Reading

Leviticus 19:1–20:21; Mark 8:11-38; Psalm 42:1-11; Proverbs 10:17

Hatred, Malice, and Slander

Whoever hides hatred has lying lips,
And whoever spreads slander is a fool.

PROVERBS 10:18 (NKJV)

Let me introduce you to two ugly sisters who are born out of hatred. They are Malice and Spite. And ladies, if we give them any kind of place in our souls, we will find that it is very hard to keep them in check. Even if we try to hide them, they will break out and have a life of their own.

Definitions:

- *Malice* implies a deep-seated animosity that delights in causing others to suffer or in seeing them suffer.
- *Spite* suggests a mean desire to hurt, annoy, or frustrate others, usually with petty, vindictive acts.

It's interesting that just two words after *malice* in the dictionary is the word *malign*, which is slander. Slander is merely hatred turned into words.

So let's be honest. In Texas they say, "You have a burr under your saddle." That burr keeps jabbing the horse, making him buck and kick. Do you have a burr of hatred that is rubbing you and making you mean? This hatred is really killing you—it will destroy your life, not just others'. Will you go to the Cross? Will you kneel all by yourself today and say, "Lord Jesus forgive me, wash me, free me with the power of your cleansing blood"?

Make It Personal . . . Live It Out!

God has some strong words to say about unresolved anger: "In your anger do not sin. Do not let the sun go down while you are still angry, and do not give the devil a foothold" (Ephesians 4:26-27, NIV). Do you feel your anger is justified and therefore must be relived and remembered? Oh, can't you see that is exactly how Satan gets a foothold? It may have started with someone else's sin, but now it has become yours. Ouch! Now, let's apply the ointment of the Word of God. "If we confess our sins, He is faithful and just to forgive us our sins and to cleanse us from all unrighteousness" (1 John 1:9, NKJV).

One Year Bible Reading

Leviticus 20:22–22:16; Mark 9:1-29; Psalm 43:1-5; Proverbs 10:18

Too Many Words

In the multitude of words sin is not lacking,
But he who restrains his lips is wise.

PROVERBS 10:19 (NKJV)

Here's a song with a catchy tune by Joe Jones written in 1958. You can google to listen. It goes like this . . .

You talk too much, you worry me to death,
You talk too much, you even worry my pet,
You just talk, you talk too much.

Ladies, we need to get a grip on this. Some things just don't need to be said. If you have a tendency to speak everything that crosses your mind, pause before you speak. Ask yourself, "Would I want this said to me?" Some use the excuse, "I just have to be honest." There is a time to speak and there is a time to refrain from speaking. If someone is having a bad hair day or they have gained some weight, your honesty is not kind or appreciated either.

Wives, in the heat of a discussion with your husband, your words can go south real fast. Remember what Proverbs 29:11 says, "A fool gives full vent to his anger, but a wise [woman] keeps [herself] under control" (NIV). Character assassination and belittling will never solve the issue. Some words are hard to forget once they are spoken.

And here's a prayer that can set us straight: "Let the words of my mouth and the meditation of my heart be acceptable in Your sight, O LORD, my strength and my Redeemer" (Psalm 19:14, NKJV).

We'll close with the New Living Translation: "Don't talk too much, for it fosters sin. Be sensible and turn off the flow!" (Proverbs 10:19).

Make It Personal . . . Live It Out!

Benjamin Franklin said, "A slip of the foot you may soon recover, but a slip of the tongue you may never get over." As we have looked at the need to tame our tongues, has it brought to mind something you have said that you regret? Have you blown off steam in a moment of anger or been too harsh and critical and saw it hurt someone's feelings? That is the Holy Spirit giving you a "holy tug" of conviction. There is no time like the present to make it right. Pick up the phone or write a sweet note today. If your heart is right, God will give you good words and go before you with grace.

One Year Bible Reading

Leviticus 22:17–23:44; Mark 9:30–10:12; Psalm 44:1-8; Proverbs 10:19

March

Scan this code for audio devotionals
or visit www.tyndal.es/wisdom.

Words That Nourish

The tongue of the righteous is choice silver,
but the heart of the wicked is of little value.
The lips of the righteous nourish many,
but fools die for lack of judgment.

PROVERBS 10:20-21 (NIV)

Ladies, never underestimate the power of the words that you speak. Words can be like precious silver used to add value everywhere you go and anytime you speak. Mark Twain said, "The difference between the right word and the almost-right word is the difference between lightning and the lightning bug."

This should make us excited and at the same time sober. We all know we have been foolish, even destructive, at times with our words.

So David prayed, "Let the words of my mouth and the meditation of my heart be acceptable in Your sight, O LORD, my strength and my Redeemer" (Psalm 19:14, NKJV). This is the key. For our words to be right, our hearts must be right. And so we can do what David did. We can ask the Lord himself to give us a sense of his presence and a desire to please and honor him at all times. This holds us accountable, but it also gives us a realization that he can give us his good, right, true, helpful words that bless others. He can give us insightful words for a complicated situation. He can give us a soft, peaceful word when there is tension in the air. He can give us words of encouragement for someone who is down and kind words for those who are in pain.

Make It Personal . . . Live It Out!

Words of comfort in a time of grief are nourishing, like water to a thirsty soul. The grief of loss comes in many forms. A painful divorce, a prodigal child, a failed business, even a moving away is a loss we grieve. The death of someone we love goes deepest. Please remember that when we're in grief, we don't need advice or quick-fix answers. Think of comfort as the combination of two words: *come* and *fort*. If you know someone who is grieving, will you go to that person? Just your personal presence and a kind look are a message of care. Then make your words like a fort: sheltering, supportive, and safe.

One Year Bible Reading

Leviticus 24:1–25:46; Mark 10:13-31; Psalm 44:9-26; Proverbs 10:20-21

Blessing and Beauty

The blessing of the LORD brings wealth,
and he adds no trouble to it.

PROVERBS 10:22 (NIV)

Ladies, this is a great and wonderful promise from God himself to us. The blessings of God are the only true commodity that can fill us so completely that we become full and rich, internally rich. But does "blessing" mean riches like money or health or beauty or popularity? No. These things can give us temporary happiness, but *temporary* is the key word. These things don't last, and they can't give us lasting satisfaction either. Through the years, Hollywood icons from Marilyn Monroe to Brittany Spears have been tragic illustrations. A picture is worth a thousand words. They had all the money, beauty, and popularity this world offers, but definitely those girls had troubles, lots of troubles.

So what is "blessing"? Literally it means God's favor—his smile on your life, his pleasure. And most of all, the greatest blessing is his presence, his friendship. His presence brings peace and joy even when times are hard. He comforts us in times of pain and gives us strength when we are weak. These are things that the world isn't selling and money just can't buy.

Paul the apostle is such a perfect picture of this. When he was in a Roman prison, he said, "I have learned to be content" (Philippians 4:11, NIV). It's been said that "contentment isn't getting what you want but wanting what you have."

"The blessing of the LORD brings wealth, and he adds no trouble to it" (Proverbs 10:22, NIV).

Make It Personal . . . Live It Out!

While we're on the topic of definitions, let's address the concept of beauty. There are many brokenhearted women because they look in the mirror and do not see the Hollywood version of beauty. We need a reality check. Those cover girls don't look that good when they wake up either. And remember, true beauty is more than skin deep. Beauty sometimes comes in simple packages. God raises the bar on real beauty in 1 Peter 3:4: "Rather let it be the hidden person of the heart, with the incorruptible beauty of a gentle and quiet spirit" (NKJV).

One Year Bible Reading

Leviticus 25:47–27:13; Mark 10:32-52; Psalm 45:1-17; Proverbs 10:22

Wise or Foolish?

A fool finds pleasure in evil conduct,
but a man [or woman] of understanding delights in wisdom.

PROVERBS 10:23 (NIV)

This proverb sets before us two women, a foolish woman and a wise woman. The point is not just for us to see the difference, but for us to choose who we are now and who we want to become.

Woman number one is foolish. She finds pleasure in evil conduct. She plays games that cause trouble. She takes a wicked pleasure in causing division or hurting people's feelings. She is drawn to sin, and no matter how much grief it brings her or others, she keeps going back for more. She is foolish because she never learns that the ounce of pleasure she gets in the moment of sin later delivers a pound of heartache. Second Timothy 3 tells us, "In the last days perilous times will come: For [people] will be lovers of themselves, lovers of money, boasters, proud, . . . headstrong, haughty, lovers of pleasure rather than lovers of God" (vv. 1-4, NKJV).

But woman number two is a wise woman, a woman of understanding. Psalm 1:1-2 is her mantra: "Blessed is the [woman] who does not walk in the counsel of the wicked or stand in the way of sinners or sit in the seat of mockers. But [her]delight is in the law of the LORD, and on his law [she] meditates day and night" (NIV).

So, to be wise or foolish? That is the question. The point is for us to choose. Who are we now, and then who do we want to be?

Make It Personal . . . Live It Out!

Part of becoming wise involves becoming increasingly sensitive to the red flags of warning and conviction sent by the Holy Spirit. For instance, if you're in a group of women and someone says something that triggers negative emotions in you, you might feel the desire rising to shoot back a sharp, retaliatory word. God will be faithful at the same moment to give a "check." What does that little voice sound like? It can be as simple as, "Zip your lip," "A soft answer turns away wrath," or, "Count to ten, Debbi. Count to ten."

One Year Bible Reading

Leviticus 27:14—Numbers 1:54; Mark 11:1-26; Psalm 46:1-11; Proverbs 10:23

March 4

Wicked versus Righteous

What the wicked dreads will overtake him;
what the righteous desire will be granted.
When the storm has swept by, the wicked are gone,
but the righteous stand firm forever.

PROVERBS 10:24-25 (NIV)

"What the wicked dread." Isn't that an intriguing phrase? What then do the wicked dread? Think about it. When you lie or steal something, there is that constant dread of someone finding out. If you say something mean about someone, what if they hear about it? What if you get a bad reputation for being mean?

Dread. It is like a big ol' black cloud of darkness, a fear that that thing you did will come back to haunt you. Isn't that the way of sin? You think it will add pleasure, but instead it rips you off. It does, it really does.

In contrast, living right, doing right, has its own sweet rewards. I love that our proverb tells us that doing right gives us stability. The definition of *stable* is "constant, able to maintain or return to a strong position, not likely to fall." Stability. "The righteous stand firm forever."

Let's let Jesus give us a clear picture. He said, "Therefore everyone who hears these words of mine and puts them into practice is like a wise man who built his house on the rock. The rain came down, the streams rose, and the winds blew and beat against that house; yet it did not fall, because it had its foundation on the rock" (Matthew 7:24-25, NIV).

Now that, my sisters, is standing strong even in shaky times!

Make It Personal . . . Live It Out!

Talk is cheap. It is time for us "to walk the walk." As Jesus explained, we must hear God's Word and then put it into practice. For example, James 1:27 gives a clear directive: "Pure and undefiled religion before God and the Father is this: to visit orphans and widows in their trouble" (NKJV). How can we apply this? Ask the Lord to show you. He might prompt you to buy some school supplies for a single mom's kids, or take them to youth group, or just look for them in the hall at church and give them a word of encouragement. Righteous living is doing right things.

One Year Bible Reading

Numbers 2:1–3:51; Mark 11:27–12:17; Psalm 47:1-9; Proverbs 10:24-25

Lazy Procrastination

As vinegar to the teeth and smoke to the eyes,
so is a sluggard to those who send him [or her].

PROVERBS 10:26 (NIV)

W. C. Fields said, "The laziest man I ever met put popcorn in his pancakes so they would turn over by themselves."

A sluggard is like a slug, lazy. The definition of *lazy* is "to dislike and avoid work or activity." Procrastination is the sluggard's method of operation. My Missouri grandmother used to say this is "living a day late and a dollar short."

If there is someone who works with you or for you who operates like this, it can be annoying and frustrating, like vinegar to the teeth and smoke to the eyes.

So let's apply this to ourselves and let it prompt us to not be the cause of this kind of irritation. There is joy in being faithful and diligent, even in the little things. Is there something that someone has asked you to do, and even though you said you would, you've put it off? Well, get to it. Really. Write it down and get to it. And do it with joy, because then everyone wins. It will be a pleasure to get it off the to-do list, and it will be a pleasure to the one who has been waiting for you to do it.

Jesus said, "Let your 'Yes' be 'Yes,' and your 'No,' 'No'" (Matthew 5:37, NKJV).

And in Colossians 3:23-24 we're told, "Whatever you do, do it heartily as to the Lord and not to men, knowing that from the Lord you will receive the reward"(NKJV).

Make It Personal . . . Live It Out!

Diligence is steady effort and perseverance. It is the opposite of lazy procrastination. One of the keys to diligence is to find some habits that help you become self-managing and organized. Here's one tip. I use small yellow writing pads to order my day. In my quiet time with the Lord in the morning, I often think of errands, calls, and must-do tasks. As things come to mind, I write them on a pad. Once I see them on paper, I can tackle them and then have the reward of checking them off. There is a sweet taste of victory—especially when I cross off something I have put off.

One Year Bible Reading

Numbers 4:1–5:31; Mark 12:18-37; Psalm 48:1-14; Proverbs 10:26

Don't Waste Your Life

The fear of the LORD adds length to life,
but the years of the wicked are cut short.
The prospect of the righteous is joy,
but the hopes of the wicked come to nothing.

PROVERBS 10:27-28 (NIV)

Abraham Lincoln said, "In the end, it's not the years in your life that count. It's the life in your years."

Some people think that living the godly life will only matter in eternity. They think if they shut God out and live for themselves, life will be better here. That's not so. Really, it's just not so.

I recently saw a picture of the late hotel billionaire Leona Helmsley. She looked miserable. She's not remembered for any good she did with all that she had. She is remembered for cutting two grandkids out of her will and leaving twelve million to her dog. Now that is a wasted life.

Ladies, do you know someone who has lived a mean, selfish life and now has nothing that is meaningful? They are a good example of a bad example.

God has a different destiny for us. Jesus came to give us life and life more abundantly.

Listen to what God gives us as a beautiful yet simple path for a godly, meaningful life here on earth: "He has shown you, O man, what is good; and what does the LORD require of you but to do justly, to love mercy, and to walk humbly with your God?" (Micah 6:8, NKJV).

Make It Personal . . . Live It Out!

I like to walk in old graveyards sometimes. The messages on the tombstones really make me think. I heard someone say, "There'll be two dates on your tombstone. And all your friends will read 'em, but all that's gonna matter is that little dash between 'em."

You are writing your legacy, a page every day, by the things that you do and the words that you say. Today, will you ask God to help you live with eternal purpose?

Let's Pray

Lord, I want my life to count for more than just the sum total of my trinkets and toys. Please fill my life with your purposes and use me to bring your message of love to others.

One Year Bible Reading

Numbers 6:1–7:89; Mark 12:38–13:13; Psalm 49:1-20; Proverbs 10:27-28

March 7

The Ways of God

The way of the LORD is a refuge for the righteous,
but it is the ruin of those who do evil.
The righteous will never be uprooted,
but the wicked will not remain in the land.

PROVERBS 10:29-30 (NIV)

Today let's focus on the phrase, "The way of the Lord is a refuge." Many people never understand God's ways. They read Isaiah 55:9, "As the heavens are higher than the earth, so are My ways higher than your ways" (NKJV), and they think he is too mysterious to know. But the real point is that God's ways are grander than ours; therefore we can't put God in a box. He has understanding and resources and ways of accomplishing his will that are wonderfully fresh and entirely independent of human management. Ladies, we try to run our lives with far too tight a grip on the wheel. We need to loosen up a bit and give him some room to steer.

One of the methods God uses to accomplish his great plan in our life is waiting, which involves patience. But we love quick fixes and instant gratification, not patience. Remember, Rome wasn't built in a day. It took forty years in the wilderness to prepare Moses to lead. And even Jesus waited until he was over thirty to begin his public ministry. If you've been frustrated with the waiting process, wishing God wasn't so slow, Isaiah 40:31 has a good word for you: "But those who wait on the LORD shall renew their strength; they shall mount up with wings like eagles, they shall run and not be weary, they shall walk and not faint" (NKJV).

Make It Personal . . . Live It Out!

Another phrase in our proverb today is "the righteous will never be uprooted." In the plant world, trees with shallow roots die in times of drought and are blown over by strong winds. Trees with deep roots have an anchor and aren't dependent on shallow, surface water. The message is, don't be a shallow Christian who is blown along with fads of false doctrines because you don't know your Bible. Be a Christian who searches the Scriptures and stands strong in the truth.

One Year Bible Reading

Numbers 8:1–9:23; Mark 13:14-37; Psalm 50:1-23; Proverbs 10:29-30

Wise, Godly Advice

The godly person gives wise advice,
but the tongue that deceives will be cut off.
The godly speak words that are helpful,
but the wicked speak only what is corrupt.

PROVERBS 10:31-32

Our proverb today says that the godly give wise advice and helpful words. That's so good. Let's ponder this for a moment. Even Moses at times needed advice. Remember when his father-in-law told him he needed to spread out his workload and have others help in his leadership (see Exodus 18:13-26)? Delegate. It was good advice to delegate.

Think about the times that you needed the wise counsel of a godly sister. Did you find it? When others come to you, do they expect it, and then do they find it? If so, God bless you. Women like you, my friend, are in short supply.

I'm going to talk to you about the best tool I have ever found for counseling, discipling, encouraging, and comforting others. It's the *One Year Bible*. It has been my policy for years that I will counsel someone once, but if they would like to continue, I ask them to start reading the *One Year Bible* too. I find that all of the struggles and issues I am personally dealing with are addressed consistently in my own daily reading. Also, as I read, I sense how the reading of a particular day is meeting others right where they are. Then when we do talk, we talk about God's Word and process it in the light of the things that they're going through. The fun thing is because the Lord has already spoken to them, they are the ones who point out the solutions, not me. Pretty good, huh?

Make It Personal . . . Live It Out!

There is absolutely no issue or dilemma known to man (or woman) that is not, at least in principle, addressed in the Word of God. Are you struggling with a sin or failure in your life? Do you need godly advice? Will you read Psalm 51:1-19 (listed below as one of our readings today)? As you read it, you will find words of correction, mercy, repentance, honesty, and restoration. What a package! No one knows the complications of your soul and how to fix them like God himself. Will you let his words be your last word?

One Year Bible Reading

Numbers 10:1–11:23; Mark 14:1-21; Psalm 51:1-19; Proverbs 10:31-32

Honorable Living

The LORD hates cheating,
but he delights in honesty.
Pride leads to disgrace,
but with humility comes wisdom.
Good people are guided by their honesty;
treacherous people are destroyed by their dishonesty.

PROVERBS 11:1-3

Immanuel Kant was a German philosopher. He said, "It is not necessary that whilst I live I should live happily; but it is necessary that so long as I live I should live honorably."

To live honorably. This is not a concept we hear much about in our society. Although on one hand that can be very discouraging, on the other hand, it gives us a great opportunity to live our lives in contrast. The apostle Paul wrote some incredible things when he was in a Roman jail. It is said he was chained to a Roman soldier every day. In Rome, life was very dog-eat-dog; immorality and power were more popular than integrity and virtue. It was in that atmosphere that Paul wrote these words in Philippians 2:14-16: "Do all things without complaining and disputing, that you may become blameless and harmless, children of God without fault in the midst of a crooked and perverse generation, among whom you shine as lights in the world, holding fast the word of life"(NKJV).

So no matter where you work or live, God has set you there to shine. Honesty and humility truly shine bright in the dark world. And as Samuel Johnson said, "It is better to suffer wrong than to do it."

Make It Personal . . . Live It Out!

You might not be chained to a Roman solider, but all of us have situations that we are "stuck with." Are you the only Christian in your workplace? Are the conversations there so wrong they grieve your spirit? Live honorably! Go the extra mile, give grace, don't get tangled in office politics. Honor the Lord.

Is your husband an unbeliever? Live honorably! Find ways to encourage and respect him. Never put him down with your friends at church. Share the gospel by your actions and love and thankfulness more than your words. Honor the Lord.

Are your in-laws hard to get along with? Live honorably! Don't take things too personally. Pray a lot, and honor the Lord.

One Year Bible Reading

Numbers 11:24–13:33; Mark 14:22-52; Psalm 52:1-9; Proverbs 11:1-3

March 10

Eternal Treasures

Wealth is worthless in the day of wrath,
but righteousness delivers from death.

PROVERBS 11:4 (NIV)

Wealth. It seems to hold all the answers to our worries and problems. We think, *If only I had money, life would be complete. Then I would have the luxury to concentrate on the things of God.* Many people do believe that with money all the world's problems could be solved, but the Bible tells us that at the end of all time, the things of this world—money, material things—will all burn. In others words, in the grand scheme, all of our efforts to gain material wealth will be worthless. So here is the question to ask yourself: What is real wealth to you? What do you value most of all? The answer to this question could be life altering, because the most valuable thing in this world is being delivered from death and to receive eternal life—really. Jesus said, "What do you benefit if you gain the whole world but lose your own soul?" (Mark 8:36). Salvation is offered to each of us through the precious blood of the risen Christ. Jesus is the only acceptable sacrifice. We owed a debt we could not pay. He paid a debt he did not owe. So if we choose to accept this gift, it is ours for the taking. How ironic it is that the one thing that is worth the most, eternal life, is a gift, completely free. If you haven't, will you accept this gift today? Second Corinthians 6:2 says, "Behold, now is the accepted time; behold, now is the day of salvation" (NKJV).

Make It Personal . . . Live It Out!

Mother Teresa was very poor materially, but she is now rich in eternity. She gave this wise advice: "Life is an opportunity, benefit from it. Life is beauty, admire it. Life is a challenge, meet it. Life is a duty, complete it. Life is a game, play it. Life is a promise, fulfill it. Life is sorrow, overcome it. Life is a song, sing it. Life is a struggle, accept it. Life is a tragedy, confront it. Life is an adventure, dare it. . . . Life is too precious, do not destroy it. Life is life, fight for it."

One Year Bible Reading

Numbers 14:1–15:16; Mark 14:53-72; Psalm 53:1-6; Proverbs 11:4

March 11

As It Should Be

The righteousness of the blameless makes a straight way for them,
but the wicked are brought down by their own wickedness.
The righteousness of the upright delivers them,
but the unfaithful are trapped by their evil desires.

PROVERBS 11:5-6 (NIV)

C. S. Lewis said, "Good and evil both increase at compound interest. That is why the little decisions you and I make every day are of such infinite importance."

Doing the "right thing" is like a crystal bell that rings deep in our souls. Doing the wrong thing is like the sound of fingernails on the chalkboard. "Right" sets a course that is clear and straight.

Fear not tomorrows, child of the King;
trust them with Jesus; "do the next thing."
Do it immediately; do it with prayer;
do it reliantly, casting all care;
do it with reverence, . . . safe 'neath his wing;
leave all resulting; "do the next thing."

AUTHOR UNKNOWN

Recently I came across the phrase "as it should be." Now when I am in a moment of decision, I hear this simple phrase and it helps me to make the better choice. It helps me land right; forgive quickly, give freely, or be patient "as it should be."

It helps me notice when others land right, too. As my friend bought a ticket for a retreat, she remembered a single mom who had no money—so she bought two. I thought, "Yep, that's 'as it should be.'" A teenage girl in the church made a mistake. Instead of casting her out in shame, the women came to her side and loved her. Now, that is truly "as it should be."

Make It Personal . . . Live It Out!

Did you know that every time you make a right choice, the next right choice is easier and comes more naturally? It's the same principle as erosion. Once a path for water is started, it gets deeper as more water flows through the grooves. The same is true with godly attitudes and thoughts. This is great news. Try it out. For instance, the more quickly you choose to overlook a rude action or word, the more quickly your thoughts are restored to peace. You're less uptight and more resilient for the next test.

One Year Bible Reading

Numbers 15:17–16:40; Mark 15:1-47; Psalm 54:1-7; Proverbs 11:5-6

Wicked Men Perish

Our proverb today is pretty sober. It reminds us that life is short, so don't waste it.

> *When a wicked man dies, his hope perishes;*
> *all he expected from his power comes to nothing.*
>
> PROVERBS 11:7 (NIV)

What exactly does the word *wicked* mean? Of course it means "a criminal, one guilty of crimes," but the definition also includes "one who is hostile to God, guilty of sin (against God or man), the ungodly."

Do you ever think of people like Hugh Hefner? He built his empire by influencing young women to cross lines of immorality and to be used like merchandise. He did this for a long time. His magazine introduced the lifelong addiction of pornography to many.

I wonder: as he stands before the throne of God on Judgment Day, will he see how his influence started them on a path that ruined their lives? Will he see the story of each girl? Will he see children born into the broken lives of these women? Will he see his life was only used for evil? He was an icon and model for others who opened clubs and made money stealing the innocence of women.

To the Hugh Hefners of this world, I want to say, "No amount of money will bail you out of the truth that you wasted your life and ruined others." Hefner said, "When you're living all this day by day, you have no idea what you're going to accomplish, and certainly no idea what lies ahead." So true, as the Bible clearly states: "It is appointed for men to die once, but after this the judgment" (Hebrews 9:27, NKJV).

Make It Personal . . . Live It Out!

"When a wicked man dies, his hope perishes." Just the sound of this makes you shudder. But maybe as you read it there is a ring of comfort. If you have suffered from wickedness, sexual abuse, or abuse of any kind, you may have wondered if God cares. The answer is yes. He is merciful, but he is also just. These words are for you: "Do not take revenge, my dear friends, but leave room for God's wrath, for it is written: 'It is mine to avenge; I will repay,' says the Lord" (Romans 12:19, NIV).

One Year Bible Reading

Numbers 16:41–18:32; Mark 16:1-20; Psalm 55:1-23; Proverbs 11:7

Delivered from Trouble

The righteous is delivered from trouble,
And it comes to the wicked instead.

PROVERBS 11:8 (NKJV)

Here is a very important promise: God rescues the godly from trouble. But does this mean that when you walk with the Lord, there is a bubble around you, that you will never face hardships or go through tough times?

No. Really I wish it meant that, but it doesn't. When we read the Bible, we see righteous men like Job and Joseph and even Jesus himself go through times that are worse than we can imagine.

So what kind of deliverance is this proverb talking about? The Hebrew word for *trouble* in this verse is *tsarah*, which means "tightness, distress." Hmm. Could this mean then that no matter what, nothing can press you so hard on the outside as to break you down and destroy you inside? This is the greater and really most important wall of protection, isn't it? We can lose our job or our house or even our health, but it's when these things rob our peace, our integrity, or our faith that we become bankrupt.

Paul the apostle is the perfect example. He loved the Lord and spent his life radically sharing the gospel, and yet he went through crazy, hard times. Listen to what he had to say about this in 2 Corinthians 4:8-9: "We are hard pressed on every side, but not crushed; perplexed, but not in despair; persecuted, but not abandoned; struck down, but not destroyed" (NIV). So our promise from God in this is that when hard times crush on you, he will give his strength in you.

Make It Personal . . . Live It Out!

What kind of problems are you facing right now? Health problems, a handicapped child, an aging parent, finances, a troubling lawsuit—all these things can feel like a mountain ready to crush you. But God has promised he will deliver you. David wrote the words of Psalm 56 when he was running for his life from King Saul. He had no safe place to run, but to God alone. Will you read it today and let his words and trust in God's deliverance give you hope?

One Year Bible Reading

Numbers 19:1–20:29; Luke 1:1-25; Psalm 56:1-13; Proverbs 11:8

Gossipers

With his mouth the godless destroys his neighbor,
but through knowledge the righteous escape.
When the righteous prosper, the city rejoices;
when the wicked perish, there are shouts of joy.
Through the blessing of the upright a city is exalted,
but by the mouth of the wicked it is destroyed.

PROVERBS 11:9-11 (NIV)

Our topic today is gossip. Gossipers are dealers in scandal. They are busybodies. There's an old country proverb that says, "Tale-bearers should be hung up by the tongue and tale-hearers by the ears." Well, that would fix 'em, wouldn't it—or would it? I think we should ask ourselves, *Why? Why do we sometimes slander and gossip even though we know it's ugly?* We hate it when others do it to us, don't we?

Well, the truth is, gossip is not just a matter of the tongue. Actually, it is a matter of the heart. "For out of the abundance of the heart, the mouth speaks" (Matthew 12:34, NKJV). Jerry Bridges wrote a book with the provocative title *Respectable Sins*. He says, "Indulging in gossip seems to feed our sinful ego, especially when the information is negative. It makes us feel self-righteous by comparison." I think he hits a chord there. Ouch!

Our proverb today says, "Through the blessing of the upright a city is exalted." So true, but it's not just a city. It's a home, a ministry, or a group of friends that's exalted. Ladies, what do you think? Wouldn't it be great if today the only thing we said about or to anyone was a blessing? I think it would be great.

Make It Personal . . . Live It Out!

It's been said, "Great minds discuss ideas; average minds discuss events; small minds discuss people."

Have you been the victim of gossip? It can get to you. You can't really defend your reputation because the damage is already done. In Psalm 57:1, David expressed his hope and survival technique in times like that: "Have mercy on me, O God, have mercy on me, for in you my soul takes refuge. I will take refuge in the shadow of your wings until the disaster has passed" (NIV). Will you make his words your own? In the shelter of God, your soul will find peace.

One Year Bible Reading

Numbers 21:1–22:20; Luke 1:26-56; Psalm 57:1-11; Proverbs 11:9-11

March 15

Let's Not Gossip

It is foolish to belittle a neighbor;
a person with good sense remains silent.
A gossip goes around revealing secrets,
but those who are trustworthy can keep a confidence.

PROVERBS 11:12-13

Chuck Swindoll once quoted an epitaph from an English country tombstone: "Beneath this stone, a lump of clay, lies Arabella Young, who on the 24th of May began to hold her tongue."

Arabella Young must have been a gossip. I wonder who wrote her epitaph? Was it someone whose reputation or whose friendships had been damaged because Arabella just plain talked too much?

Maybe—and now I'm going to say this with a sad pang in my heart—but maybe Arabella went to prayer meetings and brought up juicy little scraps of bad news so that everyone could be "praying about it." But have you noticed that sometimes we talk about the problems of others more than we pray about the problems of others? Shame on us. Arabella should have known that God is definitely against gossip, and we should be too. In fact, the Proverbs address the sins of the tongue over sixty times.

On the other hand, "those who are trustworthy can keep a confidence." Johann Lavater once said, "Never tell evil of a man if you do not know it for certainty, and if you know it for a certainty, then ask yourself, 'Why should I tell it?'"

Make It Personal . . . Live It Out!

Is it really a big deal if we gossip just a little bit, and only with our closest friends? Let's let Jesus answer: "But I tell you that men [and women] will have to give account on the day of judgment for every careless word they have spoken" (Matthew 12:36, NIV). Therefore, what can we do when others turn the conversation to backbiting and slander? Turn the tide. Shoot an arrow prayer: "Lord, help me to say something positive about that person." You'll see; God will give you wisdom in that moment. If the gossipers continue, kindly excuse yourself, leaving one less person to participate in their unholy huddle.

One Year Bible Reading

Numbers 22:21–23:30; Luke 1:57-80; Psalm 58:1-11; Proverbs 11:12-13

Godly Counselors

Where there is no counsel, the people fall;
But in the multitude of counselors there is safety.

PROVERBS 11:14 (NKJV)

Often when I am in an airport I go to the magazine shop and look at the headlines of all the magazines offering all kinds of advice. I am interested to see what people are reading. I wonder if they really believe everything they read in those magazines.

Our proverb today says that when there is no counsel, meaning no godly counsel, the people fall. Women are falling deep in credit card debt with nothing to show for it. Women fall by foolishly deciding to move in with their boyfriends, not knowing that statistically live-in men are ten times more likely to be unfaithful—and besides, it's just wrong. Women fall when they turn to medications to numb the pain of life, instead of turning to the Lord for comfort or grace or help in time of need.

I have a dear, wise friend named Dotty. Let me share her thoughts. She said, "In the days we live in, we need to analyze the people we turn to when seeking advice. We need to know who is steeped in the Word of God, who walks in maturity, who has and shows a deep reverence for the Lord. Those are the kinds of people we need to turn to when we are looking for those 'many counselors' to guide us. And we need to ask the Lord to make us that kind of women, able to give godly counsel to others who are in a quandary."

Make It Personal . . . Live It Out!

"In the multitude of counselors there is safety." As I have walked with the Lord over forty years, I've often thought of this advice. I am thankful to say that we have always been connected to a fellowship of believers. We have never been church hoppers or sideline sitters. I can pick up the phone and call many dear sisters and ask them for prayer and words of wise counsel. Do you have that?

Let's Pray

Lord, please help me to stop living on the edges of the family of God. Help me to become part of a church community where both life and burdens are shared.

One Year Bible Reading

Numbers 24:1–25:18; Luke 2:1-35; Psalm 59:1-17; Proverbs 11:14

Don't Cosign!

Guaranteeing a loan for a stranger is dangerous;
it is better to refuse than to suffer later.

PROVERBS 11:15

In the late sixties, the hippy movement sang about peace and love. It was seen as a great virtue to give and to share. That was definitely the good side. Unfortunately, there was not necessarily much respect for the virtues of stewardship and responsibility. Because of this, new terms came into the hippie vocabulary: terms like "being burned" or being "ripped off."

Our proverb today tells you that you do need to be cautious when you lend to someone you don't know much about. You might find later that the very reason they needed the loan is because they were careless and foolish with money when they did have it.

Okay. I really can't help saying it, but it seems kind of crazy for our government to be bailing out companies who we already know overspent. We already know they made bad decisions with the massive amount of money that they did have. In Missouri they say, "This is throwing money down a rat hole." Lending money with no accountability is throwing good money after bad, wouldn't you say?

Okay. I can't help saying one more thing about this. Our country was founded on principles, wise principles as found in the Word of God, principles of morality, principles of financial soundness, principles of right and wrong. When we disregard these, someone is going to eventually have to pick up the tab.

Make It Personal . . . Live It Out!

It's easy to decline cosigning for your cousin's brother-in-law or the bum down the street, but when it comes to close family it is a lot tougher. I know it seems unsympathetic, but when you cosign for anyone, you enable them to take a risk they might not be ready for and might suffer for later. Moms, when your kids ask you to help them start a business or loan them money, be wise. It's risky. Even though it's inconvenient, I have seen wise parents allow grown children to move back home while they save for their dreams. Then when they launch out, they can stand on their own feet.

One Year Bible Reading

Numbers 26:1-51; Luke 2:36-52; Psalm 60:1-12; Proverbs 11:15

Kindness in Action

A kindhearted woman gains respect,
but ruthless men gain only wealth.
A kind man benefits himself,
but a cruel man brings trouble on himself.

PROVERBS 11:16-17 (NIV)

This beautiful proverb lifts up to us the blessing of being a blessing. Even if we just looked at this selfishly, we would want to live right, knowing that it is right for us. "Remember this: . . . whoever sows generously will also reap generously" (2 Corinthians 9:6, NIV).

One of my favorite books in the New Testament is Philippians. And I love the odd little story in the book of Acts of how the Philippian church started. Paul had gone there because of a dream of a man saying, "Come over to help us." But when he arrived, he just came across a group of women—whom he shared the gospel with. Listen to the story in Acts 16:14-15: "One of those listening was a woman named Lydia. . . . The Lord opened her heart to respond to Paul's message. When she and the members of her household were baptized, she invited us to her home. 'If you consider me a believer in the Lord,' she said, 'come and stay at my house.' And she persuaded us" (NIV).

She was both an openhearted and kindhearted woman. She considered it an honor to offer true hospitality. Ladies, can you imagine some of the conversations that happened at her house over the next few weeks? Did she see others get saved in her own living room? Later, when the letter to the Philippians arrived, maybe it was at her house that it was first read. Lydia was a kindhearted woman who gained respect.

Make It Personal . . . Live It Out!

To be kind is to possess sympathetic or generous qualities. A kindhearted woman does kindhearted things. William Wordsworth referred to the "best portion of a good man's life" as "his little, nameless, unremembered acts of kindness and of love." When your husband is late, be kind. When a child breaks a dish, be kind. When your mom needs a ride to the doctor, be kind.

Let's Pray

Lord, help me to not miss those little moments when someone needs a kind word or touch.

One Year Bible Reading

Numbers 26:52–28:15; Luke 3:1-22; Psalm 61:1-8; Proverbs 11:16-17

March 19

Treasure in Heaven

Evil people get rich for the moment,
but the reward of the godly will last.

PROVERBS 11:18

So much has happened in our economy over the last few years. The fortunes of some have been lost. This seems like a really good time to rethink the definition of *rich*. What is rich? You've probably heard the famous statement of John D. Rockefeller. When asked, "How much money is enough?" he said, "Just a little bit more."

Frank Herbert once said, "Wealth is a tool of freedom, but the pursuit of wealth is the way to slavery." So how do we balance this? Princess Diana had her own version. She said, "They say it is better to be poor and happy than rich and miserable, but how about a compromise like moderately rich and just a little moody?" Nice try, Princess Di, but no cigar.

I think Henry Ward Beecher said it much better. He said, "No man can tell whether he is rich or poor by turning to his ledger. It is the heart that makes a man [or woman] rich. He is rich or poor according to what he is, not according to what he has." Now this is the real deal. It is not what you have inside the bank, it's what is inside of you.

But of course, Jesus said it best of all. He said, "Lay up for yourselves treasures in heaven . . . for where your treasure is, there will your heart be also" (Matthew 6:20-21, NKJV). Confirming our proverb, "the reward of the godly will last."

Make It Personal . . . Live It Out!

How do you store treasure in heaven? Is it the money you give to the church or charity? It can be. But it is also more personal and dynamic than that. In Matthew 25:35-40, Jesus explained that he values little things, like visiting someone who is sick. Let me connect this topic to the concept of "walking in the Spirit." When we are in tune with the Spirit of God, he will direct in specific ways to bless someone and to be "rich toward God."

Let's Pray

Lord, please give me eyes to see and then the will to do the things that really matter to you and for eternity.

One Year Bible Reading

Numbers 28:16–29:40; Luke 3:23-38; Psalm 62:1-12; Proverbs 11:18-19

What God Hates

They that are of a froward heart are abomination to the LORD:
But such as are upright in their way are his delight.

PROVERBS 11:20 (KJV)

Ladies, we need to think deeply about what this says. There are things that God really hates, and there are things that bless him so much, he is actually delighted. This is an astounding and inviting concept—that we personally can bring delight to the God who created the stars!

Hmm, let's see: to be an abomination or a delight? What should we choose?

First, what is it that is an abomination to God? A froward heart is an abomination. *Froward* is an old-fashioned word for distorted and false.

One of my least favorite moments for women in the Bible is found in Genesis 27. Rebekah influenced her son Jacob to lie to and deceive his father so that he could receive the blessing planned for his older brother. Jacob did not feel good about it and feared the deception would bring trouble. His mother said to him, "My son, let the curse fall on me. Just do what I say" (Genesis 27:13, NIV). Well, if you read the story, you learn that he did, but it did create a great breach in the family. Jacob had to flee from his brother's anger, and Rebekah never saw her son again. She thought she could do a wrong thing and it would turn out right—but she was wrong.

So, in contrast, let's look at what God does love. First Peter 3:3-4 says, "Let your adornment be . . . the incorruptible beauty of a gentle and quiet spirit, which is very precious in the sight of God" (NKJV).

Make It Personal . . . Live It Out!

To be froward is to be distorted, false. To be upright is to be sound, wholesome, innocent, having integrity. God hates one and loves the other. The truth is, so does everyone else. Those who know you best, behind the scenes—what would they say? Do your kids see you distort the truth and make compromises? Do you tell them to do one thing while you do the other? Do they hear you blame your husband (or ex-husband) for your bad attitude? God hates these things, and so do your kids. Just putting it frankly, it's time to knock it off!

One Year Bible Reading

Numbers 30:1–31:54; Luke 4:1-30; Psalm 63:1-11; Proverbs 11:20-21

Beauty Is as Beauty Does

Like a gold ring in a pig's snout
is a beautiful woman who shows no discretion.

PROVERBS 11:22 (NIV)

This is a ridiculous picture. A gold ring absolutely does not belong on the ugly nose of a pig. A pig lives in the mud. Likewise, a woman with no discretion acts and dresses with bad judgment and poor taste. She is just plain rude and selfish. Therefore, a beautiful face on such a woman is wasted and misplaced.

Josh Billings said, "To marry a woman for her beauty is like buying a house for its paint." Maybe he had seen men who fell for a pretty face and then lived miserable lives trying to make their beautiful wives happy. Studies have shown that the more beauty a woman has when she is young, the harder it is for her to watch herself age. So, my dear sisters, no one is saying go ahead and just let yourself get ugly. But I am saying, get over the anxiety and priority of needing to look young and beautiful.

Let's now get to the main point of this proverb. The main point is that beauty, real beauty, is more than skin deep. So although the world does not affirm this for us, we can affirm it for each other. Moms, read stories of great godly women in the past like Amy Carmichael and Corrie ten Boom, not just to your girls, but to your sons as well. These women had an inner glow and are true examples of Proverbs 31:30: "Charm is deceptive, and beauty is fleeting; but a woman who fears the LORD is to be praised" (NIV).

Because beauty is as beauty does.

Make It Personal . . . Live It Out!

Since indiscretion is ugly, let's look at the beauty of discretion. Discretion is not only noble, it is classy. It looks good on you no matter where you are or what you look like. Discretion carries an air of authority and dignity. Discretion guides us with the power to choose, to be careful, discerning, and wise. If you are a child of God, your Father in heaven is the great and noble King of the universe. Will you chose to live your life today to honor him, reflecting godly nobility and true beauty?

One Year Bible Reading

Numbers 32:1–33:39; Luke 4:31–5:11; Psalm 64:1-10; Proverbs 11:22

Righteous Desires

The desire of the righteous is only good,
but the expectation of the wicked is wrath.

PROVERBS 11:23 (NKJV)

This proverb gives a picture of contrasts. We are shown the end result of right living and the end result of wickedness. Many lives are like a car racing out of control heading straight for a cliff. We need flashing red lights that say, "Danger ahead, slow down, turn around, and drive carefully in the right direction."

So our quest today will be to discover how to cultivate good, godly desires and appetites that lead to good things. There is no better place to start than by asking God for a fresh love for him and a fresh desire for his Word.

How can we develop a fresh desire for God? Choose to read God's Word every morning, not just as a Christian duty but to know him more. I love to get up before anyone else, while it is still dark. There is something exciting about this secret time alone with God. Make a place in your house that is your "holy place," your place to meet with God. I have my *One Year Bible* there, my favorite devotionals, highlighters, pens, a journal, and my "to do" notebook.

Then, as you read, write little notes in the margin. Sometimes I write a date next to a promise as I ask the Lord to help me believe and trust him. Underline words that stand out, write out Scriptures. Stop and pray about the lessons you see and need to apply.

"Delight yourself also in the LORD, and He shall give you the desires of your heart" (Psalm 37:4, NKJV).

Make It Personal . . . Live It Out!

What is the result of spending the first half hour of the day with God? He rewires your thoughts with hope. Maybe you woke up still angry about something that happened yesterday at work, or worried about your kids, or anxious about the bills. The psalm reading for today is Psalm 65. As you read these words, let them give you fresh confidence to face your day: "God our Savior, . . . who stilled the roaring of the seas, . . . where morning dawns . . . you call forth songs of joy" (vv. 5, 7-8, NIV).

One Year Bible Reading

Numbers 33:40–35:34; Luke 5:12-28; Psalm 65:1-13; Proverbs 11:23

Refreshing Others

One man gives freely, yet gains even more;
another withholds unduly, but comes to poverty.
A generous man will prosper;
he who refreshes others will himself be refreshed.

PROVERBS 11:24-25 (NIV)

Isn't this just the opposite of what our natural instincts tell us? When our natural mind does the math, we think, *Give and you have less, hoard and you have more.* But Jesus gives us the true formula, "It is more blessed to give than to receive" (Acts 20:35, NKJV).

I learned this principle the hard way. I once slipped into a terrible time of depression. I was disappointed with situations in life, and on top of that I was feeling like a failure. And so I kept sinking deeper and deeper. Then one day, someone suggested that the best way out of depression was not to do more things for myself, but to find someone else who needed cheering. Just at that time I was invited to teach sewing to boys at a juvenile detention facility. It was a step—and I took it. It ended up that the most popular project with these troubled teens was to make teddy bears. They wanted to make pink and yellow and blue teddy bears. Then they told me the reason. They wanted to make them for their moms and little sisters and grandmothers. Then I realized they were just like me. In their troubles, they needed to give, too. Because "it is more blessed to give than to receive." It was the way out of depression for them and for me, too.

"He [or she] who refreshes others will [themselves] be refreshed."

Make It Personal . . . Live It Out!

Have you been feeling discouraged and depressed? Does it seem you just can't shake it? Will you try this formula? Will you look around your world and ask God to show you someone who is also going through a hard time? You don't have to look very far. Then will you ask him to show you something tangible you can do? I never thought sewing teddy bears would be the turning point for me. God knows what will turn you around, too. As you refresh others, he will indeed refresh you.

One Year Bible Reading

Numbers 36:1—Deuteronomy 1:46; Luke 5:29–6:11; Psalm 66:1-20; Proverbs 11:24-26

Seek Good

He [or she] who seeks good finds goodwill,
but evil comes to him who searches for it.

PROVERBS 11:27 (NIV)

Seeking good is a decision that can become a habit, and then a lifestyle, and then a life. Sadly, we can also chose to seek the bad or the dark or the ugly. This could apply to looking for the good or the bad in a person, a situation or a responsibility, or even your church.

And what are the rewards of seeking good? It is promised that we will find goodwill, or favor. The Hebrew word here is *ratson*, which actually means "delight." This makes sense. Think about it. There are some people who always look for the good in people. You just know they see the best in you. What happens? I know for me, it inspires me. I think for most of us it helps us want to rise to that view. We want to be that good person. And how do we feel about being around such a person? We are delighted! Because they are a blessing. Ladies, we need to remember this principle.

We also need to remember that when we always see the bad, the flaw, the failure in our husbands or children or friends or church, it becomes a self-fulfilling prophecy. We are not a blessing, and we discourage people. Sometimes, they give up. Why try?

The apostle Paul wrote the following words from a prison cell in Rome: "Whatever is true, whatever is noble, whatever is right, whatever is pure, whatever is lovely, whatever is admirable—if anything is excellent or praiseworthy—think about such things" (Philippians 4:8, NIV).

Make It Personal . . . Live It Out!

A few days ago I couldn't sleep. So I got up and made a list of people I wanted to pray for. By each of their names, I wrote something I appreciated about them. Then I prayed. My little list made my prayer time one of the sweetest ever as I thanked the Lord for each one. Will you do that? Before you go to bed tonight, sit down and make a list of the people in your life you care about. Then next to each name, write something good and pray with thankfulness.

One Year Bible Reading

Deuteronomy 2:1–3:29; Luke 6:12-38; Psalm 67:1-7; Proverbs 11:27

March 25

The Righteous Thrive

Whoever trusts in his riches will fall,
but the righteous will thrive like a green leaf.

PROVERBS 11:28 (NIV)

The first part of this proverb doesn't warn against having money, it warns us against putting our trust in money. The definition of *to put your trust* is "to put confidence in, to feel secure or safe in, to have your hope in."

Benjamin Franklin has a reputation for being wise about money; remember, he is the one who said, "A penny saved is a penny earned." But he also understood the dangers of money and warned, "He that is of the opinion money will do everything may well be suspected of doing everything for money."

So, ladies, are you are going through financial trouble right now? Maybe you're afraid, insecure. You're depressed. You and your husband are arguing. You're angry—maybe even angry at God. When our emotional security is too tightly linked to our financial security, then if our finances crumble, so do we. We fall, and we often drag others down in our tailspin.

Personally, I think we're going to go through some more hard years. Our economy is not going to recover quickly. Actually Elijah the prophet prayed for a time of drought—no rain for his country. Why? Because Elijah longed for revival. And revival doesn't usually come in times of prosperity. So back to the question: What or whom do you put your trust in? Corrie ten Boom, who survived a concentration camp, made a remarkable statement. She said, "You will never know that Jesus is all you need until Jesus is all you have."

Make It Personal . . . Live It Out!

"The righteous will thrive like a green leaf" is our promise for the day. Righteousness here does not mean sinless perfection. It merely describes those who chose to walk uprightly. I have known plenty of godly people who don't have much money, but their lives are rich with the fruit of the Spirit. As we read the list of fruit in Galatians 5:22-23, let's pray that God will help us thrive with such spiritual richness. "But the fruit of the Spirit is love, joy, peace, longsuffering, kindness, goodness, faithfulness, gentleness, self-control" (NKJV).

One Year Bible Reading

Deuteronomy 4:1-49; Luke 6:39–7:10; Psalm 68:1-18; Proverbs 11:28

Burden for Souls

The fruit of the righteous is a tree of life,
and he who wins souls is wise.

PROVERBS 11:30 (NIV)

I am so excited about this verse! "He [or she] who wins souls is wise." Ladies, as children of God, we need to be about our Father's business. God loves people. He really, really loves people.

Brandon Heath has a great song that's really a prayer. It's called "Give Me Your Eyes."

Give me your eyes for just one second
Give me your eyes so I can see
Everything that I keep missing
Give me your love for humanity

There's a man just to [the] right
Black suit and a bright red tie
Too ashamed to tell his wife
He's out of work, he's buying time

All those people going somewhere
Why have I never cared?

Give me your heart for the ones forgotten
Give me your eyes so I can see

Now listen to what Jesus said: "I tell you, open your eyes and look at the fields! They are ripe for harvest" (John 4:35, NIV).

Maybe you are thinking, *I can't share the gospel with others.* Please let me tell you, God never commands us to do that which he will not enable us to do. The Gospel of Mark 2:14 records the day when Matthew, the tax collector, left his old life to follow Jesus. In the next verse we read that he invited all his old friends to dinner, with one intention. He wanted them to know the Savior too.

The first person who witnessed to me was a high school friend. So many years later when I went to my high school reunion, I prayed for divine appointments, took copies of the Gospel of John to hand out, and told people how Jesus had changed my life.

Make It Personal . . . Live It Out!

Prayer is always the first place to start if you would like to share the gospel. God will show you a lonely neighbor, a troubled teen, your newly married niece who needs him. Just keep praying, and God will give you the next step. The first step might be scary, but sometimes we just have to "do it scared."

One Year Bible Reading

Deuteronomy 5:1–6:25; Luke 7:11-35; Psalm 68:19-35; Proverbs 11:29-31

March 27

Are You Growing?

Whoever loves instruction loves knowledge,
But he who hates correction is stupid.

PROVERBS 12:1 (NKJV)

Well, I would call that getting to the point! And you know what? Sometimes the truth should hurt. Psalm 32:9 says, "Do not be like the horse or the mule, which have no understanding but must be controlled by bit and bridle" (NIV).

God takes no pleasure in calling us, or anyone else, stupid or a mule. So how can we avoid these pitfalls? By being teachable. An eagerness to learn and grow and change is really a building block of wisdom and the antidote for stupidity.

May I ask you, Are you growing? One of the great thrills of being a Christian is that we can always be growing. I love to be around brand-new Christians. They have a thousand questions. But I also love to be around older Christians who are just as hungry. Have you become dull and stunted? Let me suggest three ways to spark your appetite:

1. Pick up a Christian biography. When I read about a life like D. L. Moody's or George Müller's, I feel challenged and inspired. I learn fresh insights from some of the trials and victories of their lives.
2. Sign up for women's Bible study. There are some excellent lessons written by women like Kay Arthur. Her studies teach how to dig into the treasures of God's Word.
3. Become a student of creationism. Don't be duped by the evolutionist lie. There are some exciting books and videos available that make learning about Creation a true joy.

Make It Personal . . . Live It Out!

"My beloved brethren, let every man be swift to hear, slow to speak, slow to wrath. . . . Be doers of the word, and not hearers only, deceiving yourselves" (James 1:19, 22, NKJV). Let's be open to exhortation from others and conviction of the Holy Spirit. And then let's put into action what God has shown us. Let's be teachable.

Let's Pray

Lord, help me to really be serious about corrections and change. I don't want to be stagnant and stubborn. Help me to be hungry to learn and eager to grow.

One Year Bible Reading

Deuteronomy 7:1–8:20; Luke 7:36–8:3; Psalm 69:1-18; Proverbs 12:1

March 28

Wicked Ways Backfire

A good man [or woman] obtains favor from the LORD,
but the LORD condemns a crafty man.
A man cannot be established through wickedness,
but the righteous cannot be uprooted."

PROVERBS 12:2-3 (NIV)

I like what Jon Courson has to say on this: "It's not that God will hurl down judgment on the man of wicked devices. It's simply that He will allow that man's own wicked devices to backfire on him."

As a kid, I used to love the "Road Runner" cartoons. That mangy coyote was always building elaborate contraptions to trap the road runner. He would light dynamite, but it would blow up in his face. He would set boulders to fall, but they would fall and crush him. The difference with the cartoon and real life is that the backfires happened right away. In real life, it takes longer.

So, ladies, if there is someone who is hurting you or someone you love, take heart from the words of Psalm 37:7-9: "Be still before the LORD and wait patiently for him; do not fret when men succeed in their ways, when they carry out their wicked schemes. Refrain from anger and turn from wrath; do not fret—it leads only to evil. For evil men will be cut off, but those who hope in the LORD will inherit the land" (NIV).

Bottom line: you cannot stop others from doing wrong. But you can refuse to let them pull you into it. Remember, "A good woman obtains favor from the LORD." That's a promise you can bank on.

Make It Personal . . . Live It Out!

Have you waited and prayed and waited and prayed, and yet you see no relief? You are not alone. The Bible tells us that Joseph waited thirteen years before he was delivered from slavery and prison. And it was at least nine more years before he saw his family. Then what an amazing restoration came (see Genesis 37–47)! Waiting on God is not wasted time. God is working behind the scenes and at the same time stretching and refining you. He can then use you to encourage others in hard times.

Let's Pray

Lord, help me to trust you while you work. And help me to yield to the work you are doing in me.

One Year Bible Reading

Deuteronomy 9:1–10:22; Luke 8:4-21; Psalm 69:19-36; Proverbs 12:2-3

An Excellent Wife

An excellent wife is the crown of her husband,
But she who causes shame is like rottenness in his bones.

PROVERBS 12:4 (NKJV)

I'm always interested to hear what men have to say about a verse like this. Matthew Henry said, "He that is blessed with a good wife is as happy as if he were upon the throne; for she is no less than a crown to him. . . . He that is plagued with a bad wife is as miserable as if he were upon the dunghill; for she is no better than rottenness in his bones; . . . she makes him ashamed."

Pretty strong language, but if we're honest, we know it is true.

Let's take a look at a good example.

Just before George Bush left office, I saw a program with Laura Bush. She was giving a tour of the White House. As she walked around, she was gentle and gracious—not just polite, but truly humble. She had an amazing respect for the history of the different rooms. But one of the things that was especially sweet was that she mentioned several times that she and George had gathered with their friends in certain rooms for little dinner parties. I can't even imagine what it would be like to live with the pressures they had for eight years in Washington. She clearly was not his vice president, but she was the kind of wife who knew how to create a personal oasis for her husband where wars and politics, even if for just a few hours, were secondary to what was on the menu for dessert. Good job, Laura Bush. You knew how to make even the president feel like a king!

Make It Personal . . . Live It Out!

An excellent wife is a praying wife. Sometimes our hearts get hard or cold or just distracted in our marriages. Stormie Omartian writes, in *The Power of a Praying Wife*, "When we pray, . . . our hearts become soft toward God, and we gain a renewed vision. We see there is hope. We have faith that He will restore all that has been devoured, destroyed, and eaten away." Will you kneel today and lift your husband up to God in prayer?

One Year Bible Reading

Deuteronomy 11:1–12:32; Luke 8:22-39; Psalm 70:1-5; Proverbs 12:4

Thought Life

The thoughts of the righteous are right,
But the counsels of the wicked are deceitful.

PROVERBS 12:5 (NKJV)

The word *thoughts* can also be translated as "plans." Think about it, ladies. Where do we make our plans? They start in our heads. That's where we formulate what we are going to do or say.

"The thoughts of the righteous are right." This gives us tremendous insight into the fact that our thought life is extremely important. Some say, "You are what you eat," but more important, you are what you think. Therefore, the disciplines of a godly woman must include cleansing and reprogramming her thought life with God's Word. The perfect method for that is given in Psalm 119:15: "I meditate on your precepts and consider your ways" (NIV). Are you having trouble with your thought life? Let me suggest Scripture memorization. It is much easier than you think.

My friend Sherri Youngward is the one who sings the intro to the *Wisdom for Women* broadcast every day. She has recorded a music CD of songs that are entirely Scripture. It's wonderful. You can order it on her website at sherriyoungward.com. Play it over and over while you are in your car—or working at home. Picture the words flowing over your mind to cleanse it, to unload your thoughts from the negative, and to rewire your attitudes. God's Word has power—it can entirely transform your thought life, because as you ponder his Word, you are thinking his thoughts.

Make It Personal . . . Live It Out!

Have you been plagued by destructive thoughts: condemning, fearful, anxious, doubts of God's love and goodness? Do you have anger and malice, jealous thoughts, lustful fantasies, hopeless or dark spiritual thoughts? God has given us powerful tools—prayer, his Word, and his Holy Spirit—"casting down imaginations, and every high thing that exalteth itself against the knowledge of God, and bringing into captivity every thought to the obedience of Christ" (2 Corinthians 10:5, KJV).

Let's Pray

I have tried to be free before; I need your power. Savior, you can move mountains. Please wash me with the power of your blood. Free me from the thoughts that block your light, and replace them with truth.

One Year Bible Reading

Deuteronomy 13:1–15:23; Luke 8:40–9:6; Psalm 71:1-24; Proverbs 12:5-7

Will Be Commended

A man [or woman] will be commended according to his wisdom,
But he who is of a perverse heart will be despised.

PROVERBS 12:8 (NKJV)

What does the word *commended* mean? Well, believe it or not, it means to shine with God's favor, to be praised.

I'd like to focus on the phrase "will be commended" in this proverb. Although the Proverbs deal mostly with the practical matters of everyday living here on this earth, once in a while they speak of a long off, future tense: "will be."

Child of God, maybe you are in a situation where it is hard to be a Christian. You don't fit in with the crowd. If your husband isn't saved, you aren't encouraged in the things of the Lord. Sometimes you aren't appreciated. Maybe even your kids ridicule your old-fashioned views of life. Just remember, a woman "will be commended" according to her wisdom.

Charles Wesley wrote, "Keep us little and unknown, prized and loved by God alone."

First Corinthians 15:58 reminds us, "Therefore, my beloved brethren, be steadfast, immovable, always abounding in the work of the Lord, knowing that your labor is not in vain in the Lord" (NKJV).

Never forget that for a child of God, the here and now is not all there is. Sometimes you need to zoom forward to eternity, picture being at the throne in his presence, and to hear the King of kings say to you, "Well done." Now that is *royally* being "commended."

Make It Personal . . . Live It Out!

If you are trying to be faithful, never forget that God does see. May he shine his favor on you today if . . .

you are caring for your mother with Alzheimer's. Well done.
you're a single mom, faithfully training your kids to love the Lord. Well done.
you're the only Christian in your family and yet you're shining his light. Well done.
you're a new wife trying to learn to honor your husband. Well done.
you're a teenager who has vowed to stay pure before marriage. Well done.
you're a Sunday school teacher and you pour your heart into the lessons. Well done.

One Year Bible Reading

Deuteronomy 16:1–17:20; Luke 9:7-27; Psalm 72:1-20; Proverbs 12:8-9

April

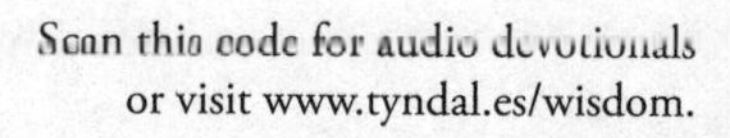
Scan this code for audio devotionals
or visit www.tyndal.es/wisdom.

Human Kindness

A righteous man cares for the needs of his animal,
but the kindest acts of the wicked are cruel.

PROVERBS 12:10 (NIV)

What this proverb is talking about is just plain decency, human kindness, and diligence. A godly man or woman is kind. There shouldn't be a mean bone in their bodies. Really, this trait carries through in all of their actions, from not neglecting to feed the dog to not neglecting to open the door for a young mommy going into WalMart with a baby in her arms. Kindness is making sure we notice the needs that are all around us and then doing what we can and what we should.

The other side of this proverb is an interesting statement: "Even the kindest acts of the wicked are cruel." Maybe this means that some acts seem kind on the outside, but in the end, they hurt more than help. Right now in the name of kindness Planned Parenthood is handing out condoms and abortions to young girls. This action is a message that you are safe if there is no physical consequence to sexual promiscuity, but when these same girls drive home after the abortions with a huge hole in their hearts, they're not prepared for the devastation. This is cruel.

Did you know that 33 percent of all American women will have an abortion, but hardly any of them ever talk about it, and some never tell anyone? It lingers as a silent shame and ungrieved grief.

My sisters, right now I have a burden for you who have this hole in your heart even after many years. Focus on the Family put out a wonderful little booklet called *Healing the Hurt*. You can order it from their website (family.christianbook.com) or download it free (www.heartlink.org) for yourself or someone you love.

Make It Personal . . . Live It Out!

A few years ago, my friend told me her testimony, which included going to an abortion clinic alone as a seventeen-year-old girl. As she finished the story, she turned and said, "Now I think you don't love me." This was my wake-up call to the pain that lingers. My friend went through an online Bible study from Healing Hearts Ministries and now leads others in their path to restoration. Will you go to their website, www.healinghearts.org, and find forgiveness and healing too?

One Year Bible Reading

Deuteronomy 18:1–20:20; Luke 9:28-50; Psalm 73:1-28; Proverbs 12:10

Get to It!

He who tills his land will be satisfied with bread,
But he who follows frivolity is devoid of understanding.

PROVERBS 12:11 (NKJV)

In our proverb today we have a picture of two ways of living.

To be *frivolous* is to be "self-indulgent, unconcerned about or lacking any serious purpose." Obviously, this is not recommended for us as godly women.

The other way of living is a get-to-it way. We are to be diligent and responsible. First things first. No job is going to be finished unless it's started. If your house is dirty or run down, daydreaming is not going to change it. Get up and do the first thing. Clean a bathroom, do a load of laundry, paint one room. Get started. With the economy the way it is, we have to stop eating out all of the time. If you're going to be out all day, put something in the Crock-Pot before you leave, and pack a sandwich for your lunch. Before you go to the grocery store, sit down with the sale flyer from the newspaper. Make your decisions about what you're going to buy according to what's on sale that week. If chuck roast and potatoes are on sale, buy several. Plan ahead. Put one in the freezer. Bake enough potatoes for several days. Take the small steps of preparation today, and you will make your dollar stretch for tomorrow.

First Thessalonians 4:11-12 has a practical good word: "Make it your ambition to lead a quiet life, to mind your own business and to work with your hands . . . so that your daily life may win the respect of outsiders and so you will not have to be dependent on anybody" (NIV).

Make It Personal . . . Live It Out!

April is spring-cleaning month, so before the weather gets nice, let's tackle an "inside job." Put on some praise music and tackle one cabinet, drawer, or closet at a time. The secret is to use three bins or boxes. Bin #1 is for trash. It is for the easy-to-identify "why was I keeping these dried-out markers or worn-out tennis shoes" kinds of items. Bin #2 is for the "give to charity or a friend" items. Bin #3 is for the keepers. These are the things you actually need and will use. As you finish, taste the victory. Good job!

One Year Bible Reading

Deuteronomy 21:1–22:30; Luke 9:51–10:12; Psalm 74:1-23; Proverbs 12:11

Trouble with Words

An evil man is trapped by his sinful talk,
but a righteous man escapes trouble.

PROVERBS 12:13 (NIV)

Second Thessalonians 1:6 says, "God is just: He will pay back trouble to those who trouble you" (NIV).

I'm reading a book called *The Leadership Secrets of Billy Graham* by Harold Myra and Marshall Shelley. Chapter 5 is titled "Loving Harsh Critics." Here's an excerpt. "All leaders get criticized. It's their response to criticism that sets them apart." When unfairly, untruthfully attacked, this was Billy Graham's response: "By God's grace I shall continue to preach the gospel of Jesus Christ and not stoop to mudslinging, name-calling, and petty little fights over nonessentials." Good job, Billy Graham.

Winston Churchill said, "By swallowing evil words unsaid, no one has ever harmed his stomach." Yes, Winston, "A righteous man escapes trouble."

So for us as women, let's also not get pulled into petty little fights. If someone has said something harsh or untrue about you, kick it to the curb. That's my new favorite visual and saying—"just kick it to the curb" and move on.

Recently I found myself really upset over some unkind things said about me. It hurt. It hurt to know that others listened. I'd be dishonest if I said that I didn't think of a few hurtful things to say back. But then I thought, *That is just not how I want to use my energy. It doesn't honor God, it doesn't feel good once it's said, and, well, it's just bad business.* So I decided to kick it to the curb, give it to God, and move on.

Make It Personal . . . Live It Out!

What if you are the one who has said something you know is wrong and hurtful? We all need to learn a very old and helpful skill called *the apology*. Here are the basics. You need to take responsibility without blaming. You need to make your apology sincere and simple. And you need to say, "I'm sorry," and mean it. Will you do it? Will you do it today?

> The first to apologize is the bravest. The first to forgive is the strongest. The first to forget is the happiest.
> —AUTHOR UNKNOWN

One Year Bible Reading

Deuteronomy 23:1–25:19; Luke 10:13-37; Psalm 75:1-10; Proverbs 12:12-14

Fools Show Annoyance

A fool shows his annoyance at once,
but a prudent man [or woman] overlooks an insult.

PROVERBS 12:16 (NIV)

Okay, ladies, let's take this one home. Honestly, do you sometimes make others feel that they have to walk on eggshells when they're around you? Let me tell you three things that are not excuses: hormones, having a bad day, being in a bad mood. Your kids or friends should never say, "Oh, you know Mom. She's in one of her moods." Shame on us.

So let's press into the second part of our proverb. "But [in contrast] a prudent man [or woman] overlooks an insult."

First Corinthians 13:5 says, "[Love] is not easily angered, it keeps no record of wrongs" (NIV). Easier said than done, yes, but totally worth doing. Let me test you on this. If you are fuming about something—a fight you had with your sister, or someone at work you're mad at—does the next little annoyance set you off like a bomb? Do you ever just vent at an innocent bystander? The key here is to defuse the bomb.

To defuse the bomb we need to empty the explosives. How do we do that? I know no better place than the foot of the Cross. Have you been cranky, edgy, irritable, short-fused? Believe 1 John 1:9: "If we confess our sins, He is faithful and just to forgive us our sins and to cleanse us from all unrighteousness" (NKJV). Kneeling at the Cross, releasing your anger—this defuses the bomb.

Make It Personal . . . Live It Out!

If you tend to build up steam over matters, will you get in the habit of asking yourself these questions? *Is this really worth fighting over? Is this worth losing sleep over? Is this worth damaging my relationship over? What do I really gain if I win or retaliate?*

Conflict is always expensive in wasted time, energy, and emotions. Will you ask the Lord to help you learn to overlook offenses? "A man's [woman's] wisdom gives him patience; it is to his glory to overlook an offense" (Proverbs 19:11, NIV).

Let's Pray

Lord, help me to come to you when the steam starts to build. I need your grace—grace for my angry heart, and grace for others too.

One Year Bible Reading

Deuteronomy 26:1–27:26; Luke 10:38–11:13; Psalm 76:1-12; Proverbs 12:15-17

Slay the Monster

Some people make cutting remarks,
but the words of the wise bring healing.

PROVERBS 12:18

Any way you slice it, words can be weapons. Let's focus on the phrase *cutting remarks.* This can refer to words that cut others down. When do we do that? What is the motive? Why would we ever want to do that? Let me say one word: *jealousy.* Jealousy can seem to Christians an acceptable sin, but you know what, that's not true. It's not acceptable to God or anyone. Shakespeare called it the "green-eyed monster."

It is a monster, and when you engage that monster, never think that the most damage comes to others. This monster cuts you down. And so I would like to ask you to say this with me: "This monster has to die." If honestly you know you have slandered or criticized harshly, would you ask yourself the question, *Was it because I was jealous?* If so, that monster has to die, because if it doesn't, it will use you and your words as weapons.

A second motive for "cutting words" is to wound, hurt for hurt. This is another monster, called *revenge.* Confucius said, "Before you embark on a journey of revenge, dig two graves."

So, my sisters, what is it going to be for us? It's been said that the greatest revenge is forgiveness—true, deep, sweet, wholehearted forgiveness. This slays the monsters and blesses the Lord. Then turn that forgiveness into words, because "the words of the wise bring healing."

Make It Personal . . . Live It Out!

We can't change the way others live and talk. But we can take the words of Ephesians 4:29-32 to heart and let them be a filter and "high bar" standard for all that we say and why we say it. "Don't use foul or abusive language. Let everything you say be good and helpful, so that your words will be an encouragement to those who hear them. And do not bring sorrow to God's Holy Spirit by the way you live. Remember, he has identified you as his own, guaranteeing that you will be saved on the day of redemption. Get rid of all bitterness, rage, anger, harsh words, and slander, as well as all types of malicious behavior. Instead, be kind to each other, tenderhearted, forgiving one another, just as God through Christ has forgiven you."

One Year Bible Reading

Deuteronomy 28:1-68; Luke 11:14-36; Psalm 77:1-20; Proverbs 12:18

Promote Peace

There is deceit in the hearts of those who plot evil,
but joy for those who promote peace.

PROVERBS 12:20 (NIV)

I feel an urgency to apply this proverb to families. There is so much intrigue and turmoil in families right now. Sisters and brothers are ganging up on each other, fighting over an inheritance, bickering over petty things.

If you're involved in trouble in your family, I suggest you go back to Genesis 37–50 and read the story of Joseph and his brothers. It's like a big soap opera, with all the elements of jealousy, bitterness, grudges, lies, deceit. Be aware that it's not just a story. It's about a real family—a family with stepmothers and stepbrothers. That adds an element that definitely makes things more complicated, and then you add the element of favoritism, and you have a real formula for trouble. I don't have to explain that to you if you're living it. It's not the Brady Bunch. Bottom line: Joseph's brothers plotted revenge against Joseph, and in the end, they were the big losers.

First Peter 3:8-9 has a formula of joy for us as an antidote. Read it carefully: "Finally, all of you, live in harmony with one another; be sympathetic, love as brothers, be compassionate and humble. Do not repay evil with evil or insult with insult, but with blessing, because to this you were called so that you may inherit a blessing" (NIV).

Make It Personal . . . Live It Out!

Families can indeed be complicated, especially with blended families, ex-spouses, in-laws, and out-laws (ex-in-laws). Everything from who is invited to Easter dinner to custody and inheritance issues can be an emotional can of worms. Let me ask you a question: When there is a conflict in your family, is there a difference between the way you respond and the way the non-Christians respond? Conflict is opportunity in disguise; really it is. It can be the best opportunity of all for you to show the grace and love and patience of Christ. Talk is cheap. This can be your "divine appointment" to walk the talk.

One Year Bible Reading

Deuteronomy 29:1–30:20; Luke 11:37–12:7; Psalm 78:1-31; Proverbs 12:19-20

Lying Lips

Lying lips are an abomination to the LORD,
But those who deal truthfully are His delight.

PROVERBS 12:22 (NKJV)

Abomination. This is pretty strong language. "Lying lips are an abomination to the LORD."

So what is lying? It's deception. Even a half-truth is a whole lie. A lie is falsehood, a fraud. It's used to cover a wrong. A lie is dishonest. It shifts the blame or slants the story. Lying is a bad habit and bad business. God hates it.

Listen to what Jesus said in John 8:44: "[The devil] was a murderer from the beginning, not holding to the truth, for there is no truth in him. When he lies, he speaks his native language; for he's a liar and the father of lies" (NIV).

For us as women, many of the things we struggle with are caused because we have listened to lies. Let me recommend to you a marvelous book by Nancy Leigh DeMoss. It's called *Lies Women Believe: And the Truth That Sets Them Free.*

This book deals with the trouble it causes women when *we* are *lied to.*

But there is another issue: that is when *we* lie. We sometimes lie to ourselves, we lie to others, and sadly we even try to lie to God. The first step to repentance, be honest that you have been dishonest. Don't blame anyone else. Then take it to the Cross. It is sin and there is a remedy for sin. With forgiveness, we can hate the lie, because God hates it. And here's the joy: each time we resist speaking that lie, we can embrace the fact that the Lord delights in a woman who speaks the truth.

Make It Personal . . . Live It Out!

Lying is indeed bad business. But we as women can sometimes put ourselves in a position to be lied to. We can sit hour after hour in front of the TV set and watch programs that mock morality and truth. Hollywood makes adultery and sex outside of marriage look harmless and normal. Many women watch talk shows that mock goodness and God. Garbage in, garbage out. The media is pushing the limits of false and phony. They call good evil and evil good. Shame on them. But if we endorse their lies by watching it—shame on us.

One Year Bible Reading

Deuteronomy 31:1–32:27; Luke 12:8-34; Psalm 78:32-55; Proverbs 12:21-23

Diligence

Diligent hands will rule,
but laziness ends in slave labor.

PROVERBS 12:24 (NIV)

Diligence is an eager determination and decision to do that which needs to be done. No dragging the feet, no slacking.

Moms, I'm afraid that we're training our children to be lazy. We are teaching them to procrastinate by allowing them to take shortcuts, put things off, and quit before the job is done. Every time they skate by with no consequences, the deeper that habit becomes.

We know how this works. When I am too lazy to pull a few weeds, they go to seed and the next spring I have thousands of weeds. Every time I put off getting a bill paid, I have a late fee. A lazy life is a wasteful life. Instead of being on top of things, they are on top of you. It's a bad way to live.

I have fought the battle of procrastination my entire life. For instance, I love a clean desk, but I hate to clean it. So let's apply two simple steps as I clean my messy desk.

1. Start small and get started. Right now I have stacks of books piled on my desk. I am going to get two shoe-box-sized bins and sort the books in two categories. Wow! That took all of five minutes.
2. Once I get started, the next step is easy. I will now sort the paperwork into two other bins. One is "to file," the other is "to do" (bills, etc.). Wow, that took fifteen minutes. In the process, I found an expired certificate (oops), and a missing phone charger (yay). Good job, Debbi.

Make It Personal . . . Live It Out!

If you have kids still at home or grandkids who stay over, it is important to impart a joyful and diligent work ethic. In the real world, benefits don't fall in place until responsibility is taken care of. We stunt kids' growth when they get to watch a movie or go out to play before they clean up a mess they've made in the family room. Teach them to pick up toys when they are at a friend's house, too. Diligence is a learned trait, and happy is the child who learns it at home.

One Year Bible Reading

Deuteronomy 32:28-52; Luke 12:35-59; Psalm 78:56-64; Proverbs 12:24

April 9

An Anxious Heart

An anxious heart weighs a man down,
but a kind word cheers him up.

PROVERBS 12:25 (NIV)

This proverb is so timely. Anxiousness is written on people's faces all around us. We know how this feels. Maybe you woke up this morning, anxious. It's like a weight on your mind, on your shoulders, and on your heart. So, you worry. For many of us, worrying almost feels like the responsible thing to do. *Well, if I don't worry, who will?* But I heard it said, "Worry does not rob tomorrow of its problems. It robs today of its strength."

Our proverb today says "a good word cheers us up." So, child of God, you need a good word. In Psalm 42:5-6, David asked himself the question *Why?* "Why are you downcast, O my soul? Why so disturbed within me? Put your hope in God, for I will yet praise him, my Savior and my God" (NIV). Listen to Jesus say to you today, "Come to me, all you who are weary and burdened, and I will give you rest" (Matthew 11:28, NIV).

Here is one more prescription for peace. Write it out and live it out—Philippians 4:6-7: "Be anxious for nothing, but in everything by prayer and supplication, with thanksgiving, let your requests be made known to God; and the peace of God, which surpasses all understanding, will guard your hearts and minds through Christ Jesus" (NKJV).

Now that's taking the weight off.

Make It Personal . . . Live It Out!

You may be thinking, *If only you knew how serious my problems are*. Please know that I am not trying to make light of the weight you have been carrying. A seriously ill child, a battle with cancer, or a child on drugs is truly more than a human heart can bear alone. God knows and cares more than you will ever know; "the LORD is close to the brokenhearted" (Psalm 34:18). Will you take a few moments to pray right now? I believe he wants to give you a fresh and comforting sense of his strength to see you through this day.

Let's Pray

Lord, I am feeling so very weak right now. You say that your grace is sufficient. I desperately need grace and hope that I am not alone. I lift my burden to you and ask that today you will carry it for me.

One Year Bible Reading

Deuteronomy 33:1-29; Luke 13:1-21; Psalm 78:65-72; Proverbs 12:25

True Friendship

The righteous should choose his friends carefully,
For the way of the wicked leads them astray.

PROVERBS 12:26 (NKJV)

Friendship. First of all, I want to say to all of us as women, *we need friends*! We need godly friends. Truly, my friendships are some of my dearest treasures. C. S. Lewis asked, "Is any pleasure in earth as great as a circle of Christian friends by a fire?"

Picture the moment that Jonathan chose David as a friend. In many ways they were light-years apart. Jonathan lived in a palace, David was just a shepherd. But 1 Samuel 18:1 says, "The soul of Jonathan was knit to the soul of David" (NKJV). Their friendship with each other was sparked because individually they each had a deep, personal friendship with God.

The advice in our proverb says to choose your friends carefully—and advises against mingling with those who have wicked traits. So let's list some traits to guard against.

- *Jealousy.* Don't get too close to someone who has jealousy issues. She will start tearing others down. And fight against that trait in yourself. Don't be jealous when your friend has other friends.
- *Pettiness.* If you are buddies with someone who is petty and critical, you will learn to be petty and critical.
- *Worldliness.* What kind of movies do you watch together? Do you have a friend who would rather go shopping than to Bible study? And would Jesus be comfortable with the things you talk about and the places you go?

Make It Personal . . . Live It Out!

Okay then, how do you make and keep good friendships? Many years ago I learned three important lessons from Proverbs 18:24: "A man [or woman] who has friends must himself be friendly, but there is a friend who sticks closer than a brother" (NKJV). First of all, don't wait for the other person to be the first one to reach out. Second, be a true friend, especially when someone is going through a hard time; it makes your bond sweeter and deeper. Third, never allow a friend to take the place of your friendship with Jesus; he is the one who sticks closer than a brother or sister.

One Year Bible Reading

Deuteronomy 34:1—Joshua 2:24; Luke 13:22–14:6; Psalm 79:1-13; Proverbs 12:26

Be Diligent

Lazy people don't even cook the game they catch,
but the diligent make use of everything they find.

PROVERBS 12:27

A lazy life is a wasteful life. Our economy is in crisis. It is time for all of us to wake up and be serious about being diligent in the everyday details of life. For godly women this is called discipline and stewardship. Even little changes can add up. It can be fun. Get your kids involved. They can clip coupons and help compare prices online. I googled the words *frugal tips* and found lots of websites with good ideas. As a young pastor's wife I learned to make a dollar stretch a mile. Here are some habits I have used for years.

- Plan meals according to what is on sale that week at the grocery store.
- When items you use a lot are on sale, stock up; buy two.
- Buy good coffee and make it at home. One bag of coffee lasts weeks and costs about the same as just three cups at Starbucks.
- Take a few snacks and water bottles in the car to avoid buying expensive snacks while you're out doing errands.
- Get out your Crock-Pot again. Throwing in a few potatoes and some chicken in the morning takes five minutes, and it is wonderful to come home to a hot meal.
- Make homemade iced tea instead of buying soda.
- A pot of homemade chicken soup, salad, and cornbread for eight costs less than dinner for two at a restaurant.

Benjamin Franklin advised, "Beware of little expenses; a small leak will sink a great ship."

Make It Personal . . . Live It Out!

Will you answer the call to be a woman of diligence? Will you then apply that diligence to your prayer life? Corrie ten Boom said, "Don't pray when you feel like it. Have an appointment with the Lord and keep it. A man is powerful on his knees." So is a woman. James 5:16 tells us, "Tremendous power is made available through a good [woman's] earnest prayer" (*THE MESSAGE*). We are not to take this great privilege and responsibility lightly. We're to be warriors, fighting with our spiritual weapon, prayer! J. Sidlow Baxter said, "Men may spurn our appeals, reject our message, oppose our arguments, despise our persons, but they are helpless against our prayers."

One Year Bible Reading

Joshua 3:1–4:24; Luke 14:7-35; Psalm 80:1-19; Proverbs 12:27-28

Be Teachable

A wise child accepts a parent's discipline;
a young mocker refuses to listen.

PROVERBS 13:1

There is a clear line drawn between someone who is wise and someone who isn't. And one of the defining marks is "a teachable spirit."

A foolish person won't learn. She already knows it all. She thinks she knows better than anyone else. So you are wasting your breath to try to talk out a problem.

Whether it is at work, in a ministry, among friends, or in a family, everyone just leaves a foolish person alone, because if you do talk to her, she is going to be offended and defensive. I hope I am not talking about you . . . and I hope I am not talking about me.

On the other hand, there are some precious people who are a delight to be friends with and to serve with. They are open, receptive, growing, and eager to learn. It's refreshing. It is easy to trust them, because they are not going to undermine people, hold grudges, or get set in a defensive box. On top of that, I feel like I am not only able to minister to them, but I always learn from them. One of the great keys is that a teachable person is constantly open, listening and learning from God!

Hebrews 3:7 warns, "The Holy Spirit says: 'Today, if you will hear His voice, do not harden your hearts as in the day of rebellion'" (NKJV).

So, who are you in this picture? And the important question now is, who do you want to be?

Make It Personal . . . Live It Out!

"A wise child accepts discipline." Are you a parent, supervisor at work, or ministry leader who sometimes has to correct or discipline someone? You can make it harder or easier to receive. The definition of *discipline* is "training that develops self-control, character, orderliness, and efficiency." Don't come down like a hammer. When you discipline, it should not be to punish, but to train. It is to help that person grow, not just for your benefit, but theirs. Next time, before you speak, will you pray? Ask God to give you words that build up and direct, not tear down and discourage.

One Year Bible Reading

Joshua 5:1–7:15; Luke 15:1-32; Psalm 81:1-16; Proverbs 13:1

April 13

Don't Speak Rashly

From the fruit of her lips a [woman] enjoys good things,
but the unfaithful have a craving for violence.
He who guards his lips guards his life,
but he who speaks rashly will come to ruin.

PROVERBS 13:2-3 (NIV)

Ladies, this is a good word for us. We will never be women of graciousness and honor until we get this area of our lives completely under the control of the Holy Spirit.

Today's proverb warns us: don't speak rashly. To speak rashly is to speak whatever you feel like speaking, with no restraint, with no thought or care. Don't do that. Don't ever do that. As Will Rogers said, "People who fly into a rage always make a bad landing."

Moms, we have to remember that children learn what they live. If you are quick to vent anger at your kids, or husband, or the clerk at the store, it will backfire on you. Either those around you will shut down, or you will see your kids "acting out" your behavior.

Many kids learn a lot about their parents' faith as they ride in the backseat going to and from church. Do they hear bickering and tension going to church, but then see another face presented as they walk in the church door? Do they hear criticism and gossip as they ride home? This is confusing and disappointing. James 1:26 tells us, "If anyone considers himself religious and yet does not keep a tight rein on his tongue, he deceives himself, and his religion is worthless" (NIV).

Make It Personal . . . Live It Out!

I have a friend who was a screamer as a young mother. As a Christian, she knew it was wrong. So she felt constantly condemned. But she couldn't stop. Just one spilled glass of milk would set her off. She was desperate and cried out to God for help. Then she heard a teaching on the Holy Spirit. She learned that he could give her strength that was beyond her own. That very day she desperately cried out to God, asking him to come and fill her with his supernatural power—and he did.

Do you feel helpless to change? Will you sit down right now and cry out to God? Ask him to fill you will his dynamite power, knowing he will, because he promised.

One Year Bible Reading

Joshua 7:16–9:2; Luke 16:1-18; Psalm 82:1-8; Proverbs 13:2-3

Soul of the Diligent

The soul of a lazy man desires, and has nothing;
But the soul of the diligent shall be made rich.

PROVERBS 13:4 (NKJV)

This proverb is not about being rich materially; it is about being rich spiritually. It answers the important question, why? Why is it that so many Christians are spiritually dry? They do not grow year after year. Why is it that they have no victory? Why don't they know God's Word? Why do they have more fruit of the flesh than fruit of the Spirit? Bottom line: *spiritual laziness.*

Amy Grant sang a song called "Fat Baby." These are the words:

I know a man, maybe you know him, too.
You never can tell; he might even be you.
He knelt at the altar, and that was the end.
He's saved, and that's all that matters to him.
His spiritual tummy, it can't take too much.
One day a week, he gets a spiritual lunch.
He's been baptized, sanctified, redeemed by the blood,
But his daily devotions are stuck in the mud.
He's just a fat, he's just a fat little baby!

So, question: How important is your own personal spiritual life to you really? There is absolutely no richer, sweeter return on an investment of time and energy than to be hungry and thirsty for righteousness. God himself makes us a wonderful promise: "The soul of the diligent shall be made rich." And you can take that to the spiritual bank!

Make It Personal . . . Live It Out!

Every day at the bottom of the page is the *One Year Bible* reading for the day. Through the years I have heard people say, "Oh, I tried reading with a schedule, but I gave up after a while." Hebrews 5:12 challenges us to grow up: "For though by this time you ought to be teachers, you need someone to teach you again the first principles of the oracles of God; and you have come to need milk and not solid food" (NKJV). Spiritual maturity only comes to those who learn to eat the manna of God's Word for themselves. Don't just rely on teachers to spoon-feed you. Will you try again? There are some valuable lessons in today's reading that will challenge you and feed you and help you to grow.

One Year Bible Reading

Joshua 9:3–10:43; Luke 16:19–17:10; Psalm 83:1-18; Proverbs 13:4

My Heart, Christ's Home

The righteous hate what is false,
but the wicked bring shame and disgrace.
Righteousness guards the man [or woman] of integrity,
but wickedness overthrows the sinner.

PROVERBS 13:5-6 (NIV)

To hate what is false—have you ever thought about how valuable it is—actually, how truly life changing and character building it is to develop a viable, clear, tangible hatred of falsehood? It is righteousness that guards our integrity, whereas wrong tears us down.

First and foremost, we need to hate anything and everything that lurks in the corners and closets of our own souls that is false and wrong. I love the little booklet *My Heart—Christ's Home*, by Robert Munger. It pictures your heart as a house. Jesus comes and walks into each room. And as he does, the light floods in. He then lets you know what is not right. Honestly, has it been a while since you asked him to do that for you? When we see things in our hearts as he sees them, it is the first step to wanting and asking him to set us free and cleanse us from whatever is false and wrong.

Next we look outward; we need to hate the false and wrong in this world. Compromise is not a part of godly living. James 4:4 asks us an important question: "Don't you know that friendship with the world is hatred toward God? Anyone who chooses to be a friend of the world becomes an enemy of God" (NIV).

Make It Personal . . . Live It Out!

The dearest idol I have known,
Whate'er that idol be,
Help me to tear it from Thy throne,
And worship only Thee.
—WILLIAM COWPER

Let's Pray

Lord, I truly do want for my heart—my entire life—to be your home. I am painfully aware I have let little compromises crowd you out. I long to be a woman of integrity and to live as a testimony that you who have begun a good work in me will complete it. Thank you that you never give up. In Jesus' name, amen.

One Year Bible Reading

Joshua 11:1–12:24; Luke 17:11-37; Psalm 84:1-12; Proverbs 13:5-6

Pretending

Some who are poor pretend to be rich;
others who are rich pretend to be poor.

PROVERBS 13:7

This proverb gives us two ends of the bad stick of being obsessed with appearances and money.

First Timothy 6:10 tells us that "the love of money is a root of all kinds of evil, for which some have strayed from the faith in their greediness, and pierced themselves through with many sorrows" (NKJV).

Pretending to be rich is a trap. First of all, who cares? Big deal! The state of many people's finances right now is the end result of thinking it is a big deal. We got caught up in thinking "bigger is better." You buy a bigger, nicer house, then your old furniture and car look shabby. So you need to upgrade your clothes, and your kids need everything new and the latest. That put many people running the rat race, and there is a trap—for the rat—in that. There is!

If you're a child of God and if you fell into the trap of living beyond your means by buying on credit, you're probably feeling very desperate right now. This is a hard lesson. I ask you to learn it and *never forget it*. Before God, ask him to break you of judging the value of people by the car they drive or the house they live in.

In Luke 12:15 Jesus warned, "Watch out! Be on your guard against all kinds of greed; a man's life does not consist in the abundance of his possessions" (NIV).

Make It Personal . . . Live It Out!

We are familiar with people who live above their means for show, but does anyone who is rich chose to live like the poor? So glad you asked. Jesus was the Prince who lived like a pauper. He made "Himself of no reputation, taking the form of a bondservant, and coming in the likeness of men. And being found in appearance as a man, He humbled Himself and became obedient to the point of death, even the death of the cross" (Philippians 2:7-8, NKJV). Somebody asked me one day, "Why would he do that?" Good question. He did it for love's sake. When was the last time you thanked him for this amazing love?

One Year Bible Reading

Joshua 13:1–14:15; Luke 18:1-17; Psalm 85:1-13; Proverbs 13:7-8

April 17

The Problem of Pride

Pride only breeds quarrels,
but wisdom is found in those who take advice.

PROVERBS 13:10 (NIV)

Pride is the topic today. Question: Do you really understand the nature of pride? It's so easy to see it in other people when they're bragging excessively about themselves or putting others down. But pride is more complicated than that. Pride doesn't always manifest itself in outward boasting. Sometimes pride takes the version of just digging in its heels. Of self-preservation at all costs. Of arrogance: no one is going to prove them wrong. This is called "stubborn pride."

Stubborn pride is really a sentence of death—emotionally, relationally, and even spiritually. It is exactly the opposite of having a soft, receptive, teachable spirit. Stubborn pride won't forgive, because everything is everyone else's fault. Stubborn pride is not a team player, because it's "my way or the highway." If a wife thinks she must always win, the husband becomes defeated. If a mother never listens to her kids' side of the story, the kids build their own world and shut her out. Stubborn pride is stuck. It isolates you.

So, dear sisters, let's be honest. Don't make this little discussion about everyone else but ourselves.

God himself has some wonderful advice in 1 Peter 5:5: "Yes, all of you be submissive to one another, and be clothed with humility, for God resists the proud, but gives grace to the humble" (NKJV).

Make It Personal . . . Live It Out!

Pride magnifies everything that is wrong with others and at the same time minimizes anything that is amiss in ourselves. That is why pride breeds quarrels. Do you bicker with your husband? Bottom line: you are irritated at not just one thing, but many. Therefore, you are never dealing with just one moment of conflict; you are piling up ten years of annoyance and reacting to it all. This is not wise. When we do that, it makes us very hard to live with. You need to clear the slate. That's not just what I say, but that is what God says: "First forgive anyone you are holding a grudge against, so that your Father in heaven will forgive your sins, too" (Mark 11:25).

One Year Bible Reading

Joshua 15:1-63; Luke 18:18-43; Psalm 86:1-17; Proverbs 13:9-10

Dishonest Gain

Wealth gained by dishonesty will be diminished,
But he who gathers by labor will increase.

PROVERBS 13:11 (NKJV)

When our nation was founded, children learned to read by reading the Bible. If the Bible were still taught in social studies and business 101 classes, the present economic crisis in our country and in our homes could have been averted.

Look at this proverb again: "Wealth gained by dishonesty will be diminished, but he who gathers by labor will increase." This gives us a solid, clear perspective on long-term financial stability.

Wealth gained by dishonesty is buying into a Ponzi or pyramid scheme. Everyone knows that for those on top to win, those on the bottom will lose. Wealth gained by dishonesty is cheating on your taxes. It's falsifying your credit application to buy more than you can afford. It's wrong, and for us as Christians, it is out of bounds. Parents, don't let your kids gain when they use shortcuts either; it erodes integrity and responsibility.

Recently I overheard a discussion between a mom and her teenage son at the store. He was trying to wear her down to buy him a new sweater. She told him that he could spend his own money. But he didn't have enough. She reminded him that he hadn't earned money because he hadn't mowed the lawn, and he knew it. A few moments later, they left the store without the sweater. Good job, mom. Your son needs a good work ethic more than he needs a new sweater. That mom loved her son enough to not cave in.

Make It Personal . . . Live It Out!

"He who gathers by labor will increase." Are you in debt? Are you struggling to get by? Let me introduce you to an amazing resource: daveramsey.com. He has lists of ways to save money and get out of debt. Here are just three you can do right away.

- Cut up your credit cards. Shred 'em. Burn 'em. Drop 'em in a trash compactor. You'll never get out of debt until you stop making debt a way of life.
- Put cash in envelopes marked for specific areas. You spend less money when you use cash.
- Listen online to *The Dave Ramsey Show*. Dave helps millions of people find hope with their money. His advice will help you, too.

One Year Bible Reading

Joshua 16:1–18:28; Luke 19:1-27; Psalm 87:1-7; Proverbs 13:11

God's Waiting Room

Hope deferred makes the heart sick,
But when the desire comes, it is a tree of life.

PROVERBS 13:12 (NKJV)

A hope deferred is a hope that is postponed. It's when we hope that something will happen, and it doesn't happen when we hoped it would happen. It takes longer—sometimes much, much longer.

If you're a mother of a prodigal child, you know only too well the heartache of this painful waiting, watching, hoping. You long for that moment when your child "comes to himself" and comes back into a restored relationship with both you and God.

But may I give you a good word? Don't hope for a shortcut. Sometimes just to have our children back and safe and comfortable, we would gladly settle. This means that we don't always have their souls and their relationship with God as our primary concern. We want them back. We don't want to see them suffer even for their own sin. We bail them out and enable their wrong behavior. But may I say to you, I know your heart breaks, but let it break over their broken relationship with the Lord more than the sorry state of their circumstances. I have seen parents come to a fresh wind of patience and hope when they shift their desire and their prayers there.

Lord, however, whenever, whatever it takes to bring my child back, let them come home to you first.

Then and only then, grieving parent, when that desire is fulfilled, it will then be for both of you truly "a tree of life."

Make It Personal . . . Live It Out!

Waiting—oh, the agony of waiting! Are you single, wondering if God has forgotten you? Are you in a difficult marriage or longing to have a child? God's waiting room can be very lonely. On the other hand, it can be the place where you become more desperate for God than you have ever been.

Let's Pray

Lord, there is no one who understands the longing of my heart like you. I am ashamed that I have been angry at times and shut you out. Help me to trust you more and to be satisfied that you can fill this longing with yourself.

One Year Bible Reading

Joshua 19:1–20:9; Luke 19:28-48; Psalm 88:1-18; Proverbs 13:12-14

Think before Acting

A person with good sense is respected;
a treacherous person walks a rocky road.
Wise people think before they act;
fools don't and even brag about it.

PROVERBS 13:15-16

This proverb clearly paints the picture that living foolishly, carelessly, thoughtlessly has hard consequences. It is a bad way to live.

And so today I'd like to talk to moms. Every child is going to make mistakes. They're going to leap before they look. It's part of immaturity and inexperience. But if the sympathetic side of you always wants to pad them from the bumps so they never experience the painful consequences of their choices, they gain nothing. In fact, since being careless is easier if they get away with it, it reinforces the weak side of them and trains them to say, "So what?"

But if, while they still live under your roof and while most of their consequences are not "life threatening," you do let them experience some painful results of their mistakes, the lessons will stick with them much longer. If they realize that the next time they spend their lunch money on a CD, no one's going to bail them out, it might—no promises, but it just might—make them think. They might learn the old principle, "Don't do the crime if you can't do the time."

So let your daughter spend all her allowance on one expensive pair of jeans, but don't bail her out when she has no money for tennis shoes or lip gloss. You both will find out no one died, really.

Make It Personal . . . Live It Out!

Wise people think before they act. It's our own responsibility to be responsible. No one is going to show up and manage our lives for us. You know the old saying: "Failing to plan is planning to fail." So, let me challenge you to honestly look at one area that you feel you are not managing well. Have you ever sat down specifically and talked to God about it? I love to sit down with a notepad. In prayer, I ask the Lord questions and ask him to give me a plan. Then—the important part—I quiet my heart to listen. Will you try it? You'll be pleasantly surprised.

One Year Bible Reading

Joshua 21:1–22:20; Luke 20:1-26; Psalm 89:1-13; Proverbs 13:15-16

Faithful Messenger

A wicked messenger falls into trouble,
But a faithful ambassador brings health.

PROVERBS 13:17 (NKJV)

Here we have a formula regarding two kinds of messengers. Of course the one that is rebuked in this proverb is the wicked one. So who is that? Who is a wicked messenger? First of all, a messenger is one who passes along a message about someone or something. And a wicked person is someone guilty of sin against God or man.

So the wicked messenger is someone who *knowingly distorts* information. I will apply this to us women in the body of Christ. As Christians, we're all held accountable. So I know I have shared this before, but here are five guidelines that can dramatically help us keep our words in check and our message Christ honoring. When we pass along information, especially about others, we need to ask ourselves

- Is it true? Are we sure?
- Is it fair? Are we fairly representing someone? Or are we slanting the facts a little to make them look bad, or ourselves good?
- Is it kind? Would you want someone to say this about you?
- Is it necessary? *Really?* Is it necessary that I say this? Some things are better left unsaid.
- Here is a big, very insightful, must-ask-yourself question: Do you have any ulterior motive for saying this about someone else?

Make It Personal . . . Live It Out!

The second part of our proverb today lands on a positive note: "But a faithful ambassador brings health." Let's commit to using our words today to build up and encourage.

Let's Pray

Lord, help me be an ambassador for you. Help me to cheer someone up. Help me to shine your light. Is there someone going through a hard time that you can give a helpful, hopeful promise from your Word? Show me how to build up my children in their faith. Give me insight. Show me if they are struggling. Help me be a messenger of your gospel today, telling someone you love them.

One Year Bible Reading

Joshua 22:21–23:16; Luke 20:27-47; Psalm 89:14-37; Proverbs 13:17-19

Companion of Fools

He who walks with the wise grows wise,
but a companion of fools suffers harm.

PROVERBS 13:20 (NIV)

Ladies, never underestimate the importance and power of personal influence. Therefore, women of God, make your choice of inner-circle, close friends very, very carefully.

The warning is, if your friends are foolish, willfully, consistently, unrepentantly foolish, it's going to rub off on you and cause you trouble.

So what are some foolish patterns that close, even Christian friendships sometimes allow? Let me suggest two areas: compromise and criticize. When you're with friends, do you ever give each other courage to compromise? What about that chick flick that was funny but trashy? What about books or magazines that you loan to each other or the way that you dress?

Number two: criticism. Do you allow yourselves to gripe to each other? Do you gripe about husbands, kids, family, friends, church, bad habits, bad friendship? Trust me: these things do add up and have bad results.

On the other hand, those who walk with the wise will become wise. Are there some godly women in your church? They might not have time to be buddies with you or disciple you, but if they're in Bible study and prayer meetings, go be around godly women. If there's an amazing Sunday school teacher, ask if she needs an assistant. Read Christian biographies. Even in print, wise and wonderful people can influence us with rich, wise insight.

Make It Personal . . . Live It Out!

Do you have an unhealthy friendship? What do you do—drop that friend? Do you tell her she is a bad influence? Hold on; before you say anything, will you take five days to faithfully pray for her? As you pray, the Lord might show you ways to redirect your relationship. The next step might be to honestly tell your friend that the Lord has convicted you about some of the things you do or have talked about. Then you can invite her to be your prayer partner to pray once a week. If she is a friend who was meant to be, the Lord will prepare her heart beforehand. Instead of losing a bad friend, you both might gain a wise and godly one.

One Year Bible Reading

Joshua 24:1-33; Luke 21:1-28; Psalm 89:38-52; Proverbs 13:20-23

Dare to Be Diligent

He who spares the rod hates his son,
but he who loves him is careful to discipline him.

PROVERBS 13:24 (NIV)

Discipline—what is discipline? The dictionary states that it is "training that develops self-control, character, and orderliness." So discipline—whether it involves a time-out, or docking of allowance, or staying home from a fun event—has a point. Biblical discipline is not just to punish; it is to train children—to mold and guide from wrong, hurtful patterns so they can learn to make good choices for themselves.

If that is true, why would any parent not want to discipline? Well, I think it's because it's hard; it takes discipline on our part.

We moms sometimes feel that little fear that if we don't give in to our kids' wishes and whims even when they throw tantrums, they are not going to love us.

Some think kids need their parents to be lenient buddies. *No! No!* Kids need trainers, not enablers. If there is no discipline when they hit their sister or lie to their teacher or steal from the candy counter, they don't have a negative experience to break them from doing it again. They got away with it. A child that lies to his teacher will later lie to his boss or to his wife.

So moms, discipline, but be careful and prayerful. Ask God to give you the right penalty for that child for that particular offense at that moment. Discipline is not one size fits all.

Make It Personal . . . Live It Out!

Being a mother is complicated. Just when you figure out how to raise your toddlers, they are school age, then teens, and then adults. But there is one thing you can always do for them that they will never grow out of: you can pray. These two books will ignite you to be a prayer warrior for your children: *Every Child Needs a Praying Mom*, by Fern Nichols (founder of Moms in Prayer International, formerly Moms In Touch) and *The Power of a Praying Parent*, by Stormie Omartian. Prayer connects the resources of heaven to our desperate needs here on earth.

Let's Pray

Lord, give me fresh passion to worry less and pray more for my children, entrusting them to you.

One Year Bible Reading

Judges 1:1–2:9; Luke 21:29–22:13; Psalm 90:1–91:16; Proverbs 13:24-25

Wise Women Build

The wise woman builds her house,
But the foolish pulls it down with her hands.

PROVERBS 14:1 (NKJV)

The wise woman builds. To build is to construct. It is a constructive process, taking parts and pieces, fitting them together. To build up is to make strong and healthy. But to tear down is to break down, beat down, destroy, and ruin.

Wise or foolish, a builder or tearer? The question is for each of us. Who are we? And then, who do we really want to be? This applies to married women and single women, moms and grandmas, old and young. Your house is your life, your home, relationships, integrity, your purpose for living, your life in Christ, and your testimony for Christ. As I wrote these things down, I thought, *Wow, these are the important things.*

Piece by piece I had to honestly ask myself the questions, *Have I chipped away by neglecting an important relationship or letting a little hurt linger? Have I been foolish or stubborn or lazy? Have I allowed something in my heart to linger that I know is not good or healthy or pleasing to God?*

Two pictures, two end results. Each involves not just one big choice, but a thousand little, daily choices. So, child of God, to be wise or to be foolish? That is the question. And the wonderful thing is, we get to choose.

Make It Personal . . . Live It Out!

Some women make the tragic mistake of tearing down their children's father to them or in front of them. They don't see how this tears down the child's own sense of worth. Recently a man in our church was told by his daughter that he was not invited to her wedding. Although the parents have been divorced twenty-five years, her mom refused to let him walk the bride down the aisle or even attend the ceremony. This decision was selfish and foolish.

Let me ask you a question: Are you tearing down your house? If you are, right now is the best time to pause and take it to God.

Let's Pray

Lord, please forgive me for the ways I have been selfish and foolish and for the times I have torn down. I know you can restore the years the locusts have eaten (see Joel 2:25), so please help me to build and redeem.

One Year Bible Reading

Judges 2:10–3:31; Luke 22:14-34; Psalm 92:1–93:5; Proverbs 14:1-2

Don't Sweat the Mess

Where no oxen are, the trough is clean;
But much increase comes by the strength of an ox.

PROVERBS 14:4 (NKJV)

I've always liked this practical little proverb. It makes a simple statement about realities of life.

First of all, if you've ever been around cattle, you know they leave a mess. It's a lot of work to take care of farm animals. You have to shovel manure and feed them and harness them for work. So the first part of the proverb says if you don't have an ox, you don't have any cleanup. But then who is going to pull the wagon or the plow?

Okay, so how does this apply to us? I can think of a lot of applications. First of all, it applies to people. A lot of people complain about other people. Some say, "Well I'd like to find the perfect church, but there are just too many imperfect people there." That's right. If we could just get rid of all of those people, you wouldn't have to vacuum the classrooms or clean the bathrooms. You would never have any issues to resolve. You wouldn't have to have prayer meetings or Bible studies or Christmas plays. All those things are a lot of work. In fact, you could just have empty buildings with nobody making any messes anywhere.

Or we could realize that we need each other. People are worth it. We do need to love each other and bear each other's burdens. Children in the halls, fingerprints on the doors—it's all good. All these things are signs of life, and yes, they're worth it.

Make It Personal . . . Live It Out!

Moms, when your kids are still at home, don't sweat the small stuff; redeem the time. Although Pam Tebow has a journalism degree, she chose to be a homeschool mom raising five kids. She was faithful to teach them to memorize Scripture. There must have been many days when the housework suffered as she did lessons and meals and drove kids to sports games. The Tebow family came into the spotlight when their youngest son, Tim, won the Heisman Trophy. When Tim Tebow wore John 3:16 under his eyes, millions of people googled it to find out what it means. Good job, Mom Tebow.

One Year Bible Reading

Judges 4:1–5:31; Luke 22:35-53; Psalm 94:1-23; Proverbs 14:3-4

Mockers Find None

The mocker seeks wisdom and finds none,
but knowledge comes easily to the discerning.

PROVERBS 14:6 (NIV)

The mocker. Who are the mockers in this world, and why is it they can actually seek and study, but true wisdom eludes them? Why is that? Wealth, intelligence, age, or education can't grant you either maturity or wisdom. Again, why is that?

Bottom-line reason is that mockers mock God. They mock moral absolutes. They mock the Bible and call it unreliable, although they've never read it. They mock their need for a savior because they mock the concept of sin. It's interesting that many mockers will deny that there is a heaven or a hell, but if asked where they will go when they die, they will say, "Heaven." They might have a bumper sticker that says, "Save the whales," and also one that says, "Protect the right to abort." *Hmm* . . . Save a whale, kill a baby? But of course this makes perfect sense to them. Does it not seem strange that many who reject the Bible will pick up a book with a conglomeration of New Age fables like *The Secret* and think it's profound? Why is that? Because "the mocker seeks wisdom but finds none."

So what is the true key to unlocking the storehouses of wisdom, knowledge, and discernment? The fear of the Lord.

Proverbs 9:10 tells us, "The fear of the LORD is the beginning of wisdom, and the knowledge of the Holy One is understanding" (NKJV).

Make It Personal . . . Live It Out!

Many people wonder why they don't understand or enjoy the Bible. They read the words, but don't receive the same comfort and hope they hear others talk about. Do you feel like that? First Corinthians 2:14 tells us, "The natural man does not receive the things of the Spirit of God, for they are foolishness to him; nor can he know them, because they are spiritually discerned" (NKJV). The Bible is a spiritual book. Jesus promised us that the Holy Spirit will guide us into all truth. Will you give it a try again by reading Psalm 95? Before you do, pause, still your heart, and ask the Holy Spirit to open God's Word up and show you his treasures.

One Year Bible Reading

Judges 6:1-40; Luke 22:54–23:12; Psalm 95:1–96:13; Proverbs 14:5-6

April 27

The Prudent Plan

The wisdom of the prudent is to give thought to their ways,
but the folly of fools is deception.

PROVERBS 14:8 (NIV)

Giving thought to our ways—now that is a good idea! The Hebrew word for "way" is *derek*. It means "road, course of life, or mode of action." It includes our habits and lifestyle. It's not just *what* we do day to day. It's how we do it, why we do it, when we do it, and where it leads us.

This makes me think of a wonderful Scripture, Psalm 37:23 (NKJV): "The steps of a good man [or woman] are ordered by the LORD."

I love this. This means that we don't have to think out our plans alone. The Lord is offering to be actively involved. That's why—I can't say it enough—that's why it's a tragic and foolish habit to waste a perfectly good day by not starting it out with time in God's Word, at his feet, talking to him, letting him talk to you. I often keep a little notepad to make a running list of things I feel the Lord brings to mind. Often things come up that were not even remotely what I might have thought of. Sometimes it really makes me smile, the little divine detours I sense he puts on my heart.

So, child of God, in this crazy, off-course, upside-down world, don't live a life of randomness. Acknowledge the Lord in all your ways, and he will truly direct your steps (see Proverbs 3:6).

Make It Personal . . . Live It Out!

Today was a great day for me. I started the morning by asking the Lord to help me make a "get-to-it list." I wrote down twelve things I'd been putting off for the last few weeks. I did not let myself move on to some things I wanted to do until I crossed off the last one.

Will you get out a pad, take a moment, and ask the Lord to help you make a list of things that have been nagging you? Then set a deadline. Tackle the first one. And keep going until the last one is done. Then you can reward yourself with a cup of tea and a cookie. Yep, sometimes we need a little positive reinforcement too!

One Year Bible Reading

Judges 7:1–8:17; Luke 23:13-43; Psalm 97:1–98:9; Proverbs 14:7-8

Make Amends

Fools mock at making amends for sin,
but goodwill is found among the upright.

PROVERBS 14:9 (NIV)

I once read a sharp remark by an atheist stating, "If a Christian is forgiven for stealing a cow, his neighbor is still left without his cow."

Wrong! I hope we as Christians don't really live like this atheist thinks we live. That would be wrong.

I am so thankful that the Lord has forgiven us, paying the penalty for the guilt, presence, and power of sin. But of all people, we are to live above reproach. Whenever and however possible, we are to pay our debts, and we are to make amends.

If you borrow our neighbor's lawn mower and it breaks, fix it. If you borrow somebody's car, fill it up with gas when you give it back. If you borrow an egg, pay it back with two. If you hurt someone's feelings and you know it, don't just ask God to forgive you, tell them you're sorry. Ask them to forgive you too. Really, it's good for you and good for them.

In Texas they call this "mending fences." In Missouri they call this "making it right."

In the Bible, Jesus called it, "Whatever you want others to do to you, do also to them" (see Matthew 7:12). And it's also called "loving your neighbor as yourself." Because "goodwill is found among the upright."

Make It Personal . . . Live It Out!

All right, let's really bring this home to roost. The religious leaders in Jesus' time made religious excuses for not helping their parents. Jesus told them that was wrong. We also can get so caught up in our activities at church or with our kids that we neglect important things like "honor your father and mother." That's a command. If your parents are getting older, it is your God-given assignment to help them. I know it's not easy, but God didn't say it would be easy; he just taught us that it is right.

One Year Bible Reading

Judges 8:18–9:21; Luke 23:44–24:12; Psalm 99:1-9; Proverbs 14:9-10

April 29

When Wrong Seems Right

There is a way that seems right to a man,
But its end is the way of death.

PROVERBS 14:12 (NKJV)

This proverb could be the headline of today's newspaper. We are a society of people who think we can make up the rules as we go. But in reality, because we're breaking God's laws, it's killing us.

But now let's apply this proverb not just to the external godless world around us, but to our own personal internal worlds. This may surprise you, but I feel that the Lord wants us to apply this principle to bitterness. Yes, bitterness. Bear with me on this.

"There is a way that seems right to a man, but its end is the way of death." Somehow (in a distorted way) we sometimes think that retaining anger, unforgiveness, and bitterness is the right way. We think it's right because it seems to protect our rights.

Here's how it happens. We get hurt or angry. We then nurse that emotion because someone did wrong, and that *was* wrong. So we relive it over and over. But the Bible warns us that this becomes a root of bitterness that defiles many, and so it does. It affects our thought lives, our personalities, our relationships, and because it's disobedience to God, it affects our relationships to him.

So the moral of this is be kind, tenderhearted, forgiving just as God for Christ's sake forgave you (see Ephesians 4:32). This is the right way—right for us and right for others.

Make It Personal . . . Live It Out!

Can you say, "Yes, I have allowed bitterness to ruin my life"? Would you like to break free? In Matthew 5: 44 (NKJV) Jesus gave an amazing formula. If you truly try it, it is guaranteed to give you victory.

1. Love your enemies.
2. Bless those who curse you.
3. Do good to those who hate you.
4. And pray for those who spitefully use you and persecute you.

Now, I find this impossible to do going from one to four. So I work the formula backwards, meaning the first step to victory for me is number four: pray. Once I start praying for the person, the Lord softens my heart. Then he shows me some way to bless the person, and eventually I find the ability to love.

One Year Bible Reading

Judges 9:22–10:18; Luke 24:13-53; Psalm 100:1-5; Proverbs 14:11-12

Heartache

Even in laughter the heart may ache.

PROVERBS 14:13 (NIV)

I love the tender acknowledgement of heartache in this proverb. We are all very complex, aren't we, especially us as women? We women multitask even with our emotions. There are many women all around us carrying a world of grief. They may look fine on the outside, but sometimes just one inch below the surface they have a broken heart.

My friend has a son who she fears is living on the streets. Seldom an hour goes by that she doesn't worry if he's cold or hungry or in danger. Outwardly she presses on, goes to work, goes to church; yet her heart aches.

Another friend has an alcoholic husband. Life at home is harsh and lonely. She's worried about the future. She silently slips into church, sits in the back row and sings the songs, but inwardly her heart aches.

When the checker at the store is slow, or you hear yelling in the apartment next door, or your coworker is irritable, don't just respond with impatience or annoyance. Maybe, just maybe, behind the masks they wear, just one inch deep, their hearts ache.

Isaiah 53:3 tells us that Jesus was "a Man of sorrows and acquainted with grief" (NKJV). This reminds me that when he looked into the eyes of the hopeless single mom or the struggling teenager, he didn't just see their pain, he felt it.

"Lord, please give me, give us, eyes to see the pain and to care and to be a source of your sweet comfort and hope."

Make It Personal . . . Live It Out!

Does your heart ache? Can any good ever come from suffering? John Kohlenberger, a gifted scholar, was diagnosed with advanced cancer. As a scholar, he had kept himself away from people. But his illness transformed his relationships. Instead of superficial contacts, he developed deep close bonds with others going through cancer. "My only regret," he said, "is that it took me fifty years to get here and that it took cancer to open my eyes." Cancer, caring for a handicapped child, or widowhood puts you in a "club" with others going through similar hardship. Will you look around and see who needs you to pray for them and give them words of comfort and hope?

One Year Bible Reading

Judges 11:1–12:15; John 1:1-28; Psalm 101:1-8; Proverbs 14:13-14

May

Scan this code for audio devotionals
or visit www.tyndal.es/wisdom.

Don't Believe Everything

A simple man believes anything,
but a prudent man gives thought to his steps.
A wise man fears the LORD and shuns evil,
but a fool is hotheaded and reckless.

PROVERBS 14:15-16 (NIV)

First of all, our proverb says that the simple believe anything. Here's a very important principle. Just because you have a negative thought, you don't have to believe it. Refuse to overthink and overimagine.

Ladies, let's apply this to the foolish tendency that we as women sometimes have called "jumping to conclusions." We sometimes immediately assume the worst. We all know how this happens in our heads. Your husband is late from work, your friend cancels a lunch date. You don't get a Mother's Day card. You jump to conclusions. You assume that nobody cares about you.

So, secondly, the prudent give thought to their steps. They are not hotheaded or reckless. When you find you have jumped to a negative conclusion, try this: take it to the Lord. Ask him to give you perspective. Ask him to show you what's true and to give you grace and wisdom to respond wisely. A moment of prayer can save you hours of anxiety. You'll be surprised how quickly the Lord softens your viewpoint and gives you peace when you pray. Others will be surprised how you're becoming easier to get along with, and that's a good thing.

Make It Personal . . . Live It Out!

Let's continue with the topic "a simple [woman] believes anything." Not only do we believe negative things about others, but sometimes we believe negative things about ourselves. Have you thought, *I can never change*, or, *I can never be completely forgiven for my past*? Do you worry and believe the worst will happen? Do you sometimes believe God doesn't care? These are lies; don't believe them. Herbert Lockyer, author of *All the Promises of the Bible*, calculated there are over eight thousand promises in Scripture. You need to become a "promise believer." Let me list a few to look up, write down, and believe with all your heart:

- Feeling alone? Hebrews 13:5
- Weary? Galatians 6:9
- Needing provision? Psalm 37:25; Philippians 4:19
- Afraid? Psalm 23:4; Isaiah 41:10

One Year Bible Reading

Judges 13:1–14:20; John 1:29-51; Psalm 102:1-28; Proverbs 14:15-16

Short-Tempered

Those who are short-tempered do foolish things,
and schemers are hated.

PROVERBS 14:17

Short-tempered. This means "cranky, in a bad mood."

Ladies, do your kids ever say about you, "Oh, you know Mom. She's in one of her moods"? That means, "Stay away from her. You might get hurt." A short-tempered mom screams at her child in the grocery store. She swats at him in anger. She says mean and demeaning things to him. A short-tempered wife bites her husband's head off in front of the kids or in front of others. If he lost the keys or makes a wrong turn, she says, "Can't you ever get anything right?" No, silly woman. You're the one who is not getting it right. That is uncalled for, and it is foolish.

The second part of this proverb says that schemers—those who are crafty—are hated. What does that mean? Well, being crafty is being sneaky, conniving. This includes making snide remarks and little put-downs or undermining others.

I know. All of this sounds like I'm being very harsh and critical about women who are harsh and critical. Well, I am.

The point is that unless we see these things for what they are in ourselves, we will always live short of who the Lord created us to be. Always remember: we are created to be women of honor and grace, reflecting his loving character to others.

Make It Personal . . . Live It Out!

What is another name for *short-tempered*? Impatient. One day I found myself being very impatient. I had to ask myself why. Honestly, I could see right away that it was selfishness. I was only thinking of what I needed and wanted to get done, and that made other people's issues seem less important. Ouch! Have you been short-tempered and impatient? Do you steam inside, do you vent?

Let's Pray

Lord, when those moments come, when impatience rises, put a check on my heart. Help me to see I might be making a mountain out of a molehill. Help me to take a breath, slow down, and give the situation to you.

One Year Bible Reading

Judges 15:1–16:31; John 2:1-25; Psalm 103:1-22; Proverbs 14:17-19

Kindness to the Poor

The poor are shunned even by their neighbors,
but the rich have many friends.
He who despises his neighbor sins,
but blessed is he who is kind to the needy.

PROVERBS 14:20-21 (NIV)

Today's proverb has two parts. The first tells us how it often is, but the second part tells us how it should be.

When Jesus taught us about life, he spoke about abundant life, but then he clarified the definition of *abundant*. He taught that the giving life is the rich life.

First John 3:17-18 says, "But whoever has this world's goods, and sees his brother in need, and shuts up his heart from him, how does the love of God abide in him? My little children, let us not love in word or in tongue, but in deed and in truth" (NKJV).

Here is how Jesus describes an amazing scene in Matthew 25:31, 34-40: "When the Son of Man comes in His glory, . . . He will sit on the throne of His glory. . . . Then the King will say, . . . 'Come, you blessed of My Father, inherit the kingdom: . . . for I was hungry and you gave Me food; I was thirsty and you gave Me drink; I was a stranger and you took Me in; I was naked and you clothed Me. I was sick and you visited Me; I was in prison and you came to Me.' [When they ask, 'When did we do that, Lord?'] the King will answer, . . . 'Assuredly, I say to you, inasmuch as you did it to the least of these My brethren, you did it to Me' " (NKJV).

Make It Personal . . . Live It Out!

Matthew 25 shows us that in eternity there will be a great award ceremony. But unlike the Academy Awards, it will not be for the rich and the famous. I think we'll all be surprised that some of the big, seemingly monumental accomplishments will only get honorable mention. The small, quiet, tender, compassionate acts of kindness will receive a personal thank-you from the King of kings. I want to hear that, don't you?

Let's Pray

Lord, forgive me when I shun the poor. Don't let me miss the moments that are all around me to touch someone's life with kindness, filling a need or easing a burden. In your name and for your sake, amen.

One Year Bible Reading

Judges 17:1–18:31; John 3:1-21; Psalm 104:1-23; Proverbs 14:20-21

Talk Is Cheap

All hard work brings a profit,
but mere talk leads only to poverty.

PROVERBS 14:23 (NIV)

Bottom line, girls: talk is cheap. We can apply this to every facet of our lives. Let me say that there is virtue and profit from doing our best, going the extra mile. But dragging around, putting things off, calling everything a chore is just a bad way to live.

So let me ask: Are there three areas in your life you would like to improve? Me too! It's time for spring cleaning; so let's write them down, and let's get to it—because talk is cheap.

Do you have a closet in your house you need to declutter? Write it down. Set a date: "Next Saturday declutter front hall closet." Don't put it off. Get to it. You'll love the results, because "all hard work brings a profit."

Maybe you need some spring cleaning in a relationship. Don't put it off. Ask the Lord to give you one tangible step to build a bridge with someone. Sometimes it's hard to be the first one to take that step, but remember: our proverb today says, "All hard work brings a profit."

And how about spring cleaning in your spiritual life? How about decluttering a negative habit? How about reading a psalm a day for the next week? You know what they say: "If there's dust on your Bible, there's dirt in your life."

All hard work, though, brings a profit.

Make It Personal . . . Live It Out!

Did you know that in most churches 10 percent of the people do 90 percent of the work? If you are not involved in serving in some way at your church, chances are you also don't feel very connected. There is no better way to build deep, lasting friendships within the body of Christ than to roll up your sleeves and jump in. There are thousands of little jobs that have to be done. Volunteer to help with vacation Bible school preparations. Join the cleaning crew or the hospitality team that makes coffee, do hospital visitation, or be part of prayer chain. Remember: all hard work brings a profit.

One Year Bible Reading

Judges 19:1–20:48; John 3:22–4:3; Psalm 104:24-35; Proverbs 14:22-24

A True Witness

A true witness delivers souls,
But a deceitful witness speaks lies.

PROVERBS 14:25 (NKJV)

This is a sober, serious, and yet exciting proverb. On the one hand, it tells us that one of the reasons people are deceived and are believing all kinds of crazy, destructive things is because there are those who are lying to them. That's right! I like it when there is a clear, easy-to-understand diagnosis.

This is what Paul wrote in 1 Timothy 4:1-2: "The Spirit clearly says that in latter times some will abandon the faith and follow deceiving spirits and things taught by demons. Such teachings come through hypocritical liars, whose consciences have been seared as with a hot iron" (NIV).

On the other hand, our proverb today says that a truthful witness saves souls. In Acts 20:26-27 Paul said, "I declare to you today that I am innocent of the blood of all men. For I have not hesitated to proclaim to you the whole will of God" (NIV).

Is there someone whose soul you really care about? Jesus said that truth is what sets people free (see John 8:32). Will you pray right now about sending them a Gospel of John, e-mailing them with a Scripture like John 3:16, or telling them you would like to share your testimony with them sometime?

After all, a truthful witness saves souls.

Make It Personal . . . Live It Out!

First Peter 3:15 tells us, "Always be prepared to give an answer to everyone who asks you to give the reason for the hope that you have. But do this with gentleness and respect" (NIV).

Are you afraid to share your faith? You don't know where to start? Bill Faye wrote a book called *Share Jesus without Fear*. He suggests conversation starters that I have used to talk to complete strangers in airplanes, on ski lifts, in hospitals, all over. My favorite question to start with is "Do you have any spiritual beliefs?" It's funny: people may pause for a moment, but then they proceed to tell me their thoughts. If you listen prayerfully and carefully, you will know where to go from there. You have broken the ice.

One Year Bible Reading

Judges 21:1—Ruth 1:22; John 4:4-42; Psalm 105:1-15; Proverbs 14:25

Strong Confidence

In the fear of the LORD there is strong confidence,
And His children will have a place of refuge.

PROVERBS 14:26 (NKJV)

In other words, those who have an awesome reverence for God the Father, Jehovah, are safe and secure and bold—not because they have confidence in themselves, but because they have an awe and an unshakable trust in the God who loves them.

Romans 8:15-17 reminds us, "You did not receive the spirit of bondage again to fear, but you received the Spirit of adoption by whom we cry out, 'Abba, Father.' The Spirit Himself bears witness with our spirit that we are the children of God, and if children, then heirs, heirs of God and joint heirs with Christ"(NKJV).

Recently I watched a YouTube video with Michael W. Smith leading a huge crowd to sing "Our God Is an Awesome God." Over and over again they sang the same stanza. As I watched the faces, each worshiper seemed to sink into some really deep place. Eyes were closed; hands were lifted. Strength and peace seemed to envelop everyone. Maybe you, too, need to reflect on these words and let them wash over your soul to give you confidence and hope.

Our God is an awesome God.
He reigns from heaven above
with wisdom, power, and love.
Our God is an awesome God.

Make It Personal . . . Live It Out!

Our proverb today speaks of strong confidence and a place of refuge. If you are battling fear right now, these words are just what you need. We often think we will never have peace and confidence unless our circumstances change and our problems are solved. But as it's been said, peace is not an absence of problems; it's the presence of God. Jesus said, "In the world you have tribulation and trials and distress and frustration; but be of good cheer [take courage; be confident, certain, undaunted]! For I have overcome the world. [I have deprived it of power to harm you and have conquered it for you.]" (John 16:33, AMP). Those are pretty strong words, spoken by a very strong Savior. Will you trust him? Will you allow him to give you peace?

One Year Bible Reading

Ruth 2:1–4:22; John 4:43-54; Psalm 105:16-36; Proverbs 14:26-27

Unload Your Guns

He who is slow to wrath has great understanding,
But he who is impulsive exalts folly.

PROVERBS 14:29 (NKJV)

Wrath is a flare-up. In the Old West they called this having a trigger finger. Shoot first; ask questions later. Ladies, this happens when you have a loaded gun. So let's get to the bottom of the real issue: wrath inside you.

The real underlying cause, if we are really honest, is unresolved anger, unforgiving anger. If you have unresolved anger, it's like the molten lava of an inactive volcano. You might think because it's cooled down, it's contained. But if you are quickly hurt or quickly annoyed or quickly offended or quickly angered, you might need to rethink the bottom line. Remember, she "who is slow to wrath has great understanding." By understanding ourselves, we can take responsibility, and we can take it to the Cross. Unresolved anger may have started with the sin of someone else, but now it's become sin in you. Once we are honest, we can be healed. "If we confess our sins, He is faithful . . . to forgive us . . . and to cleanse us from all unrighteousness" (1 John 1:9, NKJV). And this, my friend, is unloading your guns.

Make It Personal . . . Live It Out!

The definition of *wrath* is "violent rage, fury, any action carried out in great anger." If you grew up in an angry home, you know exactly what that looks like. Worse yet, you know what that feels like. I am so sorry. As a little girl, you knew it was wrong. In the book of Leviticus, laws were given to govern God's people. It was a legal system that had zero tolerance for cruelty. God hates the innocent to suffer. Sin is the source of all cruelty and suffering in the world. That's why God hates sin: because he loves you. As you go to bed tonight, may the God of all comfort wash away the memories and heal the pain of your past.

"My comfort in my suffering is this: Your promise preserves my life" (Psalm 119:50, NIV).

One Year Bible Reading

1 Samuel 1:1–2:21; John 5:1-23; Psalm 105:37-45; Proverbs 14:28-29

Envy

A heart at peace gives life to the body,
but envy rots the bones.

PROVERBS 14:30 (NIV)

Envy, that wicked scoundrel, envy. Envy shoots at others and wounds itself.

I really like what Henrietta Mears said: "The man [or woman] who keeps busy helping the one below him won't have time to envy the one above him."

Let me tell you a sad little story. Leonardo da Vinci was Italy's most celebrated artist. He was asked to submit sketches for the decorations of the Great Hall of Florence. A then young and little-known artist, Michelangelo, was also asked to submit.

The sketches of Leonardo were superb, in keeping with his genius. But when the councillors saw the sketches of Michelangelo, there were expressions of wonder and enthusiasm. News of this reached Leonardo. He also heard that someone said, "Leonardo is getting old." Sadly, Leonardo was never able to get over this. His remaining years of life were clouded with gloom and sorrow.

When I read this I wanted to say, "Noooooooooo!" But it's true. Philippians 2:3-4 gives us the beautiful antidote: "Do nothing out of selfish ambition or vain conceit, but in humility consider others better than yourselves. Each of you should look not only to your own interests, but also to the interests of others" (NIV).

Make It Personal . . . Live It Out!

Columnist Charley Reese wrote, "If malice or envy were tangible and had a shape, it would be the shape of a boomerang." That's a great visual. Now let's plug in positive words: "If kindness or generosity were tangible and had a shape, it would be the shape of a boomerang." This version is equally true. The Bible teaches that you reap what you sow. So let's not let the petty, small-hearted attitude of envy ever get the better of us. When it peeks its creepy green face in your thoughts, be proactive. The best weapon is to quickly speak kindly of the person you envy and quickly chose to lift your attitude to God. Refuse to entertain an envious thought, and the thought will lose its power.

Let's Pray

O Lord, please catch me quickly when jealousy rises. Give me victory to resist and to conquer with good.

One Year Bible Reading

1 Samuel 2:22–4:22; John 5:24-47; Psalm 106:1-12; Proverbs 14:30-31

An Eternal Perspective

The wicked are crushed by their sins,
but the godly have a refuge when they die.

PROVERBS 14:32

Life sometimes gets so hard, we can be tempted to ask, is it worth it? Is it worth it to resist evil and seek first the kingdom of God and his righteousness? If you are feeling weary right now, let's take a peek into the wonderful promises that God gives us of our future.

Paul said in Romans 8:18, "For I consider that the sufferings of this present time are not worthy to be compared with the glory which shall be revealed in us" (NKJV). As our proverb says, when they die, the godly have a refuge. In John 14:3 Jesus said, "I go and prepare a place for you, . . . that where I am, there you may be also" (NKJV).

The apostle John reported, "I saw a new heaven and a new earth, for the first heaven and the first earth had passed away. . . . [God] will dwell with them, and they shall be His people. . . . God will wipe away every tear from their eyes; there shall be no more death, nor sorrow, nor crying. There shall be no more pain, for the former things have passed away" (Revelation 21:1-4, NKJV).

As the old gospel hymn says, "Heaven is a wonderful place, filled with glory and grace. I'm gonna see my Savior's face, 'cause heaven is a wonderful place."

Make It Personal . . . Live It Out!

An eternal perspective is not a picture of "pie in the sky" or wishful thinking. Heaven is a real place. The joys that await us there will indeed far outweigh the hardships and sorrow we face on this earth. As Amy Carmichael said, we have all eternity to enjoy our rewards, and only a few short years to win them.

Let's Pray

O Lord God, help me to redeem the time and to be a good steward of all you have given me here on earth. Let my troubles remind me to cling loosely to this world and long for the day of your return to take me home to be with you.

One Year Bible Reading

1 Samuel 5:1–7:17; John 6:1-21; Psalm 106:13-31; Proverbs 14:32-33

Sin Disgraces a Nation

Righteousness exalts a nation,
but sin is a disgrace to any people.

PROVERBS 14:34 (NIV)

My first trip to a former communist nation was to Bulgaria in 1993. I was surprised at how receptive the people were and how happy they were to meet Americans. But I also remember how sad I was to see that posters of Madonna and pornographic magazines were the newest imports from the United States. I was ashamed. It was a disgrace to a nation that was once founded on godly principles.

So, what is going to happen to us as a nation? You can't look at even one facet of our society that is not in trouble with one big bottom line: sin.

Dr. Ironside said it so clearly in his commentary on this proverb: "History is but the perpetual illustration of what is here declared. Nations, like individuals, are judged according to their ways. No country has prospered long that forsook the path of national righteousness. When pride and vanity, coupled with greed and cruelty, have been in the ascendant, the hour of humbling was not far away."

Righteousness exalts a nation; so personally let's follow God's clear and simple path to restoration: "If My people who are called by My name will humble themselves, and pray and seek My face, and turn from their wicked ways, then I will hear from heaven, and will forgive their sin and heal their land" (2 Chronicles 7:14, NKJV).

Make It Personal . . . Live It Out!

Economic solutions, political maneuvering, and social programs are not the answer to the woes of a nation in crisis. Never have been, never will be. In today's *One Year Bible* reading from 1 Samuel, the people came to the prophet Samuel and said, "Appoint a king to lead us, such as all the other nations have" (1 Samuel 8:5, NIV). God gave them a tall, handsome man, Saul. But Saul was weak spiritually and ethically. The nation suffered. Will you shift your hope and energy to the only program that can make our nation great again? Will you humble yourself, seek God's face, truly repent and pray? Will you pray with your family? Will you pray with your friends? Will you pray to our great God to heal our great land?

One Year Bible Reading

1 Samuel 8:1–9:27; John 6:22-42; Psalm 106:32-48; Proverbs 14:34-35

A Soft Answer

A soft answer turns away wrath,
But a harsh word stirs up anger.

PROVERBS 15:1 (NKJV)

I really, really love this proverb. It's just brilliant! It's one of those truths that, once you get it, can help you for the rest of your life.

A *soft answer* is a gentle answer. Peter Marshall prayed, "O God, when I'm wrong, make me easy to change, and when I am right, make me easy to live with." That's a very good prayer for us.

My grandmother used to say, "You can draw more bees with honey than with vinegar."

A soft answer, I think, is in most cases a short answer. In an awkward or tense situation, less is more. It's kind of like the statement, "What if they waged a war, and nobody showed up?" When someone says something that could stir you up, don't bite the bait. Send up an arrow prayer: quickly ask the Lord to give you grace and wisdom and gentleness to navigate and not agitate. *Lord, help me be an instrument of your peace, and help me bite my lip and hold my tongue.*

I made a list of four soft answers. Try them out. Say them softly and sincerely and just see if they help.

- Say, "I'm sorry. Please forgive me."
- Say, "Thank you. Thank you so much."
- Say, "How can I help? What can I do?"
- People love it when you ask, "Tell me, what do you think?"

Make It Personal . . . Live It Out!

I just got a very unkind e-mail. Awwww! My first reaction was to hit the reply button and write back exactly what I thought. But before I sent it, I stopped and prayed, "O Lord, this hurts. I need to answer these harsh words, don't I? Shouldn't I try explain my side?" I could sense a simple, direct answer to my heart: "No, it won't help. They don't want to listen right now." I know it's true. So, by the grace of God, I will leave it in his hands. How about you? Next time you feel in a hurry to answer a critical e-mail, will you wait and pray before you hit the send button? You won't regret harsh words if you do not write them.

One Year Bible Reading

1 Samuel 10:1–11:15; John 6:43-71; Psalm 107:1-43; Proverbs 15:1-3

Words of Healing

The tongue that brings healing is a tree of life.

PROVERBS 15:4 (NIV)

We live in a hurting, wounded world. Jesus lived surrounded by a world of hurt too. I just love that day that he walked in the synagogue, picked up the scroll of Isaiah, and read these words: "The Spirit of the Lord is on me, because he has anointed me to preach good news to the poor . . . [and] proclaim freedom for the prisoners" (Luke 4:18, NIV).

This is our message too. We do have the words of hope for a lost and dying world. We do.

We have been given the ministry of reconciliation. So we need to speak it out. I'm over sixty now, and you know what? I love it. I feel that I can, without reservation, go up to someone—a total stranger who looks sad—and tell them with full confidence God loves them. I can give them a Gospel of John and tell them with full confidence it can change their life. I can talk to a young woman struggling with sin and with full confidence tell her that sin will destroy her life. With surrender, Christ can set them free. Words do have power.

In our ministry we began to go to orphanages in Russia. We love to take gifts and crafts and have fun with the children. But also I feel it's vital to talk to them about the wonderful promises of God found in the Word of God. Because "the tongue that brings healing is a tree of life."

Make It Personal . . . Live It Out!

Do you need healing? Life can be very painful. You need words that bring you comfort and hope. Let me recommend three books that will give you insight and encouragement. The first is written by Philip Yancey: *Where Is God When It Hurts?* Another book I recently discovered is *Grieving the Loss of Someone You Love*, by Raymond R. Mitsch and Lynn Brookside. The third, of course, is the book of Psalms.

One Year Bible Reading

1 Samuel 12:1–13:23; John 7:1-30; Psalm 108:1-13; Proverbs 15:4

True Treasure

There is treasure in the house of the godly,
but the earnings of the wicked bring trouble.

PROVERBS 15:6

Isaiah 33:6 tells us, "Wisdom and knowledge will be the stability of your times, and the strength of salvation; the fear of the LORD is His treasure" (NKJV).

Five years ago the status symbol was a new car and a big house at any cost, but I just heard that the new status symbol is to be debt-free. Funny how times change. I'm glad that it's time to rethink the definitions of *rich* and *treasure*.

Let me tell you a little story I read in *Chicken Soup for the Woman's Soul*. A wise woman was traveling in the mountains and found a precious stone in a stream. The next day she met another traveler, who was hungry. The wise woman opened her bag to share her food. The hungry traveler saw the precious stone in the wise woman's bag, admired it, and asked her to give it to him. The wise woman did so without hesitation. The traveler left, rejoicing because he knew the jewel was worth enough to give him security for the rest of his life. But a few days later he came back, searching for the wise woman. When he found her, he returned the stone and said, "I've been thinking. I know how valuable this stone is, but I give it back to you in the hope that you can give me something much more precious. If you can, give me what you have within you that enabled you to give me that stone."

This little story redefines the definition of *treasure*.

Make It Personal . . . Live It Out!

"There is treasure in the house of the godly." What are your greatest treasures? I have several friends who have very loved, worn, shabby Bibles. They have hundreds of notes written in the margins and even a few tearstains on the pages. They have specifically written one of their children's names inside the cover of each so that Bible will be given to that child when the mother dies. If you have children or grandchildren, this is a wonderful tradition. Will you invest your labor and love in the things that will outlive you?

One Year Bible Reading

1 Samuel 14:1-52; John 7:31-53; Psalm 109:1-31; Proverbs 15:5-7

Delighted in Prayer

The LORD hates the sacrifice of the wicked,
but he delights in the prayers of the upright.

PROVERBS 15:8

"The LORD hates the sacrifice of the wicked." Those are pretty strong words. So why? Why would he? A sacrifice would be something given, seemingly, to the honor of God. But for him to hate it, there must be something amiss. Maybe there are strings attached. Maybe it's a cover-up for unrepentant sin, a hidden agenda. Or is it really not given to God at all, but so the giver would be honored—like the hypocrites? Jesus said, "Assuredly I say to you, they have their reward" (Matthew 6:2, NKJV). So even if they gave a million dollars, if all they wanted was applause from others, they'll never get any applause from heaven. On the other hand, it might surprise them and you that the Lord just loves it when we pray. Imagine that!

So maybe you wish you could do great things for God. Maybe you feel you're small and insignificant. Maybe you wish your tithe check were bigger. Don't you worry. "God loves a cheerful giver" (2 Corinthians 9:7, NKJV), and he blesses our gifts and efforts. But the truth is, he doesn't need them. It's you he's after. That's why he loves it when you come to him in prayer. He loves it when you talk to him, when you ask his opinion, when you look to him for strength and comfort. He loves prayer—because he loves you.

Make It Personal . . . Live It Out!

I believe that God is calling his people back to be people of prayer. Do you have prayer partners whom you pray with regularly? Do you go to the prayer meetings at your church? Do you take a moment in your day to just be alone with the Lord and pray? Some people think that prayers are the gifts we give God. But actually, prayer is the gift he gives us. Will you still your heart right now? I love to slip to my knees; it helps me put my entire being in a position of reverence before him. Will you simply call upon your Father who is in heaven and cast all your care upon him?

One Year Bible Reading

1 Samuel 15:1–16:23; John 8:1-20; Psalm 110:1-7; Proverbs 15:8-10

The Shadow of Death

Death and Destruction lie open before the LORD—
how much more the hearts of men!

PROVERBS 15:11 (NIV)

I don't know if there's anything more mysterious to us as mortals than death.

A few years ago I visited a lady in Australia who had just a few weeks to live, and she knew it. As we chatted, I asked her, "Carmen, do you know what happens one minute after you die?"

She said, "I have no idea."

Here she was so close to eternity, and yet it was a complete mystery.

I've never been so glad to be able to open the Word of God right then and read to her the description of heaven. I then read and explained to her how she could go there. Then I asked her the question, "Carmen, is there anything that could keep you from saying yes to God's gift of salvation right now? Would you like to say yes, asking for forgiveness for your sins and receiving the Savior into your heart?"

She said yes. Death and destruction had been lying before her, but she chose life.

I'll never forget that day with Carmen. She died physically a few weeks later, but the Lord knew her heart. He knew that what she needed most was not a few more days on this earth. She needed a Savior.

Maybe as you read this today, you need to know that the Lord knows your heart too, and he loves you with an everlasting love.

Make It Personal . . . Live It Out!

Death is a mystery to all of us. Like Carmen, many have no idea what lies on the other side of that thin veil that separates life here from eternity. Fear of death lingers in the back of many people's thoughts. If someone you love is terminally ill or has died, or if you have a serious illness, only God's living and powerful words can lift your sorrow. Will you turn to Psalm 23 and read it aloud? As you do, picture the the Lord walking you through your sorrow. "The LORD is my shepherd, I shall not want. . . . Yea, though I walk through the valley of the shadow of death, I will fear no evil; for You are with me" (Psalm 23:1, 4, NKJV).

One Year Bible Reading

1 Samuel 17:1–18:4; John 8:21-30; Psalm 111:1-10; Proverbs 15:11

Frowns Make Wrinkles

A glad heart makes a happy face;
a broken heart crushes the spirit.

PROVERBS 15:13

Did you know you use an average of forty-three muscles for a frown, but you only use an average of seventeen muscles for a smile? Every two thousand frowns creates one wrinkle. So let's figure this out. If you frown ten times a day, you will get two new wrinkles almost every year.

So, ladies, never underestimate the power of joy. It's good for you. It's good for your face, and it's good for those around you. In fact, the Bible tells us that "the joy of the LORD is your strength" (Nehemiah 8:10) and "a cheerful heart is good medicine" (Proverbs 17:22).

God never meant us to be gloomy, negative Christians. Have you ever noticed that the first three fruits of the Spirit listed are love, joy, and peace? Can you imagine if those were the traits that you were known for? Can you imagine?

So let me give you a key that my husband taught me long ago, which will entirely cheer up a gloomy attitude.

Thankfulness. One day when I was very discouraged, he came behind me and sang a little song: "Count your blessings. Count them one by one. Count your many blessings. See what God hath done." I have to admit, I didn't really want to cheer up. I wanted to keep my little frump, but in spite of myself, I couldn't shake that little song, and the song brought little pictures of blessings with them, and they brought a smile.

Make It Personal . . . Live It Out!

Are you in a frump? Eeyore (Winnie the Pooh's friend) always looked at the downside of any situation. Have you been doing that? I do that sometimes too. Then I remember: "The joy of the LORD is your strength." Moping around only makes you feel like moping around. Let's break up that dark cloud hanging over your head with a "count your blessings" list. In the margin on this page, write down seven blessings in your life. Go ahead—do it now. Then thank the Lord for each one. Come on. Don't you see? Life has rays of joy for you. You do have reasons to smile.

One Year Bible Reading

1 Samuel 18:5–19:24; John 8:31-59; Psalm 112:1-10; Proverbs 15:12-14

Best Things in Life

Have you opened the newspaper the last few days and the front page had nothing but bad news? Our proverb for today is written "for such a time as this." It's all about looking on the bright side even when times are tough. It's been said, "Suffering is inevitable, but misery is optional." So read it carefully, dear child of God. This is good for our souls.

All the days of the oppressed are wretched,
but the cheerful heart has a continual feast.
Better a little with the fear of the LORD
than great wealth with turmoil.
Better a meal of vegetables where there is love
than a fattened calf with hatred.

PROVERBS 15:15-17 (NIV)

My friend just had a new grandbaby. I gave her a picture frame with the inscription "The best things in life are not things."

Let me share a story that illustrates this. My husband grew up in a very poor home, but his mom had a big open-heart/open-door policy. Even though she had nine kids herself, there was always room at her table for somebody else. There were young Marines on weekends and neighbor kids after school.

George remembers eating oatmeal every single morning of his childhood, but to add variety, his mom occasionally put in food coloring. One day it was green. Another day it was orange. Their home was living proof that it is better to have a bowl of oatmeal where love is than to have bacon and eggs where love isn't.

Make It Personal . . . Live It Out!

"Godliness with contentment is great gain" (1 Timothy 6:6, NKJV). Do you believe that? Even if your kids don't have all the material things you would like to give them, do you believe they can still have a great childhood? They can. Invite your kids' friends over for game night with popcorn and brownies. Guaranteed, they will have as much fun as they would on an expensive outing. Teen girls love to make crafts and cupcakes. And how about you? If your budget is too tight for dinner out, make a candlelight dinner for your husband after the kids are in bed. Or invite some girlfriends over for a soup-and-salad potluck and an old black-and-white, classic movie.

One Year Bible Reading

1 Samuel 20:1–21:15; John 9:1-41; Psalm 113:1–114:8; Proverbs 15:15-17

Patience Calms Quarrels

A hot-tempered man stirs up dissension,
but a patient man calms a quarrel.

PROVERBS 15:18 (NIV)

Extended families really are a gift from God. I know some people that have nobody in this world—no cousins, or sisters, or Uncle Harrys. But as we know, wherever there is a mix of people, things sometimes get messy: misunderstanding, hurt feelings, petty jealousy.

In Genesis 37 we read the story of Joseph. He's always been one of my favorite characters. He was young, handsome, and his father's favorite, too. But sadly, the other brothers knew it. Then when their father Jacob made Joseph a beautiful new coat, it was insult added to injury. It was visual evidence that Dad loved Joseph more. One thing led to another. Their anger became more than a quarrel. It almost became murder.

Well, for 90 percent of this story Joseph is an amazing example of integrity, faithfulness, and patience, but I just wish in the beginning when they were all young, he had played things differently. I wish he had not flaunted his coat or his dream. I wish he had not brought his father a bad report about his brothers.

But then again, he was just seventeen years old. Twenty-two years later, when he had become older and wiser, he truly was a beautiful example that a patient man can calm even a very old quarrel.

Make It Personal . . . Live It Out!

Some relational storms do not die down quickly; they take patience—sometimes lots of patience. If we are in a hurry and force people to "get over it," we just might make matters worse. We need to let people calm down. But at the same time, we need to stay calm, forgive, and keep the door open. Is someone you work with hot tempered? Or do you have a hot-tempered neighbor, teenage son, or brother-in-law? The important principle for us is, *keep calm*. Don't get riled up too; that just contributes to the trouble. Keep calm, pray, be patient. Ten years from now no one will even remember what the quarrel was about.

One Year Bible Reading

1 Samuel 22:1–23:29; John 10:1-21; Psalm 115:1-18; Proverbs 15:18-19

Honor Father and Mother

A wise son brings joy to his father,
but a foolish man despises his mother.

PROVERBS 15:20 (NIV)

A wise son is our topic today. Moms, if you're raising a son right now, you have a wonderful and yet incredibly challenging responsibility. We cannot—we must not—raise our kids randomly. We must have well-defined, godly, and God-given objectives.

Most of us would like our kids to be healthy, wealthy, and wise. But if you could only choose one out of three, would wisdom be your first choice? I'm just asking.

Yes, of course, I know: we as moms cannot make our sons or daughters become anything. They have their own first choices. But we can create an atmosphere where wisdom is honored above athletic skill or even academic achievements, because it's been said, "You can get all As and still flunk life."

Do you teach your son to honor older people, to honor his grandparents, his pastor? Do you hold him accountable? Do you teach him to keep his word? Do you talk about integrity and honesty and noble behavior and purity?

And moms, do you pray for your sons? The world, the flesh, and the devil are seeking to destroy them. Will you stand in the gap by praying on your knees?

Make It Personal . . . Live It Out!

"Honor your father and your mother, that your days may be long upon the land which the LORD your God is giving you" (Exodus 20:12, NKJV). God's instruction is clear and universal. We as mothers, we as daughters, we as women of God need to honor God by taking this very seriously too. May your children never see you be rude or hateful to your parents, even when provoked. It erodes their sense of duty about honoring you. Teach your daughter to notice how her boyfriend treats his mother. It is a sign of how he values motherhood. And lastly, be a woman of honor in all areas: it will make it much easier for your children to honor you.

Let's Pray

Lord, help me to be faithful to your command to honor my own parents. Help me not be irritated when they are needy or forgetful. May my honor of them be an honor to you.

One Year Bible Reading

1 Samuel 24:1–25:44; John 10:22-42; Psalm 116:1-19; Proverbs 15:20-21

Godly Advice

Plans go wrong for lack of advice;
many counselors bring success.

PROVERBS 15:22

Ladies, this proverb tells us we need others. We need others to give us input, godly counsel, so we don't get tunnel vision.

I'm going to apply this to two different areas: number one, mothering; number two, ministry.

1. Mothering. I have never met a mom who said, "I've got it. I have this mothering thing figured out." Because just when you think you get the hang of navigating a strong-willed boy out of the terrible twos, your older daughter is entering preteen hypersensitivity. So we need friends. We need older, godly moms to give us insight. We need prayer partners. And ladies, we need to be these things for others too.
2. Ministry. Plans, including ministry plans, can go wrong for lack of advice. I love to work with a team. I love to have good, deep prayer before any planning is done. Then I love to sit around a table and hear other women's input and insight. In business this is called participative management. In ministry this is called body life. When others have a say, there's ownership. When there's ownership, people feel they are included and needed. "Many counselors bring success."

Make It Personal . . . Live It Out!

Plans go wrong for lack of advice in lots of areas. There are times when we really need others to give us insight.

- When we are angry or hurt, we can make big decisions in a moment that cause us trouble for years.
- After a loss of someone we love, we sometimes don't know what to do next. So we get frozen and put off important matters.
- We all need some long-range financial planning.

First of all, we need to make sure the first person we consult in all decisions and planning is God. Ask him to direct you. Then be discriminating and prayerful about advice you receive from others. Finally, ask these questions: Is this wise? Is it right? Is it fair to others? Does it line up with Scripture?

One Year Bible Reading

1 Samuel 26:1–28:25; John 11:1-54; Psalm 117:1-2; Proverbs 15:22-23

Adjusting Your Thought Life

The LORD detests the thoughts of the wicked,
but those of the pure are pleasing to him.

PROVERBS 15:26 (NIV)

Our proverb today presents a positive and a negative. This is a classic style of teaching often used in the Proverbs. It's very effective, because when we see two choices side by side, it helps us realize our choices have consequences.

Today's choice deals with our thought lives. God hates it when we fixate on and mull over thoughts that are wrong. It is wrong to dwell on lustful thoughts. It's wrong to have thoughts of malice and revenge. Scientists tell us we think ten thousand thoughts a day, and quite to our dismay, all of us have wrong thoughts come to mind more than we wish.

One way to redirect our thoughts is to have a noble focus to occupy our attention. There is no better motto for life than "I must be about my Father's business" (Luke 2:49, KJV). Even though Jesus had many things thrown at him, he always moved forward with clear, pure motives because he knew his life had purpose. He couldn't waste time getting sidetracked even in his thought life. And neither can you. Pray today that God will give you a mission. Do you love kids or have a burden for the hurting? Are you drawn to the elderly, or teens, or unwed moms? Jump into serving in an area that captures your passion. Learn all you can about how to be more effective in your calling. Then when ugly thoughts come, you can just say, "Go away, I am busy with my Father's business."

Make It Personal . . . Live It Out!

Psalm 1:1-6 is an excellent Psalm to memorize. It paints a word picture regarding how our thoughts shape our actions, and then our life and then our destiny: "Blessed is the man who does not walk in the counsel of the wicked or stand in the way of sinners or sit in the seat of mockers. But his delight is in the law of the LORD, and on his law he meditates day and night. He is like a tree planted by streams of water, which yields its fruit in season and whose leaf does not wither. Whatever he does prospers" (NIV).

One Year Bible Reading

1 Samuel 29:1–31:13; John 11:55–12:19; Psalm 118:1-18; Proverbs 15:24-26

Study How to Answer

The heart of the righteous studies how to answer,
But the mouth of the wicked pours forth evil.

PROVERBS 15:28 (NKJV)

I had a teacher who used to say, "Do not engage mouth before you engage brain." Think before you speak. Better yet, in a delicate situation, pray before you speak. The more you do it, the more you will do it. It becomes a good habit.

This brings us to the whole topic of communication. Oh, how I wish we were all better communicators. Oh, how I wish we would learn to talk things out better. I really think a lot of our conflicts are because of misunderstanding, and since misunderstanding is just human, shouldn't we learn to be better in our response to it? Let's look at some principles to help us break bad communication habits.

- Don't stuff and brood. Women are experts at this. We get our feelings hurt and we stuff it. We simmer under the surface. We overthink it. We then jump to the wrong conclusions. Ladies, let's stop doing that.
- Let's stop talking to everyone else, except the person involved. Nothing is solved by this. We just widen the circle of hurt. So let's do go to the person involved first.
- Let's do pray. Let's do put ourselves in the other person's shoes. Let's do build bridges. And let's do forgive.

In closing: "The heart of the righteous studies how to answer, but the mouth of the wicked pours forth evil."

Make It Personal . . . Live It Out!

We can apply our lesson today to the need to study the person we are speaking to. This involves being an active listener. Pay attention, read body language, listen not just to the words, but the tone and emotions. Whether you are listening to your child, your mother, your boss, or a friend, try to hear people out. If you don't understand, ask them to explain. Rephrase what you think they said, and say it back to them. As you listen, ask the Lord to show you what is going on in the other person's life that is contributing to stress or anger.

Let's Pray

Lord, help me to be a peacemaker. Calm my emotions when I feel hurt or threatened. Then when I do speak, let the words of my mouth please you.

One Year Bible Reading

2 Samuel 1:1–2:11; John 12:20-50; Psalm 118:19-29; Proverbs 15:27-28

Cheerful Joy

A cheerful look brings joy to the heart,
and good news gives health to the bones.

PROVERBS 15:30 (NIV)

If you listen to a lot of news right now, you might start feeling pretty discouraged. What's going to become of us if all these bad things keep happening? Well, Jesus lived in the real world, and the people he spoke to had plenty to worry about then, too. But this is what he said to them and to us: "In the world you will have tribulation, but be of good cheer, I have overcome the world" (John 16:33, NKJV).

In Philippians 4:4 the apostle Paul says, "Rejoice in the Lord always. Again I will say, rejoice!" (NKJV). But wait a minute, Paul. You're writing from a prison cell in Rome. You are there because of trumped-up charges by mean, jealous people. Your traveling ministry has ended. You have nothing but the clothes on your back. And not to mention, you might be facing a death sentence.

So let's listen to what he said again. "Rejoice in the Lord always." That's a really good word for us right now. Circumstances and people may let you down, but the Lord never will. God promised he will never leave you or forsake you (see Hebrews 13:5).

So if you've been dragging, if your children have seen you and your husband fighting and angry over money troubles, if your thought life has been consumed with fear, I have a great prescription for you. Open your Bible to Psalm 27:14: "Wait on the LORD. Be of good courage, and He shall strengthen your heart" (NKJV).

Make It Personal . . . Live It Out!

Laughter and joy can change a cloudy day. When our fourteen-year-old nephew started losing his hair from chemo, his father, grandpa, and uncle all shaved their hair together. They took some fun, silly pictures as the family rallied around him. When my friend Carolyn lost her hair, I went with her to try on wigs. There was one we couldn't resist. It was long and very blonde, and we called it Lola. Silly fun and a blonde wig turned our day into a memory. Are you or someone you know having a cloudy day? A hot fudge sundae, holding a kitten at the pet store, or a cup of tea with a friend might be just what the doctor ordered.

One Year Bible Reading

2 Samuel 2:12–3:39; John 13:1-30; Psalm 119:1-16; Proverbs 15:29-30

Constructive Criticism

If you listen to constructive criticism,
you will be at home among the wise.
If you reject criticism, you only harm yourself.

PROVERBS 15:31-32

Constructive criticism. Is there any such thing? I know most of us just cringe when someone says, "Could I talk to you for a moment?" Especially when we sense that it may be a little talk about something we've done wrong. Maybe this is because we have never had someone who truly loved us enough to come to us and speak truth into our lives, firmly and yet kindly. Most of us are cowards about speaking honestly to others, even when it is breaking our hearts to see them make serious mistakes. Through the years, I have lost a few friends by trying.

But mostly this proverb is addressed to us. We need to be receptive, eager to grow, and eager to repent when confronted with error in our lives. So how can this happen?

- Read God's Word with personal receptivity. James 1:22 says, "Do not merely listen to the word, and so deceive yourselves. Do what it says" (NIV). Every morning I sense the Lord speaking to me. But some mornings, honestly, he has a good talking to me. Is it hard? Yes. Is it good? Yes. It is my heavenly Father, fathering me.
- When others criticize or correct you, keep your skin thick, but your heart soft. Dawson Trotman said, "There is a kernel of truth in every criticism. Look for it, and when you find it, rejoice in its value."

Make It Personal . . . Live It Out!

Our best and most consistent source of constructive criticism will always be the Holy Spirit. Jesus told us that the Spirit's job is bringing conviction for sin and guiding us into truth. So the message to you today is, will you listen? This is how it works: you hear a message on the radio about a topic and it convicts your heart. Then you hear the theme repeated in a message at church, a book someone recommends, a Scripture you read in the morning. God is talking to you. The best thing to do is simply say, "God, I hear you. Please open my ears so I understand and respond and repent. Thank you for loving me enough to not give up."

One Year Bible Reading

2 Samuel 4:1–6:23; John 13:31–14:14; Psalm 119:17-32; Proverbs 15:31-32

May 25

Humility and Honor

The fear of the LORD teaches a man wisdom,
and humility comes before honor.

PROVERBS 15:33 (NIV)

The fear of the Lord is often mentioned in the Proverbs as the pathway to wisdom. So what do you think it means to "fear the Lord"? Many think it's to be afraid of God. Some have a concept of God as the big traffic cop in the sky just waiting to catch us doing something wrong so he can punish us. But nothing could be further from the truth. God loves us. The reason that God hates sin and wants to keep us from it is that it's bad. God knows that sin is not only bad but bad for us.

So then, a proper concept of "the fear of the Lord" is reverence and respect. It is a complete trust and confidence that God's commandments and will for us are to set us free and to keep us safe and bless us. It is basically saying, "God, you are right in all your ways, and, therefore, it's only right and good to completely submit to your loving authority in every facet of our lives." When we choose to view every situation with that perspective, God will give us wisdom for the moment. Really, becoming a woman of wisdom is just the sum total of a thousand daily, wise choices.

"Humility comes before honor." James 4:10 reminds us, "Humble yourselves in the sight of the Lord, and He will lift you up" (NKJV). Now, that's a great promise.

Make It Personal . . . Live It Out!

Are you in a low, humble situation? The story of David in First and Second Samuel is both moving and instructive. He had a call on his life to be the shepherd-king of God's people. His training for that position included being unfairly treated, falsely accused, living in caves, and almost being killed. He had no one to trust or to guide him but God alone. Never underestimate how God can use your present circumstances to deepen you and prepare you for his noble purposes. Be faithful in the small things! Be a servant joyfully and willingly. And trust God with all your heart. Jesus said, "He [or she] who humbles himself will be exalted" (Luke 14:11, NIV).

One Year Bible Reading

2 Samuel 7:1–8:18; John 14:15-31; Psalm 119:33-48; Proverbs 15:33

Divine Shift

Commit your works to the LORD,
And your thoughts will be established.

PROVERBS 16:3 (NKJV)

Ladies, this proverb gives us a wonderful way to live in the midst of a complicated and troublesome world. Let's dissect it for understanding.

First step: "Commit your works." To *commit* means "to hand over, to trust." Our works are our activities, our occupations, what we make, what we do, and even what we own. Can you see it? Sometimes we feel that the weight of the world is on our shoulders, and we are constantly in a precarious balancing act. We need to do what I call the "divine shift." We need to roll it off our shoulders and roll it onto his powerful shoulders. This includes responsibility for our husband or lack of husband, our kids, our finances, our to-do lists, our work, our ministries, everything. We need a mental picture of placing everything entirely into his hands and sensing a great overwhelming load come off our hearts. Can you see that?

The second part of our proverb is a promise. "Commit your works to the LORD, and your thoughts will be established." When we feel our lives are safely in his hands, we have a freedom to live in the present with joy, with a new sense of purpose and destiny.

Psalm 37:4 says, "Delight yourself also in the LORD, and He shall give you the desires of your heart" (NKJV).

Make It Personal . . . Live It Out!

The frequent habit of experiencing the "divine shift" can literally revolutionize your life. Instead of just talking about it, will you pause and actually do it with me right now? Hold out your hands in front of you, palms up, close to your left shoulder. Now visualize the fears, problems, people, and needs that are weighing on your heart and mind today. Pause long enough to realize that the weight of them has made you weary and heavy laden. Are you ready to truly give them to God? Okay then, on the count of three, forcefully sweep your hands in front and up to your right as if you were casting them on the shoulders of the Lord. With joy and determination say, "Divine shift." Now take a deep breath, exhale, and let the peace that passes understanding wave over your heart and mind.

One Year Bible Reading

2 Samuel 9:1–11:27; John 15:1-27; Psalm 119:49-64; Proverbs 16:1-3

The Problem of Pride

The LORD despises pride;
be assured that the proud will be punished.

PROVERBS 16:5

Pride. What is it, and why does the Lord hate it? Pride can be arrogant, overbearing, and haughty.

Of course there's a pride that's good. You should be proud of your children when they do a good job or are obedient or share their toys, but pride can be dangerous when we start living through our children, pushing them to be overachievers for our own self-esteem, or when we boast to others, making them feel that their kids aren't as good as ours. The Lord hates that kind of pride.

The Lord hates pride that won't admit a mistake. The Lord hates pride that won't say we're sorry when we're wrong or when someone's hurt. The Lord hates pride that puts others down, never lets anyone else win, is critical and judgmental.

The Lord hates pride when it builds walls in families, friendships, and churches. A wall of pride keeps us isolated and lonely. So, dear sisters, let's let God melt our foolish, stubborn pride. James 4:6 says, "God opposes the proud, but he gives grace to the humble" (NIV).

Vulnerability is merely letting our imperfection show. It is being real. It is what makes us human, authentic, and lovable.

Make It Personal . . . Live It Out!

I think behind that wall of pride in some people is fear. We are afraid if people really knew how flawed we feel, they would run over us or lose all respect. Moms feel that way sometimes. They are afraid to tell their kids they made a mistake, so once they make a stand they won't listen or back down or say, "I'm sorry." Let me ask you a question. Are you in a standoff situation with your teenager, husband, or someone at work? Are you the one with the wall of pride, or is it the other person, or both? Here's a news flash that might help. If you're the first person to melt the ice, it won't kill you. No, really; it won't kill you. Make a peace offering. A latte and a muffin with a simple note can clear the air and let you both off the "pride hook."

One Year Bible Reading

2 Samuel 12:1-31; John 16:1-33; Psalm 119:65-80; Proverbs 16:4-5

Pleasing the Lord

When the L*ORD takes pleasure in anyone's way,*
he causes their enemies to make peace with them.

PROVERBS 16:7 (NIV)

There are two important parts of this proverb. Part one is to live a life that pleases God. In the early eighties Pastor Chuck Smith's wife, Kay, did an amazing Bible study series called "Pleasing the Heart of God." For me as a young woman and wife and mother, it was life changing. I learned about sweet surrender. I learned about obedience and trust and walking in the light. Thank you, Kay Smith. You not only taught this lesson; you lived it.

And so since she is one of the best examples I know of the first part—living to please the Lord—does her life also fit the second model, regarding peace with enemies? Through the years they've had many friends, but some foes, too. Some have been unkind and unfair.

But in her later years as she spoke of the people in the church, her face lit up. She always shared the sweet memories. Occasionally she would smile and say, "Oh yes, there were a few stinkers, too, but God loves them and so do I."

In a summary statement, are any and all past enemies now at peace with Kay Smith? I would say yes, because they got no traction. They did not have the ability to get her riled or bitter or mean. Her heart stayed at peace. She has been a living testimony that when a woman's ways please the Lord, he makes even her enemies to be at peace with her.

Make It Personal . . . Live It Out!

Do you have an enemy? The Bible teaches us that a soft answer turns away wrath. It instructs us to bless those who curse us, to be kind, tenderhearted, and forgiving. We know what to do, but in the heat of the moment, we fail. Are you feeling that your responses have not pleased the Lord? Condemnation is not the solution. Repentance and dependence are.

Let's Pray

Lord, here I am again. You know my heart is not right regarding this enemy. Please forgive me when I am weak. I come to you for a fresh wind of strength from the Holy Spirit. Put a lock on my tongue and your agape love in my heart.

One Year Bible Reading

2 Samuel 13:1-39; John 17:1-26; Psalm 119:81-96; Proverbs 16:6-7

May 29

Poor and Godly

It is better to be poor and godly
than rich and dishonest.

PROVERBS 16:8

In light of our economic times, this is a valuable truth.

"It is better to be poor and godly than rich and dishonest." I hope you really believe that, because there are some things that money just can't buy. Let's look at some stories of people who made hard choices.

Ruth left her country and relatives to go back to Israel with Naomi. Even though they would go as poverty-stricken widows, she said, "Your people shall be my people, and your God, my God" (Ruth 1:16, NKJV).

Mordecai challenged Esther to take a dangerous stand to save her people, saying, "Who knows whether you have come to the kingdom for such a time as this?" Her reply: "I will go to the king, . . . and if I perish, I perish!" (Esther 4:14, 16).

In Hebrews 11 we're given a wonderful list of people who accepted loss, poverty, even death for their faith and the kingdom. Noah gave up his day job to build an ark. Moses gave up his place in a palace to lead his people to freedom.

Jim Elliot, who was martyred on the mission field, said, "He is no fool who gives up what he cannot keep to gain what he cannot lose."

Paul said in Romans 8:18, "I consider that the sufferings of this present time are not worthy to be compared with the glory which shall be revealed in us" (NKJV)—because "it is better to be poor and godly than rich and dishonest."

Make It Personal . . . Live It Out!

Are you feeling poor today? Sometimes I do. Then I look at the suffering of others. I think of Christians around the world who are suffering for Christ, and I feel ashamed of myself. First Timothy 6:7-9 gives us all a reality check. Will you read it and let the words encourage you that you are richer than you think? "For we brought nothing into the world, and we can take nothing out of it. But if we have food and clothing, we will be content with that. People who want to get rich fall into temptation and a trap and into many foolish and harmful desires that plunge men into ruin and destruction" (NIV).

One Year Bible Reading

2 Samuel 14:1–15:22; John 18:1-24; Psalm 119:97-112; Proverbs 16:8-9

No Double Standards

Honest weights and scales are the LORD's;
All the weights in the bag are His work.

PROVERBS 16:11 (NKJV)

Here's the history of the reference to weights and scales.

People then did not have prepackaged things like we do now. When you went to the market to buy butter or cheese, they weighed it on a scale, and you paid per weight. In Leviticus 19 God said, "Use honest scales and honest weights." Unfortunately, some grocers would use one scale that weighed heavier when they were selling and one that weighed lighter when they were buying. That's just not right, is it?

The New Living Translation puts it this way: "The LORD demands fairness in every business deal; he sets the standard."

So, ladies, how does this apply to us? Well, if you run a business, be fair. Don't cut corners. Don't cheat anyone. I like the policy "Under promise and over deliver."

If you work in a business, give an honest day's work. If you work in day care, treat those children as you would want someone to treat yours. If you work as a cook in a restaurant, handle the food like you would want someone to handle your food.

Some Christians think they can have two lives: one that's lived inside the church and one that is lived outside in the everyday world. Not so. First Corinthians 6:20 tells us, "For you were bought with a price; therefore, glorify God in your body and in your spirit, which are God's" (NKJV).

Make It Personal . . . Live It Out!

God hates double standards. Ladies, we have a double standard when we dish it out but aren't willing to take it. Do you take offense at the smallest things? Are you offended when you feel your needs aren't met, and yet you're not truly sensitive to the needs of others? Let's apply this to your pastor and leaders at your church. You have no idea how many people's needs are constantly on their thoughts. On top of that, they have their own families and personal struggles. Your criticism can cut right to their heart. Will you pray and ask the Lord to show you one way this week to lift them up and let them know you appreciate all they do?

One Year Bible Reading

2 Samuel 15:23–16:23; John 18:25–19:22; Psalm 119:113-128; Proverbs 16:10-11

May 31

Kings Detest Wrongdoing

Kings detest wrongdoing,
for a throne is established through righteousness.
Kings take pleasure in honest lips;
they value a man who speaks the truth.

PROVERBS 16:12-13 (NIV)

Well, ladies, we don't come in contact with very many kings, do we? But we do have people who are our bosses or hold positions of responsibility that we serve under: if you're a teacher, your principal; if you're a waitress, the shift manager; if you work in a hospital, the head nurse. Whoever it is, their lives are miserable when employees under them can't be trusted, but they benefit when they have honest workers.

So this is a great opportunity for us as Christians to live out our faith in God in a practical, consistent way. Jesus said, "Let your light so shine before men, that they may see your good works and glorify your Father in heaven."

Joseph is a great example of this, even when he was unfairly put in prison. Listen to this: "The LORD was with him; he showed him kindness and granted him favor in the eyes of the prison warden. So the warden put Joseph in charge of all those held in the prison, and he was made responsible for all that was done there. . . . The LORD was with Joseph and gave him success in whatever he did" (Genesis 39:21-23, NIV).

Do you see? This warden trusted Joseph really because he *could* trust Joseph. It's a good thing.

Make It Personal . . . Live It Out!

The US Chamber of Commerce estimates that 75 percent of all employees steal at least once; half of these steal repeatedly. One of every three business failures is a direct result of employee theft. These are staggering statistics. If you work in a restaurant, or in retail, or even a doctor's office, the owner of the company has probably seen people betray his trust.

As a Christian in the workplace, you have a great opportunity to "walk the walk" in a tangible way. Be a good steward of your employer's resources. Do a job you weren't asked to do. Help someone else catch up if they're behind. Pray over a task you're working on, asking the Lord to show you if you can do it more efficiently. Even if your boss doesn't notice, the King of kings and Lord of lords does.

One Year Bible Reading

2 Samuel 17:1-29; John 19:23-42; Psalm 119:129-152; Proverbs 16:12-13

June

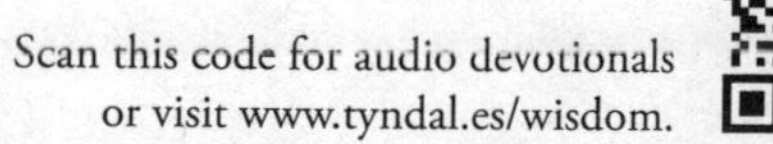
Scan this code for audio devotionals
or visit www.tyndal.es/wisdom.

Appearing Anger

The anger of the king is a deadly threat;
the wise do what they can to appease it.

PROVERBS 16:14

You might wonder what "angry kings" have to do with you. Well, we can look at the "king" as anyone who has a position of power, or authority, or influence in your life or circumstances. This could be a boss, a teacher, a board member. It could be a landlord or even someone in your family.

What then, do you do when such a person is angry? It might not be life-threatening, but we know anger can escalate and cause trouble.

The first thing you need to ask yourself is, *Have I contributed to the problem?* Yes, the "kings" in your life may be unreasonable and hard to get along with, but are you willing to look at your own responsibility? Have you undermined them? Have you given nonverbal signals of disrespect? Have you been slack in doing what they expected and required?

If the answer is yes, then it is the wise and godly thing to do what you can to appease. To appease means to pacify or quiet. Make it right, say you're sorry. Don't just do your job: do more, go the extra mile.

What if their anger is unjustified? Well, the thing is, you are still going to feel the heat of it. Wisdom still recommends that we do what we can to appease.

In either case, you will never go wrong when you begin by praying for them. May God give you insight regarding whatever has made them cranky. And may he give you grace to respond with wise and humble kindness.

Make It Personal . . . Live It Out!

I know women who are married to some very angry men. Is that you? Do you feel you can't do anything to appease his anger? I believe fear and past hurts are often the cause. It seems they vent and almost dare everyone to hate them because they believe they are unlovable. It becomes a self-fulfilling prophecy. How can you survive in such a situation? It is amazing how the psalm selection for today in *The One Year Bible* (Psalm 119:153-176) seems to be written just for you. Will you read it? Let the words give you comfort and hope.

One Year Bible Reading

2 Samuel 18:1–19:10; John 20:1-31; Psalm 119:153-176; Proverbs 16:14-15

Choosing the High Way

Our proverb today gives us an important mental picture. There are two paths in life, and each of us must choose. One path leads upward. Jesus called it the "narrow" way, that leads to life. But the other path is a slippery slope. Each step on that path leads downward. Jesus called it the "wide" way, that leads to destruction.

The highway of the upright is to depart from evil;
He who keeps his way preserves his soul.

PROVERBS 16:17 (NKJV)

Hebrews 12:1 tell us, "Let us lay aside every weight, and the sin that so easily ensnares us" (NKJV).

Dear ladies, the way of the upright is to avoid sin and everything that looks like it and leads toward it. We must develop a discernment, sensitivity, and hatred of sin within our own souls. Each time we feel a pang of jealousy, or resentment, or selfishness, or greediness, or unforgiveness, or pride, we must see it for what it is, and put it to death.

I once knew the most wonderful Christian woman who was lit up with her zeal and love for the Lord, but she let herself get hurt in a situation and became angry with another leader in her church. She wouldn't forgive. Then she became angry at others who didn't join her negative view. Her light has gone out. Yes, she is still busy with ministry things, but her light has gone out. She let her resentment linger, and it led her to the low road.

Make It Personal . . . Live It Out!

It's been said, the right way to live is to live right. So, let's get to it! I want to challenge you today to ask God to help you choose "the highway of the upright."

Read Philippians 4:4-8. Have you been worrying about everything, but praying about nothing? Stop and pray right now, lifting your burdens to God. Has it been a while since you sincerely thanked God? Pause to praise and thank him specifically for three things. Has your world been far from peaceful? Let his peace fall upon your heart and settle you. Have you been brooding over something someone did that hurt you? Ask God to wash your thoughts today and replace them with good things.

One Year Bible Reading

2 Samuel 19:11–20:13; John 21:1-25; Psalm 120:1-7; Proverbs 16:16-17

Destructive Pride

Pride goes before destruction,
and a haughty spirit before a fall.

PROVERBS 16:18 (NIV)

What a sober, serious, and important warning this is for us, dear sisters.

Pride is an overrated opinion of oneself. It is thinking you are always right or better or more important than someone else.

So how does this attitude cause destruction? Well, it does destroy relationships. Pride treats others like their feelings or wishes or opinions don't matter; only your feelings and wishes and opinions matter.

Pride can destroy our marriages. Ladies, we can start thinking and treating our husbands like they can't do anything right or say anything right. Lest we don't recognize how we communicate this, let me give you three signals we sometimes use to them.

- "Fine." We say, "Fine," to end an argument. This is our signal we are right, and they need to shut up.
- Loud sigh. This is actually a word. A loud sigh means you consider them hopeless, and you have given up on them.
- We can use the words "I'll do it myself." This means that only we can do it right.

Yes, "Pride goes before destruction" because "If mama ain't happy, ain't nobody gonna be happy."

Make It Personal . . . Live It Out!

Conflict in relationships is inevitable. It's what we do with it that matters. Here are some good guidelines.

- Don't be sarcastic or exaggerate. How do you like it when someone does that? You don't. So don't.
- Timing—don't start a serious discussion when you are tired, hungry, or in a hurry.
- Chose a place to talk that is comfortable for both of you. If you are in a public place, don't make a scene.
- Remember the goal is not to trump the other person. The goal is resolution. Keep aiming at the goal. Build some positive, affirming statements into your conversation.
- Admit your mistakes. Sincerely apologize.
- Try to find a win-win you both can live with.

One Year Bible Reading

2 Samuel 20:14–21:22; Acts 1:1-26; Psalm 121:1-8; Proverbs 16:18

Simple Childlike Trust

Our proverb today is about the sweetness of simplicity. The fast track, get ahead, me-first life has crashed all around us. For us as Christians it's time to return to the basics of humility, receptivity, and simple trust in the Lord.

It is better to live humbly with the poor
than to share plunder with the proud.
Those who listen to instruction will prosper;
those who trust the Lord will be happy.

PROVERBS 16:19-20

"It is better to live humbly." *Better* is such an ordinary word. Normally I wouldn't bother to look it up, but listen to the definition. *Better* is "pleasant, excellent, valuable, glad, happy, prosperous, and kind." It's incredible that all this good comes when we are happy and contented with the low, humble places and things in life.

Jesus talked about the high seats and the low seats one day. He said the Pharisees always make sure that they get the best seat at all times. Really? That's a lot of work. All the time you're comparing. All the time you're working things to your advantage.

But remember that day they brought young children to Jesus and the disciples wanted to send them away? They must have thought that children were not worth the Savior's time. "But when Jesus saw it, He was greatly displeased and said to them, 'Let the little children come to me . . . for of such is the kingdom of God. Assuredly, I say to you, whoever does not receive the kingdom of God as a little child will by no means enter in it'" (Mark 10:14-15, NKJV). So that's a good word.

Make It Personal . . . Live It Out!

The definition of *simple* is "not complicated, easy to do, not luxurious or elegant." There is truly no better picture of this than a child holding her father's hand. She is safe and free to enjoy the journey. Close your eyes. Can you picture yourself as that little girl with a small hand? Can you picture your Father God holding you and guiding you? "You have not received a spirit that makes you fearful slaves. Instead, you received God's Spirit when he adopted you as his own children. Now we call him, 'Abba, Father'" (Romans 8:15). Will you take a moment to pause, take a deep breath, and lean into your Father's strength and wisdom and love?

One Year Bible Reading

2 Samuel 22:1–23:23; Acts 2:1-47; Psalm 122:1-9; Proverbs 16:19-20

Pleasant Words Promote Instruction

The wise in heart are called discerning,
and pleasant words promote instruction. . . .
A wise man's [or woman's] heart guides his mouth,
and his lips promote instruction.

PROVERBS 16:21, 23 (NIV)

Often we think of wisdom springing from one's head. Being wise is being smart. But wisdom, true wisdom, dwells in the heart. Listen to the beautiful description of godly wisdom in James 3:17, "But the wisdom that comes from heaven is first of all pure; then peace-loving, considerate, submissive, full of mercy and good fruit, impartial and sincere" (NIV).

Our proverb today says, "A wise woman guides her mouth," and it is easy to learn from her. So, moms, one of your primary roles with your children is teaching. We have formal moments of teaching when we help with homework or teach them to make their beds. But be aware, there are a thousand informal teachable moments. They are learning from you all of the time, not just from what you say but how you say it. They learn from what you do and how you do it. They learn how to respond to the disappointments of life from you. What do you do when they drop the ketchup bottle, or the dog chews a shoe, or the dishwasher breaks? Little daily crises. Are we harsh? Do we vent? Do we blame?

If you realize that your words are sending the wrong message, what can you do? You don't need to wash out your mouth. You need to go to the Cross and cleanse your heart.

Make It Personal . . . Live It Out!

If you grew up in a family where scoldings and punishment were more prevalent than kindness and patience, you know in your heart that did not work. Yet we often fall into the habits we learned at home. It's time to break the mold and do things God's way. Learn to be a cheerleader. If others feel you are instructing them for their benefit and that you believe in them, learning is fun. Will you use your words to lift others up? Find something to praise. Lighten up. Give others a break. Let God's wisdom remind you that "pleasant words promote instruction."

One Year Bible Reading

2 Samuel 23:24–24:25; Acts 3:1-26; Psalm 123:1-4; Proverbs 16:21-23

Pleasant Words Are Sweet

Pleasant words are like a honeycomb,
Sweetness to the soul and health to the bones.

PROVERBS 16:24 (NKJV)

Pleasant words. I have to say that there are no words in the universe that have more power for good to us than the very words of God. Jeremiah said, "When your words came, I ate them; they were my joy and my heart's delight, for I bear your name, O LORD God Almighty" (Jeremiah 15:16, NIV).

Sweet words. The Psalms are a source of encouragement and comfort. The Proverbs give us sound, practical advice. The Epistles teach us how to live. Revelation gives us a picture of our eternal future, and the Gospels give us a fresh picture of Jesus.

Let me give you some examples that might be just the sweet, strong words that you need today to give you hope and strength.

Are you weary and discouraged? Do you feel like you just can't go on? God's Word says, "They that wait upon the LORD shall renew their strength; they shall mount up with wings as eagles" (Isaiah 40:31, KJV).

Are you lonely, feeling abandoned? "For He Himself has said, 'I will never leave you nor forsake you'" (Hebrews 13:5, NKJV).

Are you sad? Psalm 34:18 says, "The LORD is close to the brokenhearted and saves those who are crushed in spirit" (NIV).

And, last, are you worried? Are you afraid for the future? Jesus said, "Fear not, little flock; for it is your Father's good pleasure to give you the kingdom" (Luke 12:32, KJV). Remember, "the LORD is [your] shepherd; [you] shall not want" (Psalm 23:1, NKJV).

Make It Personal . . . Live It Out!

I have Scriptures all over my home. And I love to give framed Scripture to others for birthdays, to those grieving, for housewarming gifts, and always to new mothers. When I find beautiful frames at discount stores, I stock up. With all the amazing graphics you can do on the computer, along with scrapbooking supplies, it is easy to print a Scripture and add beautiful embellishments. You can go to my web page, BibleBusStop.com, to download a variety of designs. June is a month when we often give graduation and wedding gifts. Will you add a framed Scripture? Pray over the Scriptures as you give them. It is fun to see Scriptures I have given as gifts displayed in homes many years later.

One Year Bible Reading

1 Kings 1:1-53; Acts 4:1-37; Psalm 124:1-8; Proverbs 16:24

Wrong Seems Right

There is a way that seems right to a man,
But its end is the way of death.

PROVERBS 16:25 (NKJV)

This very same statement is made in Proverbs 14:12. Since repetition is the mother of learning, God must want us to understand this: that "there is a way that seems right to us, but its end is the way of death."

So, ladies, let's think about some of the ways that we might get stuck on thinking we are doing the right thing for us or for our kids, but in the end they will hurt us. Let me list a few.

It might seem right when your kids are in sports and their games are on weekends to miss church during all of baseball season, but the end of that is that your kids become detached from youth group, and they learn that a little plastic trophy is more important than honoring God.

So many single women believe that they will never be happy unless they get married. They think they must compromise morally to win a man, and that any man is better than no man at all.

Some married women think that they can only be happy if their husband changes, makes more money, or they got rid of this husband for another one. So they give up praying for their husbands. They settle for a deadness of the heart.

Sometimes we think our kids would be better off if we worked outside the home to buy them nice things. But we forget kids need a mom more than they need nice things. There are times when it seems right to be rude to your mother-in-law, or watch that racy TV show, or stop tithing when money is tight, because "there is a way that seems right to us as women, but its end is the way of death."

Make It Personal . . . Live It Out!

Can you think of an occasion when you made a decision that seemed good at the time, but it turned out bad? I can. Our human understanding is flawed and shortsighted. That's why it is exciting that God offers to make his wisdom available to us at any time. James 1:5-8 is an invitation and a promise: "If any of you lacks wisdom, let him ask of God, who gives to all liberally" (NKJV). Will you ask him to guide you today?

One Year Bible Reading

1 Kings 2:1–3:2; Acts 5:1-42; Psalm 125:1-5; Proverbs 16:25

Speak No Evil

An ungodly man [or woman] digs up evil,
And it is on his lips like a burning fire.

PROVERBS 16:27 (NKJV)

The New Living Translation puts it this way: "Scoundrels hunt for scandal; their words are a destructive blaze."

Here we look at the damage that the war of words can bring. As children of God, we must honestly look at the picture of what God is calling ungodly behavior.

It's looking for dirt on others. Are you ever eager to hear a bad report about someone else? Do you watch the scandal shows or read the scandal papers? If you hear of the sin of someone, do you ever find an inner satisfaction? That's bad.

Ungodly behavior is spreading the bad news. Are you eager to tell someone else what you know or hear even if you suspect it's only half true? Our proverb today says evil is on an ungodly person's lips like a burning fire.

James 3:6 says, "The tongue is a fire, a world of iniquity. The tongue is so set among our members that it defiles the whole body, and sets on fire the course of nature [life], and it is set on fire by hell" (NKJV).

So what do we do when we hear a bad report about someone, especially if it's a brother or a sister in the Lord? The next question is, what *should* we do?

Let me tell you: the first and sometimes the last person we should ever speak to about it is God himself. We can either be part of the problem, or we can be part of the solution by praying, because "love covers . . . a multitude of sins" (1 Peter 4:8, NIV).

Make It Personal . . . Live It Out!

James 3:9-11, 13 gives us firm warning and instruction about words. We need to post it on our phones and computer screens. Please read the words carefully and prayerfully. "With the tongue we praise our Lord and Father, and with it we curse men, who have been made in God's likeness. Out of the same mouth come praise and cursing. My brothers, this should not be. Can both fresh water and salt water flow from the same spring? . . . Who is wise and understanding among you? Let him show it by his good life, by deeds done in the humility that comes from wisdom" (NIV).

One Year Bible Reading

1 Kings 3:3–4:34; Acts 6:1-15; Psalm 126:1-6; Proverbs 16:26-27

Gossip Separates Friends

A troublemaker plants seeds of strife;
gossip separates the best of friends.

PROVERBS 16:28

Today let's have an honest, heart-to-heart talk about gossip. God hates gossip. Let's lock that in right up front.

First of all, gossip is not helpful. What good does it do to know something bad, especially when you can't do anything about it?

A very clear command of the Lord is to "Do unto others as you would have them do unto you" (Matthew 7:12, KJV). May I ask, What part of gossip, negative talk, critical comments, and slander do you want people to do to you? So think before you speak. What is your motive?

It's not fair. I never want to hear something about someone behind their back. That's not fair. The scriptural pattern is, if there is something wrong, take it to that person privately.

Human nature tends to believe the negative. If you just hear one side to a story, it sticks with you, and you can start to doubt someone you valued or trusted before. Gossip can separate even the best of friends.

So what can we do and what should we do when someone brings up negative gossip? Well, abruptly change the subject. Don't give a listening ear. When someone persists, I have actually left the room, politely but determinedly. And pray, pray that the Lord corrects the wrong, and pray that the Lord will wash your heart and make you a vessel of words of grace, not words of gossip and garbage.

Make It Personal . . . Live It Out!

Are you wondering why there are so many proverbs that address slander and gossip? Maybe it's because there is so much slander and gossip. We are desensitized. If you watch any popular sitcom on TV, mocking people is the norm. No friendship or relationship is sacred. Reality shows, Hollywood tabloids, talk shows, and really almost every show on TV has a running dialogue of cutting others down. The more we watch these things, the more it becomes the norm for us.

Let's Pray

Lord, wake me up and shake me up. I don't want to become just like the world. Please help me notice and then refuse to listen to gossip in both TV and in real life. Then, most of all, help me not be the one who speaks it.

One Year Bible Reading

1 Kings 5:1–6:38; Acts 7:1-29; Psalm 127:1-5; Proverbs 16:28-30

Silver-Haired Crown

The silver-haired head is a crown of glory,
If it is found in the way of righteousness.

PROVERBS 16:31 (NKJV)

Let me speak a word to you ladies over fifty. If you embrace this phase of your life, it can be the sweetest of all. You can be a light shining ahead of the young women all around you, because there are many young moms who don't have anyone to give them godly advice. They don't have someone to teach them how to be in the Word for themselves. They don't have anyone to teach them to respect or love their husbands. They don't know how to be homemakers, or keep a budget, or prepare balanced meals.

In Titus 2:3-5 the older women are told to "be reverent in behavior, not slanderers, not given to much wine, teachers of good things, that they admonish the young women to love their husbands and children, be discreet, chaste, homemakers, good, obedient to their own husbands, that the word of God may not be blasphemed" (NKJV).

So I'd like to challenge some of my grey-haired sisters. Let's take the next years of our life and ask the Lord how we can invest them. Ask God to show you several young women whom you can encourage. Is there a young wife you can invite over to teach her to make casseroles or pie crust or to shop for bargains at the grocery store? Is there a young woman you can take under your wing for accountability during her engagement process? Is there a young pastor's wife you can pray for every day and send notes of encouragement? Because "the silver-haired head is a crown of glory, if it's found in the way of righteousness."

Make It Personal . . . Live It Out!

If you are a young woman, indeed you are living in very challenging times. You are inundated from every angle by false information and perceptions of womanhood and motherhood, marriage and success. You indeed need someone older and wiser to encourage and guide you as Elizabeth encouraged Mary. The Lord has raised up many mentors who are available through books, websites, and videos. Let me mention two of my favorites: Fern Nichols (Moms in Prayer International, www.MomsInPrayer.org) and Emilie Barnes (author of *Survival for Busy Women*).

One Year Bible Reading

1 Kings 7:1-51; Acts 7:30-50; Psalm 128:1-6; Proverbs 16:31-33

June 11

Peace and Quiet

Better a dry crust with peace and quiet
than a house full of feasting with strife.

PROVERBS 17:1 (NIV)

Strife. What is strife? Strife is "quarrels, struggles, conflict, competition, and contention."

So let's do a little reality check. What is the present state of your heart and soul and mind? Are you constantly wrestling and reacting? Are you defensive and protective? Are you frustrated, never satisfied? We live in a world that feeds this. It's all around us, but the only time it really becomes dangerous is not when it's all around us, but when it's in us.

Our proverb today speaks of simplicity, just a crust of bread. It's enough if you have peace and quiet.

The apostle Paul is such a great example to us. We know he wrote the book of Philippians from a prison cell in Rome. Maybe some days all he had for dinner was a crust of bread, but from that cell he gave us the real secret to peace and quiet in a troubling world. He said, "Rejoice in the Lord. Again I say 'Rejoice.' The Lord is near. So be anxious for nothing, thankful for everything, and pray the peace of God will guard your hearts and minds in Christ Jesus" and "I have learned in whatever state I am to be content; for I can do all things through Christ who gives me strength" (Philippians 4:4-7, 11-12, author's paraphrase).

Make It Personal . . . Live It Out!

The joy of simple, that's want we need today. It's summer. The world outside is full of life; let's go for a walk. Stop and talk to a neighbor. Look for birds' nests in the trees. Be still: listen to the sounds all around you. Look up: just the blue of the sky or the shape of the clouds can be a simple joy. Sit and watch some busy ants. Try to find a ladybug. Take deep breaths. Have a little talk with God your Father and tell him all the things you like about the world he made.

This is my Father's world, and to my listening ears
all nature sings, and round me rings the music of the spheres.
This is my Father's world: I rest me in the thought
of rocks and trees, of skies and seas; his hand the wonders wrought.
—MALTBIE D. BABCOCK

One Year Bible Reading

1 Kings 8:1-66; Acts 7:51–8:13; Psalm 129:1-8; Proverbs 17:1

Refining Fire

The refining pot is for silver and the furnace for gold,
But the LORD tests the hearts.

PROVERBS 17:3 (NKJV)

The heat of trials and hardship to us are like the heat that the goldsmith applies to a lump of gold that he wants to make into a beautiful golden ring. Impurities are not visible, because they are imbedded in the core of that solid form. The goldsmith must hold the gold over the hottest part of the flame. As it melts into a liquid form, the impurities are released and they rise to the surface. This dross then can be skimmed away until the surface is clear. He never takes his eyes off the precious metal lest it stay in the fire too long or not long enough. How does he know that the gold is pure, fully refined? When he looks down and can see his own face reflected.

Can you see how this applies to us? Are you going through something so hard you feel you are melting down? When your child is sick in the hospital, a doctor has just found a lump, or your mom has a stroke, life changes a lot. All of a sudden the silly, frivolous things that used to seem so important just aren't. Let the dross float to the surface, things like self-reliance, self-pity, selfish ambition, jealousy, and pride.

One of the things we must remember, though, is that this is not punishment. This is the refining fire. God has trusted you to go through this really hard thing, "that the genuineness of your faith, being much more precious than gold that perishes, though it is tested by fire, may be found to praise, honor, and glory at the revelation of Jesus Christ" (1 Peter 1:7, NKJV).

Make It Personal . . . Live It Out!

How do you gain fresh hope and strength when you're in the midst of a trial? Read the Psalms. They are songs for your soul. Many were written when David was going through painful circumstances. The Psalms give you words to honestly express your lowest lows. Then they give you words of victory and confidence in God.

Let's Pray

Lord, please help me surrender to, not fight your work in my life. Help me to see your love and trust your redeeming purpose to make me a vessel fit for the master's use.

One Year Bible Reading

1 Kings 9:1–10:29; Acts 8:14-40; Psalm 130:1-8; Proverbs 17:2-3

Compassion in Action

He who mocks the poor shows contempt for their Maker;
whoever gloats over disaster will not go unpunished.

PROVERBS 17:5 (NIV)

To mock the poor or to gloat over disaster in someone's life would be to look down on people like you are better than them, not because of who they are but because circumstances put them in the low place. They are helpless, and we can view them as hopeless. But let's never forget, except for the grace of God, we could be them.

So who are those who are poor in this world, those whose lives face disaster? One very large group is foster children. They are left without a home of their own, bounced around, vulnerable and feeling like outcasts.

One church in Florida, Calvary Chapel Fort Lauderdale, became so moved by these children's plight, they knew they had to get involved. Out of this, God birthed a ministry called 4KIDS of South Florida. This is from the church's website.

"Every day in South Florida, an average of eight to twelve children are removed from their homes as a result of abuse, abandonment, or neglect. 4KIDS is an organization founded to meet the physical, emotional, social, and spiritual needs of these children. Since 1999 we have provided housing and care for thousands of children."

I'm going to close by saying I believe it's no accident that you are reading this today. I believe that God wants to stir someone's heart that God loves these children. He's not forgotten them. They are helpless but not hopeless. And maybe he'll use you.

Make It Personal . . . Live It Out!

People are poor in lots of ways besides just money. How can we put our compassion into action? Here are some tangible ways.

- Do you know of a child who has trouble with schoolwork? Offer to tutor them once a week to help with reading or math.
- Offer to give an elderly person a ride to the doctor, or help with some yard work.
- Prayer is the greatest gift. Pause and pray right now for someone going through a difficult time.
- A book or a funny card in the mail can add a smile to someone's dreary day.

One Year Bible Reading

1 Kings 11:1–12:19; Acts 9:1-25; Psalm 131:1-3; Proverbs 17:4-5

Grandma's House and Heart

Grandchildren are the crowning glory of the aged.

PROVERBS 17:6

Definitely, grandchildren are one of the sweetest gifts that God has ever bestowed. I saw a bumper sticker that said, "If I had known that grandkids were so great, I would have had them first."

I remember that moment when first I saw my granddaughter, Hannah. It was definitely love at first sight. When she was three, I gave her a little pink suitcase. When she packed it, that meant she was coming to Grandma's house. One day I was waiting for her to come and spend the night. She was excited. I was excited. Then came her little, wild knock. I ran to throw open the door, and she threw up her arms and said, "It's your girl!" I loved it.

With grandchildren, grandparents have that great privilege of being a source of unconditional love. Being a child growing up in this complicated world right now is not easy. I want to challenge you. Pray for your grandchildren even if they're not born yet. Pray for them faithfully. Pray Scripture for them. Pray the promises of God for them and invest in them spiritually.

Let me recommend some excellent resources to keep at your home for the times they come to visit. Kenneth Taylor compiled a wonderful, must-have children's Bible called *The Bible in Pictures for Little Eyes*. Keep a library of good Christian movies. And invest in nature movies like *Incredible Creatures That Defy Evolution* that show the wonder of God's creation.

Make It Personal . . . Live It Out!

Let me speak to those who have adult prodigal children. Don't let your heart despair because your grandchildren are not raised in a godly home. One of my dearest friends, Jan Vance, became an incredible woman of God largely because her grandparents were a godly influence. Whenever you can, plant seeds in your grandchildren's lives. Always tuck in a Christian music CD along with their birthday gifts. When they are teenagers, they especially need your prayers. They especially need your unconditional love. God has entrusted you with the wonderful and holy opportunity of letting "your light so shine . . . that they may see your good works and glorify your Father in heaven" (Matthew 5:16, NKJV).

One Year Bible Reading

1 Kings 12:20–13:34; Acts 9:26-43; Psalm 132:1-18; Proverbs 17:6

June 15

Don't Buy the Lie

Eloquent speech is not fitting for a fool;
even less are lies fitting for a ruler.

PROVERBS 17:7

This proverb tells us that we don't always get what we expect. We do not expect a fool to speak with eloquence. We expect to be able to tell immediately that someone is speaking foolishness because it will sound stupid. It would immediately sound wrong. But that's just not the way it is. Remember, Satan is the king of smoke and mirrors. He could be called "Slick Satan." In Genesis 3 he masked his intentions when he spoke with Eve. His words sounded both logical and appealing. He insinuated that God was withholding something good from her—something that she needed and that she really wanted. Satan made it seem that God is stingy. Eve listened and acted on this lie. But God was withholding the fruit from the tree only because it would bring her pain. Eve was a foolish woman.

As wise, godly women, we must be discerning. Don't believe every dressed-up lie you hear on a talk show or in a book, no matter how eloquently it's presented.

We must be Bereans. According to the book of Acts, the Bereans took what they heard and then searched the Scriptures to see if it lined up with God's Word. Sometimes a foolish lie merely takes a nugget of truth and twists it into a dangerous deception. The better we know the truth, the less likely we will be tricked into falling for the fancy fake.

Make It Personal . . . Live It Out!

If you are reading this right now and there is someone—maybe at the office, at the gym, or on the Internet—who is giving you a line, tempting you to do something you know is wrong, *wake up*! If you are lonely as a single or in an unhappy marriage, you are especially vulnerable. Three days ago a woman came to me sobbing. She is having an affair with a man at work, and her heart is now torn. She knows it will only bring devastation to her four kids and destroy their home.

Please, I want to beg you, call out to God right now and ask him to guard your heart. If you have already fallen, call out to him in repentance. He is the God of grace and truth.

One Year Bible Reading

1 Kings 14:1–15:24; Acts 10:1-23; Psalm 133:1-3; Proverbs 17:7-8

Love Covers

He who covers a transgression seeks love,
But he who repeats a matter separates friends.

PROVERBS 17:9 (NKJV)

What does that mean? It means it's easy to love someone who covers your back. So if you want to be loved, be lovable. Look for the best in others because it brings out the best in others. On the other hand, most of us know people who have something bad to say about everybody: a critical spirit, nagging, assuming the worst. It wears you out and drags you down. I think most of us already have this little internal voice that rags at us: *You're a failure. No one needs you. Why can't you get it right?* Come on, my friends, let's choose to be the voice that says to others, "Hey, you can do it. Try again. I do have confidence in you."

Now let's apply this. Did your husband do something stupid? Forget about it! Let that little event be buried, and throw away the shovel. Did your son strike out or fail math? Did your daughter get a fender bender? Did your sister gain a few pounds? Cover their backs. In these things, won't we just give others a break? Can we be a safety net and soft landing in their times of private pain, problems, and failures?

I just love this definition of a friend: a friend is someone who sees you fail and doesn't think you're a failure. Even better, Peter said, "Above all, love each other deeply, because love covers a multitude of sins" (1 Peter 4:8, NIV).

Make It Personal . . . Live It Out!

When I forget that I make mistakes too, I am harder on others. Admit it: so are you. Let's let Jesus set us straight: "Do not judge, or you too will be judged. For in the same way you judge others, you will be judged, and with the measure you use, it will be measured to you. Why do you look at the speck of sawdust in your brother's eye and pay no attention to the plank in your own eye? . . . You hypocrite, first take the plank out of your own eye, and then you will see clearly to remove the speck from your brother's eye" (Matthew 7:1-3, 5, NIV).

One Year Bible Reading

1 Kings 15:25–17:24; Acts 10:24-48; Psalm 134:1-3; Proverbs 17:9-11

Beware of Bears!

Better to meet a bear robbed of her cubs
than a fool in his folly.

PROVERBS 17:12 (NIV)

Here's a warning. Don't mess with mamma bear's cubs. She can be vicious. This kind of unleashed force is compared with the crazed and out-of-control behavior of a fool.

When does this happen, and what does it look like? Divorce court is a classic example. It can be a crazy, revenge-at-any-cost place. Jealousy is foolish, and those who are prone to it can destroy friendships and ministries. Family feuds over inheritance can be unleashed, acting out of old resentments from childhood. Have you ever heard the phrase *scorched earth*? When an enemy army came across the border into Russia, Peter the Great burned miles and miles of his own people's farms and crops, just so the invading army would have no food. Scorched earth.

So child of God, if you are in the way of some foolish person's warpath, here are some things to remember.

- Reason and right usually will not stop them.
- Don't answer their crazy folly with your own crazy folly.
- Really, the only safe place is higher ground.

Psalm 46:1 says, "God is our refuge and strength, a very present help in time of trouble" (NKJV).

Hebrews 4:16 reminds us, "Let us therefore come boldly to the throne of grace, that we may . . . find grace to help in time of need" (NKJV).

Make It Personal . . . Live It Out!

When someone recklessly vents her anger, it often falls on the innocent. This is a good warning to us as mothers. We as women can let frustrations and bitterness seethe against our husbands (or ex-husbands). Then all of a sudden, some little thing that a child does triggers that anger, and they get the full truckload dumped on them. It's confusing and painful and entirely unfair. If this has happened, it's not too late to make amends. Will you go to your child and ask for forgiveness? Read Ephesians 4:26 together. Then ask your child to kneel and pray with you at the throne of grace.

One Year Bible Reading

1 Kings 18:1-46; Acts 11:1-30; Psalm 135:1-21; Proverbs 17:12-13

Quit Quarrels!

Beginning a quarrel is like opening a floodgate,
so drop the matter before a dispute breaks out.

PROVERBS 17:14

Ephesians 4:26 says, "Be angry and do not sin: do not let the sun go down on your wrath" (NKJV). Truthfully, sometimes I'm so frustrated that I'm not quick on my feet. I can never think of that clever, sharp thing to shoot back in a moment of anger. But in reality I am thankful. It's sometimes better to be tongue-tied.

So much trouble is caused when tempers flare and words are used as weapons. One harsh word leads to one hurtful word, which leads to hateful looks and actions, and the damage goes deeper and deeper the longer it goes on. Stop. Just stop. Someone said, "The one that forgives, ends that quarrel." And George Herbert said, "He who cannot forgive others destroys the bridge over which he himself must pass."

In Genesis 13:8-9 Abram's herdsmen had a conflict with Lot's herdsmen. There were territory issues; so Abram went to Lot and said, "Please let there be no strife between you and me, . . . for we are brethren. Is not the whole land before you? . . . If you take the left, then I will go to the right" (NKJV).

Good job, Abram—and good example. He could have fought for his rights and probably won, but he laid down his rights and gave first choice to Lot. In the end, Abram did win, because "blessed are the peacemakers."

Make It Personal . . . Live It Out!

I have a conflict in a relationship right now. The situation that caused the conflict can't be done over. It's history. So now I have a decision to make. I can replay the details and events over and over in my mind. But that only keeps the frustration fresh. In twenty years, none of those details will matter at all. What matters is that I really do care about the other person. Before God, I have committed to let love rule. When angry thoughts pop up in my mind, he helps me turn them to prayer.

Do you have an unresolved disagreement or argument? As our proverb today says, let's drop the matter. And then let love rule.

One Year Bible Reading

1 Kings 19:1-21; Acts 12:1-23; Psalm 136:1-26; Proverbs 17:14-15

June 19

Fools are Foolish

Why is there in the hand of a fool the purchase price of wisdom,
Since he has no heart for it?

PROVERBS 17:16 (NKJV)

This is an interesting question. Why does a fool get any of the good benefits that could make him wise and true and good if he wanted, and yet he wastes every opportunity? They are wasted on him.

Why do we sometimes see godly parents who do all that they can for their children while the children do all they can to ruin the parents' lives? They choose wild friends, break all the family rules meant to guide and protect them, and break their parents' hearts.

Why? Why do some people have a Christian in their life who never gives up on them, who year after year invites them to church, shares the gospel, and prays for their souls? And yet, year after year—nothing. They become more and more set on believing anything the liberal media says and rejecting everything that God says.

Why, why do some of the dearest Christian wives have husbands who choose to live a life and in a world apart? They have no idea why their wife has joy and peace even when there are hard times. There's a Bible in their kitchen and Scriptures on their walls, but these husbands' hearts seem like block walls.

Why? Why do all these foolish people get all these chances to know the truth? Because "God so loved the world that He gave His only begotten Son. . . . God did not send His Son to condemn the world, but that the world through Him might be saved" (John 3:16-17, NKJV).

Make It Personal . . . Live It Out!

Let's turn this question back on ourselves. Is there an area of your life that foolishness has repeatedly conquered? Are you still foolish with your money, with your words, with your temper? Why? Why do you yield when you know it only brings trouble?

Let's pray and seek both the insight and power of God himself to break the grip of our weak natures.

Let's Pray

Lord, I am asking you. Help me understand why I keep failing to grow past some of the weak habits in my life. Please give me fresh resolve for victory, confident that "I can do all things through Christ who strengthens me" (Philippians 4:13, NKJV).

One Year Bible Reading

1 Kings 20:1–21:29; Acts 12:24–13:15; Psalm 137:1-9; Proverbs 17:16

A Faithful Friend

A friend loves at all times,
And a brother is born for adversity.

PROVERBS 17:17 (NKJV)

This proverb shows us why we need friends. It also shows us not just what we need in a friend, but what we need to be as a friend. The question is, who are you?

Everyone loves a winner. Everyone loves to know and be with someone who has a lot going for them and is well respected by the well-respected people. It's fun to be in the right circle. Even in churches and ministries there are "in" and there are "out" circles. That's human nature, but deep bonds aren't made in shallow pools.

In the Bible we see a picture of friendship between Jonathan and David. The true test of that friendship was when David was an outcast. It was not politically correct for Jonathan to stay close to David. He could have distanced himself and played it safe. But he made a choice. He would pay the price to walk alongside his friend as the underdog, because that's when his friend needed him the most. "Tried and true" means there is a trial that shows who is true. Again, the question is, who are you?

But no discussion of a friend could ever be complete without speaking of the friend who is truest and sweetest of all. "What a friend we have in Jesus, all our sins and griefs to bear. Can we find a friend so faithful? Who will all our sorrows share? Jesus knows our every weakness; take it to the Lord in prayer."

Make It Personal . . . Live It Out!

Now, honestly ask yourself, *Am I a friend who loves at all times?* After I wrote this sentence, I immediately thought of someone who has moved to a new city. It's hard to start over. She has been on my heart. So I stopped and picked up the phone just to let her know I'm thinking of her. This week, let's do more of that. As you drive to church on Sunday, will you ask the Lord to give you a "be a friend" moment? Reach out to someone who is new, a widow, the mother of a handicapped child, or a woman still reeling from a recent divorcee. As you fill the friendship cup of others, your own cup becomes full.

One Year Bible Reading

1 Kings 22:1-53; Acts 13:16-41; Psalm 138:1-8; Proverbs 17:17-18

Calming Quarrels

Anyone who loves to quarrel loves sin.

PROVERBS 17:19

Are you argumentative? Do you feel that you constantly have to have the last word, prove your point, show why others are wrong? Do you have to have an opinion on everything?

When there is a controversy on the news in politics, do you feel that you have to follow all the details, although there is nothing you can do about it? Do you get angry at people on talk shows but continue to watch them?

Whenever there is some sort of conflict at church, do you get involved or at least need to know about it? Do you take sides and then defend your position?

I hope I'm not stepping on anyone's toes. Wrong. I hope I am. As a matter of fact, I really hope this is hitting home with someone out there. Arguing is not good. Our proverb is very matter of fact: "Anyone who loves a quarrel loves sin." If you think that's blunt, listen to Ecclesiastes 10:12: "Words from a wise man's mouth are gracious, but a fool is consumed by his own lips" (NIV).

So calm down. Let it go. Second Timothy 2:24 says, "The Lord's servant must not quarrel; instead, [she] must be kind to everyone, able to teach, not resentful" (NIV).

James 1:20 says, "Man's anger does not bring about the righteous life that God desires" (NIV).

Make It Personal . . . Live It Out!

Are bickering and blaming part of your family culture? God's Word has some good insight in James 4:1-3: "What causes fights and quarrels among you? Don't they come from your desires that battle within you? You want something but don't get it. You kill and covet, but you cannot have what you want. . . . You quarrel and fight. You do not have, because you do not ask God. When you ask, you do not receive, because you ask with wrong motives, that you may spend what you get on your pleasures" (NIV).

Let's Pray

Lord, when someone is irritable or irritating, help me to keep a quiet heart and a silent tongue.

One Year Bible Reading

2 Kings 1:1–2:25; Acts 13:42–14:7; Psalm 139:1-24; Proverbs 17:19-21

Joy Is Good Medicine

A cheerful heart is good medicine,
but a crushed spirit dries up the bones.

PROVERBS 17:22 (NIV)

I want to ask you some questions. Are you a child of God? Is the great God of the universe your heavenly Father? Does he love you with an unfailing love? Has he forgiven your sins and washed you white as snow? Is he faithful to his promises? Do you believe that he will never leave you or forsake you? Is God your fortress and strength? Do you believe that your name is written in the Book of Life? When you woke up this morning, did you remember that in your Father's house are many mansions, and Jesus left to prepare a place for you? Did you remember that Jesus said, "In the world you will have tribulation, but be of good cheer, I have overcome the world" (John 16:33, NKJV)?

No matter what circumstance we are facing today, we have every good reason in the world to be of good cheer!

George Müller was best known as the "Father of Orphans." Meeting the needs of thousands of children taught him to look to God and God alone for all their needs. Despite all of this responsibility, it's said he had the cheerful countenance of a child himself. This is what he said was his secret: "The Lord taught me that the first business I needed to attend to every day was to have my spirit happy in the Lord, to nourish my inner man." This he did by starting his day in God's Word: reading, stopping to pray, and then reading more until all of the weight rested on God's broad shoulders, not his.

Make It Personal . . . Live It Out!

Is the weight of your world resting on your shoulders today? Do you feel crushed and dry? This is not good. I'll venture to say you don't have any joy. Did you forget that the joy of the Lord is your strength?

On May 26, I taught you how to do the "divine shift." Put your palms out and picture your burdens in your hands. Now lift those burdens up and off your shoulders and onto the broad shoulders of the Lord. Breathe in deeply. Breathe out. Now let his joy flow into you like good medicine.

One Year Bible Reading

2 Kings 3:1–4:17; Acts 14:8-28; Psalm 140:1-13; Proverbs 17:22

Bribery or Bonus?

Our proverb today gives us insight into one of the reasons we see so much unfairness in the world.

A wicked man accepts a bribe in secret
to pervert the course of justice.

PROVERBS 17:23 (NIV)

Secret bribes, hidden agendas. There is injustice in the courts, in politics, at the office, even in families and churches. Things aren't always fair, are they?

But God gives us a picture of how it ought to be in Deuteronomy 16:19: "Do not pervert justice or show partiality. Do not accept a bribe, for a bribe blinds the eyes of the wise and twists the words of the righteous" (NIV).

A bribe doesn't have to be money. It can be anything that is given to "encourage" someone to do or allow something that is wrong. Judas was bribed by money to betray Jesus. Pilate was bribed by political pressure and popularity to condemn Jesus. Peter was bribed by his own instinct to protect himself to deny Jesus. Bribes can come from the outside, and they can come from the inside. Bottom line: whatever you get out of it, it is always wrong to cave in to wrong.

God gives us a simple and yet wonderful contrast to this with a formula to live rightly before him and others—Micah 6:8: "He has shown you, O man [or woman], what is good; and what does the LORD require of you but to do justly, to love mercy, and to walk humbly with your God?" (NKJV). Elisabeth Elliot used to boil it down into one little motto for life: "Do the next thing."

Make It Personal . . . Live It Out!

They say bribery will get you everywhere. Some parents live by that motto. When their toddler throws a tantrum, they bribe him by giving him what he wants so he will stop crying. Teens often badger their moms to override their dads' decisions. This rewards bad behavior. Bribery gets you somewhere, all right—but to the wrong place! If you have fallen into that trap, try a new technique, "positive reinforcement." When your children do a chore well, share, work hard on an assignment, catch them being good. Reward them with words and occasionally with a "serendipity" bonus treat or benefit.

One Year Bible Reading

2 Kings 4:18–5:27; Acts 15:1-35; Psalm 141:1-10; Proverbs 17:23

Prodigals

Today's topic is prodigals and those who love them.

Sensible people keep their eyes glued on wisdom,
but a fool's eyes wander to the ends of the earth.
A foolish child brings grief to a father
and bitterness to a mother.

PROVERBS 17:24-25

Notice that the first part of our proverb is the official diagnosis of why children are prodigals. They did not choose wisdom. Something foolish caught their eye, and step-by-step they made choices that took them further and further from what was right and good, and further and further not just from you, but from God.

In Luke 15:13-14 Jesus said, "The younger son gathered all together, journeyed to a far country, and there wasted his possessions with prodigal living. But when he had spent all, there arose a severe famine in that land, and he began to be in want" (NKJV).

For us as mothers this is hard. We hate to see our children suffer. We want to fix it for them, but as Vance Havner says, "If somebody would have given him a bed and a sandwich, the prodigal never would have gone home."

So, moms, what can we do? Pray. I have a friend who has a prodigal daughter. No, she's not doing drugs or living on the streets. She is a prodigal because of bitterness and hardness of heart. This mom asks the Lord often, "Is there anything I can do?" Repeatedly, the Lord draws near, comforts her heart, and tells her, *Pray*.

"The effective, fervent prayer of a righteous [mom] avails much" (James 5:16, NKJV).

Make It Personal . . . Live It Out!

"A foolish child brings . . . bitterness to a mother." Moms, this is a clear warning for us. We have to be very careful to guard our hearts. Rebellion, stubbornness, thoughtlessness, broken promises, foolish choices—all these bring disappointments to a mother. If you know you have become angry and hard because of frustration and grief, will you come with me now to the throne of grace?

Let's Pray

Lord, you know the deep sorrow I feel over this child, and you know it has hardened my heart. Please restore me and help me to draw close to you for the comfort and peace I need. Make me wise and yet tender, trusting in you.

One Year Bible Reading

2 Kings 6:1–7:20; Acts 15:36–16:15; Psalm 142:1-7; Proverbs 17:24-25

The Slippery Slope

It is wrong to fine the godly for being good
or to punish nobles for being honest!

PROVERBS 17:26

Right now in our society there is a lot of pressure: pressure to punish those who take a stand for what's right. It is not politically correct to speak up against abortion or to speak for morality.

Some would like to pass laws that would penalize doctors and nurses who refuse to perform abortions because of moral convictions.

Some would like to pass laws making it a hate crime to oppose gay marriage or to object that gay sexuality be taught to your first-grader in school. It's interesting and sad that in our schools a teacher can dress up as a witch at Halloween but not sing Christmas carols. It is legal for a teacher to assign an R-rated novel but not to pray in the classroom. Bottom line, Christians: as the darkness of the world gets darker and darker, it will cost us more and more to stand up for truth, to share that Jesus is the only Way and Truth and Life.

Alan Redpath wrote, "We are prepared to serve the Lord only by sacrifice. We are fit for the work of God only when we have wept over it, prayed about it, and then we are enabled by Him to tackle the job that needs to be done. May God give to us hearts that bleed, eyes that are wide open to see, minds that are clear to interpret God's purposes, wills that are obedient, and a determination that is utterly unflinching as we set about the tasks He would have us to do."

Make It Personal . . . Live It Out!

They say that if you put a frog into a pot of boiling water, it will leap out. But if you put it in cool water, then gradually turn up the heat, the frog won't become aware of the threat until it's too late. When gradual changes in a society are a slippery slope downward, we cannot remain complacent. We aren't all called to picket and march. But we are all called to pray: "If My people . . . will humble themselves, and pray and seek My face, and turn from their wicked ways, then I will hear from heaven, and will forgive their sin and heal their land" (2 Chronicles 7:14, NKJV).

One Year Bible Reading

2 Kings 8:1–9:13; Acts 16:16-40; Psalm 143:1-12; Proverbs 17:26

Silence Is Golden

A truly wise person uses few words;
a person with understanding is even-tempered.
Even fools are thought to be wise when they keep silent;
when they keep their mouths shut, they seem intelligent.

PROVERBS 17:27-28

Don't you just love how much we are learning in the book of Proverbs about words? Here we learn that sometimes silence is golden. Of course there are many times when it's good to talk things out, when it's good to speak encouraging words, to be friendly, to instruct, to share your faith.

But there are also times when actions speak louder than words. Many people say that when they're grieving, they don't need people to come and make conversation. They don't need people to give them lots of advice to try to cheer them up. They just need the comfort of companionship, a listening ear, someone to cry with them or just to let them know they care.

Our proverb today says, "A truly wise person uses few words." So let me give a final little list of times when less is more.

- Complaining. If you have the urge to complain, truthfully, save your breath. No one really wants to hear about it.
- Criticizing. That's a ditto.
- Sarcasm. Somehow we think sarcasm is clever. Actually, it's not. It often has a mean edge, and it's a really bad habit.
- And last but not least, gossip. If you can't stop, try duct tape. No, really. Whatever it takes, just knock it off.

Make It Personal . . . Live It Out!

I'm still smiling about the bluntness of our proverb today: "Even fools are thought to be wise when they keep silent; when they keep their mouths shut, they seem intelligent."

Let's make a list of things we can do that show "actions speak louder than words." I have a strained relationship with a friend who is not ready to "talk it out." I have expressed care and concern in words, but now I need to "walk the talk." Do I really care? Then God is calling me to be faithful to pray for her. God is asking me to continuously refuse bitter, angry thoughts. And God is calling me to speak kindly of her when her name is mentioned. And when I can't, silence is golden.

One Year Bible Reading

2 Kings 9:14–10:31; Acts 17:1-34; Psalm 144:1-15; Proverbs 17:27-28

Friendliness Is Fun!

An unfriendly man pursues selfish ends;
he defies all sound judgment.

PROVERBS 18:1 (NIV)

Our topic today is unfriendliness. It's interesting that here we're told unfriendliness is selfish, and it's not good judgment either. As it has been said, "A life wrapped up in itself makes a very small package."

And God agrees. God created us to love and need people (not in an unhealthy way, not in a way that puts people above God). Jesus said, "All will know that you are My disciples, if you have love for one another" (John 13:35, NKJV).

In 1964 Barbra Streisand sang a song called "People": "People who need people are the luckiest people in the world. We're children needing other children, and yet letting our grown-up pride hide all the need inside, acting more like children than children."

Ladies, let's be friendly. This can be a lonely world. Wouldn't it be nice if just by being friendly today we could make someone's day? Here are some random little friendly things to do.

- Look at the name tag on the waitresses or checkers at the store and say hi to them by name. Ask them if they know that God loves them.
- Tell somebody today that they're right, or they're smart, or they did a good job.
- Smile at someone who looks lonely—an elderly woman, a weary mom.
- And here's a good one: let someone go ahead of you when you're stopped in traffic.

Make It Personal . . . Live It Out!

Now let me give you a few tips on going from friendliness to relationship. I love going to church. I love the worship and the teaching. And I love seeing God's people. But most of us know we can stay very shallow and really not know anyone. Let's be intentional. This Sunday, put a little notepad in the back of your Bible for the express purpose of learning a new name. While you're at it, ask the person you meet for a prayer request too. Then through the week pray for the person by name. If you do that every week for three months, you will know twelve new names. More important, you will have invested in lives with prayer. Now that's being friendly.

One Year Bible Reading

2 Kings 10:32–12:21; Acts 18:1-22; Psalm 145:1-21; Proverbs 18:1

Learning to Listen

Fools have no interest in understanding;
they only want to air their own opinions.

PROVERBS 18:2

Well, this is quite a statement. Fools, it appears, only think there is one side to the story: their side. Forget about trying to help them understand your side. Their minds are made up. I think most of us know of someone like that. But the most important thing we can learn today about this is . . . not to be like that.

James 1:19 tells us, "My dear brothers, take note of this: Everyone should be quick to listen, slow to speak, and slow to become angry" (NIV).

So then let's learn to be better listeners. Here are some random tips.

- Everyone knows at least one thing that you don't know. It's amazing what you can learn when you listen.
- Ask more questions. When people make statements and you don't agree, ask them why they believe that way. Maybe as they explain, you'll understand them better, but maybe they will also see they don't have a valid explanation.
- Listen with more than your ears. People give off emotional signals of how they're feeling. Pay attention.
- Let others speak first. Hear them out. Don't interrupt.
- Use affirming and confirming statements like "I hear what you're saying." Sometimes repeat a key word back to them.
- And one of the most important things you'll ever do when you listen is give eye contact.

Make It Personal . . . Live It Out!

Since we're on the topic of learning to be a good listener, may I ask you a very important question? Do you know how to listen to the voice of God? Jesus said, "My sheep hear My voice, and I know them, and they follow Me" (John 10:27, NKJV). Are you born again; does his Spirit live within you? If so, the Lord himself can and will speak to you. Here's a tool to help you. Turn to Psalm 146:1-10. As you read, underline the words or phrases that seem important. Circle two that stand out. Now write out two lessons from the two facts you circled—for example, verse 7: "The Lord gives freedom" (NKJV). Ask the Lord to speak to your heart regarding the lessons you discovered and to show you how to apply them. There—do you see? Just by pausing to listen, you hear.

One Year Bible Reading

2 Kings 13:1–14:29; Acts 18:23–19:12; Psalm 146:1-10; Proverbs 18:2-3

Life-Giving Water

A person's words can be life-giving water;
words of true wisdom are as refreshing as a bubbling brook.

PROVERBS 18:4

As I read this, it stirs my heart with a deep desire to have such a refreshing stream flow from my life. How about you? What is the source? How do we become filled with refreshing words? According to John 7:37-39, Jesus said, "'If anyone is thirsty, let him come to me and drink. Whoever believes in me, . . . streams of living water will flow from within him.' By this he meant the Spirit" (NIV). That's the secret. Let's look at three steps to take.

1. Come to Jesus. Spend time with him privately, unhurriedly, allowing his Spirit to fill and refresh you. Many Christians settle for only an occasional sip of Jesus. Developing a personal quiet time with the Lord can be the most wonderful, life-changing thing you will ever do. If you don't have this, I'd love to help. Go to my website, BibleBusStop.com. I've posted a message that will walk you through some practical steps.
2. Feed your faith! As you spend time with the Lord, your confidence builds. Learn his promises. The Holy Spirit will then prompt you to trust his promises. If there's a commandment, do it! Where there's instruction, obey it. Put feet to your faith.
3. Lastly, there is the flow. This is what Jesus promised would happen. When you have come to him, listened to his Word, are walking in the Spirit and truth, you are filled. Then you will be God's vessel ready to pour out. That's when you'll see his wisdom, love, and refreshing words flow life-giving refreshment through you to others.

Make It Personal . . . Live It Out!

Let's look at this promise in John 7:37-39 again. Jesus said, "'If anyone is thirsty, let him come to me and drink. Whoever believes in me, . . . streams of living water will flow from within him.' By this he meant the Spirit" (NIV). Are you thirsty, truly wanting to live differently, fully, and richly? God is ready, if you are.

Let's Pray

Lord, I realize I have often come to you for merely material things and physical help. Forgive me. I come to you now eager and thirsty. Please fill and overflow me with your refreshing, living water.

One Year Bible Reading

2 Kings 15:1–16:20; Acts 19:13-41; Psalm 147:1-20; Proverbs 18:4-5

Asking for Trouble

Fools get into constant quarrels;
they are asking for a beating.
The mouths of fools are their ruin;
their lips get them into trouble.

PROVERBS 18:6-7

When we were kids we used to say, "He's cruisin' for a bruisin'," "He's shooting off his mouth," or, "He's asking for trouble."

The bottom line here is that this type of fool is someone who causes others to get agitated. He riles them up, picks on them, offends them, and over all is hard to be around. Now before we start thinking of all the people we know who do that, let's try the shoe on ourselves first.

Moms, are there times when you ride one of your kids' cases? This means for some reason you're frustrated with them. Maybe you've had a few heated discussions, and now they just can't do anything right. Mom, you've got a chip on your shoulder. This wedge is just going to get deeper if you don't make peace with this. Would you go to the Cross? Would you go in your room, shut your door, and talk it out with God? Pray it out and lay it down.

Are you argumentative? Maybe it's with your husband, arguing over money or past hurts or who's supposed to take out the garbage; or with your mother, still arguing, bristling over little things she says; or it's someone at work and you argue over religion. Just log these words in one more time in your mind: "Fools get into constant quarrels. Their lips get them into trouble."

Make It Personal . . . Live It Out!

Abraham Lincoln said, "No man resolved to make the most of himself can spare time for personal contention." In our marriages, friendships, and with our kids, we have to pick our battles. Remember: some hills are not worth fighting over. Are you at odds with your teen about the style of her hair or your sister about who inherits Mom's pearl earrings? If they get their way, no one is going to die. These things involve no moral compromise or serious damage. Reserve your resolve for things that will affect bigger issues. And when you do need to stand your ground, do it for love's sake, honoring God and showing grace in the process.

One Year Bible Reading

2 Kings 17:1–18:12; Acts 20:1-38; Psalm 148:1-14; Proverbs 18:6-7

July

Scan this code for audio devotionals
or visit www.tyndal.es/wisdom.

Ms. Gossip

The words of a gossip are like choice morsels;
they go down to a man's inmost parts.

PROVERBS 18:8 (NIV)

Listen to what Matthew Henry had to say about gossips: "They pretend to be very much affected with the misfortunes of such and such, and to be in pain for them, and pretend that it is with the greatest grief and reluctance imaginable that they speak of them. They look as if they themselves were wounded by it, whereas really they rejoice in iniquity, are proud of the story, and tell it with pride and pleasure. Thus their words seem; but they go down as poison into the innermost parts of the belly."

How interesting. Matthew Henry lived three hundred years ago, and yet as I read his comments, he seems to describe the very same woman I know—the one who loves to share her juicy stories of other people's troubles. She has such a sympathetic look, you would almost think she cared, but in reality she only cares that she has the inside scoop. If you have been a victim of this Ms. Gossip, don't you wish you could tell her how much this hurts?

I need to use my final words to talk to those who have been hurt by gossip. Don't let the gossiper's poison become your poison. I need to admit to you that two years ago, I did. I have been angry at someone who wounded me with her gossip words. Now I am the one who is wrong. So if that's you, too, will you join me? I confess that bitterness is just as wrong. "Lord, please forgive us. Forgive the ones who wounded us and forgive us for being mad at them."

Make It Personal . . . Live It Out!

Have you been the victim of someone's unkind words? I have the perfect story for you. According to 2 Kings 18, Sennacherib, the king of Assyria, sent a hateful message to King Hezekiah, the king of Israel. He made sure all the people heard it. In chapter 19 we read that King Hezekiah did a remarkable thing. He didn't threaten or cower or defend himself. He simply took the letter to the temple, spread it out before the Lord, and prayed for God to see and hear. He basically said, "Lord, you read it." God did see and hear, and he did act.

One Year Bible Reading

2 Kings 18:13–19:37; Acts 21:1-17; Psalm 149:1-9; Proverbs 18:8

The Name of the Lord

The name of the LORD is a strong tower;
The righteous run to it and are safe.

PROVERBS 18:10 (NKJV)

This is a powerful and important promise to you from God himself. Are you worried today? Are you facing trouble, opposition, persecution? The name of the Lord is a strong tower. Are you fearful, discouraged, or overwhelmed? The name of the Lord is a strong tower.

We have to realize that each title, each name for God given in the Bible, is not just what he is called. Each name describes who he is. Have you lost your way? Are you confused? He is the Light of the World. Do you need direction or protection? He is the Good Shepherd. He leads you beside still waters. He restores your soul.

There is no need too great for his powerful sufficiency. For he is God almighty! Are you grieving with a broken heart? He is the God of all comfort. He is the True Vine, the Chief Cornerstone, the Everlasting Father, the Prince of Peace. He is your Emmanuel, God with us. Behold the Lamb of God who takes away the sin of the world.

So, child of God, we need to be students of, collectors of, and believers in the wonderful, manifold, and majestic names of our amazing God. And then we need to run into the presence of his person like we run to a mighty, unshakable tower, and we will be safe.

Make It Personal . . . Live It Out!

When we study the names of God, it increases our confidence in his character. We begin to know him. We learn he is trustworthy, powerful, noble, and good. Are you lacking confidence in God? Confidence is assurance, firm belief, trust, reliance. This is the substance of true faith. When our faith is shallow, we collapse and panic when trouble comes to our lives. We actually dishonor God by doubting and fretting. But when we know our God, we lean deeply into his strong and capable arms.

Psalm 139 speaks of God's omniscience. Will you turn to it and read it before you go to bed tonight? *Jehovah-shammah* is the Hebrew name meaning "the Lord is there." God knew you before you were born, and he'll be there to call on to the end of your days.

One Year Bible Reading

2 Kings 20:1–22:2; Acts 21:18-36; Psalm 150:1-6; Proverbs 18:9-10

Haughty or Humble?

Haughtiness goes before destruction;
humility precedes honor.

PROVERBS 18:12

Are we humble, or are we haughty when dealing with others?

A few days ago I was with a group of godly women, and we were discussing a problem. The problem is that in the summer sometimes women come to church wearing clothes that are very skimpy and immodest. This is very distracting and can lead the men to stumble. So the question is, how can we graciously help these women realize the need to dress modestly without being harsh and offending them? Some of my dearest friends who are now pastors' wives share that the first time they came to church, they wore a miniskirt or a halter top. It never occurred to them that this was wrong.

- Don't be haughty. Haughtiness is having or showing great pride in oneself and disdain or contempt for others. If we make women feel stupid, or flawed, or inferior, it will crush them—and maybe they will not come back.
- Pray first. Pray for wisdom, and grace, and gentle tact. In other words, be humble and sweet to this woman whom Christ died for. Listen to the wonderful advice given in 2 Timothy 2:24-26: "A servant of the Lord must not quarrel but be gentle to all, able to teach, patient, in humility correcting those who are in opposition, if God perhaps will grant them repentance, so that they may know the truth, and that they may come to their senses and escape the snare of the devil, having been taken captive by him to do his will" (NKJV).

Make It Personal . . . Live It Out!

Jesus is our most accurate and beautiful picture of true humility. Of course he was flawless, completely righteous. And yet the most desperate sinners were drawn to him. They felt safe in his presence because they *were* safe in his presence. This challenges and humbles me; doesn't it you? Honestly, how do those who are hurting or poor or lost feel in our presence? Are we haughty or humble?

Let's Pray

Lord, break my heart for the broken and weak. Help me to reflect your tender kindness to the poorest and the weakest, as you do. May your humble heart beat within me and your love shine through me.

One Year Bible Reading

2 Kings 22:3–23:30; Acts 21:37–22:16; Psalm 1:1-6; Proverbs 18:11-12

Learning to Listen

To answer before listening, that is folly and shame.

PROVERBS 18:13 (NIV)

All right, this affirms what we should already know. We need to be better listeners. I am convinced that many of our problems are because we only half understand each other. We have not learned to talk things out and hear each other out. Honestly, I wish I were better at this. My parents didn't really sit down to discuss serious issues with us when I was growing up. Still to this day, I feel I have much to learn.

Gary Smalley's book *The DNA of Relationships* has an excellent chapter called "Emotional Communication: Listen with the Heart." His points are very helpful. I'll share four of them.

1. "Listen beyond the words to the feelings." This is very important. Maybe your friend asks why you didn't arrive on time, or she says that she's angry that you forgot an appointment. Behind her anger is really a feeling that you don't care. She's hurt.
2. "Allow others' emotions to touch you." Don't say, "You shouldn't feel like that," or, "Oh, just get over it." People feel loved when they know you care.
3. "Communication is understanding, not determining who's right." If you are always trying to prove you are right and the other person is wrong, no one wins.
4. "Effective communication starts with safety." Criticism and threats cause others to shut down.

Bottom line: let's all be better listeners. Let's be quick to hear and slow to speak.

Make It Personal . . . Live It Out!

The next time you are in an important conversation, practice the art of listening carefully. This is just as valuable in a pleasant conversation as it is when there's a conflict. Here are some "active listening" skills.

- Don't multitask while listening. Glancing at your phone screen or watch or the TV is a message that you're only half there.
- Ask a few questions that show your interest.
- Reaffirm by saying things like, "That is interesting" or "I hear you."

Let's Pray

Lord, please help! I know I haven't listened to others in the same way I would like them to listen to me. Help me to be patient. And most of all, help me to listen with a heart of love.

One Year Bible Reading

2 Kings 23:31–25:30; Acts 22:17–23:10; Psalm 2:1-12; Proverbs 18:13

July 5

Sustained

The spirit of a man will sustain him in sickness,
But who can bear a broken spirit?

PROVERBS 18:14 (NKJV)

My dear friend Carolyn was diagnosed with breast cancer two years ago. After a mastectomy, she had to go through six months of chemo and six weeks of radiation. She lost all of her hair, even her eyelashes. On top of that, she has two small children to care for. But I have to say, it's been an amazing thing to watch her go through this. She is a living example of the fact that "the joy of the Lord is your strength." Sometimes drawing back from the Lord and away from fellowship is the first thing that we as women do when we are sick or going through a hard time. Carolyn did just the opposite. She continued not only to allow her friends to minister to her, she continued to minister to others.

We can endure *physical* sickness and pain, but our proverb says, "Who can bear a broken spirit?" The answer for us as women is, no one. If you are reading today and you have been wounded, if you have a broken heart, doctors can medicate, but they cannot heal you. So please write down Isaiah 61. If you read it over and over again for ten straight days, you will find it's a powerful prescription. Jesus came to heal the brokenhearted. He can turn your ashes into beauty. Jesus was a man of sorrows and acquainted with grief. In Psalm 23:3 David declared something you need to know. He said, "[The Lord] restores my soul" (NKJV). And, dear one, he can and will restore you.

Make It Personal . . . Live It Out!

Have you ever broken a bone? When you look at the X-ray, it is easy to see the jagged line. But a broken spirit can't be seen on an X-ray or MRI. Worse yet, it is sometimes hard to understand the true reason we get to the point of despair. We as women are very complicated; we don't even understand ourselves. Are you feeling low today, crushed, hopeless, hurting? God has something to say to you: "For I hold you by your right hand—I, the LORD your God. And I say to you, 'Don't be afraid. I am here to help you'" (Isaiah 41:13).

One Year Bible Reading

1 Chronicles 1:1–2:17; Acts 23:11-35; Psalm 3:1-8; Proverbs 18:14-15

Two Sides to the Story

The first to present his case seems right,
till another comes forward and questions him.

PROVERBS 18:17 (NIV)

Let's always remember there are two sides to a story. Moms, when one of your kids comes running in crying his eyes out and blaming his brother, there are two sides to the story.

When someone at church gets mad at the pastor or a Sunday school teacher or a Bible study leader, there are two sides to the story. When your newlywed daughter calls and wants to vent about her new husband, there are two sides to the story.

So here are some tips to help us sort out facts from fiction.

- Consider the source. The other day I heard someone go on and on about someone. It was critical and unfair, but I considered the source. That person is often critical and unfair, so I took it with a grain of salt.
- Consider the motive. Do you detect a pang of jealousy, or bitterness, or malice? Malice has a way of twisting the truth.

And lastly, when you are telling your side of the story, be honest. Don't slant the details in your favor. I'm saying this to me as much as to you. We can all be guilty of this. But a little trick that helps me keep right is to try to tell the story as if the other person were present. Let's not say something behind someone's back that we wouldn't say to their face.

Make It Personal . . . Live It Out!

It's been said that "a half-truth is a whole lie." Sometimes we listen to the half-truths of our own inner voices and feelings. Don't trust your emotions; they often lie to you. Once the disciples were crossing over the Sea of Galilee with Jesus when a huge storm hit their boat. Jesus remained peacefully sleeping. They woke him with the words, "Don't you care that we're going to drown?" (Mark 4:38). Do you wonder that today? Do you look at the pieces of your life and wonder if God knows or cares? The disciples forgot that Jesus was right there with them in the storm. This is the whole truth. Will you call out to him and ask him to calm the waves of fear and turmoil, not just around you, but in you?

One Year Bible Reading

1 Chronicles 2:18–4:4; Acts 24:1-27; Psalm 4:1-8; Proverbs 18:16-18

Build a Bridge

An offended friend is harder to win back than a fortified city. Arguments separate friends like a gate locked with bars.

PROVERBS 18:19

Today we're going to talk about the offended friend. I feel confident that someone reading today has a serious rift with someone whom you used to be close to. I can see you now. You have your emotional arms folded like a fortified city.

William Blake once said, "It is easier to forgive an enemy than to forgive a friend." I think he must have spoken from experience. So how do we forgive and forget with someone we trusted and loved so deeply? They say, "The wounds that come from the closest, wound the deepest."

Such rifts are as old as humanity. Esau was angry with Jacob. Joseph's brothers were angry with Joseph. Even Paul and Barnabas had a serious disagreement and separation. And in the fourth chapter of the book of Philippians, Paul addressed two women, Euodia and Syntyche. Who knows how their problem got started, but when Paul writes, they are stuck. He reminds them that their names are written in the Book of Life. Maybe he was hinting that their mansions in heaven might be next door to each other, so they'd better make up now. What is so serious that we can't just build a bridge and get over it?

First John 4:20-21 challenges us. "If someone says, 'I love God,' and hates his brother [or sister], he is a liar. . . . And this commandment we have from Him: that he who loves God must love his brother also" (NKJV).

Make It Personal . . . Live It Out!

What is the secret to restoring broken relationships? First, stop being so stubborn. Begin to surrender your own hurt feelings. Let go of your pride; hang on to love. Be tenacious! Never give up on love. Never stop remembering the good that is in the other person. "No one has ever seen God. But if we love each other, God lives in us, and his love is brought to full expression in us" (1 John 4:12). So keep going back to Jesus, asking him to fill you with his compassion and grace. Then, walk it out. Ask him to give you a tangible action to build a bridge of kindness. Then, do it, because "love never fails" (1 Corinthians 13:8, NKJV).

One Year Bible Reading

1 Chronicles 4:5–5:17; Acts 25:1-27; Psalm 5:1-12; Proverbs 18:19

Words to Remember

The tongue has the power of life and death,
and those who love it will eat its fruit.

PROVERBS 18:21 (NIV)

Today, let's talk about the amazing power of words for good.

I will never get tired of remembering what is said in Proverbs 31:26 about the godly woman: that "on her tongue is the law of kindness" (NKJV). Let's make that our personal motto. Let's be proactive in this.

I read a story about a teacher who asked her students to write down the nicest thing they could think of about each of the other students in their class. She compiled the lists and gave each of them the comments others had written about them. Many were surprised; all were smiling as they read them. A few years later, Mark, one of the students, was killed in Vietnam. His teacher and many of those same students attended the funeral. His father had Mark's wallet. He carefully removed a worn piece of paper. "We thought you might recognize this," he said. It was the very list Mark had received in her classroom. Other students gathered around. Charlie sheepishly smiled, "I still have my list; it's in my desk drawer." Marilyn said, "Mine is in my diary." Vicki opened her purse and showed her worn and frazzled list to the group. "I carry it at all times. I think we all saved our lists."

It seems like such a small thing, to speak kind words into another's life. But this story reminds us that these are the words we are all starving to hear. They are like seeds that go deep and change our lives for good.

Make It Personal . . . Live It Out!

You cannot do a kindness too soon, because you never know how soon it will be too late.

I'm going to ask you to join me today in declaring this day a day of kind, encouraging, loving, and thoughtful words. For the next twenty-four hours, I challenge all of us to be on a mission.

Let's Pray

Lord, please bring people to mind and people in my path who need to know they are valued. Use my words as weapons of hope to defeat discouragement. Use my words to build up those who feel weary and torn down.

One Year Bible Reading

1 Chronicles 5:18–6:81; Acts 26:1-32; Psalm 6:1-10; Proverbs 18:20-21

She Does Him Good

He who finds a wife finds a good thing,
And obtains favor from the LORD.

PROVERBS 18:22 (NKJV)

Clearly, God's design for the role of a wife is for her to bring good to his life. The definition of *good* is "pleasant, excellent, valuable, kind, right, a benefit."

In the account of Creation (see Genesis 1 and 2) each time God created something, he said, "It is good." But then, after he created Adam, the Lord God said, "It is not good that man should be alone; I will make him a helper comparable to him" (Genesis 2:18, NKJV).

Dear ladies, I'm talking to all of us: whether you're single or married, God's original plan was for us is to be a blessing, that our presence in any situation would be helpful. I'm afraid that many women look for a man to fill their missing gaps, never realizing they were created to be givers, not just takers.

Proverbs 31:10-12 says, "Who can find a virtuous wife? For her worth is far above rubies. The heart of her husband safely trusts her; so he will have no lack of gain. She does him good and not evil all the days of her life" (NKJV).

My good friend Jeanette is a great example. Let me tell her story. Jeanette has several grown children, but her husband Ken longed for a son. Then the opportunity arose for them to adopt a little baby boy. What should she do? This meant a big lifestyle change for her. But Jeanette said yes. She chose to honor her husband, and their little boy Ben has been a blessing to them both. Good job, Jeanette!

Make It Personal . . . Live It Out!

There are a lot of miserable women in the world. They are dissatisfied with what they have, dissatisfied with their situations, dissatisfied with how people treat them. You can see it on their faces. If they are married, their husbands are miserable too. They make sure of it. Misery loves company. If you have fallen into the "poor me" hole, it's time to climb out. Let change begin with you. Today is the day to ask God how you can "do good" to your husband. If that's not been your goal lately, it might shock him. Pray for him, cook his favorite dinner, "do him good."

One Year Bible Reading

1 Chronicles 7:1–8:40; Acts 27:1-20; Psalm 7:1-17; Proverbs 18:22

Friendly

A man [or woman] who has friends must himself be friendly,
But there is a friend who sticks closer than a brother.

PROVERBS 18:24 (NKJV)

I believe that two of the great skills that we can learn in this life are first to treasure our friends, but more than that, to learn to be a friend who is a treasure to others.

A few days ago I had a no-good, terrible, full-of-frustration day. Probably the bottom line was that I was grumpy. I was tired. I was trying to multitask, and nothing was going smoothly. Anyway, I was grumpy. Then my friend tried to help, and I was grumpy to her. What was her response? She showed up later with a silly card of a little girl crying because her ice cream had spilled on her lap. It made me laugh—laugh at myself—and she laughed with me. Good job, Barbie!

Emily Dickinson, when pondering prosperity and fame said, "My friends are my estate." I have to agree. True friends love you through thick and thin.

Samuel Coleridge said, "Friendship is a sheltering tree."

It's been said, "A friend is someone who understands your past, believes in your future, and accepts you today as you are. A friend is someone with whom you dare to be yourself." I will add, a true, godly friend is someone who sees your weaknesses and does not talk about them behind your back. She prays for you, forgives you, and stirs you up to grow.

Proverbs 18:24 says, "A [woman] who has friends must [herself] be friendly, but there is a friend who sticks closer than a brother" (NKJV).

Make It Personal . . . Live It Out!

Are you feeling lonely today? Do you wonder why you just don't seem to connect and make lasting friendships? Let me ask you a question: Are you harboring resentment because someone let you down in the past? Do you often rethink past wounds? Maybe you've put a guard up, fearing you'll be hurt again. Don't be so afraid of pain—it's part of life. Will you ask the Lord to soften and change you?

Let's Pray

O Lord, this wall around my heart is shutting me off from giving and receiving true friendship, I see that. Please help me to forgive and to open my heart again.

One Year Bible Reading

1 Chronicles 9:1–10:14; Acts 27:21-44; Psalm 8:1-9; Proverbs 18:23-24

The Blame Game

A man's [or woman's] own folly ruins his life,
yet his heart rages against the Lord.

PROVERBS 19:3 (NIV)

Jon Courson says, "A foolish man doesn't listen to the Lord, seek the Lord, or walk with the Lord; yet, when he ends up in trouble, who does he blame? The Lord."

That's right. That's exactly what we see in so many people's lives. I want to talk about how we as women sometimes make bad choices. We cause trouble, get people upset, and burn bridges, but then we blame everyone else, including God. You know what? The blame game has no winners. There's no prize. No one feels sorry for us. We just dig our own hole deeper.

So if this is you, if you find your life is a tangled mess, just stop pointing your finger at everyone else. Even if others have done you wrong, what you do now and how you live your life from this day on is entirely up to you. God is really for you. Don't shut him out and don't shut others out who love you and want to help.

Let me give you a little formula that can give you a place to start. Turn in your Bible to James 4:7-10: "Therefore, submit to God. Resist the devil and he will flee from you. Draw near to God and He will draw near to you. Cleanse your hands, you sinners; and purify your hearts, you double-minded. Lament and mourn and weep! Let your laughter be turned to mourning and your joy to gloom. Humble yourselves in the sight of the Lord, and He will lift you up" (NKJV).

No matter how deep your hole is, there is no hole so deep that the long arm of our Father in heaven cannot reach you and pull you out.

Make It Personal . . . Live It Out!

Personal responsibility is a true sign of wisdom and maturity. The day we stop blaming others—our mothers, our ex-boyfriends or husbands, our mothers-in-law, our churches, and especially God—we are finally growing up.

Once we are willing to take personal responsibility for our own actions and attitudes we can—we will—see that God is for us. He will supply all the strength and guidance we need for a rich and full life.

One Year Bible Reading

1 Chronicles 11:1–12:18; Acts 28:1-31; Psalm 9:1-12; Proverbs 19:1-3

True-Blue Friendship

Wealth brings many friends,
but a poor man's friend deserts him.

PROVERBS 19:4 (NIV)

Solomon is making a sad commentary, not on the way things should be, but on how, sadly, things often are. As we know, Solomon was very wealthy, famous, and powerful. Maybe he sometimes wondered if some of the people who seemed to be his friends really weren't. In a way, that would be very sad. J. H. Jowett once said, "The real measure of our wealth is how much we should be worth if we lost all of our money."

So what is the message and lesson for us as women? Don't be a fair-weather friend. We live in such a lonely world. Therefore Proverbs 18:24 tells us, "[She] who has friends must [herself] be friendly" (NKJV). The best way to have a friend is to be one.

You can have fun going out to lunch or shopping with a friend, but when you walk with her through hardship, you are bonded for life. When David was out of favor and living as a fugitive, Jonathan was a true friend to him. First Samuel 23:16 tells us, "Then Jonathan . . . arose and went to David in the woods and strengthened his hand in God" (NKJV).

Proverb 17:17 says, "A friend loves at all times, and a [sister] is born for adversity" (NKJV).

Let me close by sharing some fun, important, sweet things friends have done that blessed me. Jewell stopped by with a basket of fruit from her garden. Lynne sent me a package in the mail. Peggy called to talk about what we read that morning in *The One Year Bible*. Maggy called to pray, and Christy sent some pictures her kids had colored for me.

Make It Personal . . . Live It Out!

Did you know that God can give you "divine insight"? He can. Would you like to be his ambassador of love? Close your eyes and pray, "Lord, is there someone who needs a message of cheer?" Keep asking until he puts someone on your heart. Then ask him to give you a secret way to deliver something to impart joy, a serendipity. Secretly deliver a pot of flowers, money in an envelope, a gift card for groceries, an uplifting book . . . Let the Lord show you. I guarantee, you will be the one with the biggest smile at the end of the day.

One Year Bible Reading

1 Chronicles 12:19–14:17; Romans 1:1-17; Psalm 9:13-20; Proverbs 19:4-5

July 13

Poor

All the brothers of the poor hate him;
How much more do his friends go far from him!
He may pursue them with words,
Yet they abandon him.

PROVERBS 19:7 (NKJV)

When you are going through hard times, it is so much harder when you are alone. Our proverb today states that when we need companionship, comfort, and the help of others the most, that is often when we are the least likely to find it. Job found out that was true. Listen to his pitiful words in Job 19:14, 19: "My relatives have failed, and my close friends have forgotten me. . . . And those whom I love have turned against me" (NKJV). Wow! He is feeling really low, and we have to remember that he had done nothing wrong. It was not because of his own sin against God or others that he was afflicted.

If you are in a place where you feel really, really poor and really, really alone, who can you turn to? There is no one better than the Lord himself. He has given us the book of Psalms to comfort and encourage us. As I read the Psalms, I always see that I am not the only one who is going through struggles and feeling discouraged. But then the words lead me from that low place to higher ground. They remind me that the Lord has not forgotten or forsaken me. One of the reasons I love reading *The One Year Bible* is that it lays out a psalm to read every day.

Today's reading includes Psalm 10:14: "But you, O God, do see trouble and grief; you consider it to take it in hand. The victim commits himself to you; you are the helper of the fatherless" (NIV).

Make It Personal . . . Live It Out!

Abraham Lincoln wasn't just a great president; he was a great man. He was born in poor conditions, his son Willie died at only eleven, he faced intense political opposition and then saw the country endure a civil war. Like Jesus, he was a man of sorrows and acquainted with grief. And yet he knew one of the great secrets of life: "To ease another's heartache is to forget one's own." Will you seek to do that today?

One Year Bible Reading

1 Chronicles 15:1–16:36; Romans 1:18-32; Psalm 10:1-15; Proverbs 19:6-7

Testimonies

He [or she] who gets wisdom loves his own soul;
he who cherishes understanding prospers.

PROVERBS 19:8 (NIV)

Bottom line: the wise, godly life is the good life.

Wives, no matter where you live or who your husband is, the wise wife is the blessed wife. I know a woman who has a very cranky husband. He's stubborn, prideful, and refuses to go to church, but God has given her the sweetest, most powerful dose of wisdom and joy. She is a light to everyone around her. Years ago the Lord gave her the verse "The wise woman builds her house, but the foolish pulls it down with her hands" (Proverbs 14:1, NKJV). Well, she could see that even though her husband was making bad choices, she didn't need to. She chose to "delight herself in the Lord," and he's prospered her, in spite of her circumstance.

I have another friend who is single, actually divorced. Her husband of many years lived a secret life, and then he left her. Her husband's aging father lived with them and remained when his son left the family. Janie was brokenhearted but not bitter. She chose to walk the path of humility and grace. Her father-in-law remained under her care for many years. Her daughters initially struggled with feelings of betrayal and abandonment. Now they are both married and serving God. Janie clung to the rock of God's love; she remained close to her church family and continued to choose wisdom. Her life is living proof that God prospers the godly.

Make It Personal . . . Live It Out!

What's your story? Is there a time when a big storm hit your life? Did you cry out to God? Did you see his faithfulness in the hardship? Then you have a testimony. Your testimony can encourage others. Revelation 12:11 says, "They have defeated [Satan] by the blood of the Lamb and by their testimony." Draw out three circles on a paper. In the first circle, write out your dilemma (life without Christ, or a hardship as a believer). In the second, write out how God sent help and hope. In the third circle, describe the fruit and joy of seeing God's hand in your life. That's your testimony. Now, will you share it with someone?

One Year Bible Reading

1 Chronicles 16:37–18:17; Romans 2:1-24; Psalm 10:16-18; Proverbs 19:8-9

Slow to Anger

The discretion of a man [or woman] makes him slow to anger,
And his glory is to overlook a transgression.

PROVERBS 19:11 (NKJV)

The New Living Translation phrases it, "Sensible people control their temper; they earn respect by overlooking wrongs."

Discretion is a word we seldom hear, and truthfully, something we seldom see, either. The Hebrew word is *sekel*, which first of all means "intelligence," but it is not an intelligence that is just kept in your head. It is an intelligence that gives you good sense, good judgment that translates into wise actions. Discretion is applied here as we respond to disappointments, frustrations, and the failures of others. Are we quick to anger or slow? This is the true test.

Ladies, let's take this for a test-drive in our daily living. When we see a dirty dish in the sink or socks left on the floor, does it tick us off? When someone takes our parking spot or scratches our car, when our kids lose their math books or our husband forgets our birthday, does it tick us off? When our friend does not return our phone call or the bank makes a mistake, does it tick us off? In the course of our days, hundreds of things can go wrong. If we respond with anger, even a quiet smolder, this is bad, unintelligent living—bad for us and bad for others. On the other hand, think of a time when you made a mistake and someone was patient with you, gracious, and sweet. What a surprise! What a breath of fresh air! It's been said, "To err is human; to forgive, divine."

Make It Personal . . . Live It Out!

I spoke a word in anger to one who was my friend.
Like a knife it cut him deeply, a wound that was hard to mend.
That word, so thoughtlessly uttered, I would we could both forget.
But its echo lives and memory gives the recollection yet.
—C. A. LUFBURROW IN "THE ECHO"

If we don't learn from our mistakes, we are destined to repeat them. Grace wins friends and influences people. Practice grace, speak grace, and grace will come back to you.

One Year Bible Reading

1 Chronicles 19:1–21:30; Romans 2:25–3:8; Psalm 11:1-7; Proverbs 19:10-12

Drip . . . Drip . . . Drip . . .

The contentions of a wife are a continual dripping. . . .
But a prudent wife is from the Lord.

PROVERBS 19:13-14 (NKJV)

Contention. *Contention* means "argumentative, ready to pick a fight."

Our proverb today tells us that "the contentions of a wife are a continual dripping"—drip, drip, drip. Have you ever heard a description of Chinese water torture? The victim is trapped in place. Water is slowly dripped on the forehead so he can see each drop coming. Over a long, unceasing time, he is driven frantic. Drip, drip, drip, never really letting up. When one drop lands, you know there's another coming. Can you see that we as women can do that when we get into the habit of being negative? Sharp little looks, negative words, criticisms, put-downs, never letting our husbands be right or respected. This is maybe even worse than physical torment. It pierces the soul. Do you see how this wears everyone down?

On the other hand, a prudent wife is from the Lord. Yes, indeed a wife that is gracious and wise, she's a gift. "Every good gift . . . is from above" (James 1:17, NKJV). And so we as wives, and as women in any relationship, have to know that God can and will change us. If we have fallen into a bad, negative habit, this would be a perfect time to be honest with the need to change. It is also a great time to look up, call out, and ask the Lord himself to make us prudent wives who are blessings.

Make It Personal . . . Live It Out!

A survey was done asking men why they cheated on their wives. You'll be surprised at the number four reason: "My wife is a nag. She thrives on making me feel like dirt, nagging, fighting, and putting me down." Of course, that is not a good excuse, but evidently it has driven many men away seeking silence and/or support. A prudent wife might have just as many issues to deal with in her marriage, but she handles them kindly. Will you take this to heart?

One Year Bible Reading

1 Chronicles 22:1–23:32; Romans 3:9-31; Psalm 12:1-8; Proverbs 19:13-14

Instructions for Life

He who obeys instruction guards his life,
but he who is contemptuous of his ways will die.

PROVERBS 19:16 (NIV)

The Message puts it this way: "Keep the rules and keep your life; careless living kills."

Maybe you're one of those people who never reads the manuals. You open the box when you get a new appliance, plug it in, and keep pushing buttons until it kind of does what you want it to do. Don't ask me how I know. Well, those of us who do that realize we never really get the most out of that appliance, and by the time we figure that out, we've lost the manual. But sometimes it's more than annoying. It's dangerous to neglect reading the instructions. I once wanted to strip old wax from my floor. I thought, *I'll mix bleach and ammonia. That will clean it really well.* I hadn't read on the label that that combination is toxic. An hour on my knees breathing the fumes sent me to the hospital with lung damage.

My story is a good illustration of how we can create toxic situations in our lives by not applying the sound, practical instruction of the Proverbs.

Let me share a string of proverbs that, like a string of pearls, when obeyed, will guard your life:

- A soft answer turns away wrath (15:1, NKJV).
- He who trusts in riches will fall, but the righteous will flourish (11:28, NKJV).
- An excellent wife is a crown of her husband, but she who causes shame is like rottenness in his bones (12:4, NKJV).
- The way of a fool is right in his own eyes, but he who heeds counsel is wise (12:15, NKJV).
- Do not be wise in your own eyes; fear the Lord and depart from evil (3:7, NKJV).

Make It Personal . . . Live It Out!

As you have read the Proverbs the last few months, are there a few that have really stood out? Have they pricked your heart, and yet you haven't applied them? It's been said, "To know and not to do is not to know at all." In James 1:22, God speaks frankly to us: "Don't just listen to God's word. You must do what it says. Otherwise you are only fooling yourselves."

One Year Bible Reading

1 Chronicles 24:1–26:11; Romans 4:1-12; Psalm 13:1-6; Proverbs 19:15-16

Kindness to the Poor

He who is kind to the poor lends to the LORD,
and he will reward him for what he has done.

PROVERBS 19:17 (NIV)

One thing I have learned in my life is you can't outgive the Lord.

Sometimes I think about that little boy in John 6 who gave his entire lunch to Jesus so that the rest of the five thousand people there that day could eat. It's ridiculous that he thought his little lunch could make any difference. And of course there is the fact that he must have considered that if he gave up his lunch, he would then have no lunch. But because the little boy had just heard Jesus teach the Sermon on the Mount, he had heard him say, "Do not worry about your life, what you will eat or what you will drink; nor . . . what you will put on. . . . But seek first the kingdom of God and His righteousness, and all these things shall be added to you" (Matthew 6:25, 33, NKJV). And since he was still young and still able to believe that what God says is more valid than what circumstances seem to say, he did it. He gave it all. In that moment of letting go of his lunch, he put himself entirely, completely in the Lord's hands, voluntarily. *Hmmmm.* Can I have a little word with you now? Have you ever really done that? Can you imagine what this little boy felt like as he saw what the Lord did with his lunch?

So if God puts a holy tug on your heart as you see a need, don't be afraid. God has a wonderful economy. Trust him, because "he who is kind to the poor lends to the LORD, and he will reward him for what he has done."

Make It Personal . . . Live It Out!

Let me give you an example. Do you believe in protecting the unborn? Are you pro-life? Put your money where your mouth is! Many women resort to abortion because they feel absolutely desperate. I have several friends whose life's passion is to provide resources and support and counseling through crisis pregnancy centers. Behind each of them is a little army of loving people, each doing a small part. Some give money, some provide rides to doctor's appointments, some crochet baby blankets, some are on call for personal and emotional care. Make a difference; get involved.

One Year Bible Reading

1 Chronicles 26:12–27:34; Romans 4:13–5:5; Psalm 14:1-7; Proverbs 19:17

July 19

A Word to Moms

Discipline your children while there is hope.
Otherwise you will ruin their lives.
Hot-tempered people must pay the penalty.
If you rescue them once, you will have to do it again.

PROVERBS 19:18-19

Adam Clark said, "This is a hard precept for a parent. Nothing affects the heart of a parent so much as a child's cries and tears. But it is better that the child may be caused to cry when the correction may be healthful to his soul, than that the parent should cry afterwards when the child is grown to man's estate and his evil habits are sealed for life."

The Duke of Windsor commented, "The thing that impresses me most about America is the way parents obey their children." So sad.

Recently my friend Christy stayed with us for a few days with her three small children. It was a blessing to see what a loving and wise mother she is. What I loved was that they had freedom to just be children, and yet even the four-year-old boy understood there are boundaries. This was clear in the moment when her son crossed the boundary and was too rough with his little sister. Christy intervened. She not only stopped the bad behavior, but she took the time to explain why and to pray with him. Accidents like spilled milk or broken cups were dealt with like they should be, as accidents. But issues of character and kindness and truth and right were dealt with quickly, lovingly, and yet firmly. Good job, Christy!

Make It Personal . . . Live It Out!

Our proverb today advises us to be quick to discipline but slow to anger. Moms, a hot temper is a very unhelpful parenting tool. It teaches the kids to be afraid of you. They will distrust you, or avoid you, or copy you. Oh, dread the day you see your bad behavior displayed in their bad behavior. Discipline, on the other hand, helps children to feel secure. If boundaries are explained, kids learn the whys along with the whats. Have you failed in the past? Who hasn't? Today is a new day.

Let's Pray

O Lord, it is such a responsibility to raise children rightly. I feel overwhelmed and underequipped. And so I turn to you, the perfect Father. Please guide me with your wisdom, and cover my mistakes.

One Year Bible Reading

1 Chronicles 28:1–29:30; Romans 5:6-21; Psalm 15:1-5; Proverbs 19:18-19

God's Good Plans

Listen to advice and accept instruction,
and in the end you will be wise.
Many are the plans in a man's heart,
but it is the LORD's purpose that prevails.

PROVERBS 19:20-21 (NIV)

We live in a world with information overload. Advice comes at us from all directions. But above all, God wants to play the primary role of mentor and advisor in our lives. His Word is full of explanations and examples of both good and bad choices and the results of each.

This is one of the reasons I never get tired of encouraging people to read *The One Year Bible*. There are so many Christians who just aren't personally familiar with the lessons from Abraham's life, or Lot's life, or Saul's and David's lives. They're not reading the Proverbs every day or the Epistles. If that's you, please pray about picking one up and starting to read today. God wants to meet you with fresh manna and timely advice from his Word.

A few years ago I was struggling with some big decisions. I had been praying, asking the Lord to direct. It just so happened that I was with some friends at the Grand Canyon. As I watched the sunset, I was overwhelmed with the power and majesty of a God who would create such a masterpiece. The next morning, I opened my *One Year Bible* to read the psalm for the day. As I read the words, I could sense the Lord's voice saying in Psalm 32:8, "I will instruct you and teach you in the way you should go; I will guide you with My eye" (NKJV).

And so that morning, surrounded by the Grand Canyon, I felt secure, surrounded by the God who made it.

Make It Personal . . . Live It Out!

I want to ask you a question. Do you live the majority of your days making your own decisions and plans? Honestly, how often do you ask God's opinion? He is interested in both the major and minor issues—because he is interested in you. He knows what lies ahead. Listen to his voice say to you, "For I know the plans I have for you. . . . They are plans for good and not for disaster, to give you a future and a hope" (Jeremiah 29:11).

One Year Bible Reading

2 Chronicles 1:1–3:17; Romans 6:1-23; Psalm 16:1-11; Proverbs 19:20-21

Audience of One

The fear of the LORD leads to life:
then one rests content, untouched by trouble.

PROVERBS 19:23 (NIV)

When you respect and honor the Lord, when you value his Word above all other opinions, when you trust and obey him even when it puts you out of favor with popular opinion, you are living before what has been called "the audience of one. Before all others you have nothing to gain, nothing to lose, and nothing to fear." As Max Lucado states it, you are looking for only the "applause of heaven." Trouble may come, you may suffer externally, but it is well with your soul. Paul said, "In all these things, we are more than conquerors through Him who loved us" (Romans 8:37, NKJV).

Daniel met an incredible challenge when a law was invoked that made it illegal to pray (see Daniel 6). Daniel had a decision. He could either fear and honor God, or fear and honor man. He chose God. He prayed. He was caught and sentenced to death, then thrown into a pit of hungry lions. This just doesn't seem right! He was delivered from the lions' den. And his trust was a testimony of confidence in a God who is with you and sustains you in any dark and dangerous pit.

Charles Gordon wrote, "The more one sees of life, the more one feels, in order to keep from shipwreck, the necessity of steering by the Polar Star, i.e., in a word, leave to God alone, and never pay attention to the favors or smiles of man; if he smiles on you, neither the smile or frown of men can affect you."

Make It Personal . . . Live It Out!

What does it look like to fear the Lord as you face daily, seeming ordinary issues of life? Daniel is famous because of his lions' den event, but most of his life consisted of daily honesty and integrity in the workplace. "Daniel soon proved himself. . . . They couldn't find anything to criticize or condemn. He was faithful, always responsible, and completely trustworthy" (Daniel 6:3-4). He didn't steal pencils or check personal e-mail on company time. He was a good example of a good example. Will you be faithful to honor God in the little things? Then when the big challenges come, "you will have nothing to gain, nothing to lose, and nothing to fear."

One Year Bible Reading

2 Chronicles 4:1–6:11; Romans 7:1-13; Psalm 17:1-15; Proverbs 19:22-23

Don't Learn the Hard Way

If you punish a mocker, the simpleminded will learn a lesson;
if you correct the wise, they will be all the wiser.

PROVERBS 19:25

Have you ever noticed that a foolish person has to always learn the hard way? They're mockers. Mockers think they are above the rules. They think that the warnings and principles of God's Word don't apply to them.

Ladies, is there an area of disobedience you just don't think you have to give up?

Maybe it's the way you treat your mother. You resent needing to help her, you resent some things in the past, you're always on edge with her. Your sour attitude will come back to haunt you, because it doesn't just hurt your mother; it dishonors God. Maybe there is a secret sin in your life that you keep hanging on to. The Holy Spirit keeps sending pangs of conviction; you know it's wrong. Do you realize you aren't just neglecting his influence; you are mocking his authority in your life? This is a foolish decision. Do you have to wait until the consequences of that sin come crashing in on you before you get it?

On the other hand, the wise are tender to the prompting of the Holy Spirit. So let me ask you a question. When you read your Bible, or listen to a message from God's Word, are you hungry to learn and change and grow? Do you take his lessons and promptings to heart? Are you tired of learning the hard way? I am! Let's then be quick to hear the Lord's correction—because a word to the wise is sufficient.

Make It Personal . . . Live It Out!

Has it been a while since you sensed the conviction of the Holy Spirit? That's not necessarily a good sign. I find that some of the most mature and deeply godly people I know are increasingly sensitive to sin in their lives. They don't live in condemnation, but they have a passion for purity—not just in others, but in themselves. Remember what God said to the Laodicean church: "I correct and discipline everyone I love. So be diligent and turn from your indifference" (Revelation 3:19).

One Year Bible Reading

2 Chronicles 6:12–8:10; Romans 7:14–8:8; Psalm 18:1-15; Proverbs 19:24-25

Mom and Dad

Children who mistreat their father or chase away their mother
are an embarrassment and a public disgrace.

PROVERBS 19:26

To "mistreat a father." As I say that term, I think of daughters whose fathers are undeserving of respect or love or forgiveness. Truthfully, they deserve to be mistreated because they mistreated their daughters. Once again, all I can say is, "Two wrongs don't make a right."

Fatherhood is both a position and a role. If you have a father who is still alive, even if he was a bad dad, you, as a child of God, are assigned to him. There is a strong possibility that no one else on the face of the earth prays for him or shows true agape love to that man. If he doesn't deserve it—and many don't—then it is even more a work of the Spirit of God's grace within you to enable you to love the unlovable. Jesus told us, "If you just love those who love you, well big deal!"

Let me tell you the real key here. Let God the Father play the role of father to you. Let him father you, fill your cup, affirm you, and encourage you. Then your heart will not be so needy. You will be free and full to love as you were created to love.

Secondly, it is a shameful thing to chase away your mother. Don't do that either. For some women, their mothers just yank their chains. They can't stand to be around them. Again, if you are a child of God, that is not an option. You are assigned by God himself to love her. "Love is patient, love is kind . . . love never fails" (1 Corinthians 13:4, 8, NIV).

Make It Personal . . . Live It Out!

Now let's turn the tables here and be blunt. If you are a mother, don't make it hard for your kids to love you. Do you micromanage? Do you nag? Are you hard to please? Do you fail to listen to your kids? If they are married, do you criticize their spouses? Don't nitpick; save your advice for the big issues. Enough said? In other words, be a woman who is easy to love and respect.

One Year Bible Reading

2 Chronicles 8:11–10:19; Romans 8:9-25; Psalm 18:16-36; Proverbs 19:26

Prone to Wander

Stop listening to instruction, my son,
and you will stray from the words of knowledge.

PROVERBS 19:27 (NIV)

Two things are distinctly linked here; they present a warning and reality. If you stop listening to God's Word, you will stray. There's an old hymn with the words "Prone to wander, Lord, I feel it, prone to leave the God I love."

I hope you know your human nature well enough to know that your heart is prone to wander too. Have you heard it said, "If there's dust on your Bible, there's dirt in your life"? Never underestimate the power of the world, the flesh, and the devil to subtly plant seeds of desire that will pull you away. But then never underestimate the power of God's Word to keep you safe, and—if you stray—to pull you back, cleanse you, and restore you.

So if you do not read God's Word every day as your anchor and food, you are vulnerable. Mere head knowledge is not enough either. Henry Blackaby says, "God's people have head knowledge but little heart and life experience with God." Blackaby recommends that you keep a journal as you read. "When you sense God speaking to your heart," he says, "don't let those thoughts get away from you. Write them down so you can review them." He also is a great advocate of application. Each day ask the question, "God, what do you want me to do in response to today's reading?"

O to grace how great a debtor
Daily I'm constrained to be!
Let Thy goodness, like a fetter,
Bind my wandering heart to thee.

—ROBERT ROBINSON IN "COME, THOU FOUNT OF EVERY BLESSING"

Make It Personal . . . Live It Out!

I have been walking with the Lord for many years. I have known many, many people who at one time were "on fire for the Lord."It seemed they couldn't get enough of the things of the Lord. They loved the Word and worship. They loved fellowship. But then they got distracted or just busy with life. They slipped away and now are far away. Is that you? Oh, please listen: come back. It's not too late. Come home to God the Father; come back to fellowship with the Lord Jesus. Return to the joy of being filled again with the Holy Spirit.

One Year Bible Reading

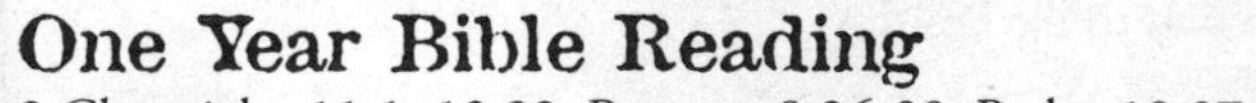

2 Chronicles 11:1–13:22; Romans 8:26-39; Psalm 18:37-50; Proverbs 19:27-29

Sober and Safe

Wine is a mocker and beer a brawler;
whoever is led astray by them is not wise.

PROVERBS 20:1 (NIV)

Augustine once said, “Drunkenness is a flattering devil, a sweet poison, a pleasant sin; whoever has it, has not himself.”

First of all, I want to say I’m not a legalist regarding alcohol. I know many Christians drink a glass of wine with meals and never have even a small problem. But, on the other hand, 1 Corinthians 8:9 says, “Beware lest somehow this liberty of yours becomes a stumbling block to those who are weak” (NKJV).

So I’ll share just a couple of reasons that my husband and I have chosen not to include alcohol in our lives for the sake of others.

- Children. You never know if one of your children or their friends or your grandchildren will see your small liberty as a big endorsement. My parents had a well-stocked liquor cabinet. As a teen, one of my friends talked me into taking some out of each bottle and watering it down. It was easy, and I liked it. It wasn’t long before we were drinking away from home.
- Others are watching, needing a role model. I once sat in the bar area of a restaurant with my sister drinking a Coke. The entire time I wondered if some little gal from Bible study would see me, think I was drinking, and be disappointed because someone in her life had ruined her life by drinking, or that she would be weakened in her resolve to stay out of the bars herself. To me, some liberties are just not worth the risk.

Make It Personal . . . Live It Out!

Is God spoiling your fun when he warns against drinking? Here are some sobering statistics. According to the Centers for Disease Control and Prevention, alcohol abuse killed an average of some eighty thousand Americans each year from 2001 to 2005 (the most recent report available), shortening the lives of these people by an average of thirty years. An average of thirty-six thousand people died each year from cirrhosis of the liver and other alcohol-related conditions, while forty-three thousand died in accidents. Because of alcohol, children grow up in poverty and abuse, marriages are ruined, and lives left in shambles.

Are you a closet drinker? Has it created a loss or danger? Will you pray and ask the Lord to lead you to help and to freedom?

One Year Bible Reading

2 Chronicles 14:1–16:14; Romans 9:1-24; Psalm 19:1-14; Proverbs 20:1

Stop Striving

The wrath of a king is like the roaring of a lion;
Whoever provokes him to anger sins against his own life.
It is honorable for a man to stop striving,
Since any fool can start a quarrel.

PROVERBS 20:2-3 (NKJV)

Six volatile words stand out: *wrath, roaring, provokes, anger, striving,* and *quarrel.* They paint a picture of the kind of troubling atmosphere many of us can sometimes find ourselves in. It is true, we cannot always avoid the fact that people around us and people who have authority over us are sometimes grumpy. They are sometimes even dangerously agitated. We can't always change them, but we do have the power of choice for ourselves. We can choose not to growl back. God calls this honorable. I like the blunt comment: "Any fool can start a quarrel." It's been said, "He who angers you, conquers you."

Gary Smalley, in his book *The DNA of Relationships*, says, "In every power struggle, people become instant adversaries; they take up opposing positions and try to crush their opponent. And do you know what? Every time that happens, Satan is very pleased."

Well then, if you are a child of God, pleasing Satan by fueling strife should just not be an option. Jesus said, "Blessed are the peacemakers, for they shall be called the children of God" (Matthew 5:9, KJV). And in Philippians 4:5 we have this good word: "Let your gentleness be evident to all. The Lord is near" (NIV).

Make It Personal . . . Live It Out!

Ever hear the expression "don't tangle with a bear robbed of her cubs"? Most angry people are upset because they feel robbed of something called "happiness." They might be taking their frustration out on you, but it often isn't about you at all. They are just venting. What they really are lacking is joy.

Joy comes from the Lord. So how's your joy quotient? Have you thanked the Lord for his love yet today? Did you remember your name is written in heaven, your sins are forgiven, and God's thoughts toward you are as numerous as the sands of the sea? If so, rejoice. Let the joy of the Lord be your shield and your strength.

One Year Bible Reading

2 Chronicles 17:1–18:34; Romans 9:25–10:13; Psalm 20:1-9; Proverbs 20:2-3

Are You Lazy?

The lazy man will not plow because of winter;
He will beg during harvest and have nothing.

PROVERBS 20:4 (NKJV)

The New Living Translation puts it this way, "Those too lazy to plow in the right season will have no food at the harvest."

And so today, the topic of wisdom has to do with diligence and timeliness. Solomon said these famous words about the importance of timing:

[There is] a time to plant, and a time to [reap]; . . .
A time to break down, and a time to build up;
A time to weep, and a time to laugh;
A time to mourn, and a time to dance; . . .
A time to gain, and a time to lose;
A time to keep, and a time to throw away; . . .
A time to keep silence, and a time to speak.

ECCLESIASTES 3:2-4, 6-7 (NKJV)

The important lesson for us as women is not to let the opportunity to do the right and important thing pass by. There are certain moments that just don't come again. In planting a crop, if you don't plow, you can't plant the seeds. If you don't plant, nothing will grow. This applies to every area of our lives. It applies to relationships. We need to invest in them. It applies to being faithful in the small things you are responsible for. Moms, this applies to paying attention to those teachable moments with your kids, and it applies to your spiritual life, too. A diligent seeking after the things of God will never leave you empty handed or empty hearted.

To help you, I have put some exciting resources on my website that will help you invest in your spiritual life. The address is BibleBusStop.com.

Make It Personal . . . Live It Out!

Diligence brings a crop of good things, but neglect brings only regrets. Begin today! Plant faith seeds in your soul. Romans 10:17 tells us, "Faith comes from hearing, that is, hearing the Good News about Christ." Here's a great exercise that will bear good fruit. Think of a quality you need in your life, such as joy, peace, faith, or purity. Then go to the concordance in the back of your Bible and look up five Scriptures on that topic and write them out. Read them often, and you will see the seeds grow and bear fruit.

One Year Bible Reading

2 Chronicles 19:1–20:37; Romans 10:14–11:12; Psalm 21:1-13; Proverbs 20:4-6

A Living Legacy

The godly walk with integrity;
blessed are their children who follow them.

PROVERBS 20:7

Integrity. *Integrity* means completeness, rightness, and uprightness. This is living right with God and right with man. What a rare but wonderful thing this is to behold. Those around us—children, families, neighbors, and even strangers—are blessed by a life that is a blessing.

Let me tell you a little story from the book *Our Daily Bread.*

Newsman Clarence Hall followed American troops around Okinawa in 1945. He came upon a small town that stood out as a beautiful example of a Christian community. He wrote, "We had seen other Okinawan villages, uniformly down-at-the-heels and despairing; by contrast, this one shone like a diamond in a dung heap. Everywhere we were greeted by smiles and dignified bows. Proudly the two old men showed us their spotless homes, their terraced fields . . . and granaries."

Hall saw no jails and no drunkenness, and divorce was unknown. He learned that an American missionary had come there thirty years earlier. While he was in the village, he'd led two elderly townspeople to Christ and had left them with a Japanese Bible. These new believers studied the Scriptures and started leading their fellow villagers to Jesus. Hall's jeep driver said he was amazed at the difference between this village and the others around it. He remarked, "So this is what comes out of only a Bible and a couple of old guys who wanted to live like Jesus."

Make It Personal . . . Live It Out!

Do you ever think, What is my legacy? When you leave a room, or leave a job, or eventually leave this earthly life, what effect will you leave behind? Will others remember unselfish acts of thoughtfulness and service? Will they remember that they saw Jesus in you?

Second Corinthians 2:14 says, "Thank God! He has made us his captives and continues to lead us along in Christ's triumphal procession. Now he uses us to spread the knowledge of Christ everywhere, like a sweet perfume."

Let's Pray

Lord, this really makes me think. I have a Bible, but do the words on the pages truly live in my life? I want to make a difference for good. Today, may my life reflect yours, expressing the sweet fragrance of Christ.

One Year Bible Reading

2 Chronicles 21:1–23:21; Romans 11:13-36; Psalm 22:1-18; Proverbs 20:7

July 29

A Pure Heart

Who can say, "I have kept my heart pure;
I am clean and without sin"?

PROVERBS 20:9 (NIV)

Horace Smith said, "When a proud man thinks best of himself, then God and man think worst of him."

I remember J. Vernon McGee talking about one of his roommates in college. He came home one day and said, "J. Vernon, I have attained sinless perfection." The problem was that from then on when anything went wrong, he would consider it everyone else's fault.

Jesus spoke in Luke 18:11-14 about those who trusted in themselves, thought that they were righteous, and despised others. So he told the story of two men in the Temple, a Pharisee and a tax collector. "The Pharisee stood up and prayed about himself: 'God, I thank you I am not like other men—robbers, evildoers, adulterers—or even like this tax collector. I fast twice a week and give a tenth of all I get.' But the tax collector stood at a distance. He would not even look up to heaven, but beat his breast and said, 'God, have mercy on me, a sinner.' I tell you, [said Jesus] that this man, rather than the other, went home justified before God. For everyone who exalts himself will be humbled, and he who humbles himself will be exalted" (NIV).

Whenever I read this story, I'm embarrassed for the Pharisee. How could he be so full of himself that he doesn't see how ridiculous this looks to God? Then I remember Jesus didn't tell this story just so that the Pharisee would get it. He told it so I would.

Make It Personal . . . Live It Out!

We can be very much like the Pharisee in this story. David went to the Lord with a deep desire to be like an open book, longing for him to cleanse and change him. Will you pray these words, and then still your heart, asking God to be completely honest with you? "Search me, O God, and know my heart; test me and know my anxious thoughts. Point out anything in me that offends you, and lead me along the path of everlasting life" (Psalm 139:23-24).

One Year Bible Reading

2 Chronicles 24:1–25:28; Romans 12:1-21; Psalm 22:19-31; Proverbs 20:8-10

A Child's Conduct

Even children are known by the way they act,
whether their conduct is pure, and whether it is right.

PROVERBS 20:11

Henry Wadsworth Longfellow wrote this poem:

There was a little girl, who had a little curl, right in the middle of her forehead.
When she was good, she was very good indeed,
But when she was bad she was horrid.

So what's a mother to do? What do we do when we're worried about our child's behavior? How can we raise godly children?

The number one answer is, pray! Never underestimate the power of a praying mom. Let me tell you about a wonderful ministry called Moms in Prayer (originally Moms In Touch). Fern Nichols (the founder) is a mom just like you. Let me quote from their website: "When her sons entered junior high, she had the same apprehensions. But overriding those fears was a deep trust that God, and only God, could protect and keep her children. Only God could change the lives of friends and coaches and teachers. She knew that if moms gathered together to cry out to God for the needs and concerns of children and schools, that He would not only hear those prayers, but answer them. Fern called like-minded moms who gathered each week to pray for their children and school, and thus began the first Moms In Touch group, now called Moms in Prayer. What started so simply in 1984 has grown into a worldwide community of praying moms in every state and in more than 140 countries around the world." What a wonderful resource. You can google Moms in Prayer and get connected in a group or start one in your church or school.

Make It Personal . . . Live It Out!

"Even children are known by the way they act." Recently scientists have discovered many interesting facts regarding DNA. They have concluded that personality type is written in the DNA code. If your child is quiet and pensive or talkative and social, he or she was born with that bent. Each personality has strengths and weaknesses. Don't try to make a quiet child into a social butterfly. But don't allow her to withdraw and become disconnected from people either. As parents, we can reinforce and encourage noble character, diligence, and stewardship. Again, bottom line: be your children's best fan and their most faithful prayer warrior.

One Year Bible Reading

2 Chronicles 26:1–28:27; Romans 13:1-14; Psalm 23:1-6; Proverbs 20:11

Look and See!

Ears that hear and eyes that see,
the LORD has made them both.

PROVERBS 20:12 (NIV)

When was the last time you thanked God for the ability to see and hear? Have you ever wondered what it would be like if you couldn't? We are so immersed in man-made, artificial sights and sounds that we often neglect the amazing wonders of God's natural world. And so, just for fun, I want to invite you to go outside and look around.

Since it is summertime, there are lot of bugs to see. Even the little ant is intriguing. Look at those skinny little legs. Did you know that an ant can lift fifty times its weight? That's like you picking up three automobiles at one time. Sunflowers are fun to watch: the sunflower faces the sun at all times throughout the day, starting the day facing east and ending it facing west.

Have you ever gotten up just to watch the sun rise? It is a mysteriously majestic sight. Then in the cool of the night, lie on the grass to stare up at the stars like when you were a kid. Drink in the wonder and beauty.

And what sounds in God's world are you missing? The sounds of birds early in the morning, the sound of a child's laughter, a kitten's sweet little purr. I love the sound of crickets on a summer night. Here's a little cricket trivia: if you count the number of chirps in fifteen seconds and then add thirty-seven, the number you get will tell you the approximate outside temperature (Fahrenheit). Now that's astounding!

Make It Personal . . . Live It Out!

Even though we do have eyes and ears, we often miss another facet of life completely. We don't notice the faces and silent tears of people just a few feet away. Should we? I believe the answer is yes. Whether it's the homeless man on the corner or the lonely woman next door, God wants you to see them as people he loves.

Let's Pray

First of all, I can't ever remember saying thank you, Lord, for giving me sight and hearing. I realize now they are both a gift and responsibility. Thank you. Help me to really look around me every day to see your wondrous works.

One Year Bible Reading

2 Chronicles 29:1-36; Romans 14:1-23; Psalm 24:1-10; Proverbs 20:12

August

Scan this code for audio devotionals
or visit www.tyndal.es/wisdom.

August 1

Lazy

Do not love sleep or you will grow poor;
stay awake, and you will have food to spare.

PROVERBS 20:13 (NIV)

Laziness verses diligence is the topic of this practical proverb. This is not an encouragement to be a workaholic, but it is an encouragement to use our time wisely. Don't sleep in but don't fritter away your waking hours either.

I remember as a young mother always feeling frustrated. I just did not know how to manage my time or my home. Then I came across a wonderful little book called, *Sidetracked Home Executives: From Pigpen to Paradise,* by Pam Young and Peggy Jones. I loved that it was written by two women who did not naturally have it all together. They learned out of desperation, and their book helped me, too. This is really the Titus 2 principle. Paul told Titus to encourage the older women to teach the younger women "to love their husbands and children, to be self-controlled and pure, [and] to be busy at home" (Titus 2:4-5, NIV). So many women grew up in our society without learning some very basic things about making a home. So if we share with each other what we've learned to make our homes better, we will build each other up, and we all need that.

Would you like to be a better, wiser steward of your time? Ask the Lord to show you resources. Emilie Barnes also has some wonderful books on this subject. And maybe there is a woman you know—an older godly woman—whom you could ask to pray for you and teach you some things that she has learned about being a good steward of her time and her home.

Make It Personal . . . Live It Out!

Moms, relishing the slower pace of summer is not being lazy. During the school year it seems you have to rush, rush, rush. Take advantage of small opportunities to savor the moment. If it's hot outside, go to the public library to read for the afternoon. Check out books on local birds and bugs. Pack a picnic and walk to the park in the cool of the evening. Invite the neighborhood kids to a Bible story time with a craft and snack. Some night, surprise your family by announcing that the main course for dinner is ice cream and peaches.

One Year Bible Reading

2 Chronicles 30:1–31:21; Romans 15:1-22; Psalm 25:1-15; Proverbs 20:13-15

Money Matters

Food gained by fraud or deceit tastes sweet to a man,
but he ends up with a mouth full of gravel.

PROVERBS 20:17 (NIV)

Fraud or deceit is lying. It's wrong. It's untruthful. It's a sham.

To someone who deceives, there is a pleasure in the sense of cleverness felt after getting away with a successful fraud. I recently looked over the paperwork of an older woman who had trustingly invested most of her life savings in an account that would tie her money up, with little gain, for many years. The broker had spent one hour, gotten her signature, and made thousands of dollars immediately. That must have seemed like a very sweet deal to him. Maybe he went out to dinner that night thinking how clever he was. But in reality, who is the biggest loser? This dear woman lost only money. The broker who took advantage of her gained a poverty of soul like a mouthful of gravel.

We can also turn this around, because the consumer can be just as deceitful. There has been an epidemic of people falsifying their credit applications to get loans to buy that sweet car, or house, or vacation, but now they can't afford the payment. This, too, is like a mouthful of gravel.

This would be a good time to insert Proverbs 3:6: "In all your ways acknowledge [the Lord], and He shall direct your paths" (NKJV). So do you want to do something? Do you have a decision? Are you making a choice? Pause and pray, "Lord, is this right? Is it good? Does it please you?" This one little pause will help you avoid ending up with a mouthful of gravel.

Make It Personal . . . Live It Out!

As wise, godly women, let's be good stewards of our money. But more than that, let's be generous. Recently a young mom with small children came into church. She had some immediate needs. My friend wanted to help but saw she only had a dollar in her purse. Then she remembered some cash tucked away. It was for a frivolous item she wanted to buy later. She dug it out and slipped it to the woman. The thankful tears in that young mom's eyes went deep into my friend's heart. She left that day not poorer but richer.

One Year Bible Reading

2 Chronicles 32:1–33:13; Romans 15:23–16:9; Psalm 25:16-22; Proverbs 20:16-18

Ban Gossip!

He who goes about as a talebearer reveals secrets;
Therefore, do not associate with one who flatters with their lips.

PROVERBS 20:19 (NKJV)

Ladies, *talebearer* is an old-fashioned word for a gossip—someone going around telling stories she knows or thinks she knows—and a talebearer's favorite thing to tell is secrets and inside stories.

There are two sides to this, and both are warnings.

First, be careful. Don't be flattered when someone comes to share an inside scoop on someone. Be aware it won't be long before she'll be gossiping to someone else about you. Don't listen to stories, because it's hard to forget them once you've heard them, even when you know they're not true. Proverbs 26:22 says, "The words of a talebearer are like tasty trifles, and they go down into the inmost body" (NKJV). Friendships, families, and even churches have been torn apart by gossip.

And, secondly, don't *be* a gossip. It's been said that you have become a mature person when keeping a secret gives you more satisfaction than passing it along. William King once said, "A gossip is one who talks to you about other people. A bore is one who talks to you about himself. And a brilliant conversationalist is one who talks to you about you."

So gossip is just plain bad business. If our heart's desire is to truly please God and bless people, let's be done with gossip. Let's ban it. Let's not listen to it, or enjoy it, or pass it along.

Make It Personal . . . Live It Out!

Do you wish the world were better? Let me tell you what to do.

Set a watch upon your actions, keep them always straight and true.
Rid your mind of selfish motives, let your thoughts be clean and high.
You can make a little Eden of the sphere you occupy.
Do you wish the world were wiser? Well, suppose you make a start,
By accumulating wisdom in the scrapbook of your heart;
Do not waste one page on folly; live to learn, and learn to live.
If you want to give men knowledge you must get it, ere you give.

—ELLA WHEELER WILCOX IN "WISHING"

One Year Bible Reading

2 Chronicles 33:14–34:33; Romans 16:10-27; Psalm 26:1-12; Proverbs 20:19

Mom and Dad

Whoever curses his father or his mother,
His lamp will be put out in deep darkness.

PROVERBS 20:20 (NKJV)

These are sobering words. There are some instructions in the Bible that can be hard to understand. But God's command to honor your parents is not one of them. Why is it then that so many, even Christians, have allowed themselves to completely disregard this?

Some people wonder, Do we really need family relationships? It is sometimes a lot easier to love people from afar or short term. Can't good friends fill the family gap? Chuck Swindoll said, "A family is a place where principles are hammered and honed on the anvil of everyday living." Yes, there are challenging times and personalities. That's when we must rely upon the Lord to help us love them through the good and bad.

Have you let your parents' flaws get under your skin? Be aware: if you can't let something go, if you can't resist the urge to be rude or unkind, it really reflects back on you. You are the child who has never grown up. It's your own inner glow and integrity that, like a lamp, is shut off and dark.

So, ladies, let me ask you, has it been a while since you called your mom to let her know you love her? If she's getting old and kind of cranky, don't take it personally. My mom told me, "Honey, getting old isn't for sissies." If one of your parents lives alone, it's especially important for them to hear your voice and for you to check up on them. You have the divinely appointed opportunity to be a bright spot in their day and a comfort in their life.

Make It Personal . . . Live It Out!

Are you thinking as you read this, *I wish I could pick up the phone and call my mom or dad, but they are gone*? Whether they died last month or many years ago, there is still a hole in your heart, you still miss them. Let me tell you, there are many older women—men, too—who would love for you to adopt them. Invite them to birthday parties or take them to lunch after church. Pray and ask the Lord to put someone in your life and on your heart. Both of you will be richer; you'll fill two holes for the price of one.

One Year Bible Reading

2 Chronicles 35:1–36:23; 1 Corinthians 1:1-17; Psalm 27:1-6; Proverbs 20:20-21

Relinquishing Revenge

Do not say, "I'll pay you back for this wrong!"
Wait for the LORD, and he will deliver you.

PROVERBS 20:22 (NIV)

Sometimes we are shocked when someone does something mean or unfair to us. How dare they? How could they? Wrong just hits us hard. But the greater blow is when we internalize it and brood over it and replay it, and—worst of all—let our thoughts fixate on how we'll get even. This is when the spider, the devil himself, has us in his wicked web. We become consumed, and often it becomes not eye for eye, but revenge wanting to wound deeper and escalate the damage. Ladies, please don't get tangled in that horrible trap. Take it directly to the Lord and surrender it to him.

Romans 12:17-19 says, "Repay no one evil for evil. . . . If it is possible, as much as depends on you, live peaceably with all men. Beloved, do not avenge yourselves, but rather give place to wrath; for it is written, 'Vengeance is Mine, I will repay,' says the Lord" (NKJV).

First Peter 3:9 says, "Don't retaliate with insults when people insult you. Instead, pay them back with a blessing. That is what God has called you to do, and he will bless you for it."

Remember, Jesus did not promise that everything in this life would be fair, or good, or right. In fact, he said, "In this world you will have tribulation, but be of good cheer, I have overcome the world" (John 16:33, NKJV).

Make It Personal . . . Live It Out!

The last part of our proverb today makes an intriguing promise, "Wait for the LORD, and he will deliver you." What does that mean? How does it relate to our desire for retribution when we are wronged? Well, one thing for sure is that it means we must be patient. I wish it weren't so, but sometimes it takes a long time for the scales to be balanced. That's why we must quickly surrender our offenses into the safekeeping of the Lord. The longer we hold on to them, the more pain we endure. What about the deliverance part? Well, if you do indeed surrender every part of the situation to the Lord, you will see a miracle occur. You will wake up one day and realize you are completely delivered—free from its grip.

One Year Bible Reading

Ezra 1:1–2:70; 1 Corinthians 1:18–2:5; Psalm 27:7-14; Proverbs 20:22-23

The Lord Directs Our Steps

The LORD directs our steps,
so why try to understand everything along the way?

PROVERBS 20:24

Life does sometimes seem like a mystery. Even in the course of a day we will have a neat little plan, and somewhere along the way interruptions and even disasters can come unexpectedly and quite uninvited. I am going to ask you an important question: When that happens, what happens to you? Honestly? Are you in the habit of responding with frustration or anger? I have to admit, I sometimes do. This is true when I have a tight grip on what we call "my life," "my plan," "my way," "my will," and "my timing."

But then we come across the Scripture that says, "Trust in the LORD with all your heart, and lean not on your own understanding" (Proverbs 3:5, NKJV).

James 1:2-3 says, "Count it all joy when you fall into various trials, knowing that the testing of your faith produces patience" (NKJV). And, of course, Romans 8:28 says that "all things work together for good to those who love God, to those who are the called according to His purpose" (NKJV).

So I want to leave you with a challenge today. Maybe you have a situation that you don't understand. Will you look up? Will you ask God to make this an adventure? Will you ask him to help you trust him completely and then to help you look for the treasures and lessons he has for you in this situation?

Always remember, we do not know what the future holds, but we do know who holds the future.

Make It Personal . . . Live It Out!

I love to hear testimonies, stories about people facing the curveballs and hardballs life throws at them. Sometimes it breaks my heart to hear of a tragedy or extreme hardship. However, a testimony is not a testimony until they share the "but God" part. This is when they tell how God used that very tragedy to place them in a position of being used to reach a soul, or to see his hand supply supernaturally, or to completely change the course of their previous path. Are you in the depths of a valley or facing a roadblock in life? God is writing your book. Will you trust? Will you yield? Will you follow his lead?

One Year Bible Reading

Ezra 3:1–4:23; 1 Corinthians 2:6–3:4; Psalm 28:1-9; Proverbs 20:24-25

The Searchlight of God

A wise king scatters the wicked like wheat,
then runs his threshing wheel over them.
The LORD's light penetrates the human spirit,
exposing every hidden motive.

PROVERBS 20:26-27

This proverb describes getting to the bottom of things. A wise leader realizes that people do not always have pure motives. Even in a church or family there are sometimes hidden agendas that are not good or godly.

So how does this apply to you and me? Well, I have learned many times through the years that we as women are complicated. Sometimes we do things within friendships or ministries or families that are destructive, but we somehow mask them as right, even to ourselves. The Bible tells us, "The heart is deceitful above all things, and desperately wicked; who can know it?" (Jeremiah 17:9, NKJV). Actually, when it comes to women, men are always complaining that they don't understand us. The truth is, we women sometimes don't understand ourselves.

Again, our proverb says, "The LORD's light penetrates the human spirit, exposing every hidden motive." This might seem like bad news, but actually it's good news. Why would we want to be blind, deceiving our own hearts? Let's let the light of God's Word shine deeply in us. Let's let it show the truth to us and give us the grace to be honest before God, and then let's ask him for the courage and strength to change.

Make It Personal . . . Live It Out!

When the Lord's searchlight shows you an attitude or action that is not right, how can you actually make that change? It's easy to shrug it off until you are blind to it again. I find that I see the clearest as I read his Word in the morning. When he speaks to my heart, I write a note in my journal or the margin of my *One Year Bible*. Then, instead of just moving on in my reading, I quiet my heart and let him speak. Prayer must always include listening as well as speaking to God. Can you change in your own strength? No. 'It is not by force nor by strength, but by my Spirit,' says the LORD of Heaven's Armies" (Zechariah 4:6).

Let's Pray

Holy Spirit, Spirit of power, change me. Make my heart right, ready to walk in the light.

One Year Bible Reading

Ezra 4:24–6:22; 1 Corinthians 3:5-23; Psalm 29:1-11; Proverbs 20:26-27

The Power of Love

Love and faithfulness keep a king safe;
through love his throne is made secure.

PROVERBS 20:28 (NIV)

Ladies, let's apply this proverb to our own realm. No, we are not literal kings—or queens, for that matter. But we do have areas of influence that the Lord has entrusted to us, and we need to have God's perspective on success and true security.

Love and faithfulness are given as the most important factors to make us safe and secure. That is not exactly how things are portrayed in the media. For a woman to be safe, it's said she needs to look out after herself first. She must defend her rights at any cost. But we can look at all the broken homes and lonely lives to see this is a formula for disaster, not success.

In the Bible, Queen Esther is the perfect example of doing a risky thing for love's sake. Her predecessor was Queen Vashti. She was beautiful and powerful, but she used her rights to defend her rights. This cost her both her position and her marriage. Later when Esther became queen, she faced a dilemma. The rights and even the lives of innocent people were threatened. She could remain silent and stay secure, or she could risk her position and speak out. Her cousin Mordecai challenged her that maybe she had attained her position "for such a time as this" (Esther 4:14, NIV). Love compelled her to be faithful to a higher responsibility. God honored her and used her to save many. I have a feeling that by showing an inner beauty, she gained respect, not only from those she helped but from her husband, too.

Make It Personal . . . Live It Out!

The theme of today's proverb is "the power of love." Amy Carmichael said, "You can give without loving, but you cannot love without giving." Let's let the words of 1 Corinthians 13:4-8 ignite our hearts with a passion to love: "Love is patient and kind. Love is not jealous or boastful or proud or rude. It does not demand its own way. It is not irritable, and it keeps no record of being wronged. It does not rejoice about injustice but rejoices whenever the truth wins out. Love never gives up, never loses faith, is always hopeful, and endures through every circumstance. . . . Love will last forever!"

One Year Bible Reading

Ezra 7:1–8:20; 1 Corinthians 4:1-21; Psalm 30:1-12; Proverbs 20:28-30

Divine Intervention

The king's heart is in the hand of the LORD,
Like the rivers of water;
He turns it wherever He wishes.
Every way of a man is right in his own eyes,
But the LORD weighs the hearts.

PROVERBS 21:1-2 (NKJV)

The book of Esther (chapters 5 and 6) tells an intriguing story that illustrates this truth. Evil Haman hated all Jews, especially Esther's cousin Mordecai. As the king's trusted advisor, Haman was a dangerous foe. One day he went home from the palace to plot Mordecai's death on a gallows. He planned to present the plan to the king the following morning for approval. "That night the king could not sleep. So one was commanded to bring the book of the records, . . . and they were read before the king" (Esther 6:1, NKJV). As he listened, he learned that Mordecai had once saved his life by exposing a plot to kill him. The next morning he ordered Haman to honor Mordecai royally. Needless to say, the villain's plot was foiled. Such a turn of events! Coincidence? No, it was divine intervention.

Jon Courson comments, "Because God is on the throne, we don't have to panic about government policies. . . . We're not to perspire, pout, panic, or plot. Instead, we're to pray, knowing that God is in complete control. And as we do, we'll be at peace."

Has someone in power made decisions that make you feel powerless? As you look at the current economy and the government, are you worried? Are you discouraged? Are you fearful? Remember, always remember: God is on the throne, and his throne is called the "throne of grace."

Make It Personal . . . Live It Out!

All of us can think of people we disagree with. We would love to change their minds. More important, we would love to change their hearts. But there are hearts that will never change. We see that with Pharaoh when Moses said, "Let my people go." What do we do with the two realities: God changes hearts, but some refuse to be changed? We need to make sure we are not the latter, stubborn and stuck. Believe it or not, you and I are sometimes wrong. Sometimes we are the ones who need "divine intervention."

Let's Pray

Lord, here I am with an open heart. May it be like water in your hand.

One Year Bible Reading

Ezra 8:21–9:15; 1 Corinthians 5:1-13; Psalm 31:1-8; Proverbs 21:1-2

Pleasing the Lord

The LORD is more pleased when we do what is right and just than when we offer him sacrifices.

PROVERBS 21:3

The topic today is pleasing the Lord. There is hardly a topic that intrigues and excites me more. Can you imagine: God—who designed the beautiful intricacy of the snowflake, the majestic flight of the eagle, and the rocky heights of Mount Everest—can be pleased with ordinary people like you and me? Enoch was a man who lived at a time in history when men were dangerously wicked. But contrary to the trend and flow of others, Enoch walked with God. "He was known as a person who pleased God" (Hebrews 11:5).

This stirs my heart. I want to please the Lord, don't you? What then does that mean? What can we do? God owns the cattle on a thousand hills; he doesn't need our money. His divine power can move mountains, but we are weak, merely human. Today's proverb gives us an important clue: the Lord is pleased when we do right. When we read about Enoch, we're not told of any big and mighty deeds that he accomplished. He didn't pastor a big church or win any big wars. It appears he was just like us, living an anonymous little life, facing whatever came his way. But he wasn't anonymous in heaven. This is the mystery and the wonder of the Christian life. There must be a secret element. The big and little battles in our souls regarding choices and surrender are seen and applauded and ultimately empowered by the same God who flung the stars into place.

Today, then, you and I choose. I choose the walk with God. May we sense his presence, honor his ways, and hear his sweet voice saying, "Well done, my child. Well done."

Make It Personal . . . Live It Out!

"We ask God to give you complete knowledge of his will and to give you spiritual wisdom and understanding. Then the way you live will always honor and please the Lord, and your lives will produce every kind of good fruit . . . as you learn to know God better and better" (Colossians 1:9-11).

Let's return to the sweet simplicity of lifting our hearts to our Father in heaven and simply living to please his heart.

One Year Bible Reading

Ezra 10:1-44; 1 Corinthians 6:1-20; Psalm 31:9-18; Proverbs 21:3

August 11

Haughty Is Not Holy

Haughty eyes, a proud heart,
and evil actions are all sin.

PROVERBS 21:4

Once in a while we need to look up a word like *haughty*. It means "disdainfully proud; snobbish; scornfully arrogant; full of contempt and arrogance."

I once knew a woman who was very rich, and very tall, and very talented. I was poor and young. I am very short and often felt inadequate. I remember whenever I was in her presence I felt small and flawed. She had a way of looking down or even looking past people. But she was a good example to me—of a bad example. I learned what it felt like to be looked at with scorn and disdain. More important, I learned that I never wanted others to feel such a look from me.

Haughty eyes show a proud heart. The eyes are said to be the window to the soul. Sometimes I look in someone's eyes, and I see darkness. Jesus said, "The lamp of the body is the eye. If therefore your eye is good, your whole body will be full of light. But if your eye is bad, your whole body will be full of darkness" (Matthew 6:22-23, NKJV).

A haughty look can make you cringe; as they say, a look can kill. But just one sweet look of kindness sends a message more powerful than words. Picture with me a look of friendliness to someone who's new in church, a look of compassion for a new widow, a look of understanding to a mother of a prodigal, and a look of forgiveness to someone who has made a mistake. Yes, child of God, that's the way it should be.

Make It Personal . . . Live It Out!

I'm sorry to say it, but sometimes churchy religious people can be very haughty. The Pharisees were haughty; they looked down on sinners like they were above them. Many people leave the church because they have felt contempt when they needed compassion. Listen, the church is not a showcase of shiny people. It's a hospital, a safe haven; it's a family. Even at best we are all just poor beggars telling other beggars where to get bread. I love the church because when we truly live what we are, God uses us to circle the wagons around the lonely and broken. Won't you do that? If not now, when? If not you, who?

One Year Bible Reading

Nehemiah 1:1–3:14; 1 Corinthians 7:1-24; Psalm 31:19-24; Proverbs 21:4

Foolishness Has Consequences

In today's Wisdom for Women we will read these three verses carefully. God is not only giving us information about the results of being wise in life, he is also showing us that foolishness will eventually ruin our lives. My husband often paraphases Galatians 6:7: "You reap what you sow." Then he says, "You can't plant potatoes and think you will pick tomatoes."

The plans of the diligent lead to profit
as surely as haste leads to poverty.
A fortune made by a lying tongue
is a fleeting vapor and a deadly snare.
The violence of the wicked will drag them away,
for they refuse to do what is right.

PROVERBS 21:5-7 (NIV)

The Proverbs used to be read in our public schools, and parents read them to their children. But many children are being educated about morality and integrity from watching TV, the Internet, and music videos. Maybe it would be more correct to say they are learning immorality and to be unethical. I know it's easy to turn on the Disney Channel or cartoons to keep your kids occupied and entertained, but sometimes we need to sit down and watch what they're watching. Stars of these shows become their heroes, but many of these stars are not heroes at all.

Maybe we can't change what others are doing, but we can make a choice to seek to be wise in our own lives and in our own homes. Unless we, as godly mothers, as godly women, have a moral anchor, the strong currents of outright wickedness that are pulling people down all around us will pull us and our families into that same dark hole.

Make It Personal . . . Live It Out!

Let's not go with the flow. Jesus said we, as God's people, are to be bright shining lights. "No one lights a lamp and then puts it under a basket. Instead, a lamp is placed on a stand, where it gives light to everyone in the house. In the same way, let your good deeds shine out for all to see, so that everyone will praise your heavenly Father" (Matthew 5:15-16). This is our mission and privilege. People all around us are lost; may it be our passion to shine God's love like a lighthouse in the dark night.

One Year Bible Reading

Nehemiah 3:15–5:13; 1 Corinthians 7:25-40; Psalm 32:1-11; Proverbs 21:5-7

A Quarrelsome Woman

Better to live in the corner of a roof
than to share a house with a quarrelsome wife.

PROVERBS 21:9 (NIV)

This description is a wake-up call for us as women. Oh, how easy it is to slip into the pattern of nagging and complaining. Somehow we, as women, almost feel it's our duty. If we don't point out everyone's flaws and mistakes, who will?

I thought I would quote a man, Matthew Henry, on this subject. He says, "What a great affliction it is to a man to have a brawling, scolding woman for his wife, who upon every occasion, and often upon no occasion, breaks out into a passion, and chides either him or those about her. . . . It makes a man ashamed of his choice and his management."

One of the habits a woman can get into is feeling she's entitled to be in a bad mood. When we're in a bad mood, we can be easily annoyed, critical, and harsh. We can bite someone's head off because "we're in a bad mood." You know what? We are not entitled to do that, and no one else is entitled to be on the receiving end. So, girls, let's just knock that off. Really.

There it is. This is not pretty. So then, how can we break this bad habit? I think the first step is to see that it's not just annoying to others, it's wrong.

Ask the Lord to forgive you. Ask others to forgive you. Then ask the Lord to fill you afresh with his loving, gentle, and kind Holy Spirit.

Make It Personal . . . Live It Out!

Have you been harsh, irritable, and quick to anger, but you don't know how to change? The first step is desire. Do you want to change? If so, good. The next step is to look at the source. Have you let resentment from your past or present pile up? We do that, you know. Will you take it to the Cross and ask the Lord to set your heart free to forgive? The next step is to kneel and ask the Lord to fill you completely and freshly with his Holy Spirit. "The Holy Spirit produces this kind of fruit in our lives: love, . . . patience, kindness, . . . gentleness, and self-control" (Galatians 5:22-23).

One Year Bible Reading

Nehemiah 5:14–7:73a; 1 Corinthians 8:1-13; Psalm 33:1-11; Proverbs 21:8-10

Trust and Obey

If you punish a mocker, the simpleminded become wise;
if you instruct the wise, they will be all the wiser.

PROVERBS 21:11

Basically, the Lord is telling us we can either learn the hard way or the easy way. So many people have a trail of scars and baggage because they made bad choice after bad choice. Oh, how the Lord would love to spare us from all that. James MacDonald puts it bluntly: "Choose to sin, choose to suffer." From start to finish, the Proverbs implore us not to sin so that we do not suffer.

D. L. Moody said, "The Scriptures were not given to increase our knowledge but to change our lives." A wise person learns from instruction. So true learning of God's Word must include application. As Howard Hendricks says, "Application is the key to Christian education; for to know and not to do is not to know at all." James tells us, "Don't just listen to God's word. You must do what it says. Otherwise, you are only fooling yourselves" (James 1:22).

So how can we establish a life-changing pattern of growing in godliness and wise living? "Developing a Quiet Time" at the back of this book is a user-friendly guide that gives simple, helpful steps. Becoming a daily Bible reader is definitely an important first step. As you read, look for and write down a lesson you can apply. Pause to pray, asking the Lord to personally help you walk it out. Our God is our heavenly Father. Let him father you, instruct, mentor, and direct you. He will give you strength and joy as you yield and follow his guidance.

Make It Personal . . . Live It Out!

Let me give you an example of how the Lord instructs us in his Word. In Nehemiah 9:19-21 the people recounted the faithfulness of God when the Israelites journeyed through the wilderness. "In your great mercy you did not abandon them. . . . The pillar of fire showed them the way. . . . You sent your good Spirit to instruct them . . . giving them manna from heaven. . . . Clothes did not wear out."

As you read this account, make it personal. Stop and recount the many times God has been faithful to you. Consider the challenges you are facing today. Ask yourself, Is God good? Is he able? Then pray, asking him to help you stop fretting and begin trusting him to see you through.

One Year Bible Reading

Nehemiah 7:73b–9:21; 1 Corinthians 9:1-18; Psalm 33:12-22; Proverbs 21:11-12

Simple Giving

Those who shut their ears to the cries of the poor
will be ignored in their own time of need.

PROVERBS 21:13

One of the greatest pursuits we can ever have in this life is to be a person after God's own heart as David was. This might seem like an odd expression to some, because they do not really think of the almighty, sovereign God as having a heart. But all through the Bible we see a God who loves, and who is tender toward the weak, hurting, and poor. Jesus told us that when you visit the lonely or feed the hungry, "inasmuch as you do it to the least of these, you do it to him" (Matthew 25:40, paraphrased).

It's amazing how seemingly small moments can impact our lives in large ways. My grandfather was a Missouri farmer. He never had much money, but he was rich in all the things a little girl like me admired. He had baby chicks and calves in the spring. And he could turn a brown patch of dirt into a wonderland of vegetables and watermelons. He purposely grew more than he needed. One day we loaded his old car to the brim with everything from green beans to potatoes. Then we delivered them to the family whose father was out of work, to the widow down the road, and to the single mom with lots of kids.

My grandfather taught me how to fish and drive a tractor and milk a cow. But this day of simple giving was his greatest lesson. No, he didn't have much money, but to me he was the richest man in the world.

Make It Personal . . . Live It Out!

Proverbs 31 describes my personal hero, the wise, godly woman. She was industrious and creative, but she was also tenderhearted and generous. It says in verse 20, "She extends a helping hand to the poor and opens her arms to the needy."

Will you simply bow your head right now and ask God to use you to fill a specific need? Then be open and eager to see who and where and what and how.

Let's Pray

Lord, open my ears, my eyes, and my heart to someone in need. Help me recognize your holy tug and follow your lead.

One Year Bible Reading

Nehemiah 9:22–10:39; 1 Corinthians 9:19–10:13; Psalm 34:1-10; Proverbs 21:13

Peace Offering

A gift given in secret soothes anger,
and a bribe concealed in the cloak pacifies great wrath.

PROVERBS 21:14 (NIV)

Of course, God would never endorse the use of gifts and bribes to pervert justice. But what this is saying is that a gift given in a subtle, gentle way can disarm someone's anger. Look at the story of Nabal and Abigail (see 1 Samuel 25). David's men had been a great benefit in providing protection to Nabal's flocks. David sent a message asking that Nabal provide food for David's troops, but Nabal was rude and selfish. He refused. David was furious. In response, he determined to attack and kill Nabal's entire household. When wise Abigail heard, she immediately gathered a generous amount of food and met David on the way. She bowed and asked him to take the gift and save himself from taking revenge into his own hands.

And for us, what can we learn from this? Would it sometimes be helpful to soften someone's anger with a gift? I think so. Have you and your husband been arguing over bills and finances? Has there been tension and stress in the house? How about surprising him by cooking his favorite dinner some night and having it ready when he comes home? Now that's building a bridge.

Maybe you have tension with your mother-in-law. A sweet card and a bouquet of flowers might melt the ice. If you have a teenager in the house, there are times when you feel you are always doing battle, laying out rules and consequences. How about ordering pizza and letting him invite his friends? Has your friend been cold because her feelings were hurt? Need a peace offering? I highly recommend chocolate.

Make It Personal . . . Live It Out!

"A gift given in secret soothes anger." Our proverb today reminds us that when we have a tiff with someone, not everyone needs to know. Relationships are best restored privately and personally. Is there someone you need to hold an olive branch out to? Won't you do it today? Be a peacemaker! Sincerely extend a gift of gentle kindness and reap the blessing of reconciliation.

One Year Bible Reading

Nehemiah 11:1–12:26; 1 Corinthians 10:14-33; Psalm 34:11-22; Proverbs 21:14-16

August 17

Chasing Pleasure

He who loves pleasure will become poor;
whoever loves wine and oil will never be rich.

PROVERBS 21:17 (NIV)

Chasing pleasure will eventually leave you with nothing, not even pleasure. It will leave you empty and needy, full of shame and condemnation.

When you're in high school or college, it is tempting to look at the kids who are in the popular party scene as lucky. When you're young, it's easy to feel like maybe you're missing the good things in life by being a Christian. But my sister just went to her high school reunion. She saw a man there who had been handsome and popular, but he never grew out of the party scene. Now he looks old and haggard and lonely.

Maybe you are the prodigal. Maybe you have chosen the pleasures of this world and are realizing it has left you far from where you should be in life. Alan Redpath used to say, you can have a saved soul and yet still have a wasted life.

Read the story of the Prodigal Son in Luke 15:13-18: "[He] set off for a distant country and there squandered his wealth in wild living. After he had spent everything . . . he began to be in need . . . and hired himself out to a citizen of that country, who sent him to feed pigs. He longed to fill his stomach with the pods that the pigs were eating, but no one gave him anything. When he came to his senses, he said, . . . 'I am starving to death! I will set out and go back to my father and say to him: Father, I have sinned against heaven and against you'" (NIV). Then this man went home.

So if this is your story, it's not too late. The Father is waiting and wanting to welcome you home.

Make It Personal . . . Live It Out!

Are you haunted with regrets because of mistakes in the past? Many women turn to alcohol and drugs to dull the pain of their childhoods. Then the addicted lifestyle brings more wounds and shame. Jesus came to restore your soul. Are you ready? *The Healed and Set Free* Bible study by Tammy Brown was written specifically to address the haunting darkness of the past. It will guide you to understand and then allow the Lord to speak truth and love and healing to your broken places.

One Year Bible Reading

Nehemiah 12:27–13:31; 1 Corinthians 11:1-16; Psalm 35:1-16; Proverbs 21:17-18

Crabby? Give Thanks!

It is better to live alone in the desert
than with a [crabby], complaining wife.

PROVERBS 21:19

Matthew Henry said, "It is better to have no company than bad company."

Solomon often spoke about women who were hard to live with. He was a man who had a thousand wives; it's hard to figure why he kept marrying. Maybe he kept hoping, *The next one will be different. The next one will be sweet. She'll appreciate me. Maybe she'll be thankful for how hard I work to give her a nice home.* Sadly, I think a lot of men think that today. *The next wife will be the good one.* That is sad for everyone.

Let's look at the key factor here that makes a woman a misery. It's complaining. This comes directly from unthankfulness. We can get so busy fixating on what we don't have that we completely forget and completely miss out on the blessings that we do have.

A while ago a darling young woman came to me. She's a single mom now living in one room with her kids in her parents' home. She said, "I drove him to it. No matter how hard my husband worked or anything he gave me, it was never enough. I always tore him down and put him down. I drove him to it, and now I have nothing."

Wives, this is a warning. If we make our husbands feel like they can't do anything right, they will eventually stop trying.

So what is the cure for a crabby, complaining heart? It's a thankful heart. Colossians 3:15 says, "Let the peace that comes from Christ rule in your hearts. . . . And always be thankful."

Make It Personal . . . Live It Out!

Psalm 103:2-5 boosts us out of the dumps by replacing discouragement with praise. Will you use these words to lift your attitude from the valley to the hilltop of thankfulness?

Let all that I am praise the LORD;
may I never forget the good things he does for me.
He forgives all my sins
and heals all my diseases.
He redeems me from death
and crowns me with love and tender mercies.
He fills my life with good things.
My youth is renewed like the eagle's!

One Year Bible Reading

Esther 1:1–3:15; 1 Corinthians 11:17-34; Psalm 35:17-28; Proverbs 21:19-20

Magnificent Obsession

Whoever pursues righteousness and unfailing love
will find life, righteousness, and honor.

PROVERBS 21:21

What motives you? What gives you the motivation to get out of bed, get dressed, and start your day? Do you have a high and noble passion and purpose for living? If you were to die tomorrow or even next year, would you say, "I made the right choices"? Of all the things that we can desire and pursue in this life, there is nothing like the pursuit of God. Jesus said, "Seek ye first the Kingdom of God and His righteousness, and all else will be added to you" (Matthew 6:33, paraphrase).

My dear, dear friend Mary Barrett was one of the most amazing worship leaders I have ever heard. Before she died of cancer, she had a bucket list. But it didn't include skydiving. Just weeks before she passed, her husband Joe drove her to Nashville to record just one more worship CD to the glory of God. She often sang the words to the song below. To her, they were more than words, they were her swan song and anthem.

Give me one pure and holy passion.
Give me one magnificent obsession.
Give me one glorious ambition for my life,
to know and follow hard after you,
to grow as your disciple in your truth.
This world is empty, pale, and poor
compared to knowing you, my Lord.
Lead me on, and I will run after you.
—MARK ALTROGGE IN "PURE AND HOLY PASSION"

As Paul the apostle said, "I press toward the goal for the prize of the upward call of God in Christ Jesus" (Philippians 3:14, NKJV).

Make It Personal . . . Live It Out!

How then can you personally and passionately pursue God? It can't be done out of duty or mere religious zeal. Trying harder, in the form of legalism and sacrificial diligence, is not the answer either. "Give me one pure and holy passion"—these words are more than a song to sing; they are a prayer to pray. It is God alone who is the spark that ignites a life. Will you take these words and from your heart ask him to give you a hunger to "follow hard after him"?

One Year Bible Reading

Esther 4:1–7:10; 1 Corinthians 12:1-26; Psalm 36:1-12; Proverbs 21:21-22

Silence Is Golden

Watch your tongue and keep your mouth shut,
and you will stay out of trouble.
Mockers are proud and haughty;
they act with boundless arrogance.

PROVERBS 21:23-24

Our mouths! Have you ever been really sorry you said something? Of course you have. All of us have. If we really desire to be wise, godly women, we must get a grip on how we use our mouths. I read this comment on the Internet: "You have the right to remain silent. Anything you say will be misquoted and then used against you."

James 1:19 tells us, "You must all be quick to listen, slow to speak, and slow to get angry." This warns us to be careful. Do not speak first and think later. Think and pray first before you speak. Then you will never have to wish you could take back the words. Here are some test questions to ask before you speak. *Is it true? Is it kind? Is it necessary? Is this the right time? Am I saying this to the right person, and will what I say bring good, or will it stir up trouble?*

Sometimes it's someone else who says something stupid or mean or rude to you. I want to tell you a little secret of life. You don't have to finish what others start. Giving up doesn't mean you are weak. Sometimes it means that you are strong enough to let go. Just hold your tongue and count to ten, and the urge to say something stupid back will pass.

David faced many complicated and frustrating situations and people. He had a prayer he must have prayed a thousand times in his life: "May the words of my mouth and the meditation of my heart be pleasing to you, O LORD, my rock and my redeemer" (Psalm 19:14).

Make It Personal . . . Live It Out!

Let's return to this profound statement: "Keep your mouth shut, and you will stay out of trouble." Why is this good advice? Because we often speak before we understand. We might give hasty advice. We sometimes take someone's comment more personally than we should. Let's learn to listen with more than just our ears. And most important, let's get in the habit of asking the Holy Spirit to give us insight and wisdom and restraint.

One Year Bible Reading

Esther 8:1–10:3; 1 Corinthians 12:27–13:13; Psalm 37:1-11; Proverbs 21:23-24

Lazy, Lazy

Despite their desires, the lazy will come to ruin,
for their hands refuse to work.

PROVERBS 21:25

What is the key element that distinguishes the lazy from the diligent? It is that the lazy "refuse to work." It's not that they can't. It's simply that they *won't* labor. The definition of the Hebrew word for *labor* encompasses many areas of endeavor. It means "to advance, to deal with, to commit, to prepare, to practice, and to finish." *Hmmm.* As I read this description, I see that when I procrastinate—which I do—I am for some reason refusing to get to something I know I should or to finish what I started.

So how do we break the habit of putting things off? Proverbs 6:6-8 says, "Take a lesson from the ants, you lazybones. Learn from their ways and become wise! Though they have no prince or governor or ruler to make them work, they labor hard all summer, gathering food for the winter."

The ant is a picture of diligence. The word *diligence* means "putting care and effort into what one does." Ants are focused, always moving forward. I love when you put something in their way—they hardly stop. They just go around it and keep moving forward. Good job, little ant!

In conclusion, the diligent life allows us to have food for our tables and hearts to share with others. Let's close with an encouraging word from Psalm 37:25-26: "Once I was young, and now I am old. Yet I have never seen the godly abandoned or their children begging for bread. The godly always give generous loans to others, and their children are a blessing."

Make It Personal . . . Live It Out!

There are lots of reasons we sometimes refuse to do something. Wives sometimes refuse to do something their husbands have asked them to do because they are angry. They won't iron a shirt or run an errand or cook his favorite meal. We can have the same attitude at work or at church or with our families. This is just another form of laziness. We are too lazy to "get over it." We let ourselves get in an emotional rut. My friend, let's not be so petty and foolish and childish. Be like the ant: just go around it and keep moving forward.

One Year Bible Reading

Job 1:1–3:26; 1 Corinthians 14:1-17; Psalm 37:12-29; Proverbs 21:25-26

Wicked Sacrifice

The sacrifice of the wicked is detestable—
how much more so when brought with evil intent!

PROVERBS 21:27 (NIV)

The term *wicked* refers to those in rebellion against God. The Hebrew word for "wicked" is *rasha'*, which means "morally wrong; actively doing wrong."

In 1 Samuel 15:22-23 God had given King Saul clear instructions about something he needed to do, but he only half did it. Then he thought he could make up for it by offering a sacrifice. The prophet Samuel came to him and said, "Has the LORD as great delight in burnt offerings and sacrifices, as in obeying the voice of the LORD? . . . To obey is better than sacrifice. . . . For rebellion is as the sin of witchcraft, and stubbornness is as iniquity and idolatry" (NKJV).

So in your life is there something that you know God has asked you to do—maybe to give up a friendship you know is not healthy? "To obey is better than sacrifice." Are you holding a grudge against your sister or against someone at work or at church? You know you should forgive: "to obey is better than sacrifice." Is there a sin that you're hiding, something you know is wrong, and the Holy Spirit is convicting you? Sometimes we try to compensate by doing or giving more to the church, thinking surely it will balance out. But "to obey is better than sacrifice."

Our proverb today says God hates the kind of sacrifice given with an unrepentant heart. But listen very carefully. It does not say he hates *you*. God loves you. The sacrifices God does love are "a broken spirit . . . and a contrite heart" (Psalm 51:17, NKJV). Primarily God doesn't want or need your money or your resources. What God really wants is you.

Make It Personal . . . Live It Out!

When God speaks to your heart and calls you to repentance, there is no time like the present. Don't cover up or run away or try to bribe God to salve your guilty conscience. You aren't kidding anyone. Jesus said, "I tell you the truth, everyone who sins is a slave to sin. . . . So if the Son sets you free, you are truly free" (John 8:34, 36). Won't you pause and take a moment with the Lord, asking him to forgive you and cleanse your soul? He can and he will.

One Year Bible Reading

Job 4:1–7:21; 1 Corinthians 14:18-40; Psalm 37:30-40; Proverbs 21:27

A False Witness

A false witness will perish,
and whoever listens to him will be destroyed forever.

PROVERBS 21:28 (NIV)

Sometimes we think it's only the gossip, the mudslinger, who is the big sinner. We think we can listen and not get mud on our faces, but our proverb today tells us this is just not so.

Have you ever heard the expression "consider the source"? Some people are always reporting on everything, putting a warped twist on things. Consider the source. I knew such a person. Each time she spoke something bad about someone, there was a hard little edge to her face, even when she covered it up with an appearance of godly concern. Eventually such people get a reputation, and all the bad things they have said about others seem to describe them. It's like the children's rhyme, "Bounce like rubber, stick like glue, bounce off them and stick on you."

On the other hand, there are some people you can trust completely. They have no interest in tearing others down. I have a wise, gracious friend, Linda. Consistently when she hears a critical comment about someone, she tactfully but firmly turns it around to say something positive. When she speaks, you can trust that "on her tongue is the law of kindness" (Proverbs 31:26, NKJV). Good job, Linda! May we be known as women who are sweet with our words and gentle to others.

Philippians 2:14-15 gives us a excellent guide: "Do everything without complaining or arguing, so that you may become blameless and pure, children of God without fault in a crooked and depraved generation, in which you shine like stars in the universe" (NIV).

Make It Personal . . . Live It Out!

Another application of the term *false witness* is one who slanders the goodness and wisdom of God. Beware of those who put a false spin on the truth. This is exactly what Satan did in the Garden of Eden. Satan told and sold the lie. But Eve bought it. He slandered God by insinuating that God doesn't know or want what is best for us. Millions of women through the ages have taken that same bait. Remember, "whoever listens to him will be destroyed forever." Be wise. The antidote of course is the Word of God. Jesus said, "You will know the truth, and the truth will set you free" (John 8:32).

One Year Bible Reading

Job 8:1–11:20; 1 Corinthians 15:1-28; Psalm 38:1-22; Proverbs 21:28-29

Victory

There is no wisdom, no insight, no plan
that can succeed against the LORD.
The horse is made ready for the day of battle,
but victory rests with the LORD.

PROVERBS 21:30-31 (NIV)

One of the interesting and yet wonderful things we learn from reading the Bible cover to cover is that life is full of humanly impossible, insurmountable situations. Even for God's people, life is sometimes very complicated. Over and over again God's people were outnumbered in battle. They were out of food and money. They faced dilemmas with no answers, and then they turned to God with empty hands and expectant hearts.

Over and over again we read of God giving them unusual answers and solutions. In all their circumstances (just like us) they had choices. Should they trust their natural instincts, or should they trust the Lord? Some, like King Saul, repeatedly refused to leave the final decisions in God's hands. Stubbornly, they used their own carnal weapons and natural wisdom. Short term, it looked good. Long term, it was a disaster. But others, like David facing Goliath, Joshua crossing the Jordon, Peter leaving his fishing business to follow Jesus, or Daniel refusing to eat the king's delicacies, saw that God's ways are much higher than our ways.

As Oswald Chambers said, "The golden rule for understanding in spiritual matters is not intellect but obedience."

"Trust in the LORD with all your heart, and lean not on your own understanding" (Proverbs 3:5, NIV), because ultimately "victory rests with the LORD."

Make It Personal . . . Live It Out!

Do you feel overwhelmed, outnumbered, and defeated by the problems of life? In times like this we sometimes think the Lord has deserted us. But be aware: he has never been closer. Troubles can press us into the promises of God, because it is then that we need them so desperately. Our problems may be bigger than we are, but they are never bigger than God. Remember, true victory is internal, not just external.

"Thank God! He gives us victory over sin and death through our Lord Jesus Christ. So, my dear brothers and sisters, be strong and immovable. Always work enthusiastically for the Lord, for you know that nothing you do for the Lord is ever useless" (1 Corinthians 15:57-58).

One Year Bible Reading

Job 12:1–15:35; 1 Corinthians 15:29-58; Psalm 39:1-13; Proverbs 21:30-31

A Good Name

A good name is more desirable than great riches;
to be esteemed is better than silver or gold.

PROVERBS 22:1 (NIV)

Immanuel Kant once said, "It is not necessary that whilst I live I live happily; but it is necessary that so long as I live I should live honorably." Is this true, or is this some old-fashioned view of values? Many would rather have a shiny, new car than an untarnished reputation.

So what are some examples of treasured names?

- John, the apostle, was called "the disciple whom Jesus loved."
- David was called "a man after God's own heart."
- Abraham was called "the friend of God."
- And Abraham Lincoln was called "Honest Abe."

Just think of the many people through the ages who, at the very mention of their name, make you think of the good that they stood for or fought for: Mother Teresa, Florence Nightingale, Corrie ten Boom, Elisabeth Elliot, Pastor Chuck Smith, and Billy Graham. But there are so, so many others whose names are not famous, but in their little sphere of influence they have a good name, a great reputation. They have a name for being a prayer warrior, or they have a name for being a faithful friend to the lonely, or a name for being true to their word. And so now, dear sisters, what is the name others would choose for you? What would you like it to be?

"A good name is more desirable than great riches."

Make It Personal . . . Live It Out!

What is your reputation? Are you known as a good listener, a friend to the underdog, compassionate and tenderhearted, faithful and diligent, a ray of God's sunshine, lover of the Word, someone with a heart for the lost? I don't know about you, but oh, how I would love to be each of these to at least somebody every day. One of the great secrets of leaving behind us a trail of kindness and goodness is having a deep desire to please the Lord. David said, "I take joy in doing your will, my God, for your instructions are written on my heart" (Psalm 40:8).

Let's Pray

O Lord, sometimes I live carelessly, not thinking how my words or attitudes affect others around me. Today, please make my life count for good.

One Year Bible Reading

Job 16:1–19:29; 1 Corinthians 16:1-24; Psalm 40:1-10; Proverbs 22:1

God Is Our Maker

The rich and the poor have this in common,
The LORD is the maker of them all.

PROVERBS 22:2 (NKJV)

Solomon was a king, and he was the son of a king. But before his father was a king, he was a shepherd. His great-grandmother was a poor widow from a foreign country, and his great-grandfather was a farmer. This gave him insight that people are people, rich or poor. As Job said, "Naked I came into this world, and naked I will return" (Job 1:21, paraphrased). The truth is, we are not human bodies with a soul. We are souls temporarily in a human body.

But our society has become very shallow. We measure people by how they dress or what they drive. Sadly, sometimes we even do this at church.

Listen to how James addressed this matter. "Suppose a man comes into your meeting wearing . . . fine clothes, and a poor man in shabby clothes also comes in. If you show special attention to the man wearing fine clothes and say, 'Here's a good seat for you,' but say to the poor man, . . . 'Sit on the floor by my feet,' have you not discriminated . . . and become judges with evil thoughts? Listen, my dear brothers: Has not God chosen those who are poor in the eyes of the world to be rich in faith and to inherit the kingdom he promised to those who love him?" (James 2:2-5, NIV).

The Bible tells us, "Man looks at the outward appearance, but the LORD looks at the heart" (1 Samuel 16:7, NKJV). And so should we. Because God loves all people. God loves the rough-around-the-edges teenager. God loves the waitress who is weary and forgot your order. God loves the old woman who is slow in the line ahead of you. God loves them, and so should we.

Make It Personal . . . Live It Out!

I have a hobby. I love to watch people at the mall, at Disneyland, in airports. I like to ponder who they are, what is going on in their lives. Our Father in heaven watches too. His loving eye is on each one; he knows the number of the hairs on their heads. Doesn't this truth make you love God even more? His heart is so big. Doesn't this make you want to be more like him? If the answer is yes, then I say, "Me too!"

One Year Bible Reading

Job 20:1–22:30; 2 Corinthians 1:1-11; Psalm 40:11-17; Proverbs 22:2-4

Guard Your Heart and Soul

Thorns and snares are in the way of the perverse;
He [or she] who guards his soul will be far from them.

PROVERBS 22:5 (NKJV)

If you look at the world around you, there are so many dangers for women, both emotionally and spiritually. Thorns and snares are meant to harm and trap. Often they are hidden. Just the bait is seen that lures us into danger. Ladies, whether you are fifteen or fifty-five, it is foolish and dangerous to be naive or careless. We must be aware and diligent to guard our hearts and our minds and our souls.

First Peter 5:8-9 gives us a strong warning: "Be sober, be vigilant; because your adversary the devil walks about like a roaring lion, seeking whom he may devour. Resist him, steadfast in the faith" (NKJV).

To devour means "to swallow up as in a dark pit." Haven't you seen women cross that line of sexual temptation and end up in a dark, life-destroying place? And when we as women fall, we take others with us—our children, our friends, and those we love.

I will leave you with a strong urging. Do not think you can watch an R-rated movie without it planting seeds and images in your mind that linger. Do not think you can read trashy novels or watch sleazy TV without causing real life to look boring and dull. Do not think you can play with an emotional affair or flirt with someone at work. It is a thorn and a snare. Remember, she who guards her soul will be safe.

Make It Personal . . . Live It Out!

"Guard your heart above all else, for it determines the course of your life" (Proverbs 4:23).

This is a sobering and yet insightful word from the Lord. He knows how we are wired. He knows that our emotions can be stirred dangerously. But God gave us emotions; they can move us to noble and compassionate purposes. We can cry with others and carry their burdens on our hearts. How do you guard your heart and soul? Be about your Father's business. If your heart is full of godly occupation, there is no room for temptation and trashy, destructive motives and interests. Amen? Amen!

One Year Bible Reading

Job 23:1–27:23; 2 Corinthians 1:12–2:11; Psalm 41:1-13; Proverbs 22:5-6

The Bondage of Debt

The rich rules over the poor,
And the borrower is servant to the lender.

PROVERBS 22:7 (NKJV)

Oh, the ball and chain of debt. It amazes me how many offers we get in the mail for credit cards, preapproved. It's easy to get the loan and easy to spend the money, but the hard part is paying it back. It's a burden. It starts out seeming that the loan company is doing you a big favor, serving you. But you end up serving the lender—sometimes for years. Oh, the ball and chain of debt. Dear sisters, we need to be wise stewards of our money. Even as Christians we can get caught up in the spend-now, pay-later syndrome.

On TV there's a commercial that asks, "What's in your wallet?" The first step to freedom is to take those cards out of your wallet and cut them up. The second step is to double up on your payments. Each month pay more than is due. This might mean that for a year you have to cut out going out to dinner or buying something new, but you'll see it will be so worth it in the long run. Then you need to cut yourself off from the sources of temptation. Stop watching the shopping channel, stop cruising the Internet, stay away from the mall. If you don't see it, you just won't even think you need it.

But the greatest antidote, as a woman of God, is to ask the Lord to fill you with new desires for things that the world isn't selling and money can't buy. "Delight yourself also in the LORD, and He shall give you the desires of your heart" (Psalm 37:4, NKJV). Instead of buying a new pair of shoes this week, find a promise in the Bible. Memorize it and take it to heart and then share it with someone else. Now, that's living rich.

Make It Personal . . . Live It Out!

Okay, admission time. I love to shop; I do. Although I'm a bargain shopper, a bargain shopper sometimes buys things just because they're cheap, not because she needs them. Guilty! I know my weakness, so I've developed a stopgap habit to curb foolish spending. Before I pay at the checkout, I ask myself, *Do I really need this?* If not, I put it back.

One Year Bible Reading

Job 28:1–30:31; 2 Corinthians 2:12-17; Psalm 42:1-11; Proverbs 22:7

The Joy of Generosity

He who sows wickedness reaps trouble,
and the rod of his fury will be destroyed.
A generous man will himself be blessed,
for he shares his food with the poor.

PROVERBS 22:8-9 (NIV)

Galatians 6:7 tells us, "A man reaps what he sows" (NIV).

The longer I live, the more I see that all the behavior the Lord warns against causes us more trouble than it ever causes anyone else. Things like bitterness, jealousy, selfishness—they all come back to haunt us and bring trouble to our own lives.

What a refreshing picture we see in contrast. "A generous man [or woman] will himself be blessed, for he shares . . . with the poor." Who wouldn't want to be blessed? This should be our goal every day. The definition of *generous* is "liberal in giving or sharing; unselfish; free from meanness or smallness of mind or character; magnanimous." Wow! We need a lot more of that in this dog-eat-dog world, don't we?

So how can we be generous and magnanimous? Be aware. Being generous is not limited to sharing money. We can be generous in extending forgiveness quickly. We can be generous in being friendly to the lonely. We can be generous doing small, random acts of kindness. We can be generous sending a card or letting someone know we care about her burden or sorrow and are praying. We can be generous just by being a blessing.

Make It Personal . . . Live It Out!

Let's not just talk about generosity; let's activate it. Surely if we ask the Lord to give us one opportunity to give today, the sun will not go down before he shows us who or where and how, be it small or great.

Let's Pray

Lord, change my heart and give me a passion to be generous. Please open my eyes and open my hand to give to someone who is needy today. Stretch me in this. Touch my heart so when I see the need, I give joyfully and gently, without making them feel humiliated or indebted. If possible, may I give secretly so the praise and thanks will go to you. I thank you in advance for the joy that will then fill my heart.

One Year Bible Reading

Job 31:1–33:33; 2 Corinthians 3:1-18; Psalm 43:1-5; Proverbs 22:8-9

The King's Friend

Throw out the mocker, and fighting goes too.
Quarrels and insults will disappear.
Whoever loves a pure heart and gracious speech
will have the king as a friend.

PROVERBS 22:10-11

A mocker or scorner is someone who will not yield or respect others. They always want their own way. Before we think of how this applies to others, may we first be honest with ourselves, and then cast out those tendencies in ourselves. Honestly, have you ever wondered why no one calls you to go to lunch? Why no one asks you to help on the retreat committee? Have you wondered why no one calls you to pray with them when they're down? Maybe, just maybe, it's because you're hard to get along with and people have given up.

Listen: the beautiful contrast to a troublemaker is someone who "loves a pure heart and gracious speech." She will enjoy the best of friendships.

One of the most beautiful pictures of friendships in the Bible is that of Jonathan and David. Jonathan was a king's son, but David was just a shepherd. It would seem they had nothing in common. But Jonathan saw something in David that he was drawn to. He saw that David viewed God as God almighty. They both believed that when we step forward in God's will, no weapon formed against us will prosper. Their friendship was forged and merged by their mutual love for God.

And so for us, what are we looking for when we seek out a friendship? What do others find in us when they look for friendship? It's been said, "We either lift others up, or we pull them down."

Make It Personal . . . Live It Out!

Although I love my friends here on earth, there is no better, truer friend than Jesus. Can you say that he is truly your friend, not just because the Bible says so, but because you've experienced it? He can be. He is available; are you? A relationship with the Lord, just like all relationships, takes time and investment and communication. The returns are beyond description. He is the Good Shepherd, the Prince of Peace, and the King Eternal. Consider this moment an invitation to draw nearer and go deeper with him.

One Year Bible Reading

Job 34:1–36:33; 2 Corinthians 4:1-12; Psalm 44:1-8; Proverbs 22:10-12

Excuses, Excuses

The lazy man says, "There is a lion outside!
I shall be slain in the streets!"

PROVERBS 22:13 (NKJV)

The lazy person is just full of excuses, isn't he? We used to live in Oregon. Both my husband and I went running very early in the morning. In the winter it was hard to go out because it was still dark at six. But sometimes it was not only dark, it was raining. When it was like this, we'd turn to each other and say, "There's a lion in the street!"

Lazy. *Lazy* means "to be averse or disinclined to work or activity."

Benjamin Franklin used to say, "He that is good for making excuses is seldom good for anything else." And Florence Nightingale said, "I attribute my success to this: I never gave or took an excuse."

So the question is, have you made an excuse for not doing the right thing, or the hard thing, or the important thing, or the next thing?

There is an area that I have to admit I am very concerned about among Christian women, particularly in regard to their spiritual lives. Although most would say that having a personal quiet time in God's Word is important, vital, and life-changing, still they put it off. They aren't consistent. I have an exciting website called BibleBusStop.com. It is full of helpful tools and practical encouragement so that there will be no excuse and no neglect. Remember the lion of laziness is really the devouring lion called Satan.

Make It Personal . . . Live It Out!

Why do we give up? Maybe it's because we feel overwhelmed, so far behind that there is no use trying. But that's not true! Right now in *The One Year Bible* we are reading 2 Corinthians. So no more excuses. Begin your habit of reading daily with just the New Testament. Just seven to ten minutes a day for the next thirty days will establish an easy and yet rich habit. Today's good word for you is from 2 Corinthians 4:16: "That is why we never give up. Though our bodies are dying, our spirits are being renewed every day."

One Year Bible Reading

Job 37:1–39:30; 2 Corinthians 4:13–5:10; Psalm 44:9-26; Proverbs 22:13

September

Scan this code for audio devotionals
or visit www.tyndal.es/wisdom.

A Deep Pit

The mouth of an immoral woman is a deep pit;
He who is abhorred by the LORD will fall there.

PROVERBS 22:14 (NKJV)

This is a very serious and sobering statement. It gives a clear picture of how powerful and dangerous a woman can be. King Solomon was a man who knew from experience that the wrong woman can bring trouble that is hard to shake. Listen to what he says in Ecclesiastes 7:26: "I find more bitter than death the woman whose heart is snares and nets, whose hands are fetters. He who pleases God shall escape from her, but the sinner shall be trapped" (NKJV).

This is a really good place to address how important it is for us as godly women to speak and act and dress like godly women, no matter what age we are. A great prayer to start our day with is "Lord, I want to please you. Help me to be aware of your presence all day." This prayer can and should affect everything, including what we wear. We need to remember that men are very visual. May we never ever be the source of trouble to any man's soul. As you go out the door, take one more look at what you're wearing. Frankly, is your neckline too low? Is your skirt too short or too tight? "Beauty is as beauty does."

First Peter 1:14-16 tells us, "As obedient children, don't be conformed to the former lusts which were yours in your ignorance, but like the Holy One who called you, be holy yourselves also in all your behavior; because it is written, 'YOU SHALL BE HOLY, FOR I AM HOLY'" (NASB).

Make It Personal . . . Live It Out!

An immoral woman is not just a pit to others; she falls into the pit herself. The sexual revolution unleashed in the late sixties and early seventies has been a whirlwind of devastation. Let me ask you, are you haunted by the sins of your past? Do you have flashbacks or shame or fear? You'd be surprised how many women, even Christian women, carry that same weight. HealingHearts.org has a Bible study written especially for you, called *The Hem of His Garment*. Will you write them today? They are ready to help.

One Year Bible Reading

Job 40:1–42:17; 2 Corinthians 5:11-21; Psalm 45:1-17; Proverbs 22:14

Dare to Discipline

A youngster's heart is filled with foolishness,
but physical discipline will drive it far away.

PROVERBS 22:15

Discipline, correction, punishment—all of these are unpopular concepts in our society.

Years ago I took a psychology class. One day the teacher walked into the classroom and threw a book against the wall. The book was *Dare to Discipline*, by Dr. James Dobson. This teacher thought and taught his students that it was outrageous for parents to inflict their values of right and wrong on their children. But Dobson states, "*Discipline and love are not antithetical;* one is a function of the other. The parent must convince himself that [loving discipline] is not something he [or she] does *to* the child; it is something he does *for* the child."

Jon Courson states, "Regardless of what psychologists say in any era, God's Word specifically tells us that a child's heart is inherently, innately in need of correction."

Young parents are often shocked to discover that their precious little one has a temper at a very early age. No one needs to teach a child to be stubborn or selfish or defiant. Our proverb tells us this foolishness is bound in his or her heart. If you look around, you'll see that not only two-year-olds throw tantrums, but some are still doing so at twenty-two and even sixty-two. Yikes.

Back to Dobson's book *Dare to Discipline*—I highly recommend it. It's especially geared toward parents raising small children. If you didn't grow up in a home where there was firm, loving discipline, it's hard to even know what that looks like. Dr. Dobson shares insights that are loving, wise, and down to earth.

Make It Personal . . . Live It Out!

Do you question why it is important to believe and apply the wisdom of God instead of following the whims of the latest psychology trend? God's wisdom is timeless. God alone knows the inner working of a child's soul; he made us. He knows that a child without training and boundaries often struggles with self-discipline and boundaries in adult life.

"While yielding to the loving leadership of their parents, children are also learning to yield to the benevolent leadership of God Himself" (James Dobson in *The Strong-Willed Child*).

One Year Bible Reading

Ecclesiastes 1:1–3:22; 2 Corinthians 6:1-13; Psalm 46:1-11; Proverbs 22:15

Getting Ahead Is Losing Ground

A person who gets ahead by oppressing the poor
or by showering gifts on the rich will end in poverty.

PROVERBS 22:16

Ladies, how do you think this applies to us? In this verse there are two things criticized: oppressing the poor and showering gifts on the rich. At first glance these two things would appear to have nothing in common, but when we think about it, we realize that both of these things are done to get ahead, to be seen, to gain, even if someone else has to lose. This kind of striving—even when giving—is just plain old-fashioned selfishness, and it's self serving.

It's been said that "the world provides enough for every man's need, but not enough for every man's greed."

In Luke 6:33 Jesus said, "If you do good to those who do good to you, what credit is that to you? For even sinners do the same" (NKJV).

And in Luke 14:12-14 Jesus said, "When you give a dinner or a supper, do not ask your friends, your brothers, your relatives, nor rich neighbors, lest they also invite you back, and you be repaid. But when you give a feast, invite the poor, the maimed, the lame, the blind. And you will be blessed, because they cannot repay you; for you shall be repaid at the resurrection of the just" (NKJV).

So the bottom line is this: Jesus said, "You will be blessed." The blessed life is the giving life. It is the life of doing little, random acts of kindness. It's adding a blessing to someone else. It's putting someone else first—just because.

Make It Personal . . . Live It Out!

Jesus did not promise us a cushy, pampered life as the formula for abundance. Quite the contrary. He said, "I tell you the truth, unless a kernel of wheat is planted in the soil and dies, it remains alone. But its death will produce many new kernels—a plentiful harvest of new lives" (John 12:24).

Let's Pray

Lord, help me to resist the selfish moments, knowing that the giving life is rich in blessing and joy.

One Year Bible Reading

Ecclesiastes 4:1–6:12; 2 Corinthians 6:14–7:7; Psalm 47:1-9; Proverbs 22:16

Rewired

Listen to the words of the wise;
apply your heart to my instruction.
For it is good to keep these sayings in your heart
and always ready on your lips.
I am teaching you today—yes, you—
so you will trust in the LORD.

PROVERBS 22:17-19

This beautiful proverb is so imploring! Please, *please* lean into God's rich, true wisdom. Don't just read God's Word or listen with your ears. Let it completely rewire you from the inside out.

Life has many complicated twists and turns. David was a man who hid God's Word deep within his heart. In 1 Samuel 24:1-32 David was fleeing for his life from King Saul. In En-gedi he and his men were hidden in a cave. Saul came in, not realizing David was there—so close David could cut off a corner of his robe. Oh, how his men would have loved for him to strike Saul dead on the spot so they all could return to their homes. But David refused. He said to his men, "The LORD forbid that I should do this to my lord the king and attack the LORD's anointed one" (1 Samuel 24:6). It's times like this that we need God's will and ways engraved deep within us. A set of pat answers and some tidy rules just don't cut it when things start screaming out of control and we have tough choices.

On a practical level, is it worth it to yield to God's will and ways? Good question. David chose to honor God instead of yielding to revenge. When he did, he set the standard for his own future reign as king. He honored God, and God then honored him.

Make It Personal . . . Live It Out!

David's example in the cave shows us what it looks like to trust the Lord, even when it goes against our own natural instincts. I have a feeling David slept very well that night. So did his men. They knew they were being led by a man of integrity. Child of God, can't you see how a life of trustful obedience is the greatest life there could ever be? We never have to look over our shoulders; we never have to fear. When we have placed ourselves entirely in the faithful hands of our almighty God, we are safe.

One Year Bible Reading

Ecclesiastes 7:1–9:18; 2 Corinthians 7:8-16; Psalm 48:1-14; Proverbs 22:17-19

The Classroom of Life

Have I not written to you excellent things
Of counsels and knowledge,
That I may make you know the certainty of the words of truth,
That you may answer words of truth to those who send to you?

PROVERBS 22:20-21 (NKJV)

God is our master instructor. His Word and his Spirit counsel and guide. Life is our classroom. No university program could ever compare with the education and insight and knowledge he imparts in even the small moments of life.

Let me tell you a story. Jean Louis Agassiz (1807–1873) is regarded as one of the greatest scientists of the nineteenth century. One day he gave a student a fish, told him to study it, and left the room. After several hours the student felt he had learned all he could, but Agassiz did not return. So he observed some more. Finally Agassiz returned with the brief comment that the student had made a fair beginning and left again. The student fell to his study in earnest and after months of investigation declared that a fish was the most fascinating of studies.

Life was indeed Agassiz's classroom. He saw the divine plan of God omnipresent in nature and could not accept Darwinism, a theory that denied the intelligent design he saw everywhere in the natural world. He concluded that if it required an intelligent mind just to study the facts of biology, "it must have required an intelligent mind to establish them."

We may not be scientists, but we can be just as eager and interested in the wonderful lessons God puts in our paths every day. Don't let your interest fade. There's always something new to learn—in his Word, from the people around us, from the storms that come our way, and from the natural wonder of his magnificent creation.

Make It Personal . . . Live It Out!

King Solomon, the author God used to write Proverbs and the book of Ecclesiastes, was also an ardent student of life. He approached every angle with curiosity. Try reading Ecclesiastes 10:1–12:14 today and picture him walking around, observing all the circumstances and details around him with the intention of gaining insight. Then try carrying your own pad of paper and making a few notes as you go about your ordinary day in our extraordinary world.

One Year Bible Reading

Ecclesiastes 10:1–12:14; 2 Corinthians 8:1-15; Psalm 49:1-20; Proverbs 22:20-21

Poor and Needy

Do not exploit the poor because they are poor,
and do not crush the needy in court,
for the LORD will take up their case
and will plunder those who plunder them.

PROVERBS 22:22-23 (NIV)

This proverb is both a warning and a promise. On one side, there's a warning. It's a warning from God himself that he cares about the poor, and just because they seem defenseless, he personally will defend them when they cry out to him. This is a warning to those who take advantage of the weak. God himself will avenge them.

On the other side of this proverb there is a promise: a promise to you who are poor, whether in money or in strength or in influence. Maybe you're a single mom, and you definitely feel poor in all three areas. Sometimes an ex-husband will go to court to reduce his obligations or to gain custody of the children, not because he cares for them, but for spite. A single mom with no funds for a good lawyer can feel defeated and forsaken. If this is you, will you turn to the God who cares for you? Don't fight wrong with wrong. Jesus said, "Blessed are the meek, for they shall inherit the earth" (Matthew 5:5, NKJV).

Listen carefully: as your first and primary line of defense, call out to your Father in heaven. Listen to the words of Psalm 46:1-2, 7: "God is our refuge and strength, an ever-present help in trouble. Therefore we will not fear, though the earth give way and the mountains fall into the heart of the sea. . . . The LORD Almighty is with us; and the God of Jacob is our fortress" (NIV).

Make It Personal . . . Live It Out!

Through the years, God has used ordinary people, like Irena Sendler, to bravely risk all to aid the needy. In 1942 the Nazis herded hundreds of thousands of Jews into the Warsaw ghetto. Granted permission to enter the ghetto as a sewer specialist, she left each day with children hidden in boxes and potato sacks.

"Can you guarantee they will live?" Irena later recalled the distraught parents asking. But she could only guarantee they would die if they stayed. Irena placed the children in non-Jewish homes, orphanages, and convents. "No one ever refused to take a child from me," she said. With the assistance of many Christians, almost 2,500 were taken to safety.

One Year Bible Reading

Song of Songs 1:1–4:16; 2 Corinthians 8:16-24; Psalm 50:1-23; Proverbs 22:22-23

Caustic Companions

Do not make friends with a hot-tempered person;
do not associate with one easily angered,
or you may learn their ways
and get yourself ensnared.

PROVERBS 22:24-25 (NIV)

Friendship, for us as women, is a wonderful and important thing. But as this proverb warns us, we need to be careful and wise about whom we buddy up with.

First Corinthians 15:33 tells us, "Do not be deceived: Evil company corrupts good habits" (NKJV).

In a godly friendship we can be iron sharpening iron. We can encourage each other, pray for each other, and best of all, fellowship, serve, and pray with each other. But as women get close, we sometimes let our guards down and allow ourselves to share the worst of what we're thinking and the worst of our attitudes. When we do this, there are sparks, but not for good. We ignite the worst in others and invite them to share the negative and destructive with us.

A woman who is angry with her husband often allows herself to tear him down and reveal his flaws, especially to her close friends. There are some women who are always angry with somebody—their mothers or friends or coworkers. Some are angry with others in the church, with leaders, or with their pastors. That anger is expressed in a constant flow of criticism. Let's not do that. And let's not be that kind of influence to our friends. And let's choose our friendships carefully so we don't unconsciously adopt habits that are ugly and hard to break.

As our proverb today says, "Do not associate with one easily angered, or you may learn their ways and get yourself ensnared."

Make It Personal . . . Live It Out!

Okay, now that we have said "distance yourself" from your angry friend, does that mean you should write her off? No. I'd venture to say she has some hurts in her past that have triggered her caustic attitude. Did she grow up with an alcoholic father? Was she abused as a child? Does she have rejection or abandonment in her past? These factors are not excuses. But they are reasons for you to be sympathetic and prayerful. It could be that her past is controlling her present. Will you partner with God to love her and pray for a breakthrough that only God can give?

One Year Bible Reading

Song of Songs 5:1–8:14; 2 Corinthians 9:1-15; Psalm 51:1-19;
Proverbs 22:24-25

Cosigners' Sadness

Don't agree to guarantee another person's debt
or put up security for someone else.
If you can't pay it,
even your bed will be snatched from under you.

PROVERBS 22:26-27

Once again we see how the Proverbs address very practical areas of our life here on earth. Some people think the Bible only talks about spiritual things. They think when it comes to our everyday living, we just have to figure it out. Nothing could be further from the truth. The Bible has instructions on all matters, including finances and godly stewardship. Money matters do matter. And as part of good financial stewardship, this proverb instructs us to not get entangled in other people's finances.

When you cosign for someone, you are legally responsible for the debt, default, or delinquency. Most people only need a cosigner because they really can't afford the loan. In those situations, you lose not only sleep but often the relationship of those you tried to help. If the loan goes sour, oftentimes, so does the relationship, which is the greatest loss of all.

So what are some principles we can apply?

- If a friend or family asks to borrow money, it's best to loan no more than you can accept losing if they never pay you back.
- Live under your means so you are able to save for emergencies and hopefully never be in a position of looking to others to bail you out.
- As we conduct our lives in this world, in all things, including finances, we are to be as "wise as serpents and harmless as doves" (Matthew 10:16, NKJV).

Make It Personal . . . Live It Out!

As we look at this topic, some might think, *Well that is hard-hearted. Aren't we to be generous and optimistic?* Yes, but being softhearted does not need to make you soft-headed. If your son or daughter wants to start a business, offer to pay for some management classes, help with some of the setup, or buy a piece of equipment that is needed. You can cheer your child on without putting both of you at risk.

One Year Bible Reading

Isaiah 1:1–2:22; 2 Corinthians 10:1-18; Psalm 52:1-9; Proverbs 22:26-27

Excellence

Do you see a man who excels in his work?
He will stand before kings;
He will not stand before unknown men.

PROVERBS 22:29 (NKJV)

This proverb absolutely contradicts the unbiblical criticism that some are "so heavenly minded, they are no earthly good." Just the opposite should be true for us as godly women. We should love excellence. When we put our hands to something, we should joyfully do all things "as to the Lord" (Colossians 3:23, NKJV).

So if you are an employee, find joy in working, doing a good job in even the little things. If you have to be there anyway, why not work with honor and diligence?

We can apply this principle of excelling in our work to our Christian service. If you are a Sunday school teacher, be the best! Pour your heart into it. Pray for those kids. Ask the Lord to give you his anointing to bring the lesson to life and make your classroom a place where kids' lives are changed.

And in your home, will you ask the Lord to teach you to work with excellence? I was in real estate for many years. Often when I came into a Christian home, I could tell. There was a beauty and comfort and order. It is evident and beautiful when a woman sees the ministry of her home as important—important enough to make it a place of blessing, a home, not just a house. The size and cost of the house are never a factor. A little paint on used furniture and some flowers can make it more appealing than a palace. Proverbs 31:27 says a virtuous woman, "watches over the ways of her household, and does not eat the bread of idleness" (NKJV). Now that's well done!

Make It Personal . . . Live It Out!

Without a doubt, God has a noble and good purpose for your life. He has given you stewardship of gifts and talents and opportunities (see Romans 12 and Matthew 25:14-30). Don't squander them, neglect them, or bury them. I feel drawn to minister to wounded women. I have been learning as much as I can, praying, reading, talking to others. I want to be faithful. How about you? What has God prompted and gifted you to do? Will you give your heart to it—to be about his business with excellence?

One Year Bible Reading

Isaiah 3:1–5:30; 2 Corinthians 11:1-15; Psalm 53:1-6; Proverbs 22:28-29

Dangerous Delicacies

When you sit to dine with a ruler,
note well what is before you,
and put a knife to your throat
if you are given to gluttony.
Do not crave his delicacies,
for that food is deceptive.

PROVERBS 23:1-3 (NIV)

What is this saying to us as women? Well, we see there is a warning that we are to enter some situations with reserve. Things are not always as they appear. Don't plunge headlong into taking part in what is set before you. Be discerning. Be wise.

In Daniel chapter 1, Daniel was invited to sit and eat at the king's table and partake of his delicacies. He refused. Do you ever wonder why? It was just food. Was he majoring on minors? No. Daniel was living in a society where compromise was commonplace. Here are some reasons he chose to distance himself.

- The king was ungodly, an idol worshiper. To come to his table would be to partake of his views, his influence, and his way of life.
- There was extravagance. Ladies, we can get a taste for rich things, and it can drive us. We can begin to think we need rich things at any cost.
- Friendships are made at tables. When we eat with others, we let down our guards and become comfortable. Be careful who you are comfortable with.

James 4:4 tells us, "Whoever therefore wants to be a friend of the world makes himself an enemy of God" (NKJV). Compromise leads to compromise, which leads to compromise.

Make It Personal . . . Live It Out!

Our children, especially when they are teens and college age, constantly find themselves in compromising situations. We call that peer pressure. Just because they seem to be doing well, don't kid yourself. One weak moment can change their lives. One taste of the delicacies of drugs or sex or pornography or alcohol can lead them to a taste for more. Don't kid yourself about the compromises you allow in your life and home either. Don't just be worried; be wise. Ask the Lord to open your eyes to give you discernment in your own life, and then you will be able to see clearly to help safeguard your family.

One Year Bible Reading

Isaiah 6:1–7:25; 2 Corinthians 11:16-33; Psalm 54:1-7; Proverbs 23:1-3

September 11

Vanity, Vanity

Do not wear yourself out to get rich;
have the wisdom to show restraint.
Cast but a glance at riches, and they are gone,
for they will surely sprout wings
and fly off to the sky like an eagle.

PROVERBS 23:4-5 (NIV)

It is hard to imagine a generation that's living more contrary to this proverb. People are driving themselves and wearing themselves out. In most homes both Mom and Dad work long hours just to get ahead. But, sadly, it's hard to find anyone who feels that enough is enough. The more money you make, the more you spend. I saw a bumper sticker that says, "I owe, I owe; so off to work I go."

For us as women, we can get caught up in the pursuit of the latest fashions, or trendy décor for our house. That too is a rabbit chase. Last year's trend often goes in this year's garage sale box. Vanity, vanity.

To be wise is to know that life is not measured in riches. Contentment is great gain. Those who have it, as Shakespeare said in *Hamlet*, "could be bounded in a nutshell and count [themselves] a king of infinite space."

So how can we make the shift? How can we shake free of the rat race?

Jesus gave us wise advice for living in Matthew 6:19-21: "Don't store up treasures here on earth. . . . Store your treasures in heaven, where moths and rust cannot destroy, and thieves do not break in and steal. Wherever your treasure is, there the desires of your heart will also be."

Make It Personal . . . Live It Out!

This is a good place to remind ourselves that having an eternal perspective will transform all our passions and pursuits.

Two little lines I heard one day, traveling along life's busy way,
Bringing conviction to my heart, and from my mind would not depart,
Only one life, 'twill soon be past, only what's done for Christ will last.
Only one life, yes only one, soon will its fleeting hours be done,
Then, in "that day" my Lord to meet, and stand before His Judgment seat;
Only one life, 'twill soon be past, only what's done for Christ will last.

—C. T. STUDD IN "ONLY ONE LIFE"

One Year Bible Reading

Isaiah 8:1–9:21; 2 Corinthians 12:1-10; Psalm 55:1-23; Proverbs 23:4-5

A Stingy Man

Do not eat the food of a stingy man;
do not crave his delicacies;
for he is the kind of man who is always thinking about the cost.
"Eat and drink," he says to you, but his heart is not with you.
You will vomit up the little you have eaten
and will have wasted your compliments.

PROVERBS 23:6-8 (NIV)

It's amazing. I've seen more stingy people who are rich than stingy people who are poor. It's a shame. For some, being rich means more to hoard, never more to give.

I have gone to homes like mansions but felt poor, hardly welcomed, and not really wanted. Be careful when you're in that atmosphere. You never want to be beholden to those who are stingy or insincere in what they give or what they do. Our proverb says we'll be sorry later.

In contrast, it's a joy to see generosity displayed. I've sat at the tables of women in Russia whose apartments were small and simple, and yet they lavished me with a warm welcome, wonderful food, and love. That's generosity.

What lesson now should we learn? Let's be generous. "God loves a cheerful giver" (2 Corinthians 9:7, NKJV), and so does everyone else. "It is more blessed to give than to receive" (Acts 20:35, NKJV). So this week let's make it a point to consciously be generous in a practical way, either in time, or kindness, or appreciative words. Don't make it a chore—*Okay. I'll do my three good deeds*. That's not the idea. Ask the Lord to show you an opportunity. You'll be amazed. It will not only make a difference in someone else's day, but it will make a difference in yours.

Make It Personal . . . Live It Out!

General William Booth of the Salvation Army was a man who spent his life in unselfish service. He once sent a Christmas greeting to his workers around the world. The message was a simple and yet profound word—*Others*. I love it. Doesn't the thought of living this day with that motto stir you? *Others!*

Let's Pray

Lord, move my heart to be outward and generous. May I see and care about what you see and care about *others*.

One Year Bible Reading

Isaiah 10:1–11:16; 2 Corinthians 12:11-21; Psalm 56:1-13; Proverbs 23:6-8

Wise Advice

Don't waste your breath on fools,
for they will despise the wisest advice.

PROVERBS 23:9

Who fits the biblical definition of being a fool? Proverbs 1:7 says that "fools despise wisdom and instruction" (NKJV). They don't need more information. They don't know because they don't want to know. I believe this is true with some who reject the existence of God. Psalm 14:1 says, "The fool has said in his heart, 'There is no God'" (NKJV). They don't know because they don't want to know.

And why do some people remain foolish in the way that they live? Why do some people keep making the same mistakes over and over? Why is it that some will never listen, even when others speak the truth in love? The reason is they don't want to change. They love their sin even though it makes them miserable. Jesus said in John 3:17, 19, "God did not send His Son into the world to condemn the world, but that the world through Him might be saved. . . . And this is the condemnation, that . . . men loved darkness rather than light, because their deeds were evil" (NKJV).

But this proverb is primarily instructing us on how we are to respond to someone who is stuck in stubborn foolishness of any kind. Don't waste your breath. You can't talk them out of it

On the other hand, mothers, if you have a stubborn, prodigal son, you can pray. If your friend is making bad decisions, you can pray. If your husband has turned his back on God, you can pray. "The effective, fervent prayer of a righteous [wo]man avails much" (James 5:16, NKJV).

Make It Personal . . . Live It Out!

Let me break some bad news. All of us, even you and I, are sometimes stubborn, short-sighted, and foolish. Yes, it's true. It is foolish to close our ears to wise counsel from others. But it is a tragic mistake to close our hearts to the nudging of the Holy Spirit. How can you tell when the Lord is speaking to you? Ask him. Do you feel a tug on your heart, a conviction in your spirit? Is there a topic or Scripture that keeps popping up? Ask God if he is trying to correct or warn or teach you something. When he confirms, your next step is to obey.

One Year Bible Reading

Isaiah 12:1–14:32; 2 Corinthians 13:1-13; Psalm 57:1-11; Proverbs 23:9-11

Learning to Learn

Apply your heart to instruction
and your ears to words of knowledge.

PROVERBS 23:12 (NIV)

What does it mean to apply your heart and your ears to learn and understand? Well, it's not a fast-food approach to God or his Word. Many of us are so busy we look for shortcuts and quick fixes in almost everything we do, but this approach just does not fly when it comes to our relationship with God. He is the God of the universe, our heavenly Father, and he deserves more.

I once saw a Bible in the store that claimed you could do all your devotional readings in one minute. The concept is you can spend sixty seconds to read several lines from the Bible and call it your devotion time. I know people are busy, but is that really devotion? To *devote* is "to set apart, to be given wholly or completely to a particular purpose." And to be devoted is to feel or show great loyalty and fondness.

May I ask, do you love to learn from God? Do you desire to know him more? Do you desire to see the truth and wisdom of God's Word change you from the inside out? God himself says to you, "Call to Me, and I will answer you, and show you great and mighty things, which you do not know" (Jeremiah 33:3, NKJV).

Jesus said, "Blessed are those who hunger and thirst for righteousness, for they shall be filled" (Matthew 5:6, NKJV). Will you ask the Lord to give you a greater hunger for his Word? Will you ask him to use his Word to speak to your heart and show you something to apply to your life today?

Make It Personal . . . Live It Out!

"Apply your heart to instruction" is our call to action today. But many wonder why they do not learn well, why they don't retain lessons they hear at church or on the radio. They don't remember what they read. Is that you? You are not alone. One big problem is focus. We are multitasking, distracted, and unfocused. Here are some simple tools. Carry a little journal to church, write a few notes, and then share what you learned with someone. When you read a book, underline or highlight things you want to remember, then review them. Pay attention, focus your heart, and learning will come.

One Year Bible Reading

Isaiah 15:1–18:7; Galatians 1:1-24; Psalm 58:1-11; Proverbs 23:12

Discipline

Do not withhold discipline from a child;
if you punish him with the rod, he will not die.
Punish him with the rod
and save his soul from death.

PROVERBS 23:13-14 (NIV)

Clearly this proverb is saying that punishment is sometimes very necessary. But this definitely is not endorsing striking a child out of anger or frustration. This is always wrong. Proverbs 27:4 cautions us that "anger is cruel, and wrath is like a flood."

Mothers, we need to make sure that when we give punishment to our children, we do it in love. But love that gives no punishment is not really love either. Sometimes a child gets locked into a behavior that, left uncorrected, could ruin their life. Picture this. When someone takes hold of a live electric wire, the voltage grabs hold of them, and they cannot let go until they die from the deadly result. The only thing that can be done is to strike them with a wooden plank at the point of contact—not to hurt them but to free them.

Years ago, our seventeen-year-old niece lived with us. She had not been used to consistent rules at home, so we had some challenges. She sometimes chafed at simple things like curfew and chores and limits regarding boys. But one night she told me about a friend at school. Our niece had been complaining to her about how tough it was to live with restrictions. Her friend started to cry. She said, "Oh, how I wish someone at home cared enough about me to just say no sometimes."

Make It Personal . . . Live It Out!

There are many ways to discipline a child, including time-outs and removal of privileges. Focus on the Family describes two more:

- Natural consequences. For example, if your child refuses to eat dinner, instead of developing a power struggle, allow him or her to go to bed without eating. He or she will naturally be hungry in the morning and will be certain to eat. (Appropriate for children two and older.)
- Logical consequences. This is a punishment that fits the crime. Suppose your child throws a ball in the house and breaks a vase. He or she could be required to work off the value of the vase or use allowance money to buy a new one.

One Year Bible Reading

Isaiah 19:1–21:17; Galatians 2:1-16; Psalm 59:1-17; Proverbs 23:13-14

Instruct, Instill, and Inspire

My son, if your heart is wise,
My heart will rejoice, indeed, I myself;
Yes, my inmost being will rejoice
When your lips speak right things.

PROVERBS 23:15-16 (NKJV)

John said, "I have no greater joy than to hear that my children walk in the truth" (3 John 1:4, NKJV). Moms, do you tell your children that they bless you? Do you catch them being good and let them know? Do you look for their strengths and tell them? We can get in the habit of pointing out their failures so often that they see themselves in our eyes as failures.

Do your children know that you value their character even more than any outward beauty or accomplishment? Sometimes we teach our kids that performance or accomplishment is the bottom line to life, and the only way they can please us is by being popular, or smart, or athletic. Will you pray about this? Will you ask the Lord to show you how to teach your kids that character matters? Will you pray and ask the Lord to show you how to teach your kids to be wise, and honest, and kind, and forgiving? Moms, teach your kids how to use the power of their words for good to encourage other kids who are discouraged. Teach them to speak the truth. Teach them to stand up for truth.

We, as moms, as women, have a powerful influence in the world around us, but the most important lessons cannot just be taught with words. They must be caught from us. It's been said, "There is no greater gift that you can give your children than a good example."

Make It Personal . . . Live It Out!

Fill your world with noble stories and songs and poems to raise the bar and challenge you. Never stop growing, and you will inspire others to follow.

There will always be something to do, my girl;
There will always be wrongs to right;
There will always be need for a noble one
And those unafraid to fight.
There will always be honor to guard, my girl;
There will always be hills to climb,
And tasks to do, and battles new
From now till the end of time.

—ADAPTED FROM "THERE WILL ALWAYS BE SOMETHING TO DO" BY EDGAR A. GUEST

One Year Bible Reading

Isaiah 22:1–24:23; Galatians 2:17–3:9; Psalm 60:1-12; Proverbs 23:15-16

September 17

Envious of the Wicked?

Do not let your heart envy sinners,
But be zealous for the fear of the LORD all the day;
For surely there is a hereafter,
And your hope will not be cut off.

PROVERBS 23:17-18 (NKJV)

It's a very natural experience to look around and see mean, selfish, ungodly people who win and prosper. Sometimes it just gets to us. We think, *God, that is just not fair. Why,* we ask, *should the bad, disobedient people get good things and those who love and serve you suffer?*

This proverb gives us instruction and encouragement and comfort. It gives us comfort knowing that we're not the only ones who sometimes feel that way. Even David felt that way. He said, "I was envious of the boastful, when I saw the prosperity of the wicked" (Psalm 73:3, NKJV). David once served under a prideful, jealous king who wanted to kill him. It is times like these that don't seem to make sense and cause us to be frustrated.

What then should we do? Our proverb today instructs us. Don't envy wicked people. All they get are their external victories and temporal prizes, but internally sin has conquered their souls, and that is too great a price. They are to be pitied rather than envied.

And, lastly, our proverb comforts us by saying, "Surely there is a hereafter, and your hope will not be cut off." Let's let Jesus have the final word. He said "In the world you will have tribulation; but be of good cheer, I have overcome the world" (John 16:33, NKJV).

Make It Personal . . . Live It Out!

In all situations, the great victory shout and defining attitude is "be zealous for the fear of the LORD all the day." To obey this does not lead us to victory; to obey it *is* victory. Have you felt discouraged seeing others who don't deserve it excel or be blessed? Our heavenly Father "gives his sunlight to both the evil and the good, and he sends rain on the just and the unjust alike" (Matthew 5:45). To "fear the Lord" in a practical way merely means to trust that your life is in his hands. Trust him when there's hardship, trust him when life isn't fair, trust him to work all things together for your good (see Romans 8:28).

One Year Bible Reading

Isaiah 25:1–28:13; Galatians 3:10-22; Psalm 61:1-8; Proverbs 23:17-18

The Way to Rags

My child, listen and be wise:
Keep your heart on the right course.
Do not carouse with drunkards or feast with gluttons,
for they are on their way to poverty,
and too much sleep clothes them in rags.

PROVERBS 23:19-21

This proverb addresses us as: my child. Jesus said we are to be childlike. But that doesn't mean childish. Look around. We live in a society that will not grow up. Sadly, I have been dealing with a single mom who hasn't. After her divorce she plunged into the party lifestyle. Her new set of friends were loud and obnoxious. Her children have not only suffered, but they are embarrassed by her. Her house is dirty and shabby. Her kids wish she would shape up and grow up.

One alcoholic writes, "I had over forty jobs. I'd work like mad for weeks without a drink, pay a few bills, and then reward myself with alcohol. Then I'd be broke again, hiding out in cheap hotels all over the country."

Is there an antidote? The best antidote for addiction is preventive medicine. "Listen and be wise: Keep your heart on the right course." Stay away from the group at the office who invite you to go out for a few drinks. Those few drinks lead to a few more drinks.

If you have been compromising—whether it's with alcohol, street drugs, or prescription drugs—will you ask the Lord to help you wake up and grow up? You can't keep blaming it on things and people in the past. The mercies of God are "new every morning" (Lamentations 3:23, NIV). God himself is ready to help.

Make It Personal . . . Live It Out!

One of Satan's tactics is to make you feel too ashamed or too hopeless to admit you need help. But admitting that we are in over our heads and that our flesh is stronger than us is always the first step to turning to God in desperation. "I know that nothing good lives in me, that is, in my sinful nature. I want to do what is right, but I can't" (Romans 7:18).

Let's Pray

God, I come to you weary and weak. Please be my strength and mighty Savior. One day at a time, walk me to wholeness and restoration.

One Year Bible Reading

Isaiah 28:14–30:11; Galatians 3:23–4:31; Psalm 62:1-12; Proverbs 23:19-21

Be Kind to Your Parents

Listen to your father who begot you,
And do not despise your mother when she is old.

PROVERBS 23:22 (NKJV)

Many women who are reading today wince when they see these words. Maybe you grew up without a father or with one who was harsh, or cold, or cruel. Maybe you've always struggled with your mother. You just cannot stand to be around her. To you this proverb doesn't sound logical or doable, at least for you in your situation. So what should we do, and how can we apply it?

My own father grew up with a dad who was a drunk. He was not mean, but he was not there. This left his family desperately poor. But it's a credit to my dad that he chose not to be bitter. He loved his dad. Later his dad sobered up and became a kind and caring grandfather. I was blessed that my father chose to honor his father and give him a second chance.

And for those of you who have a chip on your shoulder about your mom, this proverb is the Word of God; therefore, it's God who is looking you in the eye and saying, "Get over it." When you're short tempered or disdainful of your mom, it's just plain wrong. It causes your own character to be eroded.

In Ephesians 4:32 the Lord instructs us to "be kind to one another, tenderhearted, forgiving one another, even as God in Christ forgave you" (NKJV).

One final note to moms: our kids are watching and taking their cues from us. How you treat your mom or your mother-in-law, or even how you treat your ex-mother-in-law, is all a lesson to them. When we treat our family members with honor, it teaches them it's an honor to be honorable.

Make It Personal . . . Live It Out!

Are your parents getting older? Even when we know that we are to care for them, the process can be complicated. *Caring for Aging Loved Ones* by Focus on the Family is a wonderful resource. Topics include burnout; physical, emotional, and mental changes in aging; medical, financial, and legal help; elder abuse; choosing a care facility; and end-of-life decisions. It looks at what the Bible says about caregiving and the keys to effectively fulfilling that role. May God bless you and give you grace.

One Year Bible Reading

Isaiah 30:12–33:9; Galatians 5:1-12; Psalm 63:1-11; Proverbs 23:22

Lesson by Lesson

Get the truth and never sell it;
also get wisdom, discipline, and good judgment.

PROVERBS 23:23

It doesn't matter how much money or education you have, every one of us has to buy wisdom on the installment plan, lesson by lesson, truth by truth. Each time we seek God's wisdom, he gives us more. Each time we trust God's wisdom, he gives us more.

Bible Study Fellowship, founded in 1959 by A. Wetherell Johnson, is the perfect illustration that God's wisdom is sometimes delivered to us in unusual packages. Ms. Johnson was a British missionary serving in China until 1950, when Mao Tse-tung's communist regime forced missionaries to leave. She loved China deeply. With a torn heart she moved to the States. Five ladies in San Bernardino, California, asked her to teach a Bible study. Here are her words: "My heart fell! What had I come to? . . . In China there are millions who have not even heard His name. *Am I to give more to those who already have so much?*" Reluctantly she promised to pray. Dashed hopes are often the breeding ground for God's wise ways to birth great things. She did say yes, but told them she would not spoon-feed them the Bible. She prepared lesson questions to help them dig deeper using the inductive study method. Bible Study Fellowship has now grown to over one thousand classes with over two hundred thousand members in thirty-eight nations across six continents.

Has one door shut in your life, leaving you confused and sorrowful? Ask God for wisdom. "Trust in the LORD with all your heart, and lean not on your own understanding" (Proverbs 3:5, NKJV).

Make It Personal . . . Live It Out!

Our proverb for the day comes from *The One Year Bible*. This Bible arranges a daily reading in which you read a portion of the Old Testament, New Testament, a Psalm, and a Proverb every day. I have to tell you, there is nothing I look forward to more in the morning than taking my cup of coffee, my Bible, and my notebook and sitting in a secret place with the Lord. I love to take notes. I love to stop and ponder and pray, asking the Lord to teach me and show me how to apply his truth. Will you join me reading along this journey?

One Year Bible Reading

Isaiah 33:10–36:22; Galatians 5:13-26; Psalm 64:1-10; Proverbs 23:23

A Father's Child

The father of the righteous will greatly rejoice,
And he who begets a wise child will delight in him.

PROVERBS 23:24 (NKJV)

The family is in trouble. People are giving up on lasting relationships, and the fallout is dramatically affecting children. Children often end up as pawns in divorce court and child-custody battles. Are you struggling in your marriage? Please, don't give up. The quick fix of divorce is far from a quick fix.

Let me now speak to single women. When you consider a man to marry, be careful and prayerful. Are his attitudes and priorities the stuff that great fathers are made of? Is he a man of his word, is he kind, is he faithful, is he growing and desiring to become a godly man? I'm not talking about a perfect man—Adam was the last one, and that only lasted for a while. Take an honest look at his character flaws. Is he a drinker, is he selfish, does he get angry easily? Not only do all of these things affect your safety and happiness, but they will dramatically affect your children.

Consider what studies are now finding regarding the importance of a father to a daughter. Dr. Meg Meeker, author of the book *Strong Fathers, Strong Daughters: 10 Secrets Every Father Should Know*, explains that the most important factor for girls growing up into confident, well-adjusted women is a strong father with conservative values. To have one is the best protection against eating disorders, failure in school, STDs, unwed pregnancy, and drug or alcohol abuse; and the best predictor of academic achievement, successful marriage, and a satisfying emotional life.

Make It Personal . . . Live It Out!

What if your kids do not have a father in the home? Do you, as a woman, have a "father-shaped hole" in your own life? Are you destined to be just the product of a broken society? The truth is, ever since Adam and Eve fell, families have been at least somewhat dysfunctional. In Isaiah 49:15-16 God responds to your deep questions when you feel he has forgotten you. He says, "Never! Can a mother forget her nursing child? Can she feel no love for the child she has borne? But even if that were possible, I would not forget you! See, I have written your name on the palms of my hands."

One Year Bible Reading

Isaiah 37:1–38:22; Galatians 6:1-18; Psalm 65:1-13; Proverbs 23:24

A Prostitute

A prostitute is a dangerous trap;
a promiscuous woman is as dangerous as falling into a narrow well.
She hides and waits like a robber,
eager to make more men unfaithful.

PROVERBS 23:27-28

The dictionary definition of *prostitute* is "one who sells herself (body, moral integrity) for low or unworthy purposes." She is indeed a dangerous trap. But today let's look at the heartbreaking trap and pit that she falls into herself. I want to speak to and for women who have fallen.

Recently a woman told me her story. She grew up in a broken home. Her father was absent. Her bitter and lonely mom allowed many men to come into their home, along with drugs and alcohol. This was a dangerous place for a little girl. One of the men abused her repeatedly, then threatened to kill her and her mom if she ever told. Shame, pain, fear, and secrecy are a tough combination of emotions for a young soul to juggle. Her longings for male love comingled with man hatred. This combination set her up to sell herself.

As a young teen she started to experiment with drugs to kill the pain and help her cope with her out-of-control world. To supply her habit, she traded sex for drugs. So the cycle continued. Her journey began as a victim. She then became aggressive and hurtful to others, taking out her pain on anyone who got close. At her very lowest, she cried out to a God she did not know. But the wonderful part of this story is, he knew her. He heard her cry for help and in his great mercy healed and set her free.

Make It Personal . . . Live It Out!

Does this story strike a chord? It describes a world of pain but also reveals how pain can drive a woman headlong into sin. Jesus came to bring the mercy of heaven to earth.

"In all their suffering he also suffered, and he personally rescued them. In his love and mercy he redeemed them" (Isaiah 63:9).

Let's Pray

Lord, words cannot describe the feelings that surface when the closet of the past is opened. Please, pour your light and love and truth and grace into the deepest pits. Make me whole, able to live and love.

One Year Bible Reading

Isaiah 39:1–41:16; Ephesians 1:1-23; Psalm 66:1-20; Proverbs 23:25-28

A Lost Cause?

Today's proverb is a long description of the crazy, out-of-control world of drinking and drugs. If someone you love is living this life, this scene is all too familiar.

Who has anguish? Who has sorrow?
Who is always fighting? Who is always complaining?
Who has unnecessary bruises? Who has bloodshot eyes?
It is the one who spends long hours in the taverns,
trying out new drinks.
Don't gaze at the wine . . .
how it sparkles in the cup, how smoothly it goes down.
For in the end it bites like a poisonous snake. . . .
You will see hallucinations,
and you will say crazy things.
You will stagger like a sailor tossed at sea. . . .
And you will say, "They hit me, but I didn't feel it.
I didn't even know it when they beat me up.
When will I wake up
so I can look for another drink?"

PROVERBS 23:29-35

A lost-cause drunk is the picture of hopelessness. Except for the grace of God no one can return from this ruinous pit. But there is the grace of God! And his grace still works miracles. By the miracle of redemption some very unlikely people have been completely, radically, and supernaturally changed. Oswald Chambers said, "There is nothing miraculous or mysterious about the things we can explain." Many alcoholics have tried to pull themselves up by their own self-will, their desperate desire to change, or in response to the pleading of their family or friends. It's not enough. When we come to the end of ourselves, God responds, "My grace is all you need. My power works best in weakness" (2 Corinthians 12:9).

Make It Personal . . . Live It Out!

What can you do when you see someone's life going down the drain? Fear, anger, and despair are natural but not helpful. Psalm 43:5 puts words to your feelings, and then lifts you to hope in the Savior, who is mighty to save.

"Why am I discouraged? Why is my heart so sad? I will put my hope in God! I will praise him again—my Savior and my God!"

One Year Bible Reading

Isaiah 41:17–43:13; Ephesians 2:1-22; Psalm 67:1-7; Proverbs 23:29-35

Stirring Up Trouble

Don't envy evil people
or desire their company.
For their hearts plot violence,
and their words always stir up trouble.

PROVERBS 24:1-2

Ladies, this is a piece of advice we need to make sure we apply. Wicked people are troublemakers and trouble-talkers. There can be no greater trouble than a woman who is on the warpath.

There are many examples in the Bible of people who stirred up trouble with their words. On the journey to the Promised Land the Israelites grumbled many times. In Numbers 11 the rabble began to crave other food besides the manna. They were unthankful, and yet they had never missed a meal. No, they just wanted fish and cucumbers. It's been said, "Contentment is not getting what you want but wanting what you have." Well, they complained, and pretty soon everyone was unhappy. Everyone was complaining. It spread like the plague. Then Moses got discouraged. He wanted to give up. Can you see how complaining can make your husband or your pastor or your friends or your kids want to give up? Don't do that to them. But the difference between the rabble and Moses is that he took his frustration and burdens not to others but to the Lord, and the Lord sent solutions. God put his Spirit on leaders who could then help carry the burden of the people.

So the moral? Don't make friendships with complainers, whiners, gripers, or fault-finders. If there's a problem, take it to the Lord and pray for godly friends.

Make It Personal . . . Live It Out!

Griping and complaining is the shortest path to leaving you with more to gripe and complain about. Did you know that? For example, if you constantly criticize your kids about the way they put away the dishes or mow the lawn, or you put your husband down about the way he drives, or that he always forgets something when you send him to the store . . . guess what? They are not likely to want to try again. You will end up doing the dishes and going to the store all by yourself. Praise and thankfulness go a long way. Try them. For sure, others will like it—and so will you.

One Year Bible Reading

Isaiah 43:14–45:10; Ephesians 3:1-21; Psalm 68:1-18; Proverbs 24:1-2

House Beautiful

A house is built by wisdom
and becomes strong through good sense.
Through knowledge its rooms are filled
with all sorts of precious riches and valuables.

PROVERBS 24:3-4

I just returned from visiting a third-world country. Sadly, it is marred with building projects that are poorly constructed, half finished, abandoned, and vandalized. The country is rich in natural resources and spectacular beauty. But many people live in unkept shacks, their situations never improving from generation to generation. It makes me wonder.

Today's beautiful proverb pictures a stunning contrast. The key words are *built*, *wisdom*, *strong*, *good sense*, *knowledge*, *filled*, *precious riches*, and *valuables*.

I know many women who came from a life of shambles. But I have also seen those very same women completely turn toward God with desperate hope. I have seen God restore marriages, bring back prodigal children, reconnect mothers with children placed for adoption, and help women who were drug addicts become leaders and mentors to restore others.

Joshua stood at the dividing point in the Israelites' history and shouted these words: "Choose for yourselves this day whom you will serve, whether the gods which your fathers served that were on the other side of the River, or the gods of the [people] in whose land you dwell. But as for me and my house, we will serve the LORD" (Joshua 24:15, NKJV). Joshua had seen the Promised Land. He knew that nothing compared with it. As we read these words, God is throwing open the door. Will you choose today to let the Lord be the unrivaled God and ruling King of your home? He will then fill your life with precious riches: peace, kindness, fruitfulness, his strength, and most of all his presence.

Make It Personal . . . Live It Out!

"A house is built by wisdom." The building process does not happen overnight. Brick by brick it is built from the ground up. Is there a portion of your life that needs reconstruction? All right—get started! Ask God to show you where the root of the problem is. Face it honestly. Face where you have been foolish or unsurrendered. Repentance removes the rubble. Forgiveness gives you a fresh start. His Holy Spirit then empowers you and provides all the materials you need to rebuild.

One Year Bible Reading

Isaiah 45:11–48:11; Ephesians 4:1-16; Psalm 68:19-35; Proverbs 24:3-4

Spiritual Warfare

A wise man is strong;
Yes, a man of knowledge increases strength;
For by wise counsel you will wage your own war,
And in a multitude of counselors there is safety.

PROVERBS 24:5-6 (NKJV)

"Wage your war." Few of us women will ever fight on the battlefield. But be aware: there is a war raging around us. There is a battle raging to destroy our kids. There is a battle raging to destroy our concept of who we are as women, downgrading motherhood or virtue or respect for our husbands. There are battles and conflicts within our families, at work, in relationships, and even within ministries. Sometimes we definitely are facing war on many fronts. Now what we need to realize is that this is a spiritual war and must be fought, not with carnal resources, but with spiritual weapons and spiritual, godly counselors.

J. Vernon McGee gave this advice: "We need to know what the whole Bible says. We need to read Moses and Joshua and Samuel and David and Micah and Zechariah and Matthew and Paul and John. They are all our counselors. We can appeal to all of them at any time of decision."

Second Corinthians 10:3-5 gives us wisdom that will make us strong and ready. "Though we walk in the flesh, we do not war according to the flesh. For the weapons of our warfare are not carnal but mighty in God for pulling down strongholds, casting down arguments and every high thing that exalts itself against the knowledge of God, bringing every thought into captivity to the obedience of Christ" (NKJV).

Make It Personal . . . Live It Out!

Many people misunderstand what spiritual warfare is. They think if their car breaks down or their kids lose their homework, it's spiritual warfare. No. The enemy will only rattle your exterior circumstances if he thinks it will rattle you. Faith is a spiritual weapon. Obedience is a spiritual weapon against temptation. The sword of the Spirit is the Word of God. Truth may not change your outward reality, but it can transform your inner reality. God's truth shines light on the lie and helps you refocus on what is good and right and important.

One Year Bible Reading

Isaiah 48:12–50:11; Ephesians 4:17-32; Psalm 69:1-18; Proverbs 24:5-6

The Prize

Wisdom is too high for a fool;
in the assembly at the gate he has nothing to say.

PROVERBS 24:7 (NIV)

Have you ever seen a child scoot a chair up to the counter so he can reach the cookie jar? The prize of a cookie awaits him. Even if he's never seen it done, somehow he figures it out and does what it takes to climb up to get that cookie. This is called motivation. They say necessity is the mother of invention. But desire is definitely a key element.

God has set the prize of wisdom for living before us, available to everyone. James 1 tells us we can ask God and he will give wisdom. So then does the actual attainment require effort and some hard choices on our part? Is there some pain in the gain? Absolutely! Anything worthwhile is worth paying the price, pressing past obstacles, reaching higher, stretching past our lowest instincts and weakness of will. God shows us the way, but we have to choose to go the way. Foolishness has a price too, you know. Even though foolishness often gets the prize of instant gratification, the consequences always come due.

Giuseppe Garibaldi (1807–1882) was an Italian patriot, soldier, and hero who devoted his life to the cause of uniting Italy. Garibaldi had an incredibly committed volunteer army. His appeal for recruits was bold and clear: "Let him who loves his country with his heart and not with his lips only, follow me." He told his men, "I do not promise you ease; I do not promise you comfort. I promise you hardship, weariness, suffering; but I [also] promise you victory." He led others to the high road because he traveled it himself.

Make It Personal . . . Live It Out!

And so the first and real question is, do you want to be a woman of wisdom? If the answer is truly, wholeheartedly yes, pause to picture a specific question or dilemma you are currently facing. Then take that need right now to God in prayer. Ask and believe he will give you wisdom and direction. Ask him for strength and courage. And then be ready. Be ready to take that final important step when he gives you insight—to apply it.

One Year Bible Reading

Isaiah 51:1–53:12; Ephesians 5:1-33; Psalm 69:19-36; Proverbs 24:7

Villains and Bullies

A person who plans evil
will get a reputation as a troublemaker.

PROVERBS 24:8

For every great story there always seems to be a villain. My grandma called it "a snake in the woodpile." Someone always has a bone to pick, an axe to grind, a grudge to nurse. In fourth grade we had both a playground bully and a sneaky little tattletale. They started young; I wonder if they ever grew out of it.

Your kids will have bullies on their playground too,and later at the workplace, in the neighborhood, and maybe in their families. I bet even the bullies have bullies.

Taylor Swift wrote a song that asks the big question "Why ya gotta be so mean? You with your words like knives and swords and weapons that you use against me. You have knocked me off my feet. . . . All you are is mean and a liar and pathetic and alone in life and mean and mean and mean and mean. . . . Why ya gotta be so mean?"

The question then is not, will we encounter people who are harsh and mean? The question is, what do we, can we, and should we do about it?

Paul the apostle was the target of slander campaigns, beatings, and plots to kill him. When he wrote to the Christians in Rome, they were already feeling the rumblings of persecution. In Romans 12:17-19 God gave him (and us) the answer: " Never pay back evil with more evil. Do things in such a way that everyone can see you are honorable. Do all that you can to live in peace with everyone. . . . 'I will take revenge; I will pay them back,' says the LORD."

Make It Personal . . . Live It Out!

The good news for us is, what doesn't kill us, makes us stronger. Having our feelings hurt can teach us to not baby our feelings. It can break us of trying to protect our territory or reputation or rights. We are much better off when we leave every part of our lives entirely in the good hands of our good God.

Let's Pray

Lord, you are the God who sees all things. Forgive me when I get ruffled and angry when a bully threatens. Put a shield over my heart, a silencer on my tongue, and peace in my soul.

One Year Bible Reading

Isaiah 54:1–57:14; Ephesians 6:1-24; Psalm 70:1-5; Proverbs 24:8

September 29

Don't Faint

The devising of foolishness is sin, And the scoffer is an abomination to men.
If you faint in the day of adversity, Your strength is small.

PROVERBS 24:9-10 (NKJV)

Maybe you've been the victim of someone's divisive ways. Many women feel that their mothers-in-law are against them, always looking for a way to put a wedge in their families or to belittle them. A message now to that mother-in-law: this is foolishness. You are tearing down your own family. Please don't do that. No one gains.

If you are the one hurt by someone's sinful actions, do you feel that you're going to faint, shrivel up, or just give up? I have felt like that many times; we come to the end of ourselves. In times like this, God has a promise and word picture for us in Isaiah 40:31, "But those who wait on the LORD shall renew their strength; they shall mount up with wings like eagles, they shall run and not be weary, they shall walk and not faint" (NKJV).

John Wesley, founder of the Methodist church, had an unhappy marriage. His wife was jealous and vindictive. However, he often said that he attributed most of his success to his wife, for she kept him on his knees. Because he was kept on his knees, he was humble and useful.

The easy roads are crowded,
And the level roads are jammed;
The pleasant little rivers
With the drifting folks are crammed. . . .
But the steeps that call for courage,
And that task that's hard to do
In the end result in glory
For the never-wavering few.

—EDGAR A. GUEST IN "THE FEW"

Make It Personal . . . Live It Out!

Through the years, I've had my share of troublemakers. I'll be honest, I haven't always handled it well. I've let the things they do and say get under my skin. I've imagined all the clever things I could say that would set them straight. But at some point I always realize that the greatest battle is not with the troublemaker. My greatest battle is always the war within me, in my thought life and attitudes. How about you? In reality we should thank those people. Yes—as it turns out, they are just one more tool God can use to mold us and draw us close.

One Year Bible Reading

Isaiah 57:15–59:21; Philippians 1:1-26; Psalm 71:1-24; Proverbs 24:9-10

Moved with Compassion!

Rescue those being led away to death;
hold back those staggering toward slaughter.
If you say, "But we knew nothing about this,"
does not he who weighs the heart perceive it?
Does not he who guards your life know it?
Will he not repay each person according to what he [or she] has done?

PROVERBS 24:11-12 (NIV)

This proverb shatters the concept that the best way to live is to not get involved, just mind our own business. When God asked Cain, "Where is your brother," Cain answered, "Am I my brother's keeper?" (see Genesis 4:9). The answer to that is, he should have been.

The whole message of Jesus' life is that he did get involved. "When He saw the [people in the marketplace], He was moved with compassion for them, because [he saw that] they were weary and scattered like sheep having no shepherd" (Matthew 9:36, NKJV). So the question is, do I? Do you? First John 4:17 tells us "as He is, so are we in this world" (NKJV). We are called to be his arms to hug the lonely, his hands to lift and help the fallen or weak. We are to be his shoulder to cry on when others need comfort. Sometimes we feel like we shouldn't even try; the world is so needy. But just because you can't do everything, don't let that be your excuse to do nothing.

Philippians 2:4 says, "Let each of you look out not only for his own interests, but also for the interests of others" (NKJV). And Jesus said, "This is My commandment, that you love one another as I have loved you" (John 15:12, NKJV).

Make It Personal . . . Live It Out!

This is a topic I am very fired up about. Are you sitting on the sidelines while the enemy is ramping up his armies and resources? He is holding nothing back in his war against the truth, the innocent, youth, women, and children. God is rallying his people to make a difference.

Will you volunteer at a pro-life pregnancy center, invite an unchurched child to Sunday school, tutor a dyslexic student, reach out to a troubled teen, send a care package to a missionary? Ideas are flooding my head. Won't you answer the call to stand in the gap and share his love in a tangible way?

One Year Bible Reading

Isaiah 60:1–62:5; Philippians 1:27–2:18; Psalm 72:1-20; Proverbs 24:11-12

October

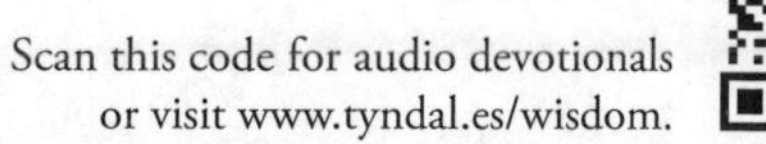
Scan this code for audio devotionals
or visit www.tyndal.es/wisdom.

Sweet like Honey

My son, eat honey because it's good,
And the honeycomb which is sweet to your taste;
So shall the knowledge of wisdom be to your soul.

PROVERBS 24:13-14 (NKJV)

It's been said, "You are what you eat." This applies not only to what you take into the body but what you feed your mind and your soul and your spirit. Honey is both sweet and fascinating. It is compared to the sweetness of the knowledge of wisdom. Lest we view this golden substance as ordinary, here are some interesting facts.

- A honeybee makes 154 trips to produce just one teaspoon of honey.
- To gather a pound of honey, a bee flies a distance equal to more than three times around the world and visits two million flowers.
- Honey has even been found in the Pharaohs' tombs, still edible after thousands of years.

Just like honey, wisdom isn't developed quickly or with little effort. Maybe that is why so many young or impatient people are not wise. Here's a good definition of wisdom: wisdom implies "a mature integration of appropriate knowledge and a seasoned ability to filter the inessential from the essential." To filter the inessential from the essential, that is a rare and valuable skill. James 3:17 describes wisdom's rich, multidimensional attributes: "The wisdom that is from above is first pure, then peaceable, gentle, willing to yield, full of mercy and good fruits, without partiality and without hypocrisy" (NKJV).

So, ladies, always remember as honey is sweet to the taste, wisdom is sweet, oh, so sweet to the soul.

Make It Personal . . . Live It Out!

James 3 lists gentleness as an attribute of wisdom. Does that surprise you? To be gentle is to be emotionally generous, kind, and patient. Why is that wiser than being overbearing and harsh? Answer: because the world is full of fragile people and delicate situations. Abraham Lincoln once said, "If you would win a man to your cause, first convince him that you are his sincere friend. Therein is a drop of honey that catches his heart." Abraham Lincoln was not weak, but like our Lord he had great inner strength under the control of compassionate kindness.

Let's Pray

Lord, gentle me, break me. Make me like you: sweet, compassionate, gentle, and kind.

One Year Bible Reading

Isaiah 62:6–65:25; Philippians 2:19–3:3; Psalm 73:1-28; Proverbs 24:13-14

Rise Again

Do not lie in wait like an outlaw against a righteous man's house,
do not raid his dwelling place;
for though a righteous man falls seven times, he rises again,
but the wicked are brought down by calamity.

PROVERBS 24:15-16 (NIV)

This could be viewed from two angles. It's first a warning, but it also includes an encouragement. Warning: if you see someone who is vulnerable or has fallen on hard times, don't pounce on him or her. Don't take advantage of anyone, especially a child of God. The Bible says that "the eyes of the LORD are on those who fear him, on those whose hope is his unfailing love" (Psalm 33:18, NIV). The selfish opportunist will be held accountable. The Lord sees and will eventually bring that person down.

But now for the encouragement. Dear sisters, many are going through hard times right now. Maybe you are. Maybe you're out of a job, or your car is broken, or you're losing your house. Although we wish that the Lord had promised us a life free of struggles and loss, he hasn't. But he has promised that he will never, ever leave us or forsake us. He has promised us wisdom in the trials, strength in our weakness, and peace that passes all understanding when we pray.

Prayer; what a gift the Lord has given us, that we can pray. Would you stop and pray right now? Listen again to our proverb. "Though a righteous man [or woman], falls seven times, [they] rise again." So humble yourself under the mighty hand of God, and He will lift you up. I know because I've been there.

Make It Personal . . . Live It Out!

When troubles push you down, there is nothing like standing on the promises of God. Hold tight to his words. Psalm 46:1-2 is a powerful promise to have written on your heart. Let it give you courage. Draw upon the comfort it brings. Let the words lift you up and give you hope!

"God is our refuge and strength, always ready to help in times of trouble. So we will not fear when earthquakes come and the mountains crumble into the sea."

One Year Bible Reading

Isaiah 66:1-24; Philippians 3:4-21; Psalm 74:1-23; Proverbs 24:15-16

People Problems

Do not gloat when your enemy falls;
when he stumbles, do not let your heart rejoice,
or the LORD will see and disapprove
and turn his wrath away from him.
Do not fret because of evil men
or be envious of the wicked,
for the evil man has no future hope,
and the lamp of the wicked will be snuffed out.

PROVERBS 24:17-20 (NIV)

This world is full of people who do evil things. Sometimes we feel threatened. Sometimes we are jealous when they win and get away scot-free. It's natural to be glad when they suffer for a change, but God wants us to live on a higher plane.

Joseph is a remarkable example of how to walk through unfair, cruel circumstances with honor and trust in the Lord and with integrity. His brothers ganged up on him, stripped him of his treasured coat, threw him in a pit, and then sold him as a slave. His hardship lasted thirteen long years. But then famine came. And he became a person who could call the shots—whether they starved to death or lived. One of the most beautiful moments in all of the Bible is when his brothers realized he could take revenge. Instead, he comforted them and said, "Don't be afraid. . . . Although you meant this for evil, God meant it for good" (Genesis 50:19-20, paraphrased).

So, ladies, do you have a situation where someone is unfair, harsh, or cruel to you? Bitterness, fear, or envy is not the answer. That keeps you under their thumb. Be aware. God has not forgotten. What goes around, truly does come around.

Make It Personal . . . Live It Out!

Difficult people come in all shapes and sizes. Toddlers throw tantrums, teens vent, bosses blame, sisters criticize. Difficult people test both our patience and our faith. As you read the encouragement found in James 1:2-4, may you discover fresh strength and motivation to endure with confidence. "Dear brothers and sisters, when troubles come your way, consider it an opportunity for great joy. For you know that when your faith is tested, your endurance has a chance to grow. So let it grow, for when your endurance is fully developed, you will be perfect and complete, needing nothing."

One Year Bible Reading

Jeremiah 1:1–2:30; Philippians 4:1-23; Psalm 75:1-10; Proverbs 24:17-20

Change Agents

Fear the LORD and the king, my son,
and do not join with the rebellious,
for those two will send sudden destruction upon them,
and who knows what calamities they can bring?

PROVERBS 24:21-22 (NIV)

So warning, do not join the rebellious. Some versions use the term, "Those given to change." Ladies, let's apply this proverb to our actions and attitudes within our church. There is no perfect church, and honestly, at times we do see things we'd like to change. There are three ways we can respond.

1. We can ignore it.
2. We can rebel and resent, or
3. We can pray.

Don't ignore the problem. Be aware; sometimes it's the Lord who is showing you an area of need to stir you up to be part of the solution.

Don't rebel or resent. Sadly, many times in churches or ministries people get impatient, and instead of trusting the Lord, they take matters in their own hands, resorting to ungodly means. They start a subversive campaign, inciting others to undermine the pastor or leaders. God will not honor actions that are dishonorable.

Pray. This is the truest and most fruitful way to bring about right changes because, first of all, it honors the Lord. It sometimes surprises me when I pray about a situation that I do feel needs changing, in prayer the Lord often changes me. He changes my perspective, and then he can show me a fresh way to play a positive and constructive role.

Make It Personal . . . Live It Out!

You are a change agent. Every day, in every way, you can live your life as part of the problem or part of the solution. It's really as simple as that. You wouldn't be reading this book if you didn't want to grow and give and make your life count for good in this world. That is your destiny, you know. Even though our lives feel small and insignificant, God can use us. Mother Teresa said, "Not all of us can do great things. But we can do small things with great love." God supplies the opportunity. All we need is the desire and willingness to respond.

One Year Bible Reading

Jeremiah 2:31–4:18; Colossians 1:1-17; Psalm 76:1-12; Proverbs 24:21-22

Justice and Mercy

To show partiality in judging is not good:
Whoever says to the guilty, "You are innocent"—
peoples will curse him and nations denounce him.
But it will go well with those who convict the guilty,
and rich blessing will come upon them.

PROVERBS 24:23-25 (NIV)

As we know, God is a kind and a merciful God, but he is also just and righteous. When he created man, he hardwired into our souls a desire for things to be right and true. Even a hardened criminal is outraged when there is no justice against someone who has done him wrong.

For there to be justice, it must be impartial. Let's apply this. As mothers, we can sometimes hold different standards for each of our children. This is not fair, and this is really not good for their souls either. Lenience is not the same as mercy. Too much lenience can cause a child to feel he or she is excused from doing the right thing when it's hard or inconvenient. So when your child has cheated on a test, or lied about Internet use, or stolen, and you know it, now both of you are accountable. If you both pretend that all is well, it's like leaving an elephant in the room and pretending it will not make a mess.

Here's a Scripture from 1 John1:8-9 that applies: "If we claim to be without sin, we deceive ourselves, and the truth is not in us. [But] if we confess our sins, he is faithful and just and will forgive our sins and purify [cleanse] us from all unrighteousness" (NIV).

Make It Personal . . . Live It Out!

Justice is one side of the coin, mercy is the other. When there has been a wrong done, are we always supposed to mete out the penalty? In most cases, no. We need to be careful, lest we play the role of traffic cop looking for what Jesus called the "speck in our brother's eye." There are many times when grace is the appropriate response. Mercy does triumph over judgment, and love covers a multitude of sins.

One Year Bible Reading

Jeremiah 4:19–6:15; Colossians 1:18–2:7; Psalm 77:1-20; Proverbs 24:23-25

Be Honest

An honest answer
is like a kiss on the lips.

PROVERBS 24:26 (NIV)

A truly honest answer—the contrast would be a dishonest answer or a half-honest answer. The Bible exhorts us to "speak the truth in love," and yet we sometimes don't.

Honesty—actually, this is a word that we really don't hear very often. As I read the dictionary definitions, they were so beautiful and the meaning so excellent, I felt it would stir us to read them.

Honesty means

- Honorable in principles, intentions, and actions.
- Sincere and frank, like an honest face.
- Gained fairly, like honest wealth.
- Genuine, truthful, and creditable. And when it applies to an honest person, it means "worthy of being trusted, truthful." An honest witness gives truthful testimony.

Since contrasts reinforce our understanding, let's look at words that describe the concept of *dishonesty*. It means "dishonorable, unjust, unfair, tricky, deceptive, deceitful, misleading, elusive, false, and hypocritical."

An honest answer, as our proverb says, "is like a kiss on the lips."

In a world so full of the false, may the Lord enable us to live and speak the truth. "And whatever you do in word or deed, do all in the name of the Lord Jesus, giving thanks to God the Father" (Colossians 3:17, NKJV).

Make It Personal . . . Live It Out!

As Christians, we sometimes put on a veneer. We never let others know we are weak, that we're hurting, that we make mistakes. This is dishonest. No, I don't think we should go around airing our dirty laundry, but pretending that you have it all together isn't good or necessary. It can make someone else feel that she is the only loser around. If she were a good Christian like you, she would never struggle. It can be a huge comfort to someone going through hard times that we are honest and let them know we've gone through similar trials without flying colors. Then you can pray with them, going together to the Cross, to be honest with God.

One Year Bible Reading

Jeremiah 6:16–8:7; Colossians 2:8-23; Psalm 78:1-31; Proverbs 24:26

First Things First

Prepare your outside work,
Make it fit for yourself in the field;
And afterward build your house.

PROVERBS 24:27 (NKJV)

The bottom line of this proverb is first things first. Necessities first, luxuries later. Good advice, especially for our generation. It seems that so many want it all, all at once and all of a sudden. Young people get the application for credit cards and start buying fun things before they even have a job. This leaves them in debt and always trying to catch up instead of getting ahead and saving.

Galileo once said, "I do not believe that the same God who has endowed us with sense, reason, and intellect has intended us to forgo their use." Good advice!

This proverb is a good exhortation to get your own life and finances in order. Since we live in a society where instant gratification is king, seldom do we see people investing in being prepared spiritually, emotionally, or financially for marriage or ministry, starting their own business, or buying a house.

So if you feel that you have not been wise and your life is out of order, the first thing to do is to acknowledge it, and then ask the Lord to give you wisdom, guidance, and self-control. God is a God of order. If you ask him, he can help you reconstruct one step at a time.

D. L. Moody liked to say, "Work as if everything depended on you and pray as if everything depended on God."

Make It Personal . . . Live It Out!

Personal responsibility, diligence, duty, steadfastness, and perseverance are great building blocks for life. Did you grow up in a home where you never saw these modeled? Join the club. But today, you get to choose. Small changes in important areas of life add up quickly. They build momentum. We become what we repeatedly do.

Let's Pray

Lord, you see the areas where I need structure and order. Forgive me for being careless and foolish. Inspire and instruct me in making wise, responsible choices.

One Year Bible Reading

Jeremiah 8:8–9:26; Colossians 3:1-17; Psalm 78:32-55; Proverbs 24:27

Off with the Old

Don't testify against your neighbors without cause;
don't lie about them.
And don't say, "Now I can pay them back for what they've done to me!
I'll get even with them!"

PROVERBS 24:28-29

In this proverb God himself is telling us two things he hates: lying and being spiteful. Both are mean. Both are destructive.

Lying—God hates it. "You shall not give false testimony against your neighbor" is one of God's top Ten Commandments (Exodus 20:16, NIV). That shows how important this is to him. It was God's plan to have an entire nation live with this principle. Just imagine what life would be like even if just Christians, God's people, decided to wholeheartedly obey this commandment. Just imagine.

Winston Churchill commented, "By swallowing evil words unsaid, no one has ever harmed his stomach."

The next issue is spitefulness, which simply means "full of spite." Colossians 3:8-9 tells us to put off ugly, useless behavior as we would take off old, dirty clothes. "Now is the time to get rid of anger, rage, malicious behavior, slander, and dirty language. Don't lie to each other, for you have stripped off your old sinful nature and all its wicked deeds." Ladies, these attitudes and actions are ugly and out of style for a godly woman. Do you remember the Disney movie *Bambi*? Thumper's father gave some good advice to his little rabbit son. He said, "If you can't say something nice . . . don't say nothing at all."

Make It Personal . . . Live It Out!

When women come to Christ, they often realize there are clothes in their closets that have to go. They're no longer the same person who put on that seductive top or those tight pants. Their desires are different, inside and out. My friend, let's continue the process of putting off old ways of living and responding. We need a fresh wardrobe of new ways to replace them. Colossians 3:10, 14 takes us on a shopping trip that will produce the kind of "extreme makeover" that really matters. "Put on your new nature, and be renewed as you learn to know your Creator and become like him. . . . Above all, clothe yourselves with love, which binds us all together in perfect harmony."

One Year Bible Reading

Jeremiah 10:1–11:23; Colossians 3:18–4:18; Psalm 78:56-72; Proverbs 24:28-29

Inch by Inch

I walked by the field of a lazy person,
the vineyard of one with no common sense.
I saw that it was overgrown with nettles.
It was covered with weeds,
and its walls were broken down.
Then, as I looked and thought about it,
I learned this lesson:
A little extra sleep, a little more slumber,
a little folding of the hands to rest—
then poverty will pounce on you like a bandit;
scarcity will attack you like an armed robber.

PROVERBS 24:30-34

It's interesting that in Solomon's day, just like ours, it's easy to spot a lazy man's or woman's house. It's neglected. This has nothing to do with the age or price range of the house. I have seen tiny, older homes that are charming and inviting simply because it's obvious someone who cares lives there.

So since our proverb describes the shabby result of neglect, let's look at how we can be diligent. Diligence is merely careful, steady effort.

When I was a young wife I heard the principle "inch by inch, anything's a cinch." I was putting off many things like planting flowers, organizing closets, or touching up paint because as a busy mom, I did not have big blocks of time to work on projects. Then I learned I could set a small goal to do just one thing each day. I actually wrote out a schedule: Monday, clean out one kitchen drawer while calling a friend. Tuesday, do two loads of laundry. Wednesday, spend fifteen minutes pulling out weeds. One of the great joys of making a list is checking things off.

"Inch by inch, anything's a cinch."

Make It Personal . . . Live It Out!

Would you like to be more diligent? A schedule, a list, and bundling—multitasking—are good tools. Get out your calendar to map out your week. List three half-hour tasks, then look for three thirty-minute blocks of time that are available. Post a note on the fridge stating your three goals and when you'll do them. As you do each task, purposely do something else like listening to a Bible study CD or praise music, or calling a friend to catch up. The time will fly by, you'll get a lot done, and you'll have fun in the process.

One Year Bible Reading

Jeremiah 12:1–14:10; 1 Thessalonians 1:1–2:8; Psalm 79:1-13; Proverbs 24:30-34

Hide and Seek

It is the glory of God to conceal a matter;
to search out a matter is the glory of kings.

PROVERBS 25:2 (NIV)

Solomon understood two things that seem to stand in conflict to each other.

1. In many ways God is mysterious. It's been said that if God were so small we could completely understand him, he would be too small for us to worship him. So think about it. Do you really understand how gravity works, or why your eye can see, or how a tiny seed can grow into a tree? If we can't grasp the mysteries of the creation, how much more so the Creator? Actually, it should thrill us that God has wisdom and understanding so vast and perfect we could explore it for all of eternity. "Oh, the depth of the riches both of the wisdom and knowledge of God!" (Romans 11:33, NKJV).

2. The fact is that even though we cannot understand everything, we need to seek to understand the things that we should understand. Kings and leaders and godly moms who take their responsibilities seriously never get tired of learning how they can grow in their ability to be and do their best. One of the first things that Solomon did when he became king was to ask God for wisdom. In 1 Kings 3:9 Solomon prayed, "Give your servant a discerning heart to govern your people and to distinguish between right and wrong. For who is able to govern this great people of yours?" (NIV).

Ladies, we live in a complicated, confusing, and challenging world, but the same God to whom Solomon went to ask for wisdom is waiting and wanting to give it to you. "Ask and you shall receive" (Matthew 7:7, paraphrased).

Make It Personal . . . Live It Out!

What does it mean "to search out a matter"? For example, I have a friend who has recently retired. She attends church and reads her Bible, but she isn't using her spiritual gifts to serve. I challenged her to "search out" God's will for this next phase of her life. Here are the steps:

1. Ask God for direction before you ask anyone else.
2. Pay attention to the stirrings he puts in your heart.
3. Look for God to open doors and send confirmation.
4. Step out to do what he is leading you to do.

One Year Bible Reading

Jeremiah 14:11–16:15; 1 Thessalonians 2:9–3:13; Psalm 80:1-19; Proverbs 25:1-5

October 11

The Right Seat

Do not exalt yourself in the king's presence,
and do not claim a place among great men;
it is better for him to say to you, "Come up here,"
than for him to humiliate you before a nobleman.

PROVERBS 25:6-7 (NIV)

Jesus said, "Whoever exalts himself will be humbled, and whoever humbles himself will be exalted" (Matthew 23:12, NKJV).

I have to tell you a little story. A few years ago I invited my sister to go to a Harvest Crusade. We arrived a little late. The ushers kept directing us higher and higher in the stadium until finally I could see that we would be sitting as high and far as you could get from the platform and the speakers. My heart sank. In a very pathetic silent voice I said, *But, Lord, I have hoped and waited many years for my sister to say yes and come to something like this. And now how could it be that we get the very worst seat?* In less than a second I heard the quiet voice of the Lord respond, *But, Debbi, will you not rejoice? Here she is. She came, and she is not complaining about the seat.* And then he pointed out, *All the other people in the top row—are they not just as important as your sister?*

Of course, Lord. I am so sorry. Thank you for setting me straight, and thank you that we do have a seat. It became one of those personal little moments, Father to daughter.

Well, seconds later my cell phone rang. It was my friend. She had saved us seats on the very first row. I had to say, *Thank you, Lord, for humbling me, and thank you, Lord, that when I did get a good seat, it was a blessing from you.*

Make It Personal . . . Live It Out!

Life sure is full of curveballs and detours. They may seem random, but when your life is in God's hands, you can see his fingerprints in the details. Even a seat in a stadium can be a teachable moment. In this case, the position of the seat was not as important as the position of my heart. Will you take your disappointments to your Lord, then leave the final results to him? A humble seat can become a holy moment.

One Year Bible Reading

Jeremiah 16:16–18:23; 1 Thessalonians 4:1–5:3; Psalm 81:1-16; Proverbs 25:6-8

Don't Widen the Circle

If you argue your case with a neighbor,
do not betray another man's confidence,
or he who hears it may shame you
and you will never lose your bad reputation.

PROVERBS 25:9-10 (NIV)

J. Vernon McGee said, "You could cause a great deal of trouble by criticizing your neighbor to the man down the street. If your neighbor has faults, go and talk to him personally." Unfortunately, one of the things that we as women often do when we're upset is widen the circle. It is really easy for us to talk to everyone around us except the person involved. Many new wives learn a painful lesson about this. She has a fight with her husband. In a moment of anger she tells her mom. Then later she makes up with her husband and all is forgotten—except by Mom. That young wife needs to keep her inner circle small and her mouth shut.

The truth is, many times when we are offended by a friend or someone at church or a relative, at the root of it is merely a big misunderstanding. I am sad to say I remember hurting a dear friend a while back. Several times when we were supposed to get together, I canceled at the last minute. She thought it meant that I did not value her friendship. Truthfully I was just overextended. I am thankful that my dear friend did not go around criticizing me to others. Now our friendship is restored, and I am more careful and hopefully more considerate.

Make It Personal . . . Live It Out!

Integrity is only proven true when it is tested. And it will surely be tested when you are in a conflict with someone. It is natural to want to build allies and rehearse your case. It is natural to share only your side of the issue. I'm ashamed to say, I've been guilty. But in the long run it downgrades people's trust in you, not just your foe. Next time, in the heat of the moment, when the temptation tugs to share gory details, resist. Let the moment pass, and then rejoice in the victory.

One Year Bible Reading

Jeremiah 19:1–21:14; 1 Thessalonians 5:4-28; Psalm 82:1-8; Proverbs 25:9-10

A Word Fitly Spoken

A word fitly spoken is like apples of gold
In settings of silver.
Like an earring of gold and an ornament of fine gold
Is a wise rebuker to an obedient ear.
Like the cold of snow in time of harvest
Is a faithful messenger to those who send him,
For he refreshes the soul of his masters.

PROVERBS 25:11-13 (NKJV)

An appropriate word spoken at the right time for the right reason and in the right way is both valuable and beautiful. Ladies, can you see how much our world is lacking for women to speak up for right, and true, and good things?

Uncle Tom's Cabin is one of the most tender, spiritual, and moving books I have ever read. It was written at a time when slaves were treated as merchandise, even women and children. It woke people up and caused them to care. When Abraham Lincoln met the author, Harriet Beecher Stowe, he said, "So you're the little woman who wrote the book that started this great war." Her words were used to stir others to do the right thing. Words—words can have great power for good.

Jon Courson says, "If you have a heart that wants to obey the Lord and learn of him, you'll receive the word of a wise reprover as gladly as you would receive a beautiful, gold earring."

I'll close today with Proverbs 15:31-32: "He who listens to a life-giving rebuke will be at home among the wise. He who ignores discipline despises himself, but whoever heeds correction gains understanding" (NIV).

Make It Personal . . . Live It Out!

God often sends a message of rebuke, exhortation, warning, or comfort in the form of a story or a word picture. Nathan the prophet confronted David's sin by telling the story of a little lamb that was stolen. Jesus taught us not to worry by looking at the well-fed birds. Of all the books you will ever read, you will never learn more about yourself and the meaning of life than from reading God's Word. His Word is powerful, it is light, it breaks strongholds, it heals broken hearts, it gives hope, it transforms your thoughts. Most of all, the greatest benefit is that in his Word, God reveals himself. It indeed is a word fitly spoken.

One Year Bible Reading

Jeremiah 22:1–23:20; 2 Thessalonians 1:1-12; Psalm 83:1-18; Proverbs 25:11-14

Patience and Gentleness

Through patience a ruler can be persuaded,
and a gentle tongue can break a bone.

PROVERBS 25:15 (NIV)

Patience and gentleness are the attributes of wisdom highlighted today. Both are also important fruits of the Spirit of God in our lives. This means that when we yield our lives more and more to the presence and leading and the fullness of the Holy Spirit, his character not only dominates but actually becomes our character. Our impatience and rudeness are replaced. This is really, really good news not only for us but for everyone we come in contact with.

In our proverb, first of all, we're told that being patient with a ruler can be persuasive. Interesting. Ladies, let's apply this to someone in your life whom you want to persuade—perhaps your boss, or your husband, or a leader you serve under. You have a good idea. You have a good plan, and you'd like to present it. Wisdom says don't shove it down someone's throat. Don't be pushy or bossy or critical. That is not the way to win friends or influence people.

Thomas Fuller once said, "Kindness is the noblest weapon to conquer with." So true. Think about it. If someone is trying to persuade us, they will win us more with honey than with vinegar. And so if you have a hard situation, be gentle. If you don't get your way, be gracious. "Through patience a ruler can be persuaded, and a gentle tongue can break a bone." "A gentle answer turns away wrath" (Proverbs 15:1, NIV).

Make It Personal . . . Live It Out!

Once again, wisdom blazes a path of goodness before us and invites us to travel the high road. Each time we accept and submit to God's way, anxiety and frustration fall by the wayside. Fighting and feuding are unnecessary. Patience is the key ingredient. So the challenge to you and me is, will we trust God? Even if he does not work the solution on your timetable (which he usually doesn't), will you wait and trust?

Let's Pray

Lord, this is sometimes very hard. Impatience rises up and wants to take over. I need your Holy Spirit to impart your peace, giving me grace to wait on you.

One Year Bible Reading

Jeremiah 23:21–25:38; 2 Thessalonians 2:1-17; Psalm 84:1-12; Proverbs 25:15

Full or Fulfilled?

Have you found honey?
Eat only as much as you need,
Lest you be filled with it and vomit.

PROVERBS 25:16 (NKJV)

Sometimes it's hard to imagine, but too much of a good thing can be a bad thing. This can apply to most of the enjoyable pleasures of life.

Whenever we go to Disneyland, we are very excited. Since the cost of admission is expensive, most people come early and stay late. We are in line with hundreds of others who can't wait to enter in. But as we are leaving, we are surrounded by hordes of people who are literally dragging; too much junk food combined with sensory overload makes going home to a quiet house and soft pillow the epitome of wonderful.

God has created us to need balance. "All work and no play make Jack a dull boy, but all play and no work make Nancy a spoiled girl."

The Bible tells us, "Let your moderation be known to all men" (Philippians 4:5, KJV).

How can we apply this to life? Be careful. Don't go overboard. We, as women, can sometimes get obsessive and compulsive. Some of us like to shop, but we can get into the habit of shopping too much, spending too much for things that we don't need. For instance, crafts and craft supplies can become addictive. Some of us forget what we have and don't even use what we buy. After a while we're sick of it all. We can go overboard with toys and sports for our kids. Their rooms and schedules are so crowded they are overwhelmed. We need to reel it in.

So remember, sometimes less is more.

Make It Personal . . . Live It Out!

Too often we are obsessive-compulsive regarding possessions and pleasure, but passive and conservative in our zeal for the Lord. It's time to switch the order. Revelation 3:15-16, 19 is a wake-up call: "You are neither hot nor cold. I wish that you were one or the other! . . . You are like lukewarm water. . . . I will spit you out of my mouth! . . . I correct and discipline everyone I love. So be diligent and turn from your indifference." Have you been feeling there is more to life? You are right! Only a holy fire and passion for the Lord will fulfill the yearnings in your soul.

One Year Bible Reading

Jeremiah 26:1–27:22; 2 Thessalonians 3:1-18; Psalm 85:1-13; Proverbs 25:16

Guest Etiquette

Seldom set foot in your neighbor's house—
too much of you, and they will hate you.

PROVERBS 25:17 (NIV)

Many of us have experienced those times when someone came into our homes and became a little too comfortable. They not only set their foot, they seemed to set up camp. They outstayed their welcome; meaning, when it was time to leave, they didn't.

This stretches us, doesn't it? For us as Christians maybe this is even good for us—to be stretched—because the Bible tells us to practice hospitality. Some of us might be a little out of practice. We live in a world where people often do not take the time to make others feel welcome or wanted. We have to be careful that we don't become like the innkeeper in Bethlehem who hung out a sign, "No room at this inn."

Hebrews 13:2 tells us, "Do not forget to entertain strangers, for by so doing some people have entertained angels without knowing it" (NIV). What a blessing this innkeeper missed when he turned away Joseph and his pregnant wife, Mary.

But actually, this proverb is not addressed primarily to the host or hostess; it's addressed to us when we are the guests. As guests, we are always to be a blessing. It's better to stay too short, leaving your hostess wishing you could have stayed longer, than for you to stay too long, leaving your hostess with the feeling she has had too much of you.

Make It Personal . . . Live It Out!

There are times when I am a guest, and times when I am the hostess for Bible study gatherings, dinners, or overnight stays. Here are some etiquette guidelines that will help you be a joy to have at any time.

- Your hosts have spent time and effort to prepare for your coming. Arrive with a contribution: a plate of cookies, flowers, or a special coffee.
- Be helpful. It's fun to chat as you work alongside your hostess to tidy up. For overnight stays, leave the bathroom tidy and the bed linens stripped. Your departure should not leave a burden of work behind.
- Be interested and enjoy those around you. Get to know the children.
- Be thankful. A sweet note left on the table or sent in the mail will bring a smile.

One Year Bible Reading

Jeremiah 28:1–29:32; 1 Timothy 1:1-20; Psalm 86:1-17; Proverbs 25:17

Word Weapons

A man that beareth false witness against his neighbour
is a maul, and a sword, and a sharp arrow.

PROVERBS 25:18 (KJV)

God inspired Solomon to use very graphic language to describe the brutality of slander. Words can be weapons. It's interesting that three different weapons are listed. Each would cause damage differently. Let's examine the implication of each.

Maul is an Old English word for a hammer or a club. Can you see it? This is when we just hammer away, not giving up until the other is bruised and bleeding. There is no quick death for the victim here. Maybe this could be like the wife who just can't say anything nice about or to her husband. She not only speaks about his faults, but she exaggerates. If he lost his keys five times, she calls it hundreds of times.

A sword is sharp. It cuts down and stabs. Words can be slung like a sword at arm's length, intended to slash and pierce. Word daggers are used up close, often to stab in the back. They hurt.

A false witness is like a sharp arrow. Like arrows shot from far away, some pass along ugly, unverified information about people that they don't even know.

Psalm 19:14 is the perfect prayer for us, all of us. "Let the words of my mouth, and the meditation of my heart, be acceptable in Your sight, O LORD, my strength and my Redeemer" (NKJV).

Make It Personal . . . Live It Out!

In this life we are to be wise as serpents and as harmless as doves. What does that mean? It means wise action should be free of malice. There are times when you have conflicts and valid concerns. Instead of slander, God has given us a way to approach these matters.

"If another believer sins against you, go privately and point out the offense. If the other person listens and confesses it, you have won that person back. But if you are unsuccessful, take one or two others with you and go back again, so that everything you say may be confirmed by two or three witnesses" (Matthew 18:15-16). If the person doesn't respond, the third step is to take your concern to the church (if that person is a believer).

One Year Bible Reading

Jeremiah 30:1–31:26; 1 Timothy 2:1-15; Psalm 87:1-7; Proverbs 25:18-19

The Grieving Heart

Singing cheerful songs to a person with a heavy heart
is like taking someone's coat in cold weather
or pouring vinegar in a wound.

PROVERBS 25:20

This proverb is about the incorrect way to show empathy and compassion to others.

Someone whose heart is heavy is someone who's grieving. When someone is grieving—a new widow, the mother of a terminally ill child or prodigal son—we might think our job is to cheer them up or to help them get over it. Yes, it's true that we as Christians don't grieve as others grieve, but listen: we *do* grieve. There are times we desperately *need* to grieve. Romans 12:15 encourages us to "weep with those who weep." Don't be afraid of their pain. Be willing to emotionally slip into their shoes and let their sorrow touch your heart.

When Jesus looked around at all the weary, broken people, he was moved with compassion. He was touched by the feeling of their infirmities, and he still is! As we grow in the Lord, he makes us more like him. He gives us his warm and tender mercies.

There is another matter I've noticed. Those grieving are often given an abundance of attention in the first months. After that, though, others tend to avoid them because they don't know what to say anymore. This is what we need to learn. We don't need to say much, if anything. Actually, Job's comforters were initially commendable; they came to him and sat with him in his misery. But then they opened their mouths. Sometimes the grieving just need a hug and a smile, a little human touch from someone who cares.

Make It Personal . . . Live It Out!

All of us will travel the path of grieving sometime in our lives. David called it "the valley of the shadow of death" (Psalm 23:4, NKJV). It can be a lonely time, but it can also be a holy time. As David discovered, the Lord not only saw his sorrow, he was right there with him. Don't be afraid to bring all of your doubts and fears and struggles and even anger to him.

What a friend we have in Jesus, all our sins and griefs to bear.
What a privilege it is to carry everything to God in prayer.
—JOSEPH M. SCRIVEN, "WHAT A FRIEND WE HAVE IN JESUS"

One Year Bible Reading

Jeremiah 31:27–32:44; 1 Timothy 3:1-16; Psalm 88:1-18; Proverbs 25:20-22

October 19

Doghouse

The north wind brings forth rain,
And a backbiting tongue an angry countenance.
It is better to dwell in the corner of a housetop,
Than in a house shared with a contentious woman.

PROVERBS 25:23-24 (NKJV)

Brrr! Like a cold wind and rain, both of these things make us shudder. Backbiting should be absolutely outlawed for us as godly women. We should not speak it or even listen to it. This kind of war of words is bad business, and it will show up as mud on everyone's face.

The second half of our proverb is also a stiff warning. "It is better to dwell in the corner of a housetop, than in a house shared with a contentious woman." A contentious woman is just plain trouble, trouble, trouble. She's hard to live with, so she drives people away. Men are often in the doghouse with their wives, and in some cases, I think they'd rather live in one than with a woman who is always picking on them. Because, as my grandma used to say, "If mama ain't happy, ain't nobody happy"—because she's gonna make sure nobody's happy. As most men know, "Unhappy wife, unhappy life."

So, ladies, let's be sweet. Being hard to live with doesn't solve any of the issues you're stewing about. Here is your antidote for the day: "Therefore, as the elect of God . . . put on tender mercies, kindness, humility, meekness, longsuffering; bearing with one another; . . . even as Christ forgave you, so you also must do" (Colossians 3:12, NKJV).

Make It Personal . . . Live It Out!

Dear sisters, when we emotionally put someone (our husbands for example) in the doghouse, we have banned him from our affections. Smiles and affection are replaced by frowns and coldness. We dole out little crumbs of kindness instead of being good-natured and generous. If we are not careful, what begins as an emotion develops a habit and can become our personality. Love turns the tide. Love is not just a feeling; love is first a decision, which we must then put into action. As Mitch Temple says, "The grass is greenest where you water it."

One Year Bible Reading

Jeremiah 33:1–34:22; 1 Timothy 4:1-16; Psalm 89:1-13; Proverbs 25:23-24

Good News

As cold water to a weary soul,
So is good news from a far country.

PROVERBS 25:25 (NKJV)

When you feel discouraged or lonely or helpless, oh, how good it would be to hear good news. We long to hear that help is on the way.

I heard the story of a young mom with three small children whose husband was out of town. The phone rang. What a relief to hear a cheerful voice asking how she was. "Well," she said, "the baby is sick, the dishwasher just broke, laundry is a mile high, and there are Cheerios all over the floor."

"Don't you worry," the caller said. "I am coming right over. I'll clean the kitchen, do the laundry, and take the kids to the park while you take a nap. And how is Tom?"

"Tom?" the mother asked. "My husband's name is Jack."

Silence. Then the caller said, "Oh, I must have the wrong number."

Silence again. Then with a small little voice the young mother asked, "But are you still coming?"

"Are you stilling coming?" That's a good question. So many struggling people wonder, *Is there any help on the horizon for me?*

We all could use some good news from a far country. Jesus came all the way from heaven with a message of hope. In John 14:1-3 he said, "Let not your heart be troubled. . . . In My Father's house are many mansions. . . . I go to prepare a place for you. . . . I will come again and receive you to Myself; that where I am, there you may be also" (NKJV). The good news is, yes, he is still coming!

Make It Personal . . . Live It Out!

What difference does it really make to know that this life is temporary, that this is not all there is? I believe that it can and should make a radical difference. Revelation 21:1, 3-4 says, "I saw a new heaven and a new earth, for the old heaven and the old earth had disappeared. . . . 'Look, God's home is now among his people! He will live with them, and they will be his people. God himself will be with them. He will wipe every tear from their eyes, and there will be no more death or sorrow or crying or pain. All these things are gone forever.'" Now that's really good news.

One Year Bible Reading

Jeremiah 35:1–36:32; 1 Timothy 5:1-25; Psalm 89:14-37; Proverbs 25:25-27

Temptations

Whoever has no rule over his own spirit
Is like a city broken down, without walls.

PROVERBS 25:28 (NKJV)

In ancient days the wall around a city was the first line of defense. Bandits and wild animals roamed the land; without a wall a city was vulnerable. Without self-control we are also vulnerable. Matthew Henry explained, "All that is good goes out, and forsakes [us]; all that is evil breaks in upon [us. We lie] exposed to all the temptations of Satan, and [we become] an easy prey to that enemy."

Think of about it, ladies. We have temptations calling our name everywhere we go. Temptation says, "Don't clean the house now. Watch that outrageous TV show instead." Or "It's okay—you can stop every morning to get a double mocha with whipped cream." Temptation says, "Go ahead. You don't have to control your anger. You can blow your top anytime you feel like it." But without self-control, it all adds up, inch by inch. It piles up and tears us down. We become miserable, but we forget that it's our own careless doing.

When we're ready to change, God is ready to help. He empowers you to say no. The first step is to slam the door on temptation. "Make no provision for the flesh" (Romans 13:14, NKJV). How can we do that? Confession: I have absolutely no willpower to resist rocky road ice cream. None. Last week my dear husband brought some home. After the first bowl, I wanted to sit on the couch and eat the entire half-gallon. So I took the carton outside and shoved it deep in the trash. Kind of radical? Yes. Effective? Absolutely!

Make It Personal . . . Live It Out!

Have you ever noticed that brand-new Christians sometimes become hyperlegalistic overnight? I did. Why is that? I believe it's partly a knee-jerk reaction; they are so glad to be free from their old lives, they want to leave them as far behind as possible. But I also believe the Holy Spirit is putting spiritual training wheels on them. They're like toddlers learning to walk. It's an exciting and beautiful thing to watch. Hopefully, God's Word, spiritual maturity, and self-control gradually replace mere rules. Will you ask God to put a new Christian in your life that you can invest in, encourage, and disciple as she learns to walk?

One Year Bible Reading

Jeremiah 37:1–38:28; 1 Timothy 6:1-21; Psalm 89:38-52; Proverbs 25:28

An Undeserved Curse

Like a fluttering sparrow or a darting swallow,
an undeserved curse will not land on its intended victim.

PROVERBS 26:2

As an old saying has it, "Curses are like young chickens; they always come home to roost."

Maybe you're reading today and you are in turmoil because of some unfair and untrue things that have been said about you. We can lose sleep over this. Our fear of those words can be like wild birds that you can't get your hands on. We can withdraw from people, thinking everyone is hearing and believing these things. Then worse yet, we can try to fight back with a war of words. I am sad to say I have done all of the above, and yet doing these things did not give me any peace.

So what should we and could we do? Let me give you three things.

1. If someone has slandered you, first of all, take it to the Lord. Don't you remember that Jesus was falsely accused? It helps to know that he understands. "Blessed," he said, "are those who are persecuted for righteousness' sake" (Matthew 5:10, NKJV).
2. This is the hardest. Put a guard on your mouth. Two wrongs don't make a right. The Bible tells us, "Let no corrupt communication proceed out of your mouth" (Ephesians 4:20, KJV).
3. Be patient. I know this is easier said than done, but what goes around does come around. If the harsh words that were said about you are untrue, they will not land on you. They will fly home "like chickens to roost" on the one who said them.

Make It Personal . . . Live It Out!

Have you ever been ridiculed for your faith or for taking a stand on morality? You're in good company. Just hours before Jesus was arrested and condemned to death, he said these tragic words: "If the world hates you, remember that it hated me first. The world would love you as one of its own if you belonged to it, but you are no longer part of the world. . . . This fulfills what is written in their Scriptures : 'They hated me without cause'" (John 15:18-19, 25).

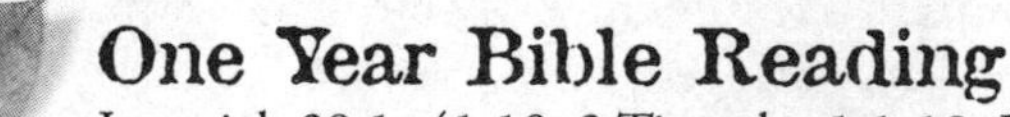

One Year Bible Reading

Jeremiah 39:1–41:18; 2 Timothy 1:1-18; Psalm 90:1–91:16; Proverbs 26:1-2

To Answer or Not to Answer

Do not answer a fool according to his folly,
or you will be like him yourself.
Answer a fool according to his folly,
or he will be wise in his own eyes.

PROVERBS 26:4-5 (NIV)

Okay. So which is it? Should we or shouldn't we get involved in discussions with foolish people? Well, the answer is sometimes yes and sometimes no.

First, don't answer a fool in such a manner that you get pulled into their whirlwind of rudeness or anger. Maybe you have a brother-in-law or a neighbor who has a chip on their shoulder. They thrive on riling people up and bringing them down to their level. First time, shame on them, but second time, shame on us. We need to learn that there are times to be the duck. This means we need to know when to let things just roll off our backs and not engage in their foolishness.

But then there are times when we should answer. For example, your teenager might say something very foolish, like, "Mooomm, why can't I do such and such? Everyone else is doing it." Or "Why do I need a curfew? You can trust me." They do not realize how all the pressures of being young can become dangerous. Just one bad decision at the wrong time can change their entire life. So, moms, listen to them and talk it out. Give them wise, logical, and truthful answers. Stay engaged, and be wise enough to pick your battles. Don't major on minors, so you can major on majors.

Make It Personal . . . Live It Out!

As we study the Proverbs we learn that wisdom is not a set of pat answers that fit into a rigid framework. Wisdom involves principles that set boundaries like the guardrails on a very tall bridge. Life is similar to the fast flow of traffic crossing the bridge. The guardrails are not to hinder our freedom; they are to keep us from falling over the edge. As we grow to respect and apply the truths of God's Word, our internal sense of right and good and noble becomes stronger and stronger.

Let's Pray

Thank you, Lord, that you have not left us to navigate this crazy life on our own. Thank you that your wisdom guides and protects and changes us from the inside out.

One Year Bible Reading

Jeremiah 42:1–44:23; 2 Timothy 2:1-21; Psalm 92:1–93:5; Proverbs 26:3-5

Poison

Trusting a fool to convey a message
is like cutting off one's feet or drinking poison!

PROVERBS 26:6

So, moms, let's apply this to the messages—foolish and dangerous messages—that are broadcast to our children. Our proverb says that trusting a fool to convey a message is foolish. It is like drinking poison. We know we can't control everything our children see and hear, but we can control what they see and hear when they're with us. When you are watching a TV show and the people on the screen are making wrong choices regarding morality or integrity or the way they dress, the way they talk, or what they talk about, that is a message. If it is wrong and we leave it on and are entertained by it, we are endorsing it. Let me say that again. It's an endorsement from us. Those foolish people are delivering a message to those you love by saying, "All that wrong behavior is not only okay, but it's even glamorous and appealing." That's a wrong message.

Also, we as parents need to be involved and aware of the things taught at school. When my daughter was in junior high, I asked to see some of the things that were to be taught in the sex education curriculum. It was appalling and undermined all that we taught at home. I chose to take her out of class for those lessons so that a foolish, immoral curriculum did not deliver a foolish, immoral lesson. That would have been like letting my daughter drink poison.

Make It Personal . . . Live It Out!

Let's now apply this proverb to ourselves. There is a strong possibility that you have or are relying on foolish sources of information to form your concept of who you are. Do you feel your life doesn't matter? Do you look at others and think God loves them more than you? If you've made bad lifestyle choices in the past, do you think you will always be a second-class Christian? These are lies. They are poison. Will you let God himself have the last word? He says, "I have loved you . . . with an everlasting love. With unfailing love I have drawn you to myself" (Jeremiah 31:3).

One Year Bible Reading

Jeremiah 44:24–47:7; 2 Timothy 2:22–3:17; Psalm 94:1-23; Proverbs 26:6-8

Be Teachable

Do you see a man wise in his own eyes?
There is more hope for a fool than for him.

PROVERBS 26:12 (NIV)

To be wise in your own eyes is to be arrogant, unteachable, unapproachable, prideful. To break us of these tendencies, let's look at a life well lived: Stephen, in the book of Acts. Did you know that 75 percent of the Bible is stories? God teaches us principles and lessons, then he illustrates them through the lives of people.

The book of Acts is the account of the early church. Just like today, problems occurred. Widows in the church were neglected. Who would take care of them? "So the Twelve called a meeting. . . . They said, 'We apostles should spend our time teaching the word of God, not running a food program. And so, brothers, select seven men who are well respected . . . full of the Spirit and wisdom. We will give them this responsibility.' . . . Everyone liked this idea, and they chose . . . Stephen (a man full of faith and the Holy Spirit)" (Acts 6:2-5).

What makes this story so appealing? Indeed, at this critical time in church history the key leaders needed to be faithful to their calling. Their decision to choose spiritual men for the lowly job of serving tables defined true kingdom ministry from then on. J. Oswald Sanders noted, "All workers must be Spirit-led and filled. Selection of kingdom leaders must not be influenced by worldly wisdom, wealth, or social status. The prime consideration is spirituality."

Stephen was a young man who was not too arrogant or too important to minister to little old ladies. In fact, he probably learned a thing or two about trust and the faithfulness of God from a few of them.

Make It Personal . . . Live It Out!

Oh, to be teachable and flexible! I want to be growing and learning to my dying day, don't you? I'm learning Spanish. When I make mistakes, people correct me. It's humbling, but it helps me learn. Actually people love to be helpful, and it's good to be on the receiving end. Let me challenge you. Is there something you've always wanted to learn? Is there a book in the Bible you've wanted to study, but haven't? Would you like to learn to share your faith or learn sign language? Be teachable. There's no time like the present.

One Year Bible Reading

Jeremiah 48:1–49:22; 2 Timothy 4:1-22; Psalm 95:1–96:13; Proverbs 26:9-12

Lions and Laziness

The lazy person claims, "There's a lion on the road!
Yes, I'm sure there's a lion out there!"
As a door swings back and forth on its hinges,
so the lazy person turns over in bed.
Lazy people take food in their hand
but don't even lift it to their mouth.

PROVERBS 26:13-15

Laziness. It's defined as "slow-moving, sluggish, idleness." Procrastination is certainly a part of this. To procrastinate is to delay, to put off till another day or time. I have to tell you I hate it when I do that. Not that we are to be workaholics and consumed with busyness, but we are to be good stewards of the time and opportunities that the Lord has given to us.

God does care about how you spend your time, because not only has he numbered your days, but if you are a child of God, your life is not your own. First Corinthians 4:2 tells us, "It is required in stewards that one be found faithful" (NKJV).

So what is *faithful*? *Faithful* means "full of faith." We need to have faith that God put us here on earth for a purpose. We can look at each day, each morning, excited. I look forward to getting out of bed and starting the day with God, reading his Word, connecting with him.

I keep a notepad by my journal. Often in my quiet time, I think of tasks that need to be accomplished. Instead of distracting me, I write them down, knowing that the Lord is ordering my steps. This helps me prioritize, gives me a plan, and a plan gets me going.

Make It Personal . . . Live It Out!

"There's a lion on the road." Did you know that fear can paralyze us and keep us from getting started? Fear of failure convinces us it's no use to go back to school—it's too late, we can't learn, we won't finish. Fear convinces us that we can't change; why even try something new? Is there a good desire that you keep pushing aside? It might be God stirring you, encouraging you to step out.

Let's Pray

Lord, I don't want to miss opportunities and blessings because of laziness and fear. Give me courage. Give me hope. And give me a firm nudge to move forward.

One Year Bible Reading

Jeremiah 49:23–50:46; Titus 1:1-16; Psalms 97:1–98:9; Proverbs 26:13-16

Mind Your Own Business

Like one who seizes a dog by the ears
is a passer-by who meddles in a quarrel not his own.

PROVERBS 26:17 (NIV)

The dictionary definition of *meddle* is "to interfere, to involve oneself in a matter without right or invitation." Some things are just not our business, are they? It is the passer-by person who certainly has no business in someone else's business. And so who are the passers-by? They are the people who have not done their homework. They just come, look at the surface of things, and think they can give a quick opinion, quick fix, or decision without knowing both sides or really all the information.

A passer-by is someone who has no vested interest. Now this is more than just being neutral. They really do not care about the long-term effect.

A passer-by is someone who is there for a moment and then moves on. They are not willing or able to be part of the solution.

And so our proverb wisely advises us today, mind your own business.

But then I feel a burden to say there is one thing that you can do. Pray. There are far too many relationships around us, even among Christians, that are fractured. Pray. If you really do care, if you want to make a difference, pray. Sometimes we need to be more than a passer-by. There is a time to be silent, but then there is a time to get involved and speak the truth in love.

Make It Personal . . . Live It Out!

Meddling—maybe you have never used that word before. Are you a mother-in-law? Oh, how tempting it is to give your unsolicited opinion. My mom was the perfect example of wisdom regarding this. In her over forty years of being a mother-in-law, I never once heard her say anything critical about her sons-in-law. She made it clear to her three daughters that she was not our sounding board for marital griping. We needed to work it out. My grandma used to say, "Too many cooks spoil the stew."

One Year Bible Reading

Jeremiah 51:1-53; Titus 2:1-15; Psalm 99:1-9; Proverbs 26:17

Not Funny

Like a madman who throws firebrands, arrows, and death,
Is the man [or woman] who deceives [their] neighbor,
And says, "I was only joking!"

PROVERBS 26:18-19 (NKJV)

H. A. Ironside commented, "Amusement at the expense of another's suffering, none but a most thoughtless and selfish person will engage in."

Deceiving your neighbor and then covering it up is the topic of this proverb.

To *deceive* is "to represent as true that which is known to be false." It is to mislead someone or to trick someone or to betray someone. Do we ever do this?

Wives, do you ever mislead your husband regarding how much money you've spent? Or have you ever betrayed a friend by sharing private information she trusted you with? Or have you ever tricked someone into doing something you knew they didn't want to do? A good way for us to realize how wrong and hurtful this is, is to remember when someone else has done it to us.

So the best lesson we can learn from this proverb is to be honest, to be fair with others. One of the greatest reputations that you can have during your life is that others can and do trust you. How wonderful it is for people to know that they are safe with you. Their reputations are safe, their money is safe, their feelings are safe, their private affairs are safe. Can you say that this is always true with you? If it isn't, if this has not always been true in the past, today is a new day, and God himself will teach you a new way.

Make It Personal . . . Live It Out!

Jesus taught us to "love your neighbor as yourself" (Matthew 22:39). This gives us a simple guideline for living. Is it easy? Not always. It isn't always easy to stay calm, or put others first, or to refuse to retaliate when hurt. But when we obey God's commandment, it's not only better for others; it's better for us. Let's take it further than just refraining from bad behavior; let's learn to be genuinely interested in people. This frame of mind stretches us past our own little worlds and interests. It teaches us that God has a big world, and he also has a big family.

One Year Bible Reading

Jeremiah 51:54–52:34; Titus 3:1-15; Psalm 100:1-5; Proverbs 26:18-19

October 29

Putting Out Fires

Without wood a fire goes out;
without gossip a quarrel dies down.

PROVERBS 26:20 (NIV)

There's a billboard along the road in Indiana that reads, "He who throws dirt . . . loses ground." Why would someone in Indiana hoist such a sign for all to see? Perhaps he'd seen way too much fighting and feuding. It was his way of saying, "Knock it off."

Conflict, differences of opinion, even arguments happen. They are just all part of life. Even great men of God like Paul the apostle and his good friend Barnabas once had a sharp disagreement. In some ways differences can be a good thing if we're committed to building bridges instead of burning them. They can stretch our patience, hone our communication skills, and most important, test our obedience to the Lord's command in Colossians 3 to forgive and forget. "If anyone has a complaint against another, even as Christ forgave you, so you also must do" (v. 13, NKJV).

I heard some great advice from a wise, older man. When you are offended or angry with someone, stop and consider, *How significant will this be in twelve months?* In the heat of the moment, molehills can seem like mountains, but over time, mountains can seem like molehills. And as our proverb tells us today, if there is no fresh wood like gossip thrown in the fire, the fire just goes out.

A four-year-old boy decided he'd try reciting the Lord's Prayer. He prayed this version: "And forgive us our trash baskets, as we forgive those who trash basket against us." Actually, if you're stewing about a conflict or quarrel with someone, that's a pretty good prayer. Now that I think of it, I think I'll pray it myself.

Make It Personal . . . Live It Out!

A quarrel, like a fire, needs fresh wood to keep it going. However, long after the flame has died, there might still be some hot coals lying under the ash. Once the heat of the moment has passed, we may think we are over it. But unless we honestly take the situation to the Lord and let his Spirit douse the lingering embers, they can rise up as flames of anger even years later.

Let's Pray

O Holy Spirit, please pour over my heart and mind. If there are lingering coals of grudges and resentment lying buried within me, wash them away. Help me to see everyone as someone you love. Change my heart so that I do indeed love them.

One Year Bible Reading

Lamentations 1:1–2:22; Philemon 1:1-25; Psalm 101:1-8; Proverbs 26:20

Rumors

Rumors are dainty morsels
that sink deep in one's heart.

PROVERBS 26:22

Rumors. If it wasn't for rumors, there'd be a lot fewer magazines in the grocery store. Our proverb today says that rumors taste good, but they go down deep in us. I really wish this proverb wasn't true, but it is, and we know it. Think about it. If we listen to a tidbit of gossip, as much as we hate to admit it, it does capture our interest. Part of us may be thinking, *That is a mean thing to say. That's probably not true.* But somehow that tidbit does stick with us. The next time we see that person, we do have a jaded view of her. And because of that, maybe we don't trust her like we did, or if she's been a friend, we distance ourself.

Isn't this just one more evidence of Satan's handiwork? I wonder when we will ever become more astute and stop falling for his insidious devices? If there was ever a scheme from the pit of hell, it's gossip, especially among the family of God.

What would happen, really, if all of us—all of us as women of God—what if we banded together and just boycotted all passing along and all listening to gossip? What if we all wore buttons that said, "Just say no!"? You might be thinking, *That will never happen.* Well, maybe everyone won't join us, but you know what? That doesn't stop us from saying, "Okay—for me, I'm done with it." Just say no, and Satan will have one less pawn in his wicked plan.

Make It Personal . . . Live It Out!

Be aware: there are some nasty rumors about God floating around out there too. And who is the perpetrator? It is none other than the enemy of our souls, the father of lies, Satan himself. You might not even realize how his lies have gone deep within your own heart. Do you doubt God's love for you? Do you wonder if he hears your prayers? Do you question if his plans for you are real and good and practical in this day and age?

Let him speak words of truth: "I love you with an everlasting love" (Jeremiah 31:3, NIV). "I will never leave you nor forsake you" (Hebrews 13:5, NKJV). "[My thoughts toward you] . . . outnumber the grains of sand" (Psalm 139:17-18).

One Year Bible Reading

Lamentations 3:1-66; Hebrews 1:1-14; Psalm 102:1-28; Proverbs 26:21-22

Phony Baloney

Like a coating of glaze over earthenware
are fervent lips with an evil heart.

PROVERBS 26:23 (NIV)

Halloween is a day of masks and costumes. The more effective the costume, the less likely you are to recognize who is behind the mask. Disguises, false fronts, pretending—for many Halloween is just a game. But for some, pretending is a way of life.

Fervent lips may say shiny, zealous words but cover up a heart with wrong motives. What you see is not what you get. Think of that day that Mary of Bethany broke the alabaster box to anoint Jesus. It was a beautiful picture of extravagant love. But Judas spoke up. "Why was this fragrant oil not sold . . . and [the money] given to the poor?" (John 12:5, NKJV). Doesn't that sound noble, even caring? "Oh, the poor. Nobody cares for the poor but me!"

John 12:6 gives us a glimpse behind the mask of Judas's heart. "This he said, not that he cared for the poor, but because he was a thief, and had the money box; and he used to take what was put in it" (NKJV). Now we see Judas didn't care about Jesus or Mary or the poor. He only cared for himself. With his lips he drew near, but his heart was far, far away.

A lot of women believe what they want to believe about a man. Some men will fervently tell you anything you want hear so they can get what they want. "Like a coating of glaze over earthenware are fervent lips with an evil heart." So the moral is, be wise. In the light, lies aren't as convincing.

Make It Personal . . . Live It Out!

In Titus 2 older women are encouraged to teach the younger women. One area of instruction that is sadly lacking involves sexuality, romance, and true love. Hollywood has conditioned girls from age two to equate a handsome face with a beautiful heart. Lust puts on a mask and calls itself love. Do young women desire instruction? I think many definitely do. There are excellent Christian books written on this subject; will you pick one up and read it? Will you pray for some young women you know? If you are single, will you bond with others to pray and hold each other accountable?

One Year Bible Reading

Lamentations 4:1–5:22; Hebrews 2:1-18; Psalm 103:1-22; Proverbs 26:23

November

Scan this code for audio devotionals
or visit www.tyndal.es/wisdom.

Big Bad Wolf

A malicious man disguises himself with his lips,
but in his heart he harbors deceit.
Though his speech is charming, do not believe him,
for seven abominations fill his heart.

PROVERBS 26:24-25 (NIV)

A malicious man may be charming, but he is up to no good. Ladies, whether you are fifteen or twenty-two or sixty-two, you need to be wise and careful. When women are lonely or dissatisfied, they become easy prey. They close their eyes to red flags and let their emotions drive them. Has that been you in the past? Is it you right now?

Please listen. We need to learn how to discern if a man who seems good is really a wolf in sheep's clothing. Why do women sometimes marry men they hardly know and later hate? Many women, even Christian women, are having sex before marriage. Sexual intimacy releases an endorphin called oxytocin, which creates emotional and physical bonding. This bonding makes you blind to flaws. This is good once you're married. But before, it can replace and short-circuit true relationship building. Sadly, many end up battered and abused, married to a stranger because they did not look before they leapt.

Wisdom is careful. Wisdom trusts God's instructions and safeguards. Be careful to observe signs of character. How does he treat the waitresses when you go out, both the pretty ones and the unpretty ones? How does he spend his money? How does he treat his family? How quickly does he get angry?

The Big Bad Wolf said, "Little Red Riding Hood, you sure are looking good." But the wolf was deceitful and disguised, and he was dangerous.

Make It Personal . . . Live It Out!

Fleetwood Mac sang these lyrics: "Close my eyes. . . . Tell me lies, tell me sweet little lies." But lies are never sweet.

God created us with a deep desire to be treasured and loved. Our desires for intimacy are not wrong. But when we go outside of his commands, when we sin, it backfires. What is a woman to do? How can you find the love you have longed for your entire life? Lift your empty cup for God to fill you and satisfy you completely. This is not a simplistic answer, although it is very simple. "Take delight in the LORD, and he will give you your heart's desires" (Psalm 37:4).

One Year Bible Reading

Ezekiel 1:1–3:15; Hebrews 3:1-19; Psalm 104:1-23; Proverbs 26:24-26

Boomerang

If you set a trap for others,
you will get caught in it yourself.
If you roll a boulder down on others,
it will crush you instead.

PROVERBS 26:27

Here God is warning us that making trouble for others will eventually boomerang back to us. Sir Walter Scott said, "Oh what a tangled web we weave, when first we practice to deceive."

Some of you know I have a great passion to encourage women to read the Bible from cover to cover. One of the wonderful benefits is that the Bible doesn't just teach life principles, but it also illustrates them through real examples in real people's lives.

The book of Esther displays a picture of someone who dug a pit for someone else and then fell in it. His name was Haman. He hated a Jew named Mordecai, Esther's cousin. His hatred wasn't based on any real wrong done to him. His hatred stemmed from the fact that he didn't get his way. That's a story in itself. And as his bitterness grew, he sought to kill not only Mordecai, but all the Jews of the land. Bitterness does that. It always widens the circle of collateral damage.

An interesting detail of the story is that Haman's wife, Zeresh, encouraged him to take revenge. She said, "Hang Mordecai. Then go and be happy." That's bad advice. But Esther took a bold step, asking her husband, the king, to intervene. End result, Haman was hung on the gallows he intended for others. Haman did not know "what goes around comes around." Haman was the rat that got caught in his own trap.

Make It Personal . . . Live It Out!

Haman is the central villain in this story. But his wife, Zeresh, fueled the fire. Instead of being the voice of reason, she encouraged him to act out his rage. When we do that, even if we don't participate in the evil actions, we are accomplices to the crime; there is "blood on our hands." Whether it's your husband or your sister or a leader you serve with that is angry, pray for them. And better yet, pray with them.

"The earnest prayer of a righteous person has great power and produces wonderful results" (James 5:16).

One Year Bible Reading

Ezekiel 3:16–6:14; Hebrews 4:1-16; Psalm 104:24-35; Proverbs 26:27

Cheap Shots

A lying tongue hates those it hurts.

PROVERBS 26:28 (NIV)

Just recently I heard someone say something harsh and critical about a woman who is a popular speaker and Bible teacher. The bottom line was they heard her accused of saying one line in a message that could be construed as endorsing something unbiblical. First of all, they never listened to the entirety of the message. Secondly, they never investigated and listened to what she said to clarify the misunderstanding. Thirdly, they took someone else's word that this woman was a false teacher. On further investigation, I discovered it all started with a website, a supposedly Christian website. The man who posted the volatile accusations has a history of taking cheap shots at people in the body of Christ who are famous or popular.

May I ask, what is that about? First of all, it's not Christian. Certainly it is not Christlike. Yes, of course, we need accountability. But cheap shots do not qualify, really. If we bite and devour each other, the family of God is weakened.

So let's get personal, and let's be honest. Do we sometimes do that? I mean, are we sometimes unfairly harsh or critical? Could it be that we tear down others because we hate the fact that they are getting some kind of attention we wish we were getting? Well, shame on us.

A child once prayed, "Dear God, make all the bad people good, and make all the good people nice."

Make It Personal . . . Live It Out!

Developing a habit of truthfulness is the best antidote for a lying tongue. We can do little to correct another's bad behavior. But God has made us personally accountable for our own. That's good. The Holy Spirit himself will prick our heart when we're amiss. That's good too. If you sense the temptation rising to exaggerate or slant or just neglect the truth, send up an arrow prayer, asking the Lord to give you grace to say what's right.

"Let your speech always be with grace, seasoned with salt, that you may know how you ought to answer each one" (Colossian 4:6, NKJV).

One Year Bible Reading

Ezekiel 7:1–9:11; Hebrews 5:1-14; Psalm 105:1-15; Proverbs 26:28

Tomorrow

Do not boast about tomorrow,
For you do not know what a day may bring forth.

PROVERBS 27:1 (NKJV)

I really love how the Proverbs cover every single facet of life. Here we come to the foolish habit of bragging. The reason that we aren't to boast about tomorrow is because even though we would like to, we can't really guarantee what tomorrow will bring, can we? Sometimes just one unexpected thing can change your entire day. Sometimes just one unexpected thing can change your entire life.

This does not mean, though, that we shouldn't be diligent or plan for the future. In fact, the Proverbs tell us to observe the good habits of the ant. If you watch an ant, he's focused, he's busy. If you put something in his way, he doesn't give up or get upset. He takes it in stride and finds a way around the obstacle. This is a good lesson for us as women. Good. Make plans. Be organized. You can have hopes and dreams for your future, for your home, for your kids, but don't get so set on them that you think they're set in stone. I love the expression "I don't know what the future holds, but I do know who holds the future."

So, dear sisters, let's savor today and be thankful. "This is the day the LORD has made; let us rejoice and be glad in it" (Psalm 118:24, NIV). The past is history, the future is a mystery, but today is a gift. That's why they call it the *present*.

Make It Personal . . . Live It Out!

Have you ever had a great plan go askew? Of course you have. Robert Burns was plowing his field one day when he overturned a little mouse's cozy nest. Perhaps he saw his own disappointments reflected in the upheaval. Sympathetically, he wrote, "Little Mouse, you are not alone, in proving foresight may be vain: The best laid schemes of mice and men go often awry, and leave us nothing but grief and pain."

Poor mousie and poor Robert. Are we left with only a fatalistic view of life, fearing fate may deal us a bad hand? Absolutely not. When we place our lives entirely in the hands of God, like David, we can say, "The LORD is my shepherd; I have all that I need" (Psalm 23:1).

One Year Bible Reading

Ezekiel 10:1–11:25; Hebrews 6:1-20; Psalm 105:16-36; Proverbs 27:1-2

Irrational

A stone is heavy and sand is weighty,
But a fool's wrath is heavier than both of them.

PROVERBS 27:3 (NKJV)

J. Vernon McGee explains, "If you have a fool angry with you, you are in trouble, because a fool has no discretion. He [or she] will say or do anything."

A fool's wrath is foolish because it's irrational. It is irrational because it's out of proportion with the offense. It is irrational because it often gathers steam instead of calming down with time. It is irrational because it's often vented on innocent bystanders. It is irrational because it has no boundaries. Fools will say or do anything when they're mad, with no sense of playing fair or thought of the consequences. It is irrational because it often begins with a response, turns into a bad habit, and becomes a cranky personality. This kind of getting mad and staying mad is heavy for everyone, because everyone loses.

I once saw a man at the airport obviously waiting for someone to arrive. He was holding an exceptionally pretty bouquet of flowers. I missed the initial greeting, but a few moments later I saw him walking behind a woman whose face was filled with wrath. He still held the rejected flowers and walked behind with shoulders stooped.

Missed moments, wasted flowers, a perpetual bad mood—all this is the end result of foolish wrath.

Make It Personal . . . Live It Out!

There's a grumpy little grouch, and he gets inside of me.
I don't like him being there! I don't like his company!

He makes me grouch and grumble at everyone I meet!

But . . . this grumpy little grouch doesn't hang around for long.
He'll vanish like a raindrop when I sing a happy song!
—JILL EGGLETON IN "GRUMPY GROUCH"

Let's Pray

Lord, you know I sometimes get in a foolish and irrational frump. When I do, wake me up and shake me out of it. Remind me to turn on some praise music and sing away the grouch.

One Year Bible Reading

Ezekiel 12:1–14:11; Hebrews 7:1-17; Psalm 105:37-45; Proverbs 27:3

A Faithful Friend

Open rebuke is better
Than love carefully concealed.
Faithful are the wounds of a friend,
But the kisses of an enemy are deceitful.

PROVERBS 27:5-6 (NKJV)

This proverb breaks the mold of thinking that silence is always golden or loving. In Matthew 18:15 Jesus tells us that we must learn how to deal with issues. He says, "If another believer sins against you, go privately and point out the offense. If the other person listens and confesses it, you have won that person back."

I can honestly say that all of my truest and dearest friends have at one time or another corrected me. This takes courage. Let me share with you some things I've learned from them, not only what they shared but how they did it.

- In love they spoke *to me*, not about me, behind my back. I'm thankful for that.
- They prayed first and spoke later. Because of that, each time the Lord prepared my heart to hear and receive.
- In love they spoke the truth, the whole truth. The combination of kindness, clarity, and boldness is not hurtful but very, very helpful.

If any of these faithful and caring friends are reading this, let me say to you, "Thank you, really, thank you." Samuel Coleridge said, "Advice is like snow; the softer it falls, the longer it dwells upon and the deeper it sinks into the mind."

Make It Personal . . . Live It Out!

"Faithful are the wounds of a friend." What an intriguing and yet winsome truth. *Faithful* means "full of faith." So first of all the friend who ventures to speak a word of correction must have faith. She must believe in you and trust that you will listen with grace. She must believe you are both humble and teachable. Speaking honestly is not easy, so she must believe you are worth the risk and effort. But lastly, a faithful friend must believe that mere words cannot change even a teachable friend. Transformation is a miracle. A faithful friend prays and believes that God, who formed our hearts, can also change them.

One Year Bible Reading

Ezekiel 14:12–16:41; Hebrews 7:18-28; Psalm 106:1-12; Proverbs 27:4-6

Bitter to Sweet

A satisfied soul loathes the honeycomb,
But to a hungry soul every bitter thing is sweet.

PROVERBS 27:7 (NKJV)

We live in a society that takes so much for granted, don't we? We eat before we're truly hungry. We buy shoes when we have ten pairs that we never wear. Kids often have more toys than they'll ever play with.

Satiated means when we have too much, we don't really enjoy any of it. But "to a hungry soul every bitter thing is sweet." That might sound like an odd statement, but think about it. Think about something you had to work for, save for, wait for. Then when you got it, you savored it. Moms, we deprive our kids of this when they get everything they want when they want it.

Let me apply this proverb in one more way. Some people who have grown up in a Christian home with loving parents become prodigals because they don't really appreciate the blessings of their parents or their heritage. But our proverb today tells us, "To a hungry soul, every bitter thing is sweet."

Pastor Greg Laurie wrote the story of his life growing up in a broken, dysfunctional home. His book is called *Lost Boy*. In it he shares the great blessing and joy he now has knowing that he has a heavenly Father who loves him and will never leave him or forsake him. Even though he's gone through a bitter tragedy with the death of his son Christopher, he is drawing deeply on the sweetness of knowing that God's grace is sufficient.

Make It Personal . . . Live It Out!

Today I spoke with a single mom who was feeling at the end of her rope. She's behind on her rent and was afraid to face her landlord. Finally she got the courage to answer his phone calls. Feeling this was the end, she had spent the morning trying to accept the inevitable. Then a small reprieve came in the form of grace and understanding. Her tears of despair turned into tears of joy. Her rent is still due. But she hung up the phone with hope in her heart. Are you at wit's bitter end? There is nothing sweeter than to see the grace of the Lord show up in your hour of need.

One Year Bible Reading

Ezekiel 16:42–17:24; Hebrews 8:1-13; Psalm 106:13-31; Proverbs 27:7-9

True Blue

Do not forsake your friend and the friend of your father,
and do not go to your brother's house when disaster strikes you—
better a neighbor nearby than a brother far away.

PROVERBS 27:10 (NIV)

Albert Barnes gives an excellent explanation. "Better is a neighbor who is really 'near' in heart and spirit, than a brother who though closer . . . by blood, is 'far off' in feeling."

So the topic of this proverb is the importance of friendships. My dear sisters, we need friends—good, true, honest, godly friends—and we need to be that for others. The Proverbs tell us that "those who are to have friends, must show themselves friendly." Don't mope around that you have no buddies, be a buddy to someone who has no buddies.

It's been said, "Money might make you wealthy, but having friends makes you rich." Helen Keller said, "Walking with a friend in the dark is better than walking alone in the light."

We live in a world of disposable relationships. But "easy come, easy go" should never apply to relationships. Benjamin Franklin understood and advised, "Be slow in choosing a friend, and even slower in changing." When you look at the life of a man like Billy Graham, it's a testimony to his character that he has close ministry friends who have stayed with him for over fifty years.

And then, there is Jesus. He is incomparable. In the last hours of his life, he taught us what loyal friendship truly looks like. John 13:1 tells us, "Having loved His own who were in the world, He loved them to the end" (NKJV).

Make It Personal . . . Live It Out!

Digging deep and being a true-blue friend is our topic today. So let me ask you, when was the last time you truly went the extra mile for someone? When was the last time you intentionally invested in making a friendship stronger? Can you honestly say you know what your closest friends are going through? Have you called and prayed with them lately? Making you feel guilty is not the point. Cheering you on to reconnect in a proactive personal way *is*. So bake some cupcakes, say a prayer, linger in a conversation, write a card. As James Taylor says, "Shower the people you love with love, show them the way that you feel."

One Year Bible Reading

Ezekiel 18:1–19:14; Hebrews 9:1-10; Psalm 106:32-48; Proverbs 27:10

Make Your Father Proud

Be wise, my son, and bring joy to my heart;
then I can answer anyone who treats me with contempt.

PROVERBS 27:11 (NIV)

Moms, when our children are little there are times when we wish we could, at least temporarily, not claim them—like when they knock over a display in a store or spill their milk in a restaurant.

But seriously, when they're older, it's a great heartache to a parent when a child goes down a wrong path. We worry. We feel pain for our child. We grieve when we see the consequences and complications bad choices bring to their life. We feel our own pain because of the lost dream we had for their life. And then, truthfully, there's a shame. We feel reproached. We wonder how we failed them. Every parent of a prodigal knows these heartaches.

But now let's apply this to ourselves, because we are daughters of God the Father. God is saying to us, "Be wise, my [child], and bring joy to my heart." We are to walk worthy of him who called us. I have to tell you, I've talked to many people who reject God because of the ungodly behavior of one of God's children or so-called children. When David fell into adultery, one of the tragic results was that it caused the enemies of the Lord to blaspheme.

Therefore, as a child of God, always remember you carry his noble name. Wherever you go, whatever you do, be a blessing. Let's make our Father proud.

Make It Personal . . . Live It Out!

Can we, mere humans, actually bring joy to the Lord of the universe? Does our behavior and character affect how others see him? Jesus said that we absolutely can and it does. "You are the light of the world—like a city on a hilltop that cannot be hidden. No one lights a lamp and then puts it under a basket. Instead, a lamp is placed on a stand, where it gives light to everyone in the house. In the same way, let your good deeds shine out for all to see, so that everyone will praise your heavenly Father" (Matthew 5:14-16). This is a sober responsibility and yet an exciting possibility. Let's do it. Let's let our lights shine. Let's make our Father proud!

One Year Bible Reading

Ezekiel 20:1-49; Hebrews 9:11-28; Psalm 107:1-43; Proverbs 27:11

Danger, Danger!

A prudent person foresees the danger and takes precautions.
The simpleton goes blindly on and suffers the consequences.

PROVERBS 27:12

As women living in this generation, this proverb can save our lives. We need to wake up. Second Timothy 3:1-6 tells us, "Know this, that in the last days, perilous times will come. For men will be lovers of themselves, lovers of money . . . without self-control . . . despisers of good . . . lovers of pleasure rather than lovers of God . . . from such people turn away! For . . . [they] creep into households and make captives of gullible women . . . led astray by various lusts" (NKJV).

This is a blow-by-blow description of what's broadcast on this season's series of sleazy, mean-spirited, sex-filled TV. It's broadcast in TV talk shows, trashy movies, and music, at school, and in the workplace. It seems everywhere people are talking about immoral and just plain wicked things. Don't be naive. Don't think you can swim in the cesspool and not get polluted.

God has given us a built-in alert system. Turn it on; tune it in. Pay attention when God gives you an inner uneasiness; that's both discernment and conviction. In our neighborhood we have rats, the kind with tails. The exterminator advised us to seal up the cracks so they can't squeeze in. *Exactly*. Take precautions. Precautions range from putting a filter on your computer to being careful about how you dress. Better safe than sorry. Or as my grandma used to say, "An ounce of prevention is worth a pound of cure."

Make It Personal . . . Live It Out!

I have a rat story. We used to leave the back door open so the dog could come and go. But one day I discovered our dog wasn't the only one making an entrance. There was evidence of a rat, a big one. I hate rats. But I didn't set a trap until I found his droppings in my kitchen. Yuck. How about you? Will you honestly and bravely look around your inner world and see if a rat of sinful, selfish, or worldly attitudes is roaming around in your thoughts or emotions?

Let's Pray

Lord, I shudder to think of a rat inside my house. Help this picture alert me to see that sin carries worse filth and disease. Have I compromised? Have I left the door open? Please cleanse my heart, make me careful, and keep me safe.

One Year Bible Reading

Ezekiel 21:1–22:31; Hebrews 10:1-17; Psalm 108:1-13; Proverbs 27:12

Softhearted or Weak Enabler?

Take the garment of him who is surety for a stranger,
And hold it in pledge when he is surety for a seductress.

PROVERBS 27:13 (NKJV)

First of all, when poeple assumes responsibility or security for another's obligation in case of default, they themselves are at risk. Therefore, this proverb advises us to not be carelessly entwined financially with others who are careless. This is not wise.

So when are we to be lenient and gracious, and when should we step back and be firm?

In the last few years we've heard the word *enabling* more and more. We know that the Lord is a gracious and merciful God. He teaches us to be kind, tenderhearted, giving, and forgiving. That will never change. But there's a difference between being softhearted and being a soft touch and a weak enabler.

When someone shows a pattern of foolish, irresponsible behavior, we are not obligated to continuously fill in the gap for them. Moms, we all know it is hard to say no, especially to your kids. But when your son finds himself in a jam because he did a business deal with a shady character or he has a girlfriend losing her car because she's a druggie, don't help him. Even if he vents his anger, don't cave in. Don't enable. When you enable, you've endangered your own self, and you have not really helped him. In Missouri they say, "That's pouring money down a rat hole."

Make It Personal . . . Live It Out!

I once took a class on ministering to the addicted. I have a deep burden for people who have fallen into addiction, and I believe that anyone can be restored—if they want to be restored. The teacher of the class was a former addict herself and knew the inside scoop. She told us, point blank, that people with addictions lie. It's what they do. They work us. They work on our sympathies; they make us feel guilty. If you are helping someone, hold that person accountable. You don't have to be hard-hearted to be wise. Ask God to give you both compassion and insight.

One Year Bible Reading

Ezekiel 23:1-49; Hebrews 10:18-39; Psalm 109:1-31; Proverbs 27:13

The Blessed Friend

He who blesses his friend with a loud voice, rising early in the morning,
It will be counted a curse to him.

PROVERBS 27:14 (NKJV)

I guess the bottom line of this proverb is, don't be annoying. As we see, this man got up and shouted cheerfully to his friend, and it went over like a lead balloon. Can you think of anyone in your life who is constantly annoying, doing little, actually harmless things but nevertheless annoying?

Let's think of things that we do that can cause friction in our friendships because we're not being sensitive to what irritates our friends.

Example: if your friend is a scheduled person, don't constantly frustrate her by showing up late. But if it's your friend who is the late one, don't badger her. Greet her with joy. Make your schedule more flexible so there is no harm done when she's late.

Does your friend feel hurt when you forget her birthday? Mark your calendar and send her a card.

Is your friend a night owl? Make it a habit to never call her before 10 a.m.

Have you lost a few pounds and your sister hasn't? Don't be annoying. Don't keep going on and on about it so she feels like a failure.

Friendship is built on a thousand thoughtful little moments. Every true friend is worth making sacrifices for. As Charles Swindoll said, "I cannot even imagine where I would be today were it not for that handful of friends who have given me a heart full of joy."

Let's face it. Friends make life a lot more fun.

Make It Personal . . . Live It Out!

Hmmm—let me ask you, do your friends think you are a joy to be around? Do your coworkers? When you arrive for Thanksgiving dinner, are you a breath of fresh air? Do you pitch in when others need a hand? When you borrow something, do you give it back on time and in good condition? Or do you call on the help of others too often? Do you nettle others over little things? Do you forget your promises? Are you unreliable? I'm just checking. It's good to do inventory once in a while. If it's time to restock the shelves of your relationships with the positive, then as Nike says, "Just do it."

One Year Bible Reading

Ezekiel 24:1–26:21; Hebrews 11:1-16; Psalm 110:1-7; Proverbs 27:14

Gripe, Gripe, Gripe

A quarrelsome [nagging] wife is as annoying
as the constant dripping on a rainy day.
Stopping her complaints is like trying to stop the wind
or trying to hold something with greased hands.

PROVERBS 27:15-16

Our topic today is nagging. Ladies, this proverb is aiming right at us and for good reason. I wish I could say I have never and will never nag my husband, but that would be flat-out lying. But one thing I do know for sure: kids hate it, husbands hate it, and friends hate it. So let's look at what nagging is, why we do it, why it's bad, and how to stop.

What is nagging? It's ragging. It's complaining and criticizing. It's not courteous because it's meant to punish.

Why do we nag? Because it just comes naturally. We see something we don't like someone doing, and we want them to change. So we say it. If there is no change, we say it again, and again, and again.

But get a grip, nagging doesn't help. I have never heard a testimony of a wife that said, "Yes, I tortured my husband with nagging a thousand times. Now he cheerfully picks up his socks."

How do we change? Turn your cares into prayers. Honestly, if socks on the floor are your pet peeve, have you ever even once taken it to the Lord? Let me suggest that for just one week every time you're annoyed and tempted to nag, zip your lip and pray instead.

Of course, our hope is that our husbands and kids *will* change, but if you try this for just one week, I guarantee you, that *you* will.

Make It Personal . . . Live It Out!

In August 2009 a Chinese man ran from his cabin on a ship. His hands were over his ears as he jumped into the Yangtze River. He couldn't take his wife's nagging anymore. True to form, his wife chased after him, leaning over the rail and ranting as he sank in the water. The question we could ask her is "When was enough, enough?"

Let's Pray

Lord, tie my tongue from nagging. Show me why I get so annoyed and can't let things go. Am I driving others away? Help me change. And please help me look on the positive and overlook the negative.

One Year Bible Reading

Ezekiel 27:1–28:26; Hebrews 11:17-31; Psalm 111:1-10; Proverbs 27:15-16

Iron Sharpening Iron

As iron sharpens iron,
so a friend sharpens a friend.

PROVERBS 27:17

My grandfather was a Missouri farmer. If his knife or his plow blades got dull, his work was much harder. So he had a grinder wheel, and he used it regularly. As the wheel spun, he held the blade just close enough to see the sparks fly but not so close as to chew away too much of the edge. I loved to watch. When he was done, the edge would be shiny and sharp and would cut anything like butter.

How does this apply to friendships? I hope this helps us see that we become dull when we isolate ourselves or just choose friends that tell us what we want to hear and never challenge us. Hebrews 10:24 says, "Let us consider one another in order to stir up love and good works" (NKJV).

Look around. Could it be that the Lord has sent people into your life to hone you?

There are sandpaper people. They grate us. This is good. Maybe God is wanting to sand off your rough edges by teaching you grace and patience.

There are those with whom, when you talk together, there are sparks. Good. I love to be around people who challenge me to trust God more fully, pray more, and step out of the boat more.

Jesus had such an interesting assortment of disciples. Peter was like Tigger. Thomas was like Eeyore. John was like Winnie the Pooh. Matthew had worked for the government, and James had worked with his hands. Variety. Variety is good for all of us. They must have had some really interesting discussions at the dinner table.

Make It Personal . . . Live It Out!

Do you shy away from friendships with people who are a little different than you? If so, you are missing out. In the family of God, there are amazing things going on. People have a passion for some important missions and ministries. Some are reaching out to prostitutes and women who are trafficked. Some serve on skid row, some minister to foster children, some to street kids or skateboarders. Come on, stretch your borders. Find a fellow believer who is out there serving her heart out for the Kingdom. And let her be iron sharpening iron.

One Year Bible Reading

Ezekiel 29:1–30:26; Hebrews 11:32–12:13; Psalm 112:1-10; Proverbs 27:17

Beauty

As a face is reflected in water,
so the heart reflects the real person.

PROVERBS 27:19

Our reflection. We as women look in the mirror to see how we look. We worry about how we look, and we want to change the way we look. But we can look good on the outside and be a mess on the inside. This might be news to some, but a person can have an unattractive exterior and yet have a beautiful heart. Always remember it is the heart that is the true picture of who you really are. That's why the Proverbs tell us, "Above all else, guard your heart, for from it flow the issues of life" (Proverbs 4:23, paraphrased).

Max Lucado wrote a storybook called *If Only I Had a Green Nose*. In the story, Willy Withit arrived in town. He was promoting the latest and greatest look that would definitely make you "with it." The first "with it" fashion was a green nose, but once everyone got the green nose, it was no longer "with it." A red nose was the new "with it." To keep up, you had to keep moving on from one color to another. Ridiculous? But how can this story sound ridiculous to us when we often are sold the same bill of goods, hoodwinked into going from one silly trend to another?

Inner beauty. Let's read what 1 Peter 3:1-4 has to say: "Be good wives to your husbands, responsive to their needs. There are husbands who, indifferent as they are to any words about God, will be captivated by your life of holy beauty. What matters is not your outer appearance . . . but your inner disposition. Cultivate inner beauty, the gentle, gracious kind that God delights in" (*THE MESSAGE*).

Make It Personal . . . Live It Out!

Believe it or not, the Disney Channel originally aired only wholesome programs. Walt Disney would be horrified if he could see what is shown on his channel today. In the 1950s, as part of *The Mickey Mouse Club*, Jimmy asked Mousketeers if they had "words to grow by." Doreen sang this sweet little song:

Beauty is as beauty does, that's what wise men say.
Now if you would be beautiful, do this every day:
Help someone who's feeling blue. Let kindness be your guide.
For beauty isn't only looks; it's what you've got inside.

One Year Bible Reading

Ezekiel 31:1–32:32; Hebrews 12:14-29; Psalm 113:1–114:8; Proverbs 27:18-20

Flattery and Praise

Fire tests the purity of silver and gold,
but a person is tested by being praised.

PROVERBS 27:21

Isn't this a different angle on the concept of refining and testing? We as Christians often think that our testing is just limited to trials and hardships, but here we see that the praise and popularity of people can provide another kind of proving ground.

It's been said, "Flattery is like perfume. It's okay to whiff it. Just don't drink it."

So what are the dangers of taking the praise of others too seriously and letting it go to our heads? I think the best way to hate it in ourselves is to see how ugly it is in others. It's ugly to be around someone who makes you feel small because they think they are so big or smart or talented.

Here's a test. Have you recently heard someone praise someone you know? How did it feel? Did you feel threatened? Did you feel that you needed to say something critical and tear them down? Maybe it's because you only love praise when it's directed toward you.

Jesus gave us the best way to shake off this addiction to attention. In his Sermon on the Mount, he said, "When you do a charitable deed, do not sound a trumpet before you, meaning don't look to be noticed and appreciated. Those who do that, they have their reward. But when you do a charitable deed, it is to be in secret so that your Father who sees in secret will himself reward you openly" (Matthew 6:2-4, paraphrased).

Make It Personal . . . Live It Out!

We can learn a lot from the rich and famous. Hollywood puts a spotlight on the stars, but affection is fickle. One bad movie or a few wrinkles causes yesterday's favorite to be today's flop. I feel sorry for them. Lee Iacocca said, "Fame and fortune is for the birds."

There is only one kind of praise that will someday be music to our ears. On that day we will stand at the judgment seat of Christ. May we hear our Savior say, "Well done, my good and faithful servant. You have been faithful in handling this small amount, so now I will give you many more responsibilities. Let's celebrate together!" (Matthew 25:21).

One Year Bible Reading

Ezekiel 33:1–34:31; Hebrews 13:1-25; Psalm 115:1-18; Proverbs 27:21-22

November 17

Be Diligent

Know the state of your flocks,
and put your heart into caring for your herds,
for riches don't last forever. . . .
Your sheep will provide wool for clothing,
and your goats will provide the price of a field.
And you will have enough goats' milk for yourself,
your family, and your servant girls.

PROVERBS 27:23-24, 26-27

Down on the farm they say, "Take care of your sheep, and your sheep will take care of you." Although most of us no longer live on farms, there are some important principles we could learn from farm life. I spent many summers with my grandparents on the farm. I remember so clearly how diligent my grandfather was. No one had to force him to get up at 5 a.m. to milk the cows and feed them and mend the fences. He noticed if one his cows was injured. He knew if one was missing. Throughout his life he had few luxuries, but I remember homegrown, home-cooked food was the best in the world. Grandfather loved his garden, his animals, and his work. Life was simple, but life was good.

Ecclesiastes 10:15 says, "A fool's work wearies him" (NIV). Ladies, it is foolish to be resentful of the work set before us, whether it's tending the sheep, or going grocery shopping, or cooking dinner. Find joy in picking out the freshest tomatoes. Find joy in fixing a delicious sandwich for your husband tonight.

In the end, the writer of Ecclesiastes said, "It is good and proper for a man to eat and drink and find satisfaction in his . . . labor. . . . [To] be happy in his work—this is a gift of God" (Ecclesiastes 5:18-19, NIV).

Make It Personal . . . Live It Out!

Diligence is a reward in itself. For a woman, her home can be a reflection of her inner world and attitudes. Whether you live in a one-room apartment or a spacious house in the suburbs, your home is your greatest realm of influence. Attend to it. I seldom go to bed until the kitchen is clean and decluttered. Since the living room is the first room you see as you come in the front door, make it warm and welcoming. Don't complain about what you don't have and can't do. Be a good steward of what God has given you, and be thankful in the little things.

One Year Bible Reading

Ezekiel 35:1–36:38; James 1:1-18; Psalm 116:1-19; Proverbs 27:23-27

Bold as a Lion

The wicked man [or woman] flees though no one pursues,
but the righteous are as bold as a lion.

PROVERBS 28:1 (NIV)

This proverb gives us insight into the inner condition of the soul of the wicked. There's no rest, no safety, no security. This must be an awful way to live. I repeat: an awful way to live. We can see this throughout history. Evil, wicked rulers like Stalin lived in a constant state of paranoia. He was always fearing he would be killed by his own generals. In his house he had eight bedrooms, which could be locked up like safes in a bank. No one ever knew in which of these bedrooms he slept on any given night.

So how does this relate to us as women? It seems that when we harbor evil things like jealousy, bitterness, slander, or gossip in our lives, we often start fearing those very same attitudes, actions, or motives in others toward us. And if we harbor a secret sin, we live in a constant worry that someone will find out and we'll be ashamed or punished. Yikes! Sin really does become a web that closes in on us and causes us to feel trapped and threatened. Sin keeps our hearts and minds in fear and turmoil.

In contrast, "the righteous are as bold as a lion." Elisabeth Elliot advises, "Do the next thing." Speak the next right, kind word, not only to people's faces, but behind their backs.

Then just like a lion, we don't ever have to look over our shoulders.

Make It Personal . . . Live It Out!

Right living is simple living. With all the stress and complicated issues flying around us in the world, we need an internal oasis and compass. An internal compass gives us direction in moments of decision and crisis. A deep and abiding sense of God's love and goodness and presence gives you stability and joy and peace no matter what comes your way. The prophet Isaiah lived in times of difficult change and moral decline. He knew he needed to keep his focus and hope placed higher than the government and current king. And so he turned to God; will you? "[God] will keep in perfect peace all who trust in [him], all whose thoughts are fixed on [him]!" (Isaiah 26:3).

One Year Bible Reading

Ezekiel 37:1–38:23; James 1:19–2:17; Psalm 117:1-2; Proverbs 28:1

Internal Rebellion

When a country is rebellious, it has many rulers,
but a man [or woman] of understanding and knowledge maintains order.

PROVERBS 28:2 (NIV)

As we watch world events in the news, it's easy to see how unstable a country becomes when there is rebellion against the loving, righteous ways of God. There are wars and factions because there's no true moral, ethical, or spiritual base. There is chaos. The country and the people of that country get torn apart. It's important to know that this is true not only within a nation, but within our own personal lives and within our homes.

We as women have a great position of influence for good or for bad. We are keepers of the home. It's been said, "As goes the woman, so goes the home; as goes the home, so goes the nation." Maybe you've been living with split priorities and a divided heart. Maybe you have been wondering why your world and your home and your inner life is filled with chaos and rebellion.

So, may I say to you, there is no greater decision that you can make for your life than to decide to order each day starting with time in God's Word and with prayer. It will change the tone of your entire day to begin by visualizing God on the throne. He alone is the true and best ruler, not just in heaven, but here on earth over you, in your heart, and over your day.

Will you stop right now and ask him to take his rightful place in your life and bring order?

Make It Personal . . . Live It Out!

We may think we've surrendered and yet still have a stubborn streak of rebellion. We can be deeply immersed in Christian service, Bible study, and prayer meetings, and yet a corner of our hearts is very far away. How can that be? Unfortunately, we cubicle our lives. Some parts belong to God; some parts are entirely ours. We hold the reins. It can be very subtle. Let me name one classic culprit: bitterness. Frankly, harboring unforgiveness is in direct violation of a very core issue with God. He is dead set against it. Today, right now, will you open the access to your heart and let him rein that in and put it to death? He is waiting to help.

One Year Bible Reading

Ezekiel 39:1–40:27; James 2:18–3:18; Psalm 118:1-18; Proverbs 28:2

Pecking Order

A poor man who oppresses the poor
Is like a driving rain which leaves no food.

PROVERBS 28:3 (NKJV)

What warning do we see as women? The picture is given of a driving rain, one that just pounds the earth leaving no good result. When does that happen? It happens when someone who is poor pushes down someone else who is already poor. The definition of *poor* in this case is "one lacking strength, power, stamina, or resilience."

Mothers, can you see that sometimes when a mom is at her lowest and weakest, she sometimes takes it out on her kids? A mom who takes out her frustration on her kids is like a cold, harsh, driving rain right in her own home. Children have no way of knowing why all of sudden a harsh word or punishment is thrown their way.

Moms, I know life can sometimes feel overwhelming. Are you a single mom or a mom with an unsupportive husband? Do you feel there's too much to do; you can't keep up? Are you feeling weak, weary, hopeless? Let me tell you, there is hope and help, even if you've failed.

Will you kneel down right now, if you can, and go to your Father in heaven? Go to him asking for mercy and grace for yourself. Ask him to help you to bestow mercy and grace on your children. He wants to. He can, and he will.

"[Cast] all your care upon Him, for He cares for you" (1 Peter 5:7, NKJV).

Make It Personal . . . Live It Out!

In the barnyard, chickens have a pecking order. There is usually one hen that is bossy, pecking and pulling out the tail feathers of those she dominates. She actually doesn't have to be the biggest, just the meanest. Knowing this, when I raised baby chicks, I kept them in an isolated pen until they were big enough to hold their own in "big-chicken world." The playground at school, team sports, the office, and even church can have a pecking order. First lesson: don't be a bossy hen. Second lesson: don't peck back. Third lesson: don't let it get to you. Talk it out and pray it through when it happens to you or your kids. Then stay clear of the bossy hens.

One Year Bible Reading

Ezekiel 40:28–41:26; James 4:1-17; Psalm 118:19-29; Proverbs 28:3-5

Honest and True

Better to be poor and honest
than to be dishonest and rich.

PROVERBS 28:6

On one side we see someone who is poor but has a true and honest character, contrasted with one who is rich and yet not true and not honest. First of all, let's make sure we notice this is not telling us that just because you're poor, you're good, or just because you're rich, you're bad.

So let's look at what God is saying. Who is rich? When we think of rich or poor, we often think in terms of money. But think about how, as women, we can be rich or poor in lots of other material, physical, and even immaterial things like beauty or circumstances or health.

Maybe you've seen a beautiful, rich, popular woman, but she's mean. She's sneaky. She doesn't even want to be honest or fair or right or kind. God is saying to us that all these rich things that the world says are better don't make you better. On the other hand, hopefully we've noticed a woman who has a handicap, is not pretty, or has hard life circumstances that many would consider poor, and yet she has an inner beauty, integrity, and honesty. You can trust her. You like her. You want to be around her.

God is saying she is better off, really, and we are better off to know and be such women.

Make It Personal . . . Live It Out!

Dishonesty is a dangerous thing, for it twists your ability to think and function. Are you living a double standard? That is spiritual dishonesty. Right now, there is an epidemic of Internet affairs. Women—even married women—are cruising the Internet, reconnecting with old boyfriends, sharing personal struggles with men they meet in chat rooms. It often begins because of loneliness, the emotional void that develops in an unhappy marriage. But the secret fulfillment of the affair is like a drug. It becomes addicting. Just like a drug, every taste leaves you wanting more. Oh, dear girl, this lie is leading to trouble and danger and darkness in your soul. Come to the light. Cut the ties. Let truth and right and good overrule and overcome.

One Year Bible Reading

Ezekiel 42:1–43:27; James 5:1-20; Psalm 119:1-16; Proverbs 28:6-7

The Privilege of Prayer

God detests the prayers
of a person who ignores the law.

PROVERBS 28:9

How can it be that the word *detest* could ever be connected to prayer? It's a warning! Those who willfully disobey, who ignore God's Word—their prayers are hindered, ignored, and even despised. Prayer is a gift. Never forget that. It is a gift and a privilege. Prayer is an amazing thing. It's a wonder that we, mere humans, are not just able but invited to have direct communication with the God of the universe. We could never imagine having the president of the United States' personal cell phone number. But in a real sense, we have God's. Prayer gives us close, intimate, personal access and communication with the Lord any time of the day and night.

Martin Luther once said, "To be a Christian without prayer is no more possible than to be alive without breathing."

But sin causes static on the phone lines with God. As John Bunyan stated, "Prayer will make a man cease from sin, or sin will entice a man to cease from prayer."

So if you are feeling distant from God, like your prayers are hitting a block wall in the sky, *maybe they are*. Is there a commandment, instruction, or warning in God's Word you are ignoring? Sin opens our thoughts to the voice of the enemy of our souls. The enemy delights in building a wall between you and God, because then he has you all to himself. But the good news is, God is bidding you to come back. Confess your sin. "He is faithful and just to forgive us our sins and to cleanse us from all unrighteousness" (1 John 1:9, NKJV).

Make It Personal . . . Live It Out!

Not only personally, but as a nation, sin can separate us from God. On the 2011 National Day of Prayer, Joni Eareckson Tada lifted up desperate words. Let's join in her prayer:

> Almighty God, you are our Mighty Fortress, our refuge and the God in whom we place our trust. As our nation faces great distress and uncertainty, we ask your Holy Spirit to fall afresh upon your people—convict us of sin and inflame within us a passion to pray for our land and its people. . . . Send a spirit of revival and may it begin in our own hearts.

One Year Bible Reading

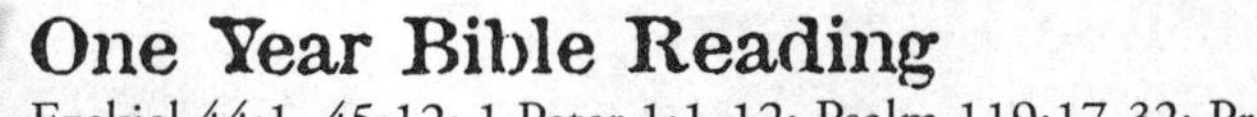

Ezekiel 44:1–45:12; 1 Peter 1:1-12; Psalm 119:17-32; Proverbs 28:8-10

Seeing the Invisible

A rich man may be wise in his own eyes,
but a poor man who has discernment sees through him.

PROVERBS 28:11 (NIV)

Hans Christian Andersen wrote an intriguing story called "The Emperor's New Clothes."

Once upon a time, there was a vain emperor who loved beautiful new clothes. As it happened, two swindlers arrived in town announcing they could weave a cloth with a strange quality. It would be entirely invisible to anyone who was unfit for his office and unforgivably stupid.

This is marvelous, thought the emperor. *Such robes will give me superior wisdom!*

He then paid the swindlers handsomely so they could begin their work immediately.

Well, the story goes that the swindlers pretended to weave his new clothes, and the king pretended to put them on. The townsfolk pretended to admire them as he paraded through the town. Only one child with discernment shouted the obvious truth: "The Emperor has no clothes!" And he didn't.

"A rich man may be wise in his own eyes, but a poor man who has discernment sees through him."

King Solomon was one of the richest kings who ever lived. As God inspired him to write the words of this proverb, I wonder if he put down his pen and pondered. Did he think about the gentle young man who made his shoes, or his gardener who loved simple, pure beauty, or the old wife of the baker with her kind, clear gaze? Did he all of a sudden see himself through their eyes and wonder, *Who is the true nobility?*

Make It Personal . . . Live It Out!

Things are not always as they appear. Even if people around us don't see the truth, our hearts can rest with assurance that God sees all things with perfect clarity. He gives mothers "eyes in the back of their heads" to detect trouble with their kids. When there are dishonest shenanigans in the office, he'll reveal red flags. Checks in your spirit can indeed be insight from the Holy Spirit.

Let's Pray

Lord, help me to see with your eyes. Let me see people with your eyes of love. And give me discernment to be wise and careful.

One Year Bible Reading

Ezekiel 45:13–46:24; 1 Peter 1:13–2:10; Psalm 119:33-48; Proverbs 28:11

True Success

When the godly succeed, everyone is glad.
When the wicked take charge, people go into hiding.

PROVERBS 28:12

This is both a beautiful and a tragic picture of the effect that we can have on people around us every day. We can make people glad or sad.

Maybe you're a waitress, or a nurse, or you work at Walmart. You can be a blessing. You can be the fragrance of Christ, even in the midst of a worldly atmosphere. Do you remember the story of Joseph? "When his master saw that the LORD was with him and that the LORD gave him success . . . Potiphar put him in charge of his household, and he entrusted to his care everything he owned" (Genesis 39:3-4, NIV). Here we see Potiphar was glad to find someone who not only worked hard but was someone he could trust. Joseph was also put in charge of the other servants, and we can be sure they were glad too, because a godly boss is a good boss.

But the wicked have an entirely different effect on those around them. The definition of *wicked* in this case is "one who sins against God and man." People don't trust them. When someone who is wicked is in charge, things are not going to be fair. People are going to be treated harshly or rudely. No one feels safe, because no one *is* safe.

Ladies, these very same principles can be applied to our place of influence in our homes. So the true test of real success is, are those around us blessed because we're a blessing?

Make It Personal . . . Live It Out!

Motherhood, marriage and homemaking, missions and ministry are often seen as lower levels of success. Climbing the corporate ladder and having a job title might seem to carry more influence and prestige. But nothing really matters that doesn't have eternal value—nothing. Romans 12:1-2 sets our sights on success that never fades: "And so, dear . . . sisters, I plead with you to give your bodies to God. . . . Let them be a living and holy sacrifice. . . . Don't copy the behavior and customs of this world, but let God transform you into a new person by changing the way you think. Then you will learn to know God's will for you, which is good and pleasing and perfect."

One Year Bible Reading

Ezekiel 47:1–48:35; 1 Peter 2:11–3:7; Psalm 119:49-64; Proverbs 28:12-13

Holy Fear

Blessed is the man [or woman] who always fears the LORD,
but he [or she] who hardens his heart falls into trouble.

PROVERBS 28:14 (NIV)

What does it mean to "fear the Lord"? Should we be afraid that he wants to crush or dominate or punish us? Is he the big traffic cop in the sky? Is he quick to anger, slow to forgive? I hope you don't believe that. God loves you more than you'll ever know. He is the God of all comfort and the God of all grace. Even his chastisement is for our good, to break us from sin and a ruined life.

To live in reverence of God means that we view him as a Father: a good Father; a right Father; an almighty, wise, faithful Father; a heavenly Father who deserves our respect. It's been said that "those who live in the fear of the Lord have nothing else to fear."

"The LORD takes pleasure in those who fear Him, in those who hope in His mercy" (Psalm 147:11, NKJV).

Few writers stir my heart to holy reverence like A. W. Tozer. In his book *Whatever Happened to Worship?* he writes, "When we come into this sweet relationship, we are beginning to learn astonished reverence, breathless adoration, awesome fascination, lofty admiration of the attributes of God and something of the breathless silence that we know when God is near. . . . There are very few unqualified things in our lives, but I believe that the reverential fear of God mixed with love and fascination and astonishment and admiration and devotion is the most enjoyable state and the most purifying emotion the human soul can know."

Make It Personal . . . Live It Out!

The blessed life is the end result of living in astonished reverence. What constitutes the blessed life that results from such a relation with our Creator? The whole world is grasping for the elusive key elements, true love and authentic purpose. Life is empty without them. Money can buy a diamond ring, as the Beatles sang; "but money can't buy me love." They ought to know.

Let's Pray

Lord, please keep me from wasting my life chasing artificial happiness. I want to delight in you, trust your promises, dwell in your love, and honor you as the great King of kings and Lord of lords.

One Year Bible Reading

Daniel 1:1–2:23; 1 Peter 3:8–4:6; Psalm 119:65-80; Proverbs 28:14

No Growling!

A wicked ruler is as dangerous to the poor
as a roaring lion or an attacking bear.
A ruler with no understanding will oppress his people,
but one who hates corruption will have a long life.

PROVERBS 28:15-16

This graphic word picture is addressed to leaders. Are you a leader? If you're a mom, a committee head, or supervisor at work, you're a leader. The question is, how do you use your power? Do you rule with a rod of iron? Like a bear, do you growl? Are you easily threatened? Do you bite people's heads off?

In the movie *The Wonderful Wizard of Oz*, the Wizard seemed to be a tyrant. He kept his subjects shaking in their boots. Believing that he was the only man capable of solving their problems, Dorothy and her friends traveled to the Emerald City. What high expectations they had. Of course he knew he could never meet those expectations; the plan was doomed to failure and he knew it. He kept up the guise as long as he could. But behind the smoke and mirrors he was just a little guy named Oscar from Omaha, Nebraska.

Could it be that some of the tyranny you see displayed in yourself or others is merely a front, smoke and mirrors? Fear, insecurity, a crippling sense of inadequacy will drive us to overcompensate. We can't let down our guard, because if people really knew how weak we truly felt, well . . . we don't know what they'd think. It might surprise you that many pastor's wives feel very small and inadequate for the shoes they wear. The moral of this story: let's drop the power plays, cut others some slack, and stop growling.

Make It Personal . . . Live It Out!

Weak, incompetent leadership crushes others. Strong, godly leadership is actually gentle and provides a safe environment for people to learn and grow and do their best. Does your daughter-in-law want to help with Christmas dinner? Don't micromanage; let her add her own personal touch. Do the little ones want to make cookies? The more the merrier. No big deal if a little sugar gets spilled on the floor. Be fun to be with and to work with. Getting the job done will be secondary. Seeing the joy of accomplishment shine in others—primary.

One Year Bible Reading

Daniel 2:24–3:30; 1 Peter 4:7–5:14; Psalm 119:81-96; Proverbs 28:15-16

November 27

Murder

A man burdened with bloodshed will flee into a pit;
Let no one help him.
Whoever walks blamelessly will be saved,
But he who is perverse in his ways will suddenly fall.

PROVERBS 28:17-18 (NKJV)

This proverb uses serious and extreme words like *bloodshed, fall into a pit,* and *perverse ways.* Most of us aren't around murderers. And we don't often see any open pit that anyone is likely to fall into. So how can these wise words apply to our world and our lives?

Let's look at the words *burdened with bloodshed.* The NIV says "guilt of murder." Sticks and stones may can break my bones, but mean words will always hurt me. Yes, we can murder someone's reputation with slander and gossip. We can harshly criticize. We can humiliate and put people down in front of others. We can be partial. We can be prejudiced. Many of us have seen mothers in a grocery store screaming at or belittling their children. We've seen coaches or teachers purposely neglect a child who's slow, or allow other kids to ridicule him.

Murder is a serious thing, whether it is physical or mental or emotional. Harm will come to those who harm others.

In closing, let's shift gears and look at the other side. Our proverb today is a comfort to those who are mistreated. You don't have to retaliate. They will fall in the pit they dug for themselves. You don't have to push them in. God has better things for us. We are like clay pots. He can use even the harshness of others to season and refine us like fire in a kiln. Be still; be patient. Trust him to use even this for good.

Make It Personal . . . Live It Out!

A clear conscience is a soft pillow. As our proverb today promises, "Whoever walks blamelessly will be saved." Saved from what? Saved from the torment of a guilty conscience, saved from having to cover your tracks. Life is complicated enough without all of that. Wouldn't you agree?

Let's Pray

O Lord, please shine the light of your truth on all of my ways. Do I ever murder? Are my words harsh? Am I thoughtless and careless with the feelings of others? Guard my mouth before I speak. Guard my heart against wounds from others.

One Year Bible Reading

Daniel 4:1-37; 2 Peter 1:1-21; Psalm 119:97-112; Proverbs 28:17-18

Chasing Fantasies

He who works his land will have abundant food,
but the one who chases fantasies will have his fill of poverty.

PROVERBS 28:19 (NIV)

It seems in our society today there so many young people who have never learned to work or make their bed or be responsible for any real thing by the time they're young adults. Many kids live in a fantasy world of TV, sports, dance, music, and video games. The principles of responsibility and having a work ethic are regarded as obsolete.

Charles Sykes wrote some "rules kids won't learn in school" that have been circulating in various forms on the Internet (often attributed to Bill Gates). Here are three sobering points from one of the versions.

1. Life is not divided into semesters. You don't get summers off, and very few employers are interested in helping you find yourself.
2. Television is not real life. In real life, people actually have to leave the coffee shop and go to jobs.
3. Your school may have done away with winners and losers, but life has not. In some schools they have abolished failing grades; they'll give you as many chances as you want to get the right answer. This does not bear the slightest resemblance to anything in real life.

Entitlement: as long as our kids live with a feeling that the world owes them a living, they will never wake up and smell the coffee. So as godly women, let's take joy in working hard. Let's do a good job. Let's be good stewards of our households. And let's teach our kids that work is a privilege. It's all good.

Make It Personal . . . Live It Out!

The phrase "chasing fantasies" has an interesting ring to it. What is a fantasy? The dictionary defines it as "extravagant and unrestrained imagination." In the Cinderella world of Prince Charmings and fairy godmothers a wave of the wand fixes everything. Not so in real life. Truthfully, in the Disney movie, my favorite part is not the "abracadabras." I love watching Cinderella joyfully take the humble little pieces of what she had to make her own beautiful gown. Do you have dreams? Would you like to change or make your life better? Stop fretting about what you lack. Take the pieces of what God has given you and get started. Day by day, little changes have big outcomes.

One Year Bible Reading

Daniel 5:1-31; 2 Peter 2:1-22; Psalm 119:113-128; Proverbs 28:19-20

The Poverty of Debt

Greedy people try to get rich quick
but don't realize they're headed for poverty.

PROVERBS 28:22

Get rich quick—everywhere we look, women are bombarded with images of what we should have, what we should drive, what we should wear, and how we should look. We want it all, and we want it now. In generations before us, it was accepted that it took years to slowly get the things you needed, let alone the things that you wanted. Unfortunately, young couples today are anxious to have a nice house with all new furniture and accessories. They must at the same time wear the latest clothes and drive new cars. This makes them appear rich overnight, but the sad truth is, it will take them years and years to pay for it because it was purchased on credit cards. Buy now and pay later. Later when all the interest charges are added, they will feel poor, very poor. Statistics show that the number one cause of stress, fighting, and marriage breakup is financial problems.

Amazingly, even people in their forties and fifties have been living the high life on credit. Many feel they can't tithe, can't retire, can't go on a mission trip, can't share with others in need because they have never learned to "live under their means." They were greedy to live rich, and now they are feeling poor. They forgot 1 Timothy 6:6-7: "Godliness with contentment is great gain. For we brought nothing into this world, and it is certain we can carry nothing out" (NIV).

Make It Personal . . . Live It Out!

Debt is an albatross. Are you ready to get it off your back? Dave Ramsey (www.daveramsey.com) has a "snowball plan" that will help you take some positive steps. "List your debts, excluding the house, in order. The smallest balance should be your number one priority. Don't worry about interest rates unless two debts have similar payoffs. If that's the case, then list the higher interest rate debt first. The point of the debt snowball is simply this: You need some quick wins in order to stay pumped up about getting out of debt! . . . When you start knocking off the easier debts, you will see results and you will stay motivated to dump your debt."

One Year Bible Reading

Daniel 6:1-28; 2 Peter 3:1-18; Psalm 119:129-152; Proverbs 28:21-22

What Is Wrong with That?

Anyone who steals from his father and mother
and says, "What's wrong with that?"
is no better than a murderer.

PROVERBS 28:24

Our proverb today is saying that stealing from your parents is serious. Although many people would never steal money or things, they don't give a second thought to robbing them of respect. The fifth of the Ten Commandments is, "Honor your father and your mother." It is clear that God considers this not just important to your parents, but it's important to him.

Billy Graham once said, "A child who is allowed to be disrespectful to his parents will not have true respect for anyone." I believe this is true. And this applies to grown-up children too. Being kind and respectful is a decision, then a habit, then a lifestyle.

Okay, ladies, let's make this personal. How about you and your mom? Do you bristle each time your mom makes a suggestion? Do you find you get annoyed, ignore her, or are rude to her like when you were a teenager? And do you blame her for your flaws? Some people justify their attitudes by deflecting blame. As Dr. Laurence Peters states, "Psychiatry enables us to correct our faults by confessing our parents' shortcomings." Let's not get stuck in that dead-end trap.

And so, for us as godly women, let's grow up. There is a gracious maturity in seeking to love and be good to your mom—just because she's your mom.

Make It Personal . . . Live It Out!

The holidays can bring out the best or the worst in family relationships. If your parents are getting older, they may feel especially lonely at this time. Age carries with it health issues, regrets from the past, and fear of the future. Be aware of this. If they vent, or complain, or withdraw, please don't be angry or resent the extra burden they have become. They carried you and put up with *your* crying fits once, you know. They might feel very useless right now; call and ask their advice. Ask your mom to teach you to make her special holiday dish. Take an hour to help them send a few Christmas cards. Someday, they will no longer be with you. Love them while you still can.

One Year Bible Reading

Daniel 7:1-28; 1 John 1:1-10; Psalm 119:153-176; Proverbs 28:23-24

December

Scan this code for audio devotionals
or visit www.tyndal.es/wisdom.

December 1

The Pitfalls of Pride

He [or she] who is of a proud heart stirs up strife,
But he [or she] who trusts in the LORD will be prospered.

PROVERBS 28:25 (NKJV)

It's been said, "Temper gets you into trouble. Pride keeps you there."

Before we apply this to someone else, let's see if this applies to us. Prideful. We are being prideful when we always think we have a better way or when we think we're always right. When we do this, we can make others feel inferior. We dig in our heels.

Henry Beecher once said, "A proud man is seldom a grateful man, for he never thinks he gets as much as he deserves." Maybe that's why pride always causes trouble and an atmosphere of tension. Unfortunately, pride makes us think that everything is about us. Every little slight is noted, even if unintentional. Every delay is resented. If we are the center of things, then others are on the outs. This makes us very hard to live with.

Ladies, let's be honest. Is there a conflict that you are having with a friend, your husband, or in your church, and it comes down to the fact that you are offended that you didn't get your way? Yes, maybe you think your idea or plan was best, and maybe it was, but now you're angry. If you retain that resentment, can you see in the end nobody wins, including you?

Our proverb simply and yet clearly gives us both the cause and the antidote: "A proud heart stirs up strife, but [she] who trusts in the LORD will be prospered."

Make It Personal . . . Live It Out!

Trusting God relieves us of the need and even the desire to fight our own battles. Therefore, let me challenge you. Will you allow your heart to rest by shifting your confidence to God? Trust involves patience and a willingness to accept his sometimes unusual and creative solutions. I often quote Proverb 3:5-6 to myself. It reminds me that my natural instincts and insight are limited and flawed. God sees the end from the beginning.

"Trust in the LORD with all your heart; do not depend on your own understanding. Seek his will in all you do, and he will show you which path to take" (Proverbs 3:5-6).

One Year Bible Reading

Daniel 8:1-27; 1 John 2:1-17; Psalm 120:1-7; Proverbs 28:25-26

The Gift of Giving

He [or she] who gives to the poor will lack nothing,
but he who closes his eyes to them receives many curses.

PROVERBS 28:27 (NIV)

I love what Winston Churchill said: "We make a living by what we get, but we make a life by what we give."

The Christian life is really a giving life. This is not the burden of it. This is the blessing and privilege of it. And often it's not the bigness of the gift, it's the sweetness in which it's given that blesses the one who receives.

That is what makes the story of the Good Samaritan so powerful. The story starts out with a man traveling. Thieves attacked him, stripped him, wounded him, and left him half dead. Every time I read this I think about how many women all around us are hurting and wounded, not just physically, but emotionally and morally and spiritually. In this story the first two people passed by, and we know how they felt. They were busy. It wasn't their problem.

But we do love the Good Samaritan. Pay attention to his reaction. "[He] . . . came to where [the wounded man] was. And when he saw him, he had compassion. So he went to him, bandaged his wounds . . . and took care of him" (Luke 10:33-34, NKJV).

Let me emphasize the first three important elements. He saw him, had compassion, and went to him. After Jesus told this story, he said, "Go and do likewise" (Luke 10:37, NKJV).

"My little children, let us not love in word or in tongue, but in deed and in truth" (1 John 3:18, NKJV).

Make It Personal . . . Live It Out!

Why do we sometimes pass by the poor and needy? Truthfully, we're already stretched. We're afraid we'll run short of time, energy, and resources we require for our own needs and families. But God makes an amazing promise: "[She] who gives to the poor will lack nothing." Is that true? Are you wondering, *Can I trust God to make good on his word?* You'll never know unless you step out in faith. The Good Samaritan gave up his plans for a few hours. But you can be sure there are three who never forgot it: the wounded man, the Samaritan who left the inn with joy deep in his heart, and God himself.

One Year Bible Reading

Daniel 9:1–11:1; 1 John 2:18–3:6; Psalm 121:1-8; Proverbs 28:27-28

Let Go

For people who hate discipline and only get more stubborn,
There'll come a day when life tumbles in and they break,
but by then it'll be too late to help them.

PROVERBS 29:1 (*THE MESSAGE*)

This is a sober description and a serious warning. Sure enough, we can all think of people who are hardheaded, hard-hearted, stubborn, unwilling to yield or be corrected.

Do you know how they capture monkeys in the jungle? The trap of stubbornness. A hole is drilled in a coconut shell, just large enough for a monkey to thrust in his hand. It is then filled with nuts and fastened firmly to a tree at sunset. Drawn by the scent of food, the monkey will put his hand into the shell and grasp the nuts. But the hole is too small for him to withdraw his now-clenched fist. Pull as he may, he is trapped unless he releases his nuts. This poor stubborn monkey, nothing holds him captive but himself.

But are there times that we too are just like this monkey? The answer can be right under our noses, but we are stuck because we won't give up our right to our right. Oh foolish us. Let's stop fearing discipline and change, knowing that God brings it into our life to break us of our rigid ways.

Do you want to let God do a fresh, freeing work? Write the words *Let God*. Then, strike out the *d* and you'll know the secret: *Let Go.*

"Let God transform you into a new person by changing the way you think. Then you will learn to know God's will for you, which is good and pleasing and perfect" (Romans 12:2).

Make It Personal . . . Live It Out!

All to Jesus I surrender; All to Him I freely give,
I will ever love and trust Him, In His presence daily live.
I surrender all, I surrender all,
All to thee, my blessed Savior, I surrender all.
All to Jesus I surrender; Humbly at His feet I bow,
Worldly pleasures all forsaken; Take me, Jesus, take me now.
—JUDSON VAN DEVENTER IN "I SURRENDER ALL"

One Year Bible Reading

Daniel 11:2-35; 1 John 3:7-24; Psalm 122:1-9; Proverbs 29:1

Godly Leadership

When the righteous are in authority, the people rejoice;
But when a wicked man rules, the people groan.

PROVERBS 29:2 (NKJV)

Question: Is it better to have leaders that tell us what we want to hear and constantly lean to the whims of the people and popular opinion? Or is it better to have a leader who seeks to do the right thing even if it's not popular at the moment? Undeniably we do need strong, righteous leadership in every realm of life, whether in the home, school, business, church, or a nation. Truly, in leadership integrity matters.

People are fickle. It's been said, "You can please some of the people all of the time, all of the people some of the time, but you just can't please all of the people all of the time."

And so even though we might feel frustrated that we can't change what the powers in government are doing right now, we can make a difference in our own little sphere of influence. Whether you're a mom, a ministry leader at church, or a supervisor at work, may you lead with a wonderful combination of two things: diligence and a deep reverence for God, pleasing him. May you fill your role with honor. "Whatever you do, do it wholeheartedly as unto the Lord, not just unto man" (Colossians 3:23, paraphrased). May you be fair with people; may you be honest; may you be kind.

In the Old Testament, both Daniel and Esther lived in decadent, worldly societies. Yet they chose to honor God and do the next right things. May God raise up many Daniels and Esthers "for such a time as this" (Esther 4:14, NKJV).

Make It Personal . . . Live It Out!

Are you a leader? You might not realize it, but your life is affecting others, for better or worse. We as women, do have a God-designed, God-appointed place of influence in this world. It is an honor he has trusted us with. It is a responsibility. He has charged us to be faithful. I believe every Christian should own and read the book *Spiritual Leadership*, by J. Oswald Sanders. In it he says, "If those who hold influence over others fail to lead toward the spiritual uplands, than surely the path to the lowlands will be well worn. People travel together; no one lives detached and alone."

One Year Bible Reading

Daniel 11:36–12:13; 1 John 4:1-21; Psalm 123:1-4; Proverbs 29:2-4

Flattery Will Get You Nowhere

Whoever flatters his neighbor
is spreading a net for his feet.

PROVERBS 29:5 (NIV)

We all like receiving a compliment, don't we? A word of encouragement is just that. It encourages us. But *flattery* as defined by *Webster's* is "an insincere compliment, excessive or unjustified praise." Put another way, flattery's not truthful, and in the end, it isn't kind.

So let's beware of people who lavish flattery and praise. Women, young and old, beware of a man who gives you too much of the wrong kind of attention. Beware. There may be a hidden agenda at work. An old folk saying is "Flattery looks like friendship, just like a wolf looks like a dog."

Pastor Chuck Smith comments that "flattery is often used to soften us up and then trip us up." If we listen to enough flattery, we might begin to believe it, causing us to think too much of ourselves.

It's been said, "Flattery is like perfume. You can sniff it. Just don't drink it."

But on the other hand, many people never hear a word of praise, not ever. So if you're a Sunday school teacher, try to find one uplifting thing to say to each child before they leave class. If you're a mom, don't just point out your kids' mistakes, catch them being good. Praise them. And wives, when your husband comes home, bless him with a kind, encouraging word. It might be the only one he's heard all day.

Make It Personal . . . Live It Out!

Flattery not only puffs people up, it sets them up. Parents and grandparents often praise a child's accomplishments. We cheer the winning team or the good grades. Everyone loves a winner. But when your child strikes out or struggles with math, they may interpret your lack of praise as a statement of failure. Achievements come and go. Praise your kids when they do their best, regardless of results. Teach them to be kind to their teammate who dropped the ball; it's only a game. Show them you're their best fan—not because of what they do, but because of who they are.

One Year Bible Reading

Hosea 1:1–3:5; 1 John 5:1-21; Psalm 124:1-8; Proverbs 29:5-8

December 6

Blowing Off Steam

A fool gives full vent to his anger,
but a wise man [or woman] keeps himself under control.

PROVERBS 29:11 (NIV)

When a toddler gives vent to anger, it's called a tantrum, but when an adult does it, it's called blowing off steam and fits of rage. When two people do it together, it can escalate from screaming to violence. One thing does lead to another, and everyone loses.

Maybe you grew up in an angry home. It's sad, but many women who grew up in that kind of atmosphere create it in their own lives and homes. It's surprising, but studies show that women are getting more and more violent.

So let's look at what God says in Ephesians 4:26-27. He says, "Be angry and do not sin: do not let the sun go down on your wrath, nor give place to the devil" (NKJV).

First, when we're angry—and, honestly, sometimes we are—don't add fuel to the fire. If we sin in response to sin, we've just made matters worse.

Second, don't let the sun go down on your wrath. This speaks of keeping short tabs because we women sometimes are experts at keeping long tabs. We won't forgive, and daily our frustration adds up. We nurse a grudge, and then when the next offense comes, *kaboom*, we blow up.

The last part tells us if we're not on guard, we give place to the devil himself. Anger gives the devil a place in our thought life, attitudes, and even our personality.

So read our proverb again: "A fool gives full vent to his anger, but a wise [woman] keeps [herself] under control."

Make It Personal . . . Live It Out!

I have to admit, a few years ago my neighbor's actions finally got to me. I let loose and gave her a piece of my mind. I did not use bad language, but my words were sharp. My long years of trying to be patient were all erased by a single, two-minute venting of frustration. The only thing it accomplished was that her feelings were hurt and I am ashamed. Anger can get the better of us; then like a volcano, it erupts. How do we tame it? Our anger needs to surrender to the Savior. If it is brewing in you, will you give it to him today?

One Year Bible Reading

Hosea 4:1–5:15; 2 John 1:1-13; Psalm 125:1-5; Proverbs 29:9-11

Don't Listen to Lies

If a ruler listens to lies,
all his officials become wicked.

PROVERBS 29:12 (NIV)

Listen to this staggering quote by Adolph Hitler: "Make the lie big, make it simple, keep saying it, and eventually they will believe it."

Let's apply this attitude to the unproven theory of evolution. Although it completely contradicts the fixed and proven first law of biogenesis, "Life comes from life," it is taught in our schools as an unquestioned fact. Why? Human gullibility. It's been said, "It is easier to believe a lie that one has heard a thousand times than to believe a fact that no one has never heard."

In the movie *Expelled*, Ben Stein shows how leaders of universities and the media have built a wall around evolution, and everyone who questions it is ostracized. He also shows how this belief tends to undermine not just religion, but a belief that life has any real meaning or purpose because we're just a product of random accidents. It undermines belief in morality and a respect for human life.

Eve believed a lie in the Garden, but may we settle for nothing less than the truth. As Jesus said, "The truth will set you free" (John 8:32).

Make It Personal . . . Live It Out!

Lies have a devastating effect on both us and our children. When asked, can you give solid, biblical answers about dinosaurs, aliens, evolution, death, and why we look different? We don't need to feel threatened when our kids ask deep and thought-provoking questions. God created us with intelligence and curiosity. Their questions can challenge us to do our homework and learn some exciting information ourselves. Dr. Georgia Purdom (AnswersInGenesis.org) has created a DVD called *Kids' Most Asked Questions about Science and the Bible*. She supplies simple, Bible-based answers that parents can use with children of all ages.

One Year Bible Reading

Hosea 6:1–9:17; 3 John 1:1-15; Psalm 126:1-6; Proverbs 29:12-14

Discipline

To discipline a child produces wisdom,
but a mother is disgraced by an undisciplined child.

PROVERBS 29:15

The 1990 movie *Home Alone* with Macaulay Culkin is a classic illustration of today's proverb. Truly, a child left to himself is a disaster waiting to happen. Children need boundaries—wise, loving boundaries.

A few years ago there were flash floods in the Midwest. Two young boys hopped on their bikes and rode down to see the raging river. But they had no idea how powerful floodwater can be. They got too close and the river swept them away. Were those kids in the habit of going where they wanted, when they wanted, without permission or supervision? Had they gone places before—dangerous places—and not been disciplined?

Right now, it is hard to imagine a more morally dangerous time for children to grow up. Parents, don't kid yourselves. Dark music, violent video games, computer access to pornography, drugs, experimenting with sex, strangers in chat rooms lure them in and can sweep them away. Children have no way of discerning the dangers or understanding the consequences. Some of these are so wicked and serious that just one experience can change their life forever.

So moms, don't be ashamed to discipline your children today. If necessary, give them tough love, because if you don't, you might be brokenhearted tomorrow.

Make It Personal . . . Live It Out!

Corrective discipline is something we never grow out of the need for. For discipline to be effective, the boundaries need to be understood. Unfortunately we often have to learn from our mistakes. My sister constructed an electric fence to keep her dogs out of the flower beds. Her verbal commands went unheeded. A sharp, harmless shock got the message across. Is God cruel when he allows pain as part of our consequence for sin? Pain will not kill you. Sin will.

"For the Lord disciplines those he loves, and he punishes each one he accepts as his child. As you endure this divine discipline, remember that God is treating you as his own children. . . . No discipline is enjoyable while it is happening—it's painful! But afterward there will be a peaceful harvest of right living for those who are trained in this way" (Hebrews 12:6-7, 11).

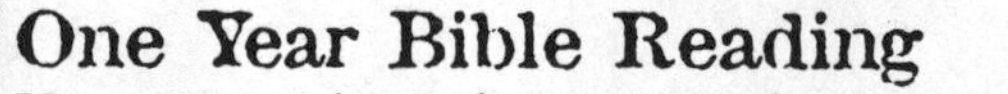

One Year Bible Reading

Hosea 10:1–14:9; Jude 1:1-25; Psalm 127:1-5; Proverbs 29:15-17

Divine Guidance

When people do not accept divine guidance, they run wild.
But whoever obeys the law is joyful.

PROVERBS 29:18

Many people view God as the divine killjoy. They bristle at the *don'ts*. They resent God telling them what they can and can't do. "Do not have false idols, do not steal, do not lie, do not commit adultery, do not murder." Jesus said, "Enter by the narrow gate that leads to life, for wide is the way that leads to destruction" (Matthew 7:13, paraphrased). Is God really confining us by giving us such guidelines? Is our nation better off now that we have taken the Ten Commandments off the courthouse walls and prayer out of schools?

Recently I was walking with my friend Lenya in an older part of town. A man who was obviously homeless came alongside her requesting assistance. Instead of giving him money she offered to buy him—Donny—a hamburger. It grieved our hearts to see how alcohol had reduced him to such brokenness. I said, "Donny, are you tired of living this life? Do you want to change?" Tears came quickly. "I cry every day," he said. "Drink has caused me to lose my kids and my family." When he was young he probably thought the wild life was the free life. Like so many, he thought could ignore God's warnings and guidelines. He thought he could beat the odds. Now he's in bondage. But, the glorious truth I could tell Donny that day is "It's not too late. You may have turned your back on God, but God has not turned his back on you. It's not too late, Donny. His power to restore is mighty." Amazing grace, how sweet the sound.

Make It Personal . . . Live It Out!

Donny's life portrays the dark side of disobedience. Sin strips us from the dignity and true freedom God created us to have. Obedience often requires some tough moments of surrender. But joy awaits us. "Whoever obeys the law is joyful." That is why studying the Proverbs is vital to us. God gives us solid practical instruction. We are then given clear pictures that describe the end result of our choices. Oh, what a kind and wise and patient Father in heaven we have. Take his instruction deep into your heart. Indeed, it's true: Father knows best.

One Year Bible Reading

Joel 1:1–3:21; Revelation 1:1-20; Psalm 128:1-6; Proverbs 29:18

Restrain

Do you see a man hasty in his words?
There is more hope for a fool than for him.

PROVERBS 29:20 (NKJV)

The theme in this proverb is wisdom with words. It deals with not just what we say but when we say it. Ladies, we will always be foolish women until we get a grip on this.

Hasty words—let's look at three principles.

1. When we speak without thinking, we say too much. Proverbs 10:19 warns us, "In the multitude of words sin is not lacking" (NKJV). I once heard someone say, "Small minds talk about people, average minds talk about things, but great minds talk about ideas." There is way too much small-minded talk, even among Christians. A good rule of thumb is, would you say exactly the same thing about someone behind their back as you would if they were present? If not, don't say it.
2. Timing. Ecclesiastics 3:7 tells us, "[There is] a time to be silent and a time to speak" (NIV). Bad times to speak are when we're emotional, when we're angry, hurt, tired, or frustrated. At such times we are in great danger of causing damage and regretting it later. Orson Card said, "Among my most prized possessions are the words that I have never spoken."
3. Attitude. David prayed, "Let the words of my mouth and the meditation of my heart be acceptable in Your sight, O LORD, my strength and my Redeemer" (Psalm 19:14, NKJV).

So we'll close with Proverbs 10:19: "[She] who restrains [her] lips is wise" (NKJV).

Make It Personal . . . Live It Out!

Wisdom restrains. The Hebrew word for *restrain* is *khasak*, which means "to keep from, to hold in check." Whether it's trying to hold back from eating a second piece of cheesecake or trying to restrain yourself from saying the wrong thing, you know it's easier said than done. The forces of our human nature seem to have a life of their own. It's a tug-of-war. Are you feeling weak, defeated? Join the club. Even Paul, the great apostle, cried out, "Oh, what a miserable person I am! Who will free me from this life that is dominated by sin and death?" (Romans 7:24). Romans chapter 8 explains the marvelous answer. Only God's Holy Spirit has the power to "restrain."

One Year Bible Reading

Amos 1:1–3:15; Revelation 2:1-17; Psalm 129:1-8; Proverbs 29:19-20

December 11

Hot-Tempered

An angry man stirs up dissension,
and a hot-tempered one commits many sins.

PROVERBS 29:22 (NIV)

Dissension and strife, being hot-tempered, and sins—all these concepts become part of the atmosphere when anger is raging in someone's soul.

To some of you reading today this does not need to be explained. You are living this. Maybe it's because of an angry husband or an angry teenager, or maybe you have an angry boss. You probably feel overpowered and powerless. Someone who is given to outbursts of anger feels at that moment that they are in control, but nothing could be further from the truth. They have lost control of themselves. Anger is their slave-master, causing them to lash out, vent, be cruel, and burn bridges by hurting even those who love them most. And what do they have after that's done? Less than nothing. There is no comfort or satisfaction. All they have is a trail of collateral damage that wraps them up in a package of shame, problems, and more sin as they seek to blame others.

If you're a victim of this, it can be a nightmare because it feels like there's nothing you can do. But there is hope. The Lord hears, and sees, and cares. In moments of outbursts, shoot up an arrow prayer. Practice putting up your shield of faith. Ask God to guard your heart and mind. And don't let them pull you into their pit. Misery loves company. So I repeat, don't let them pull you into their pit.

Make It Personal . . . Live It Out!

If you've been the brunt of someone's anger, either in the past or present, you probably have anger of your own. There are two responses, fight or flight. If you aren't a fighter, your flight pattern might have turned your anger inward. Depression is often the result. Let me ask you an important question. Are you now angry at God? Are you depressed and angry that he did not defend you? Never forget, Jesus bore the full brunt of angry men. "He is despised. . . . Surely He has . . . carried our sorrows . . . and by His stripes we are healed" (Isaiah 53:3-5, NKJV).

One Year Bible Reading

Amos 4:1–6:14; Revelation 2:18–3:6; Psalm 130:1-8; Proverbs 29:21-22

The Best Gifts

A man's pride brings him low,
but a man of lowly spirit gains honor.

PROVERBS 29:23 (NIV)

Pride, oh, the problem of pride. The dictionary says it's "an overrated self-esteem." It's arrogance, haughtiness, a feeling that we are better. Humility is just the opposite. Pride brings people down. Humility stoops down and lifts others up.

The Christmas season is the perfect time to choose to be humble. Two thousand years ago, the King of kings chose to be born in a manger. Philippians 2:4-7 gives us a beautiful pattern. "Don't look out only for your own interests, but take an interest in others. . . . Have the same attitude that Christ Jesus had. Though he was God . . . he gave up his divine privileges; he took the humble position of a slave and was born as a human being."

That very first Christmas, Jesus was the gift. He did not bring silver or gold, he brought kindness and goodness. He gave himself. In his honor, let's make kindness and goodness the key ingredients in all we do and all that we give. Do you know a widow? The holidays can be lonely; pray for her, take her shopping, hang a cheerful wreath on her door. Are your kids being inconsiderate of your wishes and needs? Let it go and love them anyway. Did your sister hurt your feelings last holiday? You be the first to call and mend the gap. Put homemade cookies in the mailbox for the mailman, shovel your neighbor's sidewalk, let a mom with little ones go ahead of you in line at the store. What if you really did humble yourself and lift others up? Well, then Christmas just might come to your house a little early.

Make It Personal . . . Live It Out!

Do you know the true story of Santa Claus? Nicholas was born during the third century in Patara, a small Greek village. His wealthy parents raised him to be a devout Christian. But they died in an epidemic while Nicholas was still young. Obeying Jesus' words to "sell all your possessions and give the money to the poor" (Matthew 19:21), Nicholas used his inheritance to assist the needy, the sick, and the suffering. He dedicated his life to serving God and was known for his generosity and love for children.

"He leads the humble in doing right, teaching them his way" (Psalm 25:9).

One Year Bible Reading

Amos 7:1–9:15; Revelation 3:7-22; Psalm 131:1-3; Proverbs 29:23

December 13

Fear of Man

The fear of man brings a snare,
But whoever trusts in the LORD shall be safe.

PROVERBS 29:25 (NKJV)

Peer pressure is a huge dilemma for most teenagers. As teens, most of us feared being different or looking different. But, sadly, many never grew out of it. The pressure to fit in and to please people can not only cause us to do wrong, but it can also keep us from doing what is right. It can keep us from speaking up for what is true and good.

Many people have never read the book of Jeremiah in the Old Testament. They think it could never apply to them living in this modern, complicated world. Not so. Recently as I read it, I felt like I was reading front page news. Man-pleasing religion, false spirituality, corrupt political shenanigans, tragic moral decline, and the rejection of godly principles—this was going on in the once-godly nation of Israel. It was heartbreaking. Even the so-called prophets of God were saying, "It's fine. We will never suffer the consequences."

But then there was Jeremiah. He had the Word of God in his hands, a deep care for the people in his heart, and God's message on his lips. He would have been much more comfortable and popular if he had just shut his eyes and shut up, but he couldn't. The Lord himself had stirred his heart.

Jeremiah stood with God, and it's been said, "Just one standing with God is a majority."

Make It Personal . . . Live It Out!

Like Jeremiah, we live in a world of compromise. Many so-called Christians are chameleons. They say they love God, but they live like the world. This is very confusing to those who don't know Christ. Even the guy at the bar has no respect for this double standard. It's time for us to live true to our faith and true to the God who is faithful to us. "Above all, you must live as citizens of heaven, conducting yourselves in a manner worthy of the Good News about Christ. Then, whether I come and see you again or only hear about you, I will know that you are standing together with one spirit and one purpose" (Philippians 1:27).

One Year Bible Reading

Obadiah 1:1-21; Revelation 4:1-11; Psalm 132:1-18; Proverbs 29:24-25

The Justice of God

Many seek the ruler's favor,
But justice for man comes from the LORD.

PROVERBS 29:26 (NKJV)

As you read this, can you picture Solomon sitting at a little desk having just written this proverb? God had given him deep insight into the way human affairs on this earth operate. He was a king, a ruler. Was he thinking of the many times people had sought his favor, hoping to get answers and help for problems that were not only over their heads but way over his? How aware he must have been that life is much too complicated for any human being to make unfair things right and to unravel life's dilemmas. God had made him wise enough to know his own inadequacies. This is true wisdom.

Other great men like Abraham Lincoln came to the same conclusion. He said, "I have been driven many times to my knees by the overwhelming conviction that I had nowhere else to go."

God is inviting you—in fact he is *urging* you—to draw the same conclusion. You also have nowhere else to go. Kings and presidents, Congress and courts of law, can never bring real solutions for a broken world full of broken souls. We need a Savior! Every single one of us needs a Savior.

But the good news is we do have a Savior—Jesus. Justice comes from the Lord. He alone is our Good Shepherd, our Strong Tower, our Comforter, our King of kings, our Bread of Life, our Prince of Peace, and our Light of the World.

Make It Personal . . . Live It Out!

Kids have a keen sense of justice. Even a four-year-old will cry out the words "It's not fair!" We may not say these words, but there are times when we think them. We long for things to be right. We fret about things we have no control of. But have you taken your concerns to God? Worry and frustration accomplishes nothing. Prayer does. Prayer links you to the faithful love of God who reigns over the universe from the throne of grace. "The LORD will work out his plans for my life—for your faithful love, O LORD, endures forever" (Psalm 138:8).

One Year Bible Reading

Jonah 1:1–4:11; Revelation 5:1-14; Psalm 133:1-3; Proverbs 29:26-27

Wise

Today's Wisdom for Women is an interesting proverb. Instead of making a wise statement, it is one man, Agur, expressing his frustration that he is not wise. Good. Good for him. Jesus said, "Blessed are the poor in spirit. . . . Blessed are those who hunger and thirst for righteousness, for they shall be filled" (Matthew 5:3, 6, NKJV).

In Proverbs 30:1 Agur says, "I am weary, O God; I am weary and worn out, O God." He goes on to say in verses 2-4,

I am the most ignorant of men;
I do not have a man's understanding.
I have not learned wisdom,
nor have I knowledge of the Holy One.
Who has gone up to heaven and come down?
Who has gathered up the wind in the hollow of his hands?
Who has wrapped up the waters in his cloak?
Who has established all the ends of the earth?
What is his name, and the name of his son?
Tell me if you know! (NIV)

Maybe you feel exactly the same. This would be a very good time to talk about how godly wisdom *is* attained.

- It's a gift from God bestowed on those who ask. Solomon asked. James 1:5-6 said we can ask too: "If any of you lacks wisdom, he should ask God, who gives generously to all without finding fault. . . . But when he asks, he must believe and not doubt" (NIV).
- God's Word is wisdom. As we read it every day, it teaches us and trains us. God's Word also warns us regarding the things that are dangerous and foolish.
- Wisdom is not just information. It must be lived—rubber meeting the road of life.
- "The fear of the LORD is the beginning of Wisdom" (Proverbs 9:10, NKJV).

Make It Personal . . . Live It Out!

Experts who study the learning process tell us that knowledge is like a magnet. The more you learn, the more the magnet in your brain becomes larger and stronger. It then attracts and absorbs information at a faster rate. It is the same with the attainment of wisdom. Each time you learn a wise principle and then apply it, your capacity and retention is increased. Wisdom becomes part of you, a second nature; "you grow wiser." May God grow you, deepen you, and cause you to become a woman who not only acts wisely, but is wise.

One Year Bible Reading

Micah 1:1–4:13; Revelation 6:1-17; Psalm 134:1-3; Proverbs 30:1-4

Be a Berean!

Every word of God is pure;
He is a shield to those who put their trust in Him.
Do not add to His words,
Lest He rebuke you, and you be found a liar.

PROVERBS 30:5-6 (NKJV)

I love the word *pure*. God's Word is pure, meaning, "free from anything inferior or contaminating." It is flawless and undiluted like pure gold or clear water.

This is a good place to talk about the importance of being Berean Christians. The Bereans did not rely upon secondhand knowledge or other people's opinions. They went directly to the Scriptures and searched them themselves.

Therefore we, too, must read the whole counsel of God. Many people get in a rut. They always just read the Psalms or just the Epistles, but the Bible has a wonderful balance from cover to cover. We miss some important truths and powerful examples from the Old Testament if we're afraid to read it. And so, as we are coming to a new year, this would be a great time to pick up a *One Year Bible* so you can begin on January 1. *The One Year Bible* is divided in 365 segments. Each day of reading includes the Old Testament, New Testament, a psalm, and a proverb. By just reading twenty to thirty minutes a day, you can read the entire Bible in one year. How exciting that is! But more than that, you will see a new victory, a new love for the Lord, a new desire to please him. Now, that's life-changing!

Make It Personal . . . Live It Out!

God's Word is a shield that protects your heart, soul, and mind from fear, lies, doubt, and temptation. As you read, be intentional. Personally embrace a lesson or instruction each day. Allow God's Word to paint images of truth that counteract falsehood. Memorize and take ownership of his promises. Our Old Testament reading in *The One Year Bible* today includes Micah 6:8. In this verse, God gives us a template for living. I have it written on a plaque at my front door to remind me that the godly life is the good life. "He has showed you, O man, what is good. And what does the LORD require of you? To act justly and to love mercy and to walk humbly with your God" (Micah 6:8, NIV).

One Year Bible Reading

Micah 5:1–7:20; Revelation 7:1-17; Psalm 135:1-21; Proverbs 30:5-6

Sweet Simplicity

Two things I ask of you, O LORD;
do not refuse me before I die:
Keep falsehood and lies far from me;
give me neither poverty nor riches,
but give me only my daily bread.
Otherwise, I may have too much and disown you
and say, "Who is the LORD?"
Or I may become poor and steal,
and so dishonor the name of my God.

PROVERBS 30:7-9 (NIV)

Simple living is our topic today. Paul said, "Godliness with contentment is great gain" (1 Timothy 6:6, NKJV). This is an interesting proverb to ponder right before Christmas. For many, Christmas is anything but simple and we are far from contented. Busyness can be an excuse, a replacement and avoidance of authenticity. We fill our days so full we don't have time to attend to the real and important. Simplicity takes discipline. It takes solitude and quietness before God. Wouldn't it be sweet if we did return to the basics? Paul said, "I have learned in whatever state I am, to be content" (Philippians 4:11, NKJV). Contentment, you see, is first a choice and then it becomes a habit.

Let's look at the simplicity of the birth of Jesus that very first Christmas. They were far from home, his mother was young. They were poor, shut out, homeless. And yet as we emotionally visit that humble little scene in the stable, it captures us. It has a majesty not found in palaces. There was joy and hope, and most of all God was near. Immanuel is the message; God with us. And when he is near, our hearts are full.

Make It Personal . . . Live It Out!

To *simplify* is "to render less complex, less embellished, more natural." Although we love the bows and the glitter of Christmas, we can get lost in them. When the shepherds arrived in the stable to see the Savior, they didn't feel underdressed. They came as they were. They had been invited and included in this holy event. All that attracted their attention was the beauty of Jesus.

Let's Pray

Lord, please help me to slow down, refocus, and be thankful. Show me if my expectation of what needs to be done has cluttered what matters most. Help me rejoice today in the sweetness of simple things and quiet moments.

One Year Bible Reading

Nahum 1:1–3:19; Revelation 8:1-13; Psalm 136:1-26; Proverbs 30:7-9

Choice Words

Do not slander a servant to his master,
or he will curse you, and you will pay for it.

PROVERBS 30:10 (NIV)

First of all, slander is mean. Can I say that again? Slander is mean. To slander is to speak or spread false information. It's harmful to another's reputation. It is to accuse someone unfairly.

Let's apply this to two servants. First, to the waitress who serves you at a restaurant, and secondly, to the servants at your church.

1. The waitress: Have you ever seen people treat their waitress like dirt? I have. They're impatient and demanding. If something is forgotten or not to their liking, they act like it's the end of the world. They tip cheap and complain to the manager. This is bad behavior for anyone, but inexcusable for the child of God. Did you ever consider that maybe this is a weary single mom working a second job? Or maybe your waitress is new, or has a migraine, or is going through a rough divorce. Have you ever thought that maybe that waitress came across your path for you to bless her instead of her just serving you? Have you ever prayed about it?
2. I feel prompted to encourage you to be kind when speaking about those who serve at your church. Don't ever think your ministry is the ministry of the critical tongue. Be kind when speaking about a Sunday school teacher or an usher or your pastor.

Make It Personal . . . Live It Out!

Our proverb today informs us that giving bad reports can backfire. The person we reported to might view us with contempt. My husband and I had a standing policy: "I can talk about my mamma, you can talk about your mamma. But you can't talk about my mamma." This does not mean we don't ever discuss concerns. Silence isn't always golden. It is the motive and method that are important. The right word, at the right time, in the right way can have the right result.

Let's Pray

Dear Lord, help me to be careful and kind. Pointing out error doesn't have to tear someone down. Help me to choose my words both carefully and kindly.

One Year Bible Reading

Habakkuk 1:1–3:19; Revelation 9:1-21; Psalm 137:1-9; Proverbs 30:10

December 19

Sober Words for Sober Times

There is a generation that curses its father,
And does not bless its mother.
There is a generation that is pure in its own eyes,
Yet is not washed from its filthiness.
There is a generation—oh, how lofty are their eyes!
And their eyelids are lifted up.
There is a generation whose teeth are like swords,
And whose fangs are like knives,
To devour the poor from off the earth,
And the needy from among men.

PROVERBS 30:11-14 (NKJV)

This describes a generation that has turned its back on God. At the risk of sounding too negative, I feel I must read 2 Timothy 3:1-7: "Know this, that in the last days perilous times will come: For men will be lovers of themselves, lovers of money, boasters, proud, blasphemers, disobedient to parents, unthankful, unholy, unloving, unforgiving, slanderers, without self-control, brutal, despisers of good, traitors, headstrong, haughty, lovers of pleasure rather than lovers of God, having a form of godliness but denying its power. And from such people turn away! For of this sort are those who creep into households [through talk shows, books, magazines] and make captives of gullible women loaded down with sins, led away by various lusts, always learning and never able to come to the knowledge of the truth" (NKJV).

Sober words for sober times. For such a generation I believe nothing will change it but revival. Revival is sparked by repentance, made holy by the blood of Christ, fueled by the Word of God, and fanned into flame by the Holy Spirit.

Make It Personal . . . Live It Out!

Arrogance, rebellion, and foolishness are sometimes symptoms of youth. Certainly, there are dangerous trends drawing young people today. On the other hand, there are many young people who are looking for true purpose and passion for living. They can see that sin and addictions have devastated some of their friends. They are hungry for God and desire to have authentic faith. Let me challenge you. If you are young, the only way to fight unholy fire is with holy fire. Be courageous, solid, and sold out. If you are older, it's time for revival in our own hearts. Will you pray? Will you join me, on our knees, praying that God will draw and restore and ignite a revival that will circle the world?

One Year Bible Reading

Zephaniah 1:1–3:20; Revelation 10:1-11; Psalm 138:1-8; Proverbs 30:11-14

A Christmas Carol

The leech has two daughters,
Give and Give! . . .
The grave,
The barren womb,
The earth that is not satisfied . . .
And the fire never [say], "Enough!"

PROVERBS 30:15-16 (NKJV)

We are nearing the end of the Proverbs. Instead of a chipper, upbeat theme, we are seeing an almost desperation. God is addressing a selfishness and emptiness that envelops and shadows.

And so on this theme, I'm thinking of that amazing story *A Christmas Carol*, written by Charles Dickens. In the story, Ebenezer Scrooge was selfish and harsh. "Give me" was his motto too, but the beauty and power of the story lies in the fact that he was given a second chance. On Christmas Eve he saw all of his life—past, present, and future—parade before him in a dream. He saw that if he did not change, people he could have helped would suffer, and he would die empty and alone. Then he awoke, and he realized he still had time to give and to be a blessing. But the best part of the story is that he did change. The good news was that it wasn't too late.

What, then, is the lesson for us? Christmas for some is the loneliest time of the year. Maybe you're feeling lonely and needy yourself. Would you close your eyes for just a moment? Can you think of a Tiny Tim who is needy, the child of a single mom, or an elderly man, or an unloved teenager? It is not too late. Maybe the stores have left the love of Christ out of Christmas, but the good news is, he can use you to put it back in.

Make It Personal . . . Live It Out!

That I may not in blindness grope, but that I may with vision clear
Know when to speak a word of hope, or add a little wholesome cheer.
That tempered winds may softly blow where little children, thinly clad,
Sit dreaming, when the flame is low, of comforts they have never had.
That through the year which lies ahead, no heart shall ache, no cheek be wet,
For any word that I have said or profit I have tried to get.
—S. E. KISER IN "A LITTLE PRAYER"

One Year Bible Reading

Haggai 1:1–2:23; Revelation 11:1-19; Psalm 139:1-24; Proverbs 30:15-16

Bitter Battles

The eye that mocks a father,
that scorns obedience to a mother,
will be pecked out by the ravens of the valley,
will be eaten by the vultures.

PROVERBS 30:17 (NIV)

Oh, my goodness. If I was not committed to taking each proverb in order, I would surely skip this one. It does not seem like a four-days-before-Christmas theme. But maybe it is. God's Word always has something to say to us. It could be that there is someone reading today who needs to hear this. Please bear with me. It's important and urgent.

First of all, this is speaking to you if you have a broken relationship full of bitterness and anger toward your parents. Please know this is going to eat you up to your dying day. I think this is the very reason that God inserted this graphic, awful word picture of ravens and vultures. Vultures only eat the dead and dying. Truly, the enemy of your soul feeds on and delights in seeing a child of God who is bitter. Bitterness is a rottenness and emotional death in you. It robs your joy and steals your peace.

Let me say, no matter what the issue is, even if it's deep and serious, may this be the Christmas that Satan gets no more mileage by tormenting you.

Now the question is, are you willing to forgive? If so, express that to the Lord right now. He is able to make you able. It would be a threefold gift: to your parents, to yourself, and to God the Father, who loves you. This may seem like the most expensive gift you've ever given. Actually, it is. Forgiveness is not only expensive, it's priceless.

Make It Personal . . . Live It Out!

Perhaps you are entirely innocent of bitterness within your family. It's those ornery folk on the outside who are the problem. At one time both William Anderson Hatfield and Randolph McCoy were simple, hospitable, home-loving mountain men. They were close friends. But once they started to feud, they never forgave and never forgot. Now their name, the Hatfields and the McCoys, are synonymous with the danger of escalating, unresolved anger. One Christmas long ago, God sent his Son to straighten us out. If you are bitter against anybody, anywhere, for any reason, will you open your heart and let him unload your guns?

One Year Bible Reading

Zechariah 1:1-21; Revelation 12:1-17; Psalm 140:1-13; Proverbs 30:17

Amaze Me!

There are three things that amaze me—
no, four things that I don't understand:
how an eagle glides through the sky,
how a snake slithers on a rock,
how a ship navigates the ocean,
how a man loves a woman.

PROVERBS 30:18-19

Four amazing things: it is good to sometimes ponder and just enjoy some of the amazing things in nature that really can't be explained. In the natural world, God has placed his signature deeply in creation.

Let's ponder the majestic beauty of an eagle soaring. It can soar at an altitude of up to ten thousand feet and achieve speeds of thirty-five miles per hour. Bald eagles weigh only ten to fourteen pounds, have seven thousand feathers, are good swimmers, mate for life, and are at the top of the food chain. All eagles are renowned for their excellent eyesight. Soaring at one thousand feet, they can identify a rabbit moving almost a mile away.

A snake has no feet, leaves no footprints, and yet, it's lightning fast. Amazing, and a little scary.

A ship on the sea weighs thousands of tons, and yet, it leaves no trail and does not sink. For thousands of years, sailing ships have been driven by the wind and the currents and navigated by the stars. Surely this is amazing.

The fourth on our list is the way a man falls in love with a woman. We never tire of a sweet love story, do we?

But the most wonderful thing of all is God's love for us. "God so loved the world that He gave His only begotten Son" (John 3:16, NKJV). Now, that's amazing!

Make It Personal . . . Live It Out!

Although all of God's creation is awesome and astounding, there is nothing quite as amazing as you. You are his masterpiece. You were created in his image. Although you spent your first half hour of life contained in one cell the size of a sugar granule, you were already *you*. As Dr. Seuss has said, "Today you are You, that is truer than true. There is no one alive who is Youer than You." No one ever possessed your exact DNA or your fingerprint. You are not a one-size-fits-all. Go to bed tonight knowing that he who flung the stars into space is watching over you with love.

One Year Bible Reading

Zechariah 2:1–3:10; Revelation 12:18–13:18; Psalm 141:1-10; Proverbs 30:18-20

The Earth Trembles

Under three things the earth trembles,
under four it cannot bear up:
a servant who becomes king,
a fool who is full of food,
an unloved woman who is married,
and a maidservant who displaces her mistress.

PROVERBS 30:21-23 (NIV)

All four of these things, first of all, just shouldn't happen. And when they do, there is trouble.

There is a tremble when a servant becomes a king. Through the ages people who rise to positions of leadership without training, experience, or wisdom often rule harshly. They rule with fear because of their own fears.

A fool doesn't know you can have a full stomach but an empty head and an empty soul. Before the prodigal fell on hard times, he was full of himself. But when he became hungry, Jesus said, he came home (see Luke 15:11-32).

The next two things that make the earth tremble are an unloved married woman and the woman who replaces her. It makes me tremble too. This is both sad and wrong. Wives, be aware. Your husbands are bombarded everywhere they go with seductive and tempting images. There are women out there who are aggressive and dedicated to winning them. So, first of all, are you praying for him every day? Secondly, I don't want to be unspiritual in this suggestion, but, girls, sometimes we need to keep up a little with the competition. Don't let yourself look drab and unkempt. And, thirdly, love him. Make your husband's home his castle.

Make It Personal . . . Live It Out!

God created a perfect world. It's hard to imagine why Eve doubted God's goodness and believed he withheld good from her. She had a perfect home, no wardrobe issues, and was married to a perfect husband (the last perfect husband). Adam was married to a perfect wife (the last one of those, too). But Eve took the bait and ate the fruit, and since that moment, our world has been full of things that shouldn't be.

If your world feels like Humpty Dumpty, broken in a thousand pieces, Jesus came to fulfill the words spoken by Isaiah the prophet. "He has sent Me to heal the brokenhearted, to proclaim liberty to the captives, and the opening of the prison to those who are bound . . . to comfort all who mourn . . . to give them beauty for ashes" (Isaiah 61:1-3, NKJV).

One Year Bible Reading

Zechariah 4:1–5:11; Revelation 14:1-20; Psalm 142:1-7; Proverbs 30:21-23

Good Things Come in Small Packages

There are four things which are little on the earth But they are exceedingly wise: The ants are a people not strong, Yet they prepare their food in the summer; The rock badgers are a feeble folk, Yet they make their homes in the crags; The locusts have no king, Yet they all advance in ranks; The spider skillfully grasps with its hands, And is in kings' palaces.

PROVERBS 30:24-28 (NKJV)

Do you ever feel little? Do you ever feel that your life doesn't matter? I think most of us feel like that at times. For many people Christmas can be the hardest time of the year. You look around and feel that you don't measure up, you don't have the picture-perfect family, you feel small, insignificant. So if that's you, God wants you to know that he has poured wisdom and beauty into weak, little things.

There's a test that's circulating on the Internet:

1. Name the five wealthiest people in the world.
2. Name the last five winners of the Miss America Pageant.
3. Name ten people who have won a Nobel Prize.

How did you do? The point is, none of us really remember the prize winners of yesterday. Here's another quiz. See how you do on this one.

1. List a few teachers who aided your journey through school.
2. Name three friends who have helped you through difficult times.
3. Think of a few people who have made you feel appreciated and special.

Easier? The lesson: the people who make the difference in your life are not the ones with the most credentials, money, or awards. They are simply the ones who care. So be yourself. Everyone else is taken.

Make It Personal . . . Live It Out!

The very first Christmas eve occurred in the little town of Bethlehem. Two great men were born there, David and Jesus. David was a man who loved God; Jesus is God who loves man. Sometimes great things and people have humble beginnings. Athlete Lance Armstrong never knew his birth father. Apple creator Steve Jobs was born to an unwed mother. Albert Einstein had a speech impediment as a child. Charles Schultz was a shy, timid teenager. Plain, ordinary, slightly flawed—do you feel that describes you? Brown paper packages tied up with string . . . these are a few of God's favorite things.

One Year Bible Reading

Zechariah 6:1–7:14; Revelation 15:1-8; Psalm 143:1-12; Proverbs 30:24-28

Come, Let Us Adore Him

There are three things that are stately in their stride,
four that move with stately bearing:
a lion, mighty among beasts,
who retreats before nothing;
a strutting rooster, a he-goat,
and a king with his army around him.

PROVERBS 30:29-31 (NIV)

Stately is "a manner that is graceful and yet weighty and dignified." It is the picture of strength under control. The lion stands above the rest.

On this Christmas day let's remember that the baby born in a manger was really a lion king. He was and is the Lion of the tribe of Judah in disguise. The eternal King of the universe chose to humble himself and become humanly confined to that little body. Immanuel—such an amazing title. Do you know what it means? "God with us." It was God in that manger so small and yet so stately.

Let's read the words of that wonderful song "Mary, Did You Know?"

Mary, did you know that your baby boy will give sight to the blind man?
Mary, did you know that your baby boy will calm a storm with his hand?
Did you know that your baby boy has walked where angels trod?
And when you kiss your little baby, you have kissed the face of God?

Merry Christmas. May you know that your Lion King became weak so you could be made strong. Now that is a King who was and is stately.

Make It Personal . . . Live It Out!

That first Christmas day there were many who had no idea that the King of the universe was near. They were busy, they were distracted. We, too, can get so caught up in all the busyness of this Christmas day and entirely shut him out.

Before the day is over, will you slip away to a quiet spot? Will you bow your head and even get on your knees if you can? Will you still your heart and let the words of another Christmas song invite you into his presence?

O come, let us adore him.
O come, let us adore him.
O come, let us adore him, Christ the Lord.

One Year Bible Reading

Zechariah 8:1-23; Revelation 16:1-21; Psalm 144:1-15; Proverbs 30:29-31

Just Stop!

If you have been foolish in exalting yourself
Or if you have devised evil, put your hand on your mouth.

PROVERBS 30:32 (NKJV)

Here we're warned of two very foolish things: exalting yourself and devising trouble.

What is the practical advice given to those who do that? Stop! Put your hand on your mouth and stop talking. It's foolish to either excuse the behavior or accuse someone else. Just stop talking.

So let's look at the foolish behavior of exalting self. In most families there is someone who is always on their high horse, belittling others, critical, bossy. Anytime we exalt ourselves, others are unexalted, whether we mean to or not. So if it's you, put your hand on your mouth, and let it be a filter saying, "In this conversation, Lord, check me. Keep me from saying anything that makes me look better than others, puts others down, or hurts other's feelings."

Secondly, have your words been used to plant little seeds of discord? In your family have you criticized your sister or brother-in-law or mother? Are you still complaining about something someone did last Christmas? If so, face it. The Bible calls that "devising evil." Shame on you. In all these things put your hand over your mouth and stop it.

"Let no corrupt word proceed out of your mouth, but what is good for necessary edification, that it may impart grace to the hearers" (Ephesians 4:29, NKJV).

Make It Personal . . . Live It Out!

Harmony and sweetness of spirit are distinct characteristics of godliness. Could you say that is your heart's desire? If it is, then it's good to do some periodic fruit inspecting. Prayerfully ponder all the interaction with people you have had over the last few weeks. Was there evidence that the Holy Spirit and all of his personality traits (love, joy, peace, patience, kindness, goodness, faithfulness, gentleness, self-control) were active and overflowing in your life? If not, would you like him to be?

Let's Pray

Dear Lord, I come to you with an honest heart. I know I fail. But with all my heart I want to grow. I'm like an empty cup; fill me with your Holy Spirit and make me more like you.

One Year Bible Reading

Zechariah 9:1-17; Revelation 17:1-18; Psalm 145:1-21; Proverbs 30:32

Calm Down

As churning the milk produces butter,
and as twisting the nose produces blood,
so stirring up anger produces strife.

PROVERBS 30:33 (NIV)

Agitation. Jon Courson comments, "Rather than letting hurt feelings heal, those who continually revisit the problems and rekindle the fire of misunderstanding will make the situation infinitely worse, as sure as stirring milk results in butter and wringing the nose brings forth blood."

Let's take an example. Your friend calls. She is livid. Her mother-in-law was domineering and rude on Christmas day. Your friend is hurt and wants to vent. Okay, what kind of friend are you, really? A carnal friend would not just be sympathetic, she would add fuel to the fire, adding criticism and reinforcing the woundedness. This does not help, and it is not true friendship, either.

As true godly friends, this very same encounter could take you both to a higher place, the Cross. First, just listen, but pray as you listen. Sometimes, when people share, they see things more clearly. Then ask, "How can I help? How can I encourage you in the Lord?" Then don't hang up until you've said, "Let's pray regarding your mother-in-law and let's pray *for* her, right now." I've heard it said that you cannot truly pray for someone and hate them at the same time.

"Blessed are the peacemakers, for they shall be called the children of God" (Matthew 5:9, KJV).

Make It Personal . . . Live It Out!

Honestly, are you annoyed, irritated, even fuming at someone right now? Anger is a dangerous thing. Here are some tips to avoid the pitfalls and traps.

- Don't call your friend to vent. Getting her riled up won't help.
- Don't just stuff your feelings either. That can turn to bitterness and resentment and depression.
- Take your anger to God, not just once, but again and again until it's gone.

Let's Pray

Lord, I come to you alone with this hurt. Please give me your grace to open my heart to release it to you. Free me of this burden. Free me from dark, angry thoughts and replace them with your peace. In Jesus' name, amen.

One Year Bible Reading

Zechariah 10:1–11:17; Revelation 18:1-24; Psalm 146:1-10; Proverbs 30:33

The Dangers of Drink

Today's Wisdom for Women is a statement by a king. He tells how his mother brought him up. He had a mother who wasn't afraid to tell him the cold, hard facts about the dangers of drinking.

So this is a message to moms. This world needs godly moms, moms who are loving, firm, consistent; moms who teach their sons and daughters that messing around with the party life will mess up their life.

An oracle his mother taught him:
O my son . . .
do not spend your strength on women,
your vigor on those who ruin kings.
It is not for kings . . . to drink wine,
not for rulers to crave beer,
lest they drink and forget what the law decrees,
and deprive all the oppressed of their rights.

PROVERBS 31:1-5 (NIV)

Sometimes we think we live in the only generation that is so immoral that we don't have a chance at protecting our kids from the temptations all around them. As I listen to the words of this mother, I can tell she was desperately worried, as every mother of a teenager would be.

And so what can we do? Like this mother, stay informed, stay involved, and stay in relationship. Some of the wisest parents I know make sure their kids' friends come to their house to hang out. They make sure they know them, they're welcome, there's lots of food, and there's love. But the most powerful thing we could ever do is to fight this battle for our teens on our knees. Moms, be praying moms. Never underestimate the power of a praying mom.

Make It Personal . . . Live It Out!

There is a dangerous new trend among Christian young people. Drinking is viewed as cool and harmless. They like how it makes them feel. They like that it lowers inhibitions. A few beers with pizza could never hurt anyone, right? For some this is true. But for others, one drink leads to another until they lose their bearings. One too many clouds judgment. Clouded judgment opens the door to danger. If this is a liberty you have allowed in your life, is it worth taking the risk? Is it worth causing a weaker sister or brother or son or daughter to stumble?

One Year Bible Reading

Zechariah 12:1–13:9; Revelation 19:1-21; Psalm 147:1-20; Proverbs 31:1-7

Be a Voice

Speak up for those who cannot speak for themselves;
ensure justice for those being crushed.

PROVERBS 31:8

Speak up. God himself is calling us to speak for those who can't. Although there's many applications, those who are most unable to speak for themselves are the unborn.

In the womb each baby is "fearfully and wonderfully made" (Psalm 139:14, NKJV). The heartbeat starts at twenty-two days from conception. Eight weeks from conception the baby has every organ in place. It can hear. It has fingerprints.

But did you know that the most dangerous place for a child to live in the United States right now is in the womb? Since 1973 over fifty million babies have died from abortion. Of this number, 93 percent of abortions were not performed because of health risks or rape. Thirty-six hundred babies die every day. That's one every twenty-four seconds.

When a baby dies in this way, there are at least two victims: the baby and the mother. I have talked to women who thirty years later have not allowed themselves to grieve. They have buried this wound. If this is you, please know that God loves you, forgives you, and has that baby safe with him in eternity.

On my website I have resources especially for you. You can go to BibleBusStop.com. It is time for you to be helped and healed. And now may I urge you to use what Satan meant for evil, for good? Will you accept God's forgiveness, and then will you accept the challenge to speak up for those who cannot speak for themselves?

Make It Personal . . . Live It Out!

Why do women chose abortion? There are many reasons. The mere fact that abortion is legal creates a false belief that it isn't wrong. Often, women see no alternative. They don't realize there are families longing for children who would gladly adopt. They think abortion is less emotionally painful than adoption. Nothing could be further from the truth. There is good news! There are crisis pregnancy centers across the nation staffed by dedicated men and women willing to stand in the gap. They provide counseling and tangible assistance to women in crisis. Will you pray? Will you help?

One Year Bible Reading

Zechariah 14:1-21; Revelation 20:1-15; Psalm 148:1-14; Proverbs 31:8-9

A True Gem

For today's Wisdom for Women we are going to read about the Proverbs 31 woman. She is my personal hero. There are so many practical lessons. Read carefully. If you learn even just one thing from her life, it's a good thing.

A wife of noble character who can find?
She is worth far more than rubies.
Her husband has full confidence in her
and lacks nothing of value.
She brings him good, not harm,
all the days of her life.
She selects wool and flax
and works with eager hands.
She is like the merchant ships,
bringing her food from afar.
She gets up while it is still dark;
she provides food for her family
and portions for her servant girls.
She considers a field and buys it;
out of her earnings she plants
a vineyard.
She sets about her work vigorously;
her arms are strong for her tasks.
She sees that her trading is profitable,
and her lamp does not go out at
night.
In her hand she holds the distaff
and grasps the spindle with her
fingers.
She opens her arms to the poor
and extends her hands to the needy.
When it snows, she has no fear for her
household;
for all of them are clothed in scarlet.
She makes coverings for her bed;
she is clothed in fine linen and purple.
Her husband is respected at the city gate,
where he takes his seat among the
elders of the land.
She makes linen garments and sells them,
and supplies the merchants with
sashes.

PROVERBS 31:10-24 (NIV)

I just love this woman. She is worth more than rubies.

Make It Personal . . . Live It Out!

King Solomon married many princesses who were high maintenance—"poodles on pillows." In contrast, a loyal, creative, industrious woman was one in a million. Must we sew, buy fields, and grow grapes to fit the Proverbs 31 mold? That's not the point. The point is, do the best with what you have. I learned to be a morning person from this portrait. As a young single woman I read that the godly wife "brings [her husband] good, not harm, all the days of her life." It rang true and right. Will you read the description again? If it stirs in your heart a noble purpose, pray about it and put it to practice.

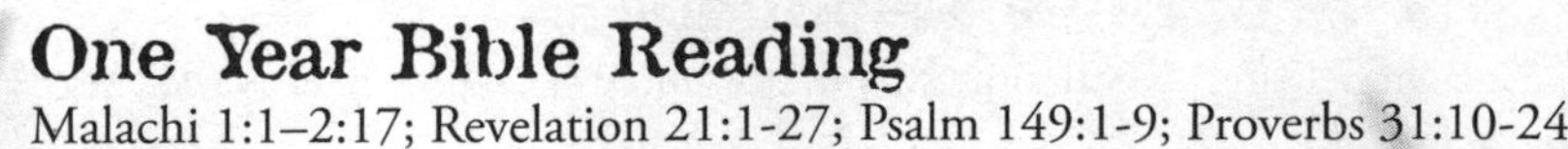

One Year Bible Reading

Malachi 1:1–2:17; Revelation 21:1-27; Psalm 149:1-9; Proverbs 31:10-24

True Beauty

Today's Wisdom for Women is the second part of the description of the godly woman. As you read this, you might feel intimidated, but please know that is not the point. She is not superwoman. As a young woman, I didn't have anyone to mentor me. I had no idea how to be a wife or how to live a life of discipline and purpose, but then I found her, the Proverbs 31 woman. She gave me a picture and a pattern, someone to learn from, and she gave me hope.

Strength and honor are her clothing;
She shall rejoice in time to come.
She opens her mouth with wisdom,
And on her tongue is the law of kindness.
She watches over the ways of her household,
And does not eat the bread of idleness.
Her children rise up and call her blessed;
Her husband also, and he praises her:
"Many daughters have done well,
But you excel them all."
Charm is deceitful and beauty is passing,
But a woman who fears the LORD, she shall be praised.
Give her of the fruit of her hands,
And let her own works praise her in the gates.

PROVERBS 31:25-31 (NKJV)

In closing, I must end with a final word for some brokenhearted mother reading right now. Although you've done your best, your child is a prodigal, and you feel like a failure. Let's look at the phrase "Her children rise up"—it's then that they call her blessed. If your child has fallen, is far from God and maybe far from you, God does hear your prayers, because remember, God the Father has a few prodigals himself.

Make It Personal . . . Live It Out!

As we finish our journey through the book of Proverbs, it is noteworthy that the last chapter concludes with a stunning picture of the godly woman. She is far from a stereotypical, straight-laced, religious stoic. A woman who personally knows, passionately reveres, and wholeheartedly trusts God has a dignity that only authentic faith and integrity can bestow. Her beauty is more than skin deep. Strength, honor, kindness, and diligence are the fabric of who she is. She is a lighthouse, shining over the troubled waters of our generation. God is wooing you, inviting you to join her ranks. Will you rise up, take your place, and take your stand for wisdom?

One Year Bible Reading

Malachi 3:1–4:6; Revelation 22:1-21; Psalm 150:1-6; Proverbs 31:25-31

Developing a Quiet Time

Using *The One Year Bible*—Called the Bible Bus

From BibleBusStop.com. Sign up for the daily "Wisdom for Women" audio devotional.

1. Begin with prayer. As you open God's Word, pause and ask God to open your spiritual eyes to see wonderful things and to open your spiritual ears to hear his voice.
2. Remember, there is therefore now no condemnation to those who are on the Bus. Although I want to encourage you to protect your personal time in the Word every day, we all have our low times—we fall off the bus.
3. Hop back on. When you do miss a reading, whether for just a few days or for a few weeks, don't try to catch up. Just start again with the current day's reading, and keep going from there. You might have time to go back and catch up later, but do not stress over it. Remember, this is not a "notch on your belt." Our goal is fellowship, not accomplishment.
4. Personalize the pace. Be realistic about your journey. If you are new to Bible reading, the mother of young children, or a student with a lot of homework, you may decide to read through just the New Testament portion this year. This reading segment will take just five to seven minutes. It is much better to be consistent with a smaller portion than to be overwhelmed with too much.
5. Keep paper and pen handy. If you write the date of your reading in a notebook, you have put yourself in the mode to "pay attention." What you are saying to God and to yourself is that you expect God to show you something or say something in his Word that is worth writing down and remembering. When you write something down, you more than double your retention. Often as you write one thought, you will see other facets of it expand and grow to a sweet, deep understanding.
6. Set a time. Everyone has a personal rhythm. One is a morning person; another is a night owl. Buy an inexpensive alarm clock, and set it for a certain time each day. This small action can help you protect your "personal appointment with Jesus."
7. Prepare a place. Keeping your *One Year Bible*, notebook, and pen in the same place all the time is a tremendous help. You can go right there and just jump in. You will find that you start viewing that place as special and holy.
8. Search for answers. A quick review of the following questions will help you anticipate and be excited about your reading.
    - What did I learn about God today in my reading?
    - What lesson about life did I learn?
    - What did I learn about myself, my attitudes, priorities, fears, failures, desires, mission, destiny?
    - Is there a lesson I can apply today?
    - What can I take from my reading and pray back to God for understanding, instruction, or help?

Building Your Life on the Rock

Many will say to me on that day, "Lord, Lord, did we not prophesy in your name and in your name drive out demons and in your name perform many miracles?" Then I will tell them plainly, "I never knew you. Away from me, you evildoers!" Therefore everyone who hears these words of mine and puts them into practice is like a wise man who built his house on the rock. The rain came down, the streams rose, and the winds blew and beat against that house; yet it did not fall, because it had its foundation on the rock.

Matthew 7:22-25 (NIV)

CP0617

For Families

The One Year® Family Devotions, Vol. 1

For Couples

The One Year® Devotions for Couples

The One Year® Love Language Minute Devotional

The One Year® Love Talk Devotional for Couples

For Teens

The One Year® Devos for Teens

For Teens
(continued)

The One Year® Devos for Sports Fans

The One Year® Be-Tween You and God

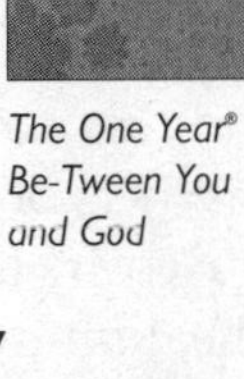

For Personal Growth

The One Year® at His Feet Devotional

The One Year® Daily Insights with Zig Ziglar

The One Year® Uncommon Life Daily Challenge

For Bible Study

The One Year® Praying through the Bible

The One Year® Praying the Promises of God

The One Year® Through the Bible Devotional

The One Year® Experiencing God's Presence Devotional

The One Year® Unlocking the Bible Devotional

It's convenient and easy to grow
with God the One Year way.
TheOneYear.com

CP0145

Additional Ministry Resources

* **Innkeeper Ministries, Inc.** (www.InnkeeperMinistries.org): A ministry dedicated to providing services that encourage, support, and edify Christian leadership in their godly pursuits.

* **Moms in Prayer International** (www.MomsInPrayer.org): Formerly Moms In Touch, this ministry impacts children and schools worldwide for Christ by gathering mothers to pray. Their website will give you information so you can find a group in your area.

* **Healing Hearts Ministries International** (www.HealingHearts.org): The Healing Hearts study for women *Binding up the Brokenhearted* and its counterpart for men, entitled *Wounded Warrior,* guide readers on a biblical journey to healing from the wounds caused by abortion. *The Hem of His Garment* also leads to healing from other wounds such as sexual abuse.

* **Blessed Hope:** A residential discipleship program for women seeking restoration from drug and alcohol addictions. You may contact them at ccbangor.org under the *Discipleship* tab.

* **Answers in Genesis** (www.AnswersInGenesis.org): This website helps us understand and answer the tough questions about Creation, evolution, and the Bible. As a scientist, wife, and mother, Dr. Georgia Purdom offers information particularly geared toward women at the companion website, AnswersForWomen.org.

CP0619